D1177593

10 —
1/23

1385/1500

MAGNOLIA

Memories & Milestones

AUTHORS

Joy Carpine
John Hendron
Rob Hitchings
Bob Kildall
Rick Malsed
Gail Martini-Peterson
Joan Santucci
Patty Small
Scott Smith
Sam Sutherland
Hal Will
Monica Wooton
Nancy Worssam

Published by
The Magnolia Community Club
2000

Magnolia: Memories & Milestones

© Copyright 2000
ISBN number pending
Printed in Canada

NO MATERIAL IN THIS BOOK MAY BE COPIED, REPRODUCED OR OTHERWISE USED WITHOUT PRIOR WRITTEN PERMISSION. INQUIRIES MAY BE SENT TO MAGNOLIA COMMUNITY CLUB, 3213 WEST WHEELER #136, SEATTLE, WASHINGTON, 98199.

WHITNEY MASON, EDITOR
Born in the hospital at Fort Lawton in 1963, Whitney Mason grew up in a house her parents remodeled at 30th Avenue West. She attended Ruth Prins pre-school, took ballet from Miss Thelma, studied piano with Mrs. Lancaster, attended Magnolia Elementary, Blaine Junior High and graduated from Queen Anne High School in 1980. She has bachelor's and master's degrees in journalism from Northwestern University and is a major in the US Marine Corps Reserves. While she currently lives in Charlottesville, Virginia, where she is the executive director for the Charlottesville Society for the Prevention of Cruelty to Animals (SPCA), she still considers Magnolia home.

PAUL LANGLAND, DESIGNER
Born on Vashon Island in 1956. Paul Langland graduated from the University of Washington in 1984 and has been in design and photography for twenty years. After working in Frankfurt, Germany, New York and Los Angeles, he has moved back home to Seattle and has been specializing in book design and production for the past 6 years. Past clients include Weyerhaeuser, Seattle Symphony, Pacific Northwest Ballet, Peterbilt, Simpson Paper and various publishers around Puget Sound.

Cover photo: Magnolia Boulevard with an infrared process. Photo by Ken Baxter, courtesy of Virginia Baxter. Circa 1970.

Page 2-3: Lighthouse at West Point with an infrared process. Photo by Ken Baxter, courtesy of Virginia Baxter. Circa 1970s.

Back cover: Moonlight taken from Magnolia Park. Photo by Hal Will, 1946.

Special thanks to the City of Seattle, Department of Neighborhoods Matching Grant Program, *Director Jim Diers and Project Supervisor Shireen Deboo, for their contributions of two $10,000 grants.*

Magnolia Community Club, Publisher, 3213 West Wheeler #136, Seattle, Washington 98199

DISCLAIMER: THE VIEWS EXPRESSED IN THIS BOOK DO NOT NECESSARILY REFLECT THE VIEWS OF THE MAGNOLIA COMMUNITY CLUB, CITY OF SEATTLE, OR DEPARTMENT OF NEIGHBORHOODS. ALL WRITERS ARE SOLE OWNERS OF THEIR MATERIAL AND ARE RESPONSIBLE FOR THE CONTENT.

The Magnolia Historical Essay Team

EDITOR HIRING TEAM:
Mimi Sheridan
Scott Smith
Nancy Worssam
Monica Wooton

DESIGNER HIRING TEAM:
Lindsay Brown
Scott Smith
Hal Will
Nancy Worssam
Monica Wooton

TREASURER:
Rob Wilson

FINAL EDIT TEAM:
Whitney Mason, Editor
Mimi Sheridan
Monica Wooton

INDEX
Hal Will
Shirley Will

PHOTOGRAPHERS TEAM:
Roy Scully
Sam Sutherland
Monica Wooton
Photo Expertise: Dan Kerlee

PROOFING TEAM:
Betty Ivie, Chair
Cindy Howell
Mimi Sheridan
Shirley Will
Nancy Worssam

PLANNING COMMITTEE:
Betty Ivie, Chair
Steve Erickson
Cindy Howell
Scott Smith
Rob Wilson
Monica Wooton

STORY CONTINUITY TEAM:
Scott Smith
Hal Will

WRITERS EDITORIAL TEAM:
Claudia Callan
Gail Martini-Peterson
Sisi Sedgewick

MAP INSERT
Hal Will
Monica Wooton

ILLUSTRATOR:
Dick Bringloe

Table of Contents

Forewords:

Yesterday Becomes Today
Leslie W. Cowan: Magnolia Community Club President 1975

The first history of Magnolia was issued in 1975 when I was president of the Magnolia Community Club (MCC). We raised the money and contracted John Murray of the *Magnolia News* to print it. Aleua Frare was our superstar who did the real work. A bored Boeing retiree, she worked tirelessly to collect information and to write *MAGNOLIA Yesterday and Today*. It is truly Aleua Frare's legacy to Magnolia.

Now, 25 years later, the "Today" of 1975 has turned into the "Yesterday" of 2000; but in an age of change, much is still the same in Magnolia. We have a nice central Village with no parking meters or traffic lights. We enter over the same three bridges from the City. The number of homes hasn't changed much, although the number of multiple-car families is amazing. Our churches are generally overflowing. The recreation center and playfields are still what they were, but have been upgraded and are better utilized. Our library is still well-used but lacks some technology enhancements. Our teenagers are still bored with night-time Magnolia.

Some long-term dreams have come true—we now have a swimming pool, a neighborhood golf center, and a marina. We also have many nice restaurants and coffee shops. The old movie theater is long gone but only slightly missed with all the video stores renting movie tapes. Many areas have been beautified and plantings enhance public areas. The mature cedar trees along Government Way and 20th Avenue West screen Magnolia eyes from the railroad presence. This was much more than we expected when we planted those wee incense cedars after our community litterthon on Arbor Day 1972. Discovery Park is a great place enjoyed by many people (we enjoyed Fort Lawton, too). The Daybreak Star Center has been developed into a regional meeting place. When the formal Magnolia Dance Club disbanded in the 1980s, it reflected the trend toward casual activities which now prevail.

Some things are not as great. The old Mom and Pop stores are mostly gone. Although, good things happen at Catherine Blaine, Lawton, and Our Lady of Fatima schools, Magnolia Elementary, Briarcliff Elementary and Queen Anne High School are closed. There has been an increase in busing and the use of private schools. The sewage plant at West Point causes concern about further growth. Traffic seems to be steadily worsening due to more cars on our roads. Interruptions on West Dravus Street and on the Magnolia Bridge have exposed the delicate balance between normal traffic flow and gridlock.

My goal in 1975 was to place a copy of *MAGNOLIA Yesterday and Today* in every Magnolia home. At the September 1975 MCC meeting, we issued a free copy to each member (of course we raised the dues from $1.00 to $3.00). It was placed on sale in local stores and a second printing released later is now sold out. Copies were donated to the City, County and State Libraries (there are currently four copies in the Magnolia Library). Magnolians really enjoyed this book.

As the reality of 2000 soon will become a memory the MCC is sponsoring a second increment of Magnolia history, MAGNOLIA: Memories & Milestones. It adds significant information and levels of detail to what is generally known about Magnolia. I hope you will add it to your library beside our first history book, and after reading it you will feel increasingly connected to Magnolia.

Brought To You By . . .

Susan Stern: Magnola Community Club President 2000

MCC is a volunteer service organization. Through its Board of Trustees and Committees, it is a focal point in the community for City, County and State agencies to have a basis of communications with the neighborhood of Magnolia—its needs, wants and desires. The MCC also participates in many activities, which engage neighbors through volunteer service projects within the neighborhood.

Since the inception of the MCC in the 1920s, hundreds of Magnolians have served on the Board, steering the neighborhood through numerous challenging waters. The MCC interacts with the City of Seattle, King County, the Port of Seattle, King County Airport (Boeing Field), the Seattle School District, the West Point Sewage Treatment Plant and the Seattle Parks and Recreation Department to name just a few.

In 1975, as a Community Club 50th anniversary project, Aleua Frare wrote *MAGNOLIA Yesterday and Today*. This manuscript was the first history solely about the neighborhood of Magnolia. This 126-page, soft-cover collection also became part of the Seattle-King County Bicentennial History Project. As the year 2000 approached, it was obvious to the MCC Board that it was time to update the original text as well as dig deeper into our colorful history.

This new history book proved to be a monumental task involving dozens of volunteers, hundreds of hours of interviews, obtaining materials, and collecting it into the volumn in your hands today. Everyone involved in this project has participated in the beginning of what we hope will be the future of all Magnolia residents—participation in its ongoing history!

One of our most valuable partners was the City of Seattle Department of Neighborhoods (DON) and we thank them profusely for the financial support in producing this book. DON awarded the MCC two $10,000 "Small and Simple" grants which assisted us in hiring a professional editor, graphics designer and printer. Businesses, early book purchases and the generosity of individuals contributing time, money and historical material enabled this book to become a reality.

Thank you to all who worked on this project. Without you, we would not be what we are today—a strong, united Seattle neighborhood, proud of our pioneer heritage and forever protecting the charm and integrity of our neighborhood. As Magnolia friends come and go, I hope they will always regard highly the privilege of living in Magnolia.

Manicotti Again!

Monica Wooton: Project Manager, *Magnolia: Memories & Milestones*

I will be retiring from a 25 year "career" of volunteerism at the end of this project. If only every one of us had the privilege of 25 years of service to devote to causes we believed in, what a better world it would be! I will personally miss Halloween pumpkin faced cup cakes, an invention of my room-mother days . . . the very most! But this (this book making process) I will not ever have to miss at all! It was an experience so rich in lessons; I will hardly have enough time to practice all that I have learned in one lifetime. What a great privilege I have certainly had. I want to publicly thank all who had a hand in my instruction!

This was an intense project with many lifetime firsts (and seconds, thirds and fourths (the re-writes alone went on and on . . .). I made silver friendships that someday I hope will be golden. My history is much improved, but I still can't tell east from west or read a map. I learned: there are just some things I'll never learn! (An old saying . . . a new epiphany for me!) And, I realized: that's what teamwork is all about (to encourage group strengths and minimize individual weaknesses). I'm happy I worked with a team.

Mostly, this was an experience in mentoring. I had many. Non-profit organizations can't always afford to buy the best; BUT, if they are good organizations the best volunteer for them. People in the top of their fields worked with us and charged nothing for their expertise and help. Their generosity will always be appreciated! The Magnolia Library was an excellent partner allowing us to hold all our meetings there and supporting us all along in our endeavor.

History-making folks from Magnolia wrote down or researched, for the first time, important stories they had spent lifetimes living or wondering about. All who worked on the project took the time to patiently explain the "whys?" that I asked (and I had as many as a three year old!). Those with many more years experience in life had to listen to me give them direction. (And, that is just counting the Modern Language Association Style Book . . .) They allowed me to get my life experience, even if they already had theirs. They role-modeled patience absolutely.

The members of the Magnolia Historical Essay Project Team were so enthusiastic and full of energy for the pieces they wrote, the project itself and the people with whom they worked. They shared information, worked unreasonable amounts of time, and watched out for each other. They cared ultimately for you: the reader! They brought a certain profession-alism to this committee you seldom see in volunteer organizations. The team, in the end of it all, made me feel blessed to have said yes to something that I would look back at and occasionally scream: "I said what?"

We are bound together now by the birthing of a book. This book has the very best parents in the whole-wide-world! Magnolia is fortunate to have had these writers, editors, photo experts, our main editor and designer, each bringing with them a definite sense of great book making, and a "sense of place" about the Magnolia they have come to know and love! I wonder how I will ever be able to transition from them . . . I will miss them so!

But, I am off! "I have done what I can do, and I am done!" (An old African expression.)

Now is the time to reacquaint myself with my gracious, understanding, very, very, very patient husband, Jonathon. He has known for over a year that an open door policy would be my style (and it was more like a revolving door, most days). His private life disappeared willingly. He put up with the midnight calls, even though we had call waiting, because on some days people just couldn't get through. He knew I had to be always, all ways accessible or I would not feel I had given my team my very best. He had his sleep disrupted as e-mail sometimes went out at 4 a.m. . . . some days I just wanted to talk jabberwocky, the nonsense of project management having gotten to me! I was a great conversationalist these past months! (He even never once recommended marriage counseling!).

Worst of all, many days I had to run away, find a special space where no one could find me, that had no curfew, where no questions were asked of me, no advice sought. Jonathon let me run away. Friends took me in . . . Finally, he noticed the phenomenon that I could go nowhere without lots of black book bags, boxes, and plastic bags. I lacked only a bellboy or a stolen grocery cart, and he stepped into that role for me as well. He was with me the night I shot the very last photo for the book at 11 p.m.

I also have four children somewhere. I must relearn their names . . . I remember it was important when we named them!

I will come upstairs and say "Hello" to my parents when they drop by to get a progress report on my well-being.

I will concentrate on my nine brothers and sisters as we plan a trip to Italy in 2002.

I will check in with those already golden friends who allowed me the year off . . . the type of thing only golden friendships can handle and survive. (I'm back!)

I will make our bed, delete my e-mail (over 2000), and make a nice red sauce with manicotti again and sit down to eat dinner with the family!

I'll listen to music again, especially Raffi, perhaps Bach? I'll make green eggs and ham for all those that kept me alive these past months by feeding me and reminding me to: EAT!

I'll write fiction again.

I will start less sentences with And, But, or However . . . (This is the sort of English up with which I will not put! -Winston Churchill). Me neither!

I will never, ever forget the privileges, pains, and prattlings I shared so openly about this wonderful Magnolia History Essay Project - Volume I, with people so bored of hearing it, but kind enough to fake it and listen anyway.

I thank every single person, archivist, organization, especially the Neighborhood Grants Department of the City of Seattle, and every Magnolia Community Club member who lent a hand.

To every person who gave a lead, an anecdote, a picture, a dollar, served as a source, as a fellow volunteer, I have the honor to present back to you a book I hope you will enjoy. A book I hope you will come to cherish . . . it is full of Magnolian pride and a special kind of caring this particular team created for our community.

I thank you for letting me work for all of you! I truly believe this is a great historical, sometimes hysterical presentation of our Magnolia community's memories and milestones.

As much as it was an adventure to write this book, it is my hope that you will experience adventure in reading it! It is not just a book of historical facts to be memorized . . . just the opposite! Instead, each essay presents a real Magnolian voice that speaks to you with the authority of historical background on the subject of which they write. This is a special

Opposite: "Enormous amount of blackberries", as a life-long Magnolia girl, I admit it . . . in eighth grade, blackberry mini-tarts were my specialty. The smell of a ripening blackberry bush in late August sunshine still brings back days of my youth. The boys can have their "dumb stunts"! Photo by Monica Wooton, 2000.

As I designed this project, I was highly influenced by the book: Lies My Teacher Told Me: Everything Your American History Textbook Got Wrong *by James Loewen. I recommend it highly!* Photo by Monica Wooton, 2000.

concert of Magnolia voices intertwined in a complicated chorus, the lines of a musical chorale, creating richer harmony of history, in a unique sound that makes up the best music that is Magnolia.

It is our hope that this collection of essays will entertain, educate, and excite you about the stories of where you come from or now belong: Magnolia (if you are just reading about us, we're happy you've come along!).

Dr. Henry Smith, first Magnolia pioneer risked everything to reach Smith's Cove. It is a story of risk-taking, written about historical figures in today's historical context, and about family. His son was a risk taker as well, whose consequences were very different.

A dedicated Magnolia citizen stands up to bureaucracy for twenty years, trying to save West Point beaches from a sewage treatment plant. It is a story of tenacity, with an ending that frustrates and inspires.

The history of Discovery Park is done by a man who spent his lifetime creating green spaces for Magnolia. He shares his unique experiences and specialized knowledge telling the story of this great Park.

One author's father disembarked at Fort Lawton years before the Korean War. On the 50th anniversary of what is called "The Forgotten War", our writer retells us the stories of the Army experience, and of finally working with veterans and the Army Reserve to plan and create a fitting commemoration for Korean War Vets at Fort Lawton. This is a story of US and Magnolian patriotism.

The book has so much more:

There are rare, one hundred year old, never published photos of the Magnolia area and early Magnolia families.

There is an interview with a woman who, as a young girl, lived with her sister and mother in an untraditional life on Magnolia in the 1920s (hyphenated names and a single parent family). This single parent became prominent in civil rights as the first woman lawyer in Seattle and later a State Senator from our district and first woman Magnolia Community Club President.

See a 1936 aerial photograph of Magnolia and compare it to how Magnolia looks today.

Remember Evelyn's Ice Creamery? There's a time-machine map of businesses in the Village, from 2000 back to its beginnings in 1927.

Now that you have this book in your hand, begin your adventure and explore!

The Magnolia History Essay Project, Volume I participants have spent many, many months creating the most interesting neighborhood history we could produce. We hope you will agree. It is with pride that we present to our community, Magnolia, a book that we are glad we wrote; and, are sure that in the reading of it you will be intrigued by the variety, quality, and amount of information we have provided for you, our fellow Magnolians, and all friends of Magnolia, wherever you live and our taking an interest in reading about us!

We proudly present to you: MAGNOLIA: Memories & Milestones. It is a song of praise about the place from which we hail!

Thankful to be a Magnolian

By Rick Malsed

This article appeared in the Magnolia News *December 1, 1999.*

Through the magic of newspaper deadlines, you're reading this about the time the Thanksgiving leftovers have run out, yet it's being written when a cold turkey sandwich is barely a gleam in the eye, just after our turkey had his second basting. We are awaiting the arrival of the outlaws from Spokane for the bird-day weekend. So please put yourself in reverse, back to the November Thursday when everyone gathers around the dinner table and reflects over their good fortunes.

Let's take a minute to share some of the many thank-able parts of Magnolia with each other before the last slice of turkey and piece of pumpkin pie disappears and the Thanksgiving warmth fades into other holiday shopping madness.

For more recent arrivals to Magnolia the list most likely includes being thankful neither end of the Magnolia (Garfield Street) Bridge is closed, the kids have a great summer swimming hole (parent parking shortage put aside), a golf day is just a five-minute drive by car, a fort that became a park full of discoveries, that Fred Meyer built on the Ballard side of the Ship Canal rather than at Fishermen's Terminal as they first wanted—(just kidding), 28th has a north-end mini park for a brief walk amongst the flowers, and that the double parking and jaywalking are still part of the Village charm and tradition.

From a 50-plus-year perspective the list of Magnolia thankfulness grows considerably. It starts with all the youthful Magnolia joys that now can fill a mid-aged mind and heart. Magnolia adventures like beach combing from 32nd's end all the way around to West Point, YMCA Day Camp at Magnolia Park and the path to the beach, Johnny's Pasture, Perkins Lane, the Goat's Trail, sledding the hills of Dravus and McGraw streets, biking everywhere on the Bluff, the Locks, Fort Lawton and those look-the-other-way MPs at the gates, the new house (our own private play grounds) building boom of the 1950s, Boots (my Lassie look-alike) waiting outside Briarcliff for class to end and her master to walk her home to 43rd Avenue West, a first girl kiss, a vanilla coke and side order of fries at Thrifty Drug after

Opposite; The Wolfe Creek Beach at 32nd Avenue West street-end. "Kayak friendly launch" spot today, yesterday's Tom's Dock, a popular swimming hole and pier of the port. Photo by Roy Scully, 2000.

junior high at Blaine, yo-yo contests every Wednesday next to J & J Pharmacy, the Village bowling alley, the Magnolia Theater (OK, and even Mrs. Chester we can now be thankful for), gas stations on every corner and Kelley's Chevron way down on 34th Avenue West (issuer of my first credit card), woods, woods, and more woods, playing Dinky Toy wars with Bob Leisy under the water tower, a *Seattle Times* paper route along the Boulevard and Magnolia Lane, the No. 19 bus when it was the "Carleton Park," and the lady who found little Ricky lost along Dravus Street in a blizzard in early 1950 and took him safely home.

The Magnolia News, *a great little neighborhood paper that runs monthly nostalgic columns of Magnolia's memories and milestones!* Photo by Monica Wooton, 2000.

Opposite: Owner-operated Italian restaurant, Luigi's is one of the "charming" businesses in the middle of Magnolia Village. Photo by Monica Wooton, 2000.

A slightly older review of Magnolia thanks includes the marked-off quarter mile (e.g., zero-to-60) along the Boulevard, the 28th Avenue West reservoir for midnight, sneak-in swimming, the closure of the Interbay open-burning dump and landfill, the near-lifetime years of medical care by the Drs. McElroy, a near-mouthful of fillings by Dr. German, and the many Village characters like Leon (shoe holes), Russ (shirts & pants) and Hugo (plants along with a twinkle from those warm, kind eyes), plus all the friends then and now from school days at Magnolia and Briarcliff Elementary, Blaine Junior High and Queen Anne High.

Collectively everyone in Magnolia, whether here just a day or a lifetime, can give thanks for all the people who make up our island kingdom, the owner-operators of the charming businesses in the Village and elsewhere around Magnolia, the Boulevard and other great neighborhood walks, the many public park spots around "town" including the just-completed renovation of the public beach area at the end of 32nd Avenue West as a kayak-friendly launch spot (the huge, old, eyesore outfall pipe on top of the beach is now buried), the charming homes and yards all around us, and the peace and seclusion that we find on the Bluff mis-named for the graceful trees along her edge which are still present after many struggles to survive.

Isn't it great, all there is thank-able about Magnolia (even after the leftovers are gone)?

Courtesy Rick Malsed and Mike Dillon, publisher, Queen Anne/Magnolia News.
Freelance writer Rick Malsed has lived on Magnolia since 1944, and is a monthly columnist for the Magnolia News.

Indians On Magnolia Before 1915

By Nancy Griffin Worssam

For at least 4,000 years before Europeans made their way to what is now Washington State, Magnolia welcomed a steady progression of Indian peoples to its bluffs and beaches. Although few Indians ever lived permanently on Magnolia, many camped here from time to time to harvest the rich natural bounty and enjoy the same beautiful landscape and vistas that give us pleasure today. The earliest of these people were quite primitive hunters and gatherers. By the time of white intrusion to this region; however, the Indian peoples who traveled through Magnolia were members of wealthy and sophisticated cultures. They counted their affluence and organized their society differently than we do; but, like us, they were conspicuous consumers, vied with one another for status, and thought rich was better than poor.

We have historical records and evidence from contemporary Indians to tell us about the lives of native peoples in the cultural region known as the Northwest Coast during the seventeenth through nineteenth centuries. We must, however, create the story of the lives of the earlier natives from archaeological remains. Sadly, archaeological vestiges are too often found by accident and arbitrarily preserved. German archaeologist Heinrich Schliemann discovered Troy by reading Homer. Contemporary archaeologists use climatic, topographic and cultural data to help them locate sites. It is far more likely that a prehistoric site is discovered by chance—erosion reveals long-buried cultural remains; a shepherd searching for a lost lamb falls into a cave, we build a road or a sewer plant. When a site is found, archaeologists use sophisticated methods of analysis to extract a remarkable amount of data, but we cannot know what the sites we haven't yet found might tell us. Thus, our understanding of prehistory changes through time as more information becomes available.

Despite this less than perfect record, we can say with reasonable certainty that the first people came to the Puget Sound Basin after the retreat of the last glacier about 13,000 years ago. These migratory hunters and gatherers moved down the Pacific Coast in small groups taking advantage of a wide range of food resources. As the years passed, old timers moved further south down the continent, newcomers arrived and the cultures evolved. Better fishing equipment, finer gathering tools, and more lethal and specialized points for spears and arrows were invented, allowing for more sophisticated subsistence activities.

Suquamish grave site of Chief Sealth at St. Peter's Roman Catholic Church, Suquamish Note the offerings at the bottom of the marker. Photo by Patty Small, 2000.

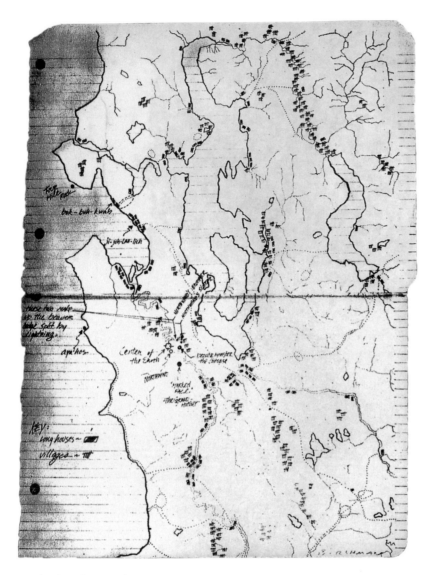

Archaeological sites in the Seattle area from David M. Buerge's "Lost Seattle." Copyright by *The Weekly*, March 6 – March 12, 1985.

The oldest archaeological evidence on Magnolia comes from analysis of a campsite with cultural remains that surfaced during construction of the sewer plant at West Point. It revealed the existence of generalized hunters/gatherers/fishers 4000 years ago. Evidence from 2,700 years ago at the same site showed that the people who camped on Magnolia at this later period were more restricted in their subsistence activities. They appeared at this time to have focused their attention quite strongly on salmon, clams and mussels, a clear sign to archaeologists that their culture was more sophisticated and had begun to foreshadow the lifestyle of the peoples who were here to greet the European and American pioneers centuries later. An archaeological assessment at Fort Lawton corroborates the West Point story but doesn't add much to it.

From historical records, archaeological analyses in other parts of the Seattle region, and extrapolation from contemporary Indian people, we know that for hundreds of years before Euro-American settlement the region was inhabited by groups of very sophisticated people whose anglicized name is Duwamish. The territory of the Duwamish people extended south along the Duwamish River as far as Renton and went north to the Sammamish River. Although the Duwamish were still semi-nomadic hunters/gatherers/ fishers, they had permanent villages in which they lived during the winter months. During the rest of the year, they followed an orderly hunting, gathering, fishing, and trading cycle. The permanent villages were located in West Seattle, on the east shore of Elliott Bay in what is now downtown Seattle and Belltown, and along the shores of Lake Washington and Lake Sammamish. An extensive village complex also existed in what is present-day Ballard on the north side of the long tidal estuary known today as Salmon Bay. A small contingent of the Ballard or Shilshole Duwamish lived on Magnolia, across the estuary from their fellow villagers.

All of these permanent villages were laid out parallel to the shorelines and consisted of hundreds of people, or perhaps even a thousand or more. Their orientation to the water reflected a lifestyle in which travel was mostly by canoe and much of the food was harvested from the waters.

It is probable that those who lived on Salmon Bay and along Lake Washington, Lake Union and Lake Sammamish had strong ties with the more southerly Duwamish but considered themselves a separate social division. They came into the historical record as Duwamish, and all Duwamish as well as the Suquamish, Snohomish, Puyallup, and other tribal groups are considered closely related by anthropologists because of the similarities of their languages. Together they are known as the Puget Sound Salish.

In the pleasant months when natural resources were at their peak, the Indians left their villages and moved from one temporary campsite to another, collecting the earth's gifts as they presented themselves in greatest abundance. It was during this time that Indians other than the Shilshole group came to Magnolia. They probably set up camp above the beaches where they would fish and collect clams and mussels and smoke them, putting vast quantities aside for trade and winter consumption. After the collecting and fishing were done, they moved on, trading their excesses with villages whose people had accumulated different provisions. This trade allowed specialization in resource collection and insured that all the Puget Sound Salish had marine, lake and forest products.

The Northwest Coast of America was rich in food, and it provided for its pre-European inhabitants a level of luxury unknown to other hunting and gathering peoples anywhere in what is now the United States and Canada. All along the Pacific Coast from northern California through the Alaskan Panhandle, these people gathered the extraordinary profusion provided by an environment of abundant woods and generous rivers and shores—berries, roots, bulbs, deer, elk, muskrat, bear, waterfowl, clams, mussels, oysters, sea mammals, and fish. Fish of all sorts were important, but particularly the salmon that came by the millions each year as they made the runs from sea to spawning ground. Rivers turned roiling red as 5 million to 10 million fish headed upstream and, on their way, favored the Indians with fish harvests that can only be dreamed about today.

Gathering basket used by Duwamish in their yearly gathering cycle. From the collection of the Burke Museum #8650

Throughout the region, these Indians had developed sophisticated tools and subsistence strategies that adapted them well to their generous environment. This allowed them to accumulate great excesses beyond their immediate needs and made them very wealthy people. Because of the wealth, their social structure became highly stratified—ranging from slaves to high nobles. There was some specialization of labor. Each person knew exactly what his or her place was within the community. Lineage was of great importance. Their political systems were quite complex. These shared social and economic practices are the hallmarks of traditional Northwest Coast Indian life. Also shared by the Northwest Coast Indians were striking art forms, the extensive use of cedar, and the potlatch, a ceremonial gathering at which the host validated and increased the family's status through elaborate gift giving. The potlatch was a central feature of social life. Not only did it serve to validate status, but it reaffirmed the social bonds and was a core economic mechanism that made possible the redistribution of wealth.

Much of Northwest Coast culture was, indeed, held in common, but the particularities of life varied according to ecological zone. The greatest riches, the most elaborate arts and the greatest attention to status occurred in northern British Columbia and the Alaskan Panhandle. Peoples living in the southern regions of the culture zone, including the Duwamish, lived very well, but had somewhat less surplus than their northern neighbors. For these southern peoples, status was not quite so finely defined, and the arts not quite so well developed. But they still had sufficient resources to establish permanent villages whose size exceeded that of any other known hunting and gathering people on the continent.

It is estimated that the Shilshole Duwamish on Salmon Bay numbered from 600 to 1,000 residents in the seventeenth century. Their cedar plank houses, lined up along the shore in a single row facing the water, could be 200 feet long. Four or five families lived in each house during the winter months. There were probably one or two long houses on the Magnolia side of the bay. At that time, it was possible to walk across the bay at low tide. The Magnolia-side villagers might well have resided there to take advantage of the plentiful fresh water supplied by a creek that drained from what is now Fort Lawton to the shore.

In winter, when all of the families returned from their various subsistence activities, the villages teemed with activity. This was the time the people sponsored potlatches, renewed social bonds, refreshed relations with the supernaturals, and repaired and made the tools necessary for the yearly round—harpoons, fish hooks, spears, and baskets.

Religious ceremonies were time consuming and elaborate. The villagers gathered to support the shamans, their religious leaders, whose job it was to reinforce the ties between humans and the spirit world, and to protect the village from threatening, malevolent forces. During the winter solstice, the most dramatic of all shamanistic ceremonies took place, marking the end of the old year and the beginning of the new. At this time of perceived danger, shamans crossed the boundaries between the human and supernatural worlds in search of souls taken by ghosts. Through powerful rituals, incantations, and deep knowledge they would recapture the souls and work to assure good fortune for villagers during the coming year. The shamans were compelling forces, and good fortune did indeed mark the lives of these people until the late eighteenth century.

In the late eighteenth century, the fortunes of the Shilshole population declined. Diseases introduced by European explorers and traders were devastating. Recurrent raids from northern tribes further decimated

Map of historic tribes in Western Washington. Courtesy of www.historylink.com

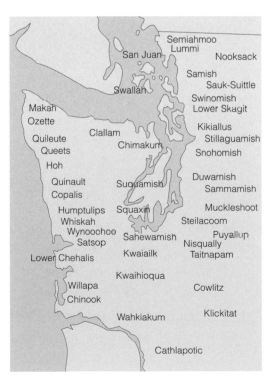

the population. The Indians in northern British Columbia, southeastern Alaska and the Queen Charlotte Islands—Haida, Tlingit, Tsimshian, Kwakiutl—with their more affluent economies and more elaborated social structures, developed an insatiable demand for riches and the status that went with them. They wanted more than they had and found that through raids they gained more status than through subsistence activities. Like the Vikings who ravaged the coasts of Great Britain many centuries before, these adventurers came by sea and assaulted without warning. They raided to take slaves and booty, avenge a wrong, mourn a death. A reason could always be found for a raid, and every successful raid brought riches that added to status in societies obsessed with social position.

Their seagoing craft were open boats, 30 to 100 feet long, 8 feet abeam, each side lined with warriors paddling in perfect synchronization. Silently they came, to wreak bloody havoc, hacking the heads off the bodies of the slain, then carrying these trophies back to their own villages along with the individuals they chose to enslave. The local inhabitants fought as best they could, escaped into the woods when it was possible, and over the long term watched their populations decline and their fortunes shrink.

Raiding intensified as local groups like the Lummis, Nisquallies and Yakima took up the practice. It escalated still further when the Hudson Bay Company established its trading post at Fort Victoria in 1843, providing new opportunities to trade stolen goods. The raids continued well into the period of settlement by people of European descent. By the time Dr. Henry Smith settled in Smith Cove on Magnolia in 1852, there were probably only a dozen Duwamish families in Shilshole.

The raiding warriors didn't distinguish between white farm settlements and Indian longhouses in their search for riches. All local inhabitants were in jeopardy. Despite the fact that these attacks had been going on throughout the Puget Sound region for generations, the white settlers in Western Washington viewed it in a very personal fashion; and, despite their generally good relations with their close Indian neighbors, they considered the raids a form of warfare.

Raiding did become war in 1855 after Isaac I. Stevens, Territorial Governor appointed by President Franklin Pierce, traveled through Washington Territory announcing to local tribal leaders that the US Government was going to purchase their lands and remove their people to reservations. The Indians didn't really understand what was going on. Few, if any of them, spoke English. But, Stevens and the other government officials never questioned the morality or legality of this. It was manifest destiny.

In 1851, the US government first began awarding land claims to the new settlers. In 1854, the Puget Sound Indian leaders and their neighbors east of the Cascades were cajoled and coerced into signing the Point Elliott Treaty which formalized the surrender of the land they used, put severe restrictions on the traditional Indian lifestyle, and condemned many to confinement on reservations. The treaty discussions were probably carried on in the Chinook jargon, a patois of about 500 words designed for trade and clearly not sufficient to explain the fine points of treaties.

Wood crafts were highly developed among the Northwest Coast Indians. Duwamish tools from the collection of the Burke Museum #25.0/358

The Indian leaders certainly did not understand the implications of the treaty, but there was much else that they didn't understand about their new neighbors. Indian misunderstandings of white culture were prevalent, as were white misconceptions about Indian ways. Both assumed that the other shared their worldview and saw the world through the same lens. But it just wasn't so.

Basic assumptions about life were in conflict. Generous hospitality was a sacred duty to the Indians who were outraged when 20 or 30 of them showed up at a homestead ready to eat and the white settlers locked them out. Whites saw land as property that could be owned. Indians used land. It could no more be owned than could the air they breathed. Cultural misunderstandings existed on almost every front and, naturally, led to hostilities as each people saw its way of life threatened.

Although the Point Elliott Treaty wasn't ratified by the US Senate until 1859, from 1851 on, whites increasingly began to take over the lands that the Indians had traditionally used. The Indians thus came to a better understanding of the full meaning of the Treaty. Relations between some Indians and the whites deteriorated rapidly. White encroachment outraged the Yakima and their neighbors, the Wenatchee. It seemed perfectly reasonable to them to take revenge through escalated raids. In January 1856, Yakima and Wenatchee warriors marched across the mountains to Seattle, the settlement in Pioneer Square, with the goal of ravaging the white settlers. In that raid, two whites were killed. Indian losses weren't documented. Tensions heightened. Secretary C. H. Mason, Acting Governor of the Washington Territory, asked for federal troops. New forts to protect the region were built at places like Bellingham and Port Townsend. By 1857, the US Army succeeded in temporarily putting a stop to all raids including those from the north. The northern attacks resumed by 1859 and finally ended in 1860. By that time traditional Indian life in the Seattle region was in its death throes. The reservation period had begun.

Not all Indians went to the reservations, however. Some Indian women were married to white men. They were spared exile, although their husbands were subject to sanctions during the hostilities. Other Indians managed to find a way to make themselves useful to the Euro-American community by providing cheap labor or establishing good trading relations. They were allowed to live on the outskirts of the white settlements.

Although there are references in some sources to other traditional Indian families on Magnolia, the last well-documented traditional Indians to reside here were Salmon Bay Charlie (Hwehlchtid or Hwelch'teed) and his wife Madellene (Chilohleeet'sa). They lived on a spit of land jutting out into Salmon Bay down the hill from what is now Discovery Park,

Although not renowned for their beadwork, the Duwamish did learn to bead in the late contact period. From the collection of the Burke Museum #1-2158

in the late nineteenth and early twentieth centuries. Their single-room wooden house was a composite of features, mixing those of the traditional long houses of the Duwamish people with the turn-of-the-century wooden houses of the recent settlers. From this house Charlie and Madellene collected seafood along the shore and took their boat out to fish. A ramp led down to the beach, and at low tide they walked to the north shore of Salmon Bay to visit their 30 or 40 Shilshole Duwamish neighbors, the last remnants of the village on the Ballard side of the Bay.

Using the subsistence techniques they had learned from their elders as children, Charlie, Madellene and the Indians on the north shore were able to carve out an acculturated existence for themselves by selling salmon, clams and berries to their white neighbors. Charlie used his traditional Duwamish canoe to get from place to place as he conducted business in the white communities. The money gained from these sales was used to purchase goods introduced by the whites. Charlie claimed to have been a headman of his people and according to oral history was said to have hosted at least one potlatch.

According to some sources, traditional indigenous life on Magnolia came to an end in 1916 when the Army Corps of Engineers completed the ship canal and dredged Salmon Bay. Madellene had died in her home shortly after the work began. Charlie was taken away to one of the reservations by the Bureau of Indian Affairs. Some sources, however, suggest that Charlie was taken away at least 20 years earlier. We do know for certain that the Army Corps of Engineers obliterated the promontory on which Charlie's house was located and displaced any remaining Indians on the Ballard side of the Bay.

In the course of its dredging, the Corps uncovered a sizable shell midden in the vicinity of Charlie's home. A shell midden is the equivalent of a prehistoric garbage dump, a rich source of cultural information for archaeologists. The dredging was not interrupted for archaeological assessment of the site, however, so whatever record was there was destroyed before it could be interpreted.

Salmon Bay Charlie collected berries and seafood to trade with his white neighbors. Nordic Heritage Museum. Courtesy of Neil Thompson. Discovery Park Archive. Circa early 1900s.

With Charlie and Madellene, the story of Magnolia's traditional Indian history comes to an end. But through intermarriage, Indian genes entered the gene pool of Seattle's early settlers; some of these descendants live here still, many with no knowledge of their connection to the native population. In addition to these, there are contemporary Indian residents, descendants of the Indians of the past, who have chosen to live in Magnolia. They enrich our neighborhood and remind us of this region's past.

Salmon Bay Charlie and officials shortly before he was taken to one of the reservations. Photo by Clarence Langstaff. Circa 1900.

Thirty years after the gathering at which the Point Elliott Treaty was introduced to the assembled Indian leaders, an early Magnolia resident, Dr. Henry Smith, "translated" the speech that Sealth or Chief Seattle gave to that assembly of territorial and Indian leaders in 1854. The speech that Smith set down for the historical record is long, eloquent, and most effective in supporting the nineteenth century white view that the Indians were destined to disappear from this earth. Considering that Smith committed it to paper 30 years after it was given and that memory is a capricious companion, considering that the original speech was most likely delivered in the 500-word Chinook trade language, it is unlikely that Smith's version is exactly true to the original. Smith's language is, however, compelling and does remind us that there was a time when only Indian people lived on or visited Magnolia. We do well to remember that heritage.

> *The soil is rich with the life of our kindred. And when the last red man*
> *shall have perished from the earth, and his memory among white men*
> *shall have become a myth, these shores shall swarm with the invisible*
> *dead of my tribe, and when your children's children shall think of*
> *themselves alone in the field, the store, the shop, upon the*
> *highway, or in the silence of the woods, they will not be alone.*

Chief Seattle (as remembered by Dr. Henry Smith)

Nancy Griffin Worssam, a Magnolia resident since 1998, is a newcomer to Seattle. She is an anthro-pologist by training and taught a broad curriculum, including courses in Native American History and Culture at Quinnipiac College in Hamden, Connecticut. As a program officer at the National Endowment for the Humanities, she worked with native groups throughout the country and represented the Endowment on the Department of Interior, Bureau of Indian Affairs, American Indian Art & Culture Review Panel. She is now a consultant who works principally with museums on strategic planning and organizational development.

Looking toward Salmon Bay from Shilshole Bay in the early twentieth century before the Locks were built. Salmon Bay Charlie's house is on the Magnolia side. White settler farms are on the Ballard side. Courtesy of Webster & Stevens Collection, Museum of History and Industry #83.10.9067. Circa 1914

Making History?
Magnolia's First Pioneer

By Monica Wooton

___

FOREWORD

Dr. Henry Smith takes on very large dimensions in the reflections of his loving daughter's reminisces and a few available paragraphs of biographers. While Ione Smith Graff's writings offer a special perspective on Smith, it is just that: a daughter's memories of a loving and fun childhood fifty years after the fact, and a strong and understandable belief in her father and his abilities. Most sources consider him a "hero" type, quietly striving to make Seattle a better place to live. Few biographers mention the extent or source of his wealth, or his moneymaking impetus. All cast him as a compassionate Seattle pioneer and leader, loving fellow settlers and native Indians equally. Yet, there is little written on his business deals. Ione is the first source found to explain how Smith acquired his acreage through a rather healthy inheritance, and then built an empire in Seattle.

REFLECTIONS OF A DAUGHTER . . .

"My father, Dr. Henry Allen Smith was born in Wooster, Ohio; April 11, 1830. He was the tenth of eleven children . . . medium height and build . . . a high forehead, a Roman nose, expressive blue eyes . . . while young, soft wavy black hair which, as I first remember him, had turned quite gray. His third generation grandfather was Baron Nicholas von Schmidt whose son, Copelton, against his parents' wishes, married the girl of his choice, Katrina, and left with her for America, arriving in Philadelphia in the year 1760. There he eventually acquired large land holding in now what is the heart of that great city."[1]

Copelton fought in the Revolutionary War. His son Nicholas decided to change the family name to Smith and that became the formal family name in America. Nicholas and his wife, who were Henry A. Smith's great grandparents, were soon killed by Indians, but their baby son, also named Nicholas, was "miraculously saved."[2]

The younger Nicholas Smith, Henry's father and Ione Smith's grandfather, grew up to be "a powerful man, physically, mentally, morally" and a preacher in the Baptist religion when he converted to the Disciples of Christ Church. The pastors of these particular congregations were required to support their churches through their own labor and business endeavors.[3]

Smith Cove Park named after Dr. Henry A. Smith, commemorating his landing here on Magnolia. When he arrived in 1852, mud-flats went from here to Dravus street. Photo by Monica Wooton, 2000.

Nicholas took contracts to dig canals and was very successful. With his earnings, he built a three-story brick church and dwelling, using the third floor as the church. It was built in Wooster, Ohio, in 1837. Henry Smith was seven years old at this time. His father would die at the age of 50, having served in the War of 1812, leaving Henry's mother, Abigail Teaff Smith, alone with Henry's youngest sister Ellender.[4]

An interesting painting of Smith's property done most likely by Emily Denny. The scene is noted for its naive style yet showing contemporary transportation. Note: the steam engine train. "The encroachment of industrial society is indicated by the ravaged portion of land in the foreground." The idealism of the setting is also evident. Museum of History and Industry Archive # 878/3.

MINISTRY OF MEDICINE

"My father entered Allegheny College, Meadville, Pennsylvania with the intention of studying for the ministry but later decided that he could do more good in the world as a physician and therefore took up the study of medicine." After Allegheny, an internship in Ohio, finishing his professional work at the office of Dr. Charles Roode and later at the University of Pennsylvania, Smith was ready to begin a medical career.[5]

Ione recounts that as a young man, Smith set out West: "One day in the spring of 1851, he told {his} mother, that he had an opportunity to travel out west . . . as a medical assistant physician." Smith's mother responded with "shock and dismay: 'People die on those trips!' to which the 22-year-old Smith replied, 'That's just why I'm going, to stop that—to keep people from dying.'" He promised to return for Ellender if it was "to his liking." "Papa's mother, being a wise woman" decided to accompany him and take Ellender, who had just finished her schooling, on the trip right then. They traveled in a covered wagon with another doctor by the name of Millard.[6]

Smith, at 22, was probably still somewhat naive about how the West and its cities developed. But, demonstrating great medical sense and unusual common sense, Smith brought cholera medicine with him, knowing that the disease was prevalent on the wagon trains. To his credit, his instincts and humanitarianism saved many lives.

When he left Ohio, he was most likely not dreaming of the bustling commerce and busy steam trains, or the active docks and lucrative worldwide trade which would all emanate from the place where he would eventually settle—the marshy southern shores of a place called Magnolia. Medicine was his vocation, agriculture his avocation by admission. And he was headed for "California Gold Country" to utilize those skills and perhaps strike it rich there.[7]

BELIEF, LOGIC AND LUCK

It was during this trip that some important information was passed on to Smith. "The Northern Pacific Railway announced plans to extend to the Puget Sound country"—a highly undeveloped part of the west of which Henry had heard glowing reports.[8] Smith did not miss the implication of the potential cash reality of railroads and cities, given his intelligence and better-than-average social background. He seemed to realize this railroad could bring with it great commerce and economic growth. Soon, this most compelling idea was the one that called Smith away from California and spurred him onward to Magnolia.

Leaving his mother and sister in Portland, Henry traveled to Puget Sound in a small canoe. Some accounts say a gruff but friendly pioneer named L. M. Collins told Smith to pack his duds promising "in three day's time I will land you in the Garden of Eden or give you my head as a football."[9] Along the harbor, Smith saw a bay flanked on both sides with good possibilities to make a railroad track and shipping piers, using fill, over vast tidelands.

Scouting the area, he found a valley between Elliott Bay and the inner harbor of Salmon Bay. There he staked a donation claim of 160 acres.[10]

The boundaries of this claim were West Barrett to West Armour Street, and 16th Avenue West to 20th Avenue West.[11] The beauty of the country struck him profoundly. He wrote about it often in his later life in poetic form in journals, some of which were published.[12]

Young Smith, working on logic, rumors and discussions with fellow settlers such as David Denny, seemed more and more vindicated in his choice of property for the potential railroad land. Smith determined that this cove was the perfect spot for shipping docks and a natural tidewater terminus for a transcontinental railroad that would someday reach Puget Sound by way of the old Indian trail across the mountains. More than 40 years later the Seattle, Eastern, Lakeshore Railway Company did reach Seattle. The great shipping piers Denny and Smith envisioned at Smith's Cove subsequently became a reality also.

DR. HENRY A. SMITH

The most "official" portrait used for Dr. Smith.
UW Special Collections
#UW 18650.

MORE THAN EXPECTED

Smith brought his mother and sister to his new land. "His mother staked a claim a bit to the north. He built a two-story frame house, with lumber which was brought to the cove on scows from Yesler's mill and then by ox-teams to the building site."[13] This luxury illustrated that Smith was a little better off than one would imagine given his age and life experiences to date.

Smith, now with a reputation as a "visionary" and the common sense of a businessman, could also see the probability of a canal connecting lakes and Salmon Bay to Puget Sound. With the bay located next to his claim, this provided potential to make financial gains.

In these early days of the densely wooded and lowly populated city, he did not stand around and dream. Smith was a man of zealous industry. He built a cabin for his mother and sister.

This US Army Corp of Engineers map shows the piers and railroad Smith envisioned many years before the reality came near Smith's Cove.

When Indians burned the cabin down, his mother and Ellender moved temporarily to the safety of the Seattle blockhouses used as shelter during the Indian War days. Smith defended the colony along with the town leaders; their main raiders were Indians from Eastern Washington. The War ended in the fall of 1856. He bought more property from settlers who fled during the conflict, raising his land holdings to 800 acres.[14]

By now, Ellender had married Charles Plummer, a wealthy town merchant, and Smith's mother kept house at Smith's log cabin, while he built her another home in the orchard near the burnt remains of the one previously destroyed.[15]

Ione wrote about her parents: "In 1862, Henry Smith married Miss Mary Ann Genevieve Phelan of Portland Oregon, a red cheeked brunette with a lithe figure . . . and a very gracious manner. Her father had immigrated from the County Cork Ireland, first settled in Madison, Wisconsin where he acquired large land holdings."[16]

At Grand Boulevard (now West Dravus Street) and 15th Avenue West, Smith decided to establish a medical practice and built an infirmary on the side of his home, continuing to grow plenty of fruits and vegetables, and raising animals. When his practice slowed down, he recognized the local population's good health. Clarence Bagley, a historian and contemporary of Smith, wrote: "They afforded him too little sickness to realize any profit on medicine, he had better work a piece of land like everyone else."[17]

Eventually, he built a fine reputation as a doctor who treated both Indians and white settlers. From then on, a medical practice of some sort continued at all three of his homes, where no one was ever turned away. If they couldn't pay him, they could help clear land. According to Smith: "They wouldn't have any money, but they always promised to send me some. I found that promises to pay didn't get much farther than their lips, so I tumbled to the scheme of setting them to work clearing up my 800 acres until they had settled their bills."[18]

Smith had a certain respect for the Indians as human beings and took the time to try to learn their language. Smith is quoted as saying, "Many persons are honestly of the opinion that Indians have no ideas above catching and eating salmon, but if they will lay aside prejudice and converse freely with the more intelligent ones . . ."[19]

Smith has been credited with the translations of Chief Seattle's speeches, and had those versions printed in papers such as *The Seattle Star*. (Questioned are Smith's ability to translate Seattle's true native speech and the possibility that the translations included Smith's own prose style. This is under study at the university level and by those in post-graduate study and research. See story on page 39.)

Typical picture of the type of land Dr. Smith would have farmed in the Interbay area where his first donation claim was made. Courtesy Paul Dorpat.

HELPING . . . A QUESTION OF . . .

Many others came to see the potential of Smith's Cove, and made claims. Due to various difficulties some homesteaders lost hope and wanted to sell. Ione offered her view on the situation that reflected how Smith's property holdings expanded: "In order to help them, Papa, who had inherited money from his father's estate, bought one claim after another and that is how he acquired over a thousand acres of land at Smith's Cove . . . "[20]

With the Civil War being fought in the East, a number of factors caused the railroad to be postponed. Those long piers were still just a dream. Despite all of this, Smith was able to increase his holdings and bank account.

Henry busied himself as he practiced medicine, farmed, and dealt in commerce, government work, and Republican politics. He was not one to seek the spotlight and worked quietly about his business:

A City of Seattle Map from the era when Washington was still a territory and not an official state. Shows early claims in the Magnolia Area. Note: Smith's claim next to Salmon Bay. Courtesy Paul Dorpat.

"No sir, I never dabbled in politics. It is true I represented King County five different times, and I was the first Superintendent of Schools King County ever had, but I never asked a man to vote for me in my life, and I never sought office. I didn't like politics and I didn't like to hold office, but Lord bless us when I found myself at Olympia. I did the best I could."[21]

FAMILY, MORE LARGE LAND HOLDINGS

As the Smiths prospered, Mary Phalen Smith gave birth to seven daughters and one son. The latest Smith address given by Ione at this time was: "Off the Bluff and toward downtown: at 2nd Avenue and James." Smith bought a 600-acre island at the mouth of the Snohomish River, and moved his family there after he felt his cove improvements were for the most part accomplished.

On the island, he began a series of experiments to reclaim tidelands, as he had read they had done in Holland. He published his fairly successful results of food development in these kinds of tidal soils. The end result of this experimentation was the discovery that certain vegetables and fruits could be grown successfully on this marshy, salty, extensive land surrounding Puget Sound and opened the potential of more land acquisitions.[22]

Smith published articles on the subject. As was his practice to write, whether it was poetry on the beauty of Puget Sound, his interpretations of a Chief Sealth speech, or agricultural practices. He left a plentiful collection of written work behind when he died—many under the pen name of Paul Garland.[23]

He built a hospital for the Indians on the Island, and often traveled by canoe to answer the call of a sick patient. Smith was eventually appointed Governor of the Tulalip Reservation. He owned and managed 12 logging camps and a general store on the island as well.[24]

A shipping bill of the
Seattle Lake Shore and
Eastern Railroad. Dr.
Smith sold much of his
land for great profit, years
after he positively believed
a train would come through
his property. Courtesy of
Paul Dorpat.

MORE . . .

In 1878, when Smith returned to Seattle and Smith's Cove, his wealth had greatly appreciated with the rise in land values. Finally, the railroad came. He sold 9,550 acres of land for $75,000. Of the experience, Smith was quoted as saying:

"The Lake Shore and Eastern Railroad finally came along and I drew up an agreement with them whereby they were to purchase my land (all but 50 acres) provided they made their terminals on Smith Cove. They did this, but when the time for operation came they informed me that they would have to run a branch to Seattle, and of course, they made their terminals there. Oh, those railroad men are smart fellows."[25]

Because of his wealth, Smith was the largest taxpayer in King County for years. Later, he was named the first superintendent of schools. He served in the legislature, and according to Bagley, "never sought office, never asked for a vote and was never defeated. While he was presiding officer in the council there was never an appeal of his rulings."[26]

In her memoirs, Ione continued:

"In 1880, my mother died. And, then my Father, in order to insure freedom, safety and proper care for us children moved us back to the Ranch (their original property in Interbay) . . . On the property was "a 2 story house with four large rooms . . . to make it big enough for the family, he added a west wing consisting of eight large rooms and a large basement. That is the house in which we children grew up."[27]

"Boulevard" located on
Grand Boulevard Street
(now West Dravus Street),
was the first "Magnolia
village that sprung up".
Courtesy of Paul Dorpat.

LIFE WRAPPED UP IN MOTHERLESS CHILDREN

From then on, Smith took primary care of his children, and according to Ione, found this to be a rewarding job. He fit in many hobbies, agricultural mainly, to round out his activities. He wanted the children to grow up back on the Ranch. This house that was located at 2827 15th Avenue West is the house most photographed as the Smith residence. It eventually was sold in a dilapidated and abandoned state nearly 20 years after the Smiths resided there, in a tax sale, for a little more than $1,000. When condemned by the City for the land for the Interbay Dump a year later, in early 1946, it was appraised at $17,000.[28]

Smith's approach to child rearing was unique in that according to Ione, "he assigned the oldest child to watch the youngest, the second oldest the next, and so on. So that each of us little ones had a loving sister to care for her."

The Indians had a friendly relationship with Smith and kept him supplied with clams, and fish, and Ione's brother Ralph Waldo hunted fowl. Extra foods were always shared with neighbors:

"We younger children had our riding ponies and the older girls rode the carriage horses. Ralph had his own horse. He always accompanied us little ones when we rode over the beautiful old logging roads whose skids were worn level. Ferns, violets and trilliums grew there in profusion. The blooming

shrubs were most beautiful; then we children lay and tromped in the warm tide-flats and pools of water, we had our very own lovely sandy bathing beach with water warmed from having come in over the tide flats."[29]

Formal education was not ignored. The children's first schoolhouse was a large room in a building that Smith owned. He later hired Miss Flora Fond, daughter of the West Point Lighthouse operator as their teacher. Ione added:

"Papa donated some land on which a schoolhouse was built and it had separate boys' and girls' cloak-rooms. . . . modern for the times. Sunday school and church services were held in the same building . . . at times we were taught in our home . . . my brother Ralph rode his horse to the Denny School. At various times my elder sisters attended the Mills Seminary, Oakland California, Annie Wright Seminary in Tacoma, and St. Ann's Convent in British Columbia . . . I finished eighth grade at the Mercer School then entered the Old Central High School in 1892."[30]

Ione reports about her home life: "It was not unusual for guests to come in the night and make themselves at home without disturbing us. All winter, day and night, logs blazed in the fireplace of our living room . . . an iron teakettle with hot water always hung on the crane. We had six outside doors, none of which were ever locked."[31]

The Smith house never seemed to be empty, as some guests would stay for more than a year:

"We never spent a winter alone at the Ranch and our Seattle friends came mostly in the summers. We had only one bathroom with running cold water and it was necessary to get hot water from a large tank at the back of our stove. All rooms had pitchers and basins, and wash stands. Harvesters, apple pickers, and sheep-shearers came seasonally bringing their own equipment."[32]

A Family Tragedy
Ione recounts:

"Ralph told Papa that he would make just one more {trip to Alaska} then settle down in Seattle, but Ralph said he wanted some of the thrills of adventure in life before settling down with his feet under a desk. Then Papa said: Why should you have to go to Alaska for adventure when you have everything right here in the State of Washington? And, Ralph replied: Why did you have to come west for adventure when you had everything in Ohio?"*[33]

2827 15th Avenue West, "The Ranch", had seen busier, happier days. The Smiths were gone at the time this picture was taken. Museum of History and Industry Archive #SHS 4322, circa late 1940s.

After a number of years during which he made several trips to Alaska, Ralph Waldo and his companion Fred Campbell drowned while exploring the Aleutian Islands in a sailboat in 1892. Their bodies were not recovered.[34]

Opposite: Dr. Henry Smith as he appeared in his later life. Now more the farmer than the gentleman.
Courtesy of Paul Dorpat.

VISION AGAIN, JUST LUCK, OR CERTAIN LOGIC . . .

". . . Just after two men had been drowned in Lake Washington . . . it became necessary to find a new source of water-supply. Therefore, when two men came out from town to ask my father's advice, . . . I heard him say: 'Cedar River is our God-given water reservoir with a constant supply of pure water from the Cedar River'...the men protested . . . it was too far away . . . it would cost too much...the city was not large enough for an undertaking. But, Papa maintained {his position}..bonds could be issued. It was not long before this development was made." The Cedar River Water Shed lasts as a protected water supply today.[35]

HARD TIMES TOOK THEIR TOLL

To Ione, Dr. Henry A. Smith's "power of accomplishment seemed to lay in the ease with which he could turn from one form of activity to another. Whatever he was doing absorbed his whole attention. If he asked me to hold a tree straight [while he planted it], I felt it a privilege."[36]

She wrote of asking her father what he considered himself to be, and he responded, "I would call myself an agriculturist because I so enjoy working with nature in accordance with God's laws which are absolute and eternal . . . " Her thoughts on his response indicate that she thought very highly of her father. ". . . to me [that] was a modest answer . . . because he was considered to be a very successful physician and surgeon, a statesman, a poet, a scholar and a writer."[37]

Smith had tried to hold onto 50 acres that might have been of a great value to him assuming the development of a canal utilizing Salmon Bay succeeded as Fishermen's Terminal. His property would be needed for its completion. Like the railroad, it seemed a progressive plan. The economic depression of 1893 devoured his large land holdings: his city block, island, buildings, and other property.

What remained were 10 lots on Queen Anne Hill. He ended up living there. His last orchard, vegetable patch, and flower garden were there. He died in 1915, at age 85, allegedly of influenza. Ione wrote that he seemed to feel that he had not done all that he wanted to do with his life, quoting him as saying one day, "I would like to live a little longer, there is so much to be learned and I know so little."[38]

"In the summer of 1893, a tragic thing happened. Papa was in an accident in which he suffered a fractured skull and internal injuries. He was sick about seven years during which period it was necessary to entrust the management of his affairs to others who grossly mismanaged them. That all happened during depression years."[39]

"When, I look back upon my childhood years, I see a kind and loving father whose main interest in life seemed to be wrapped up in his motherless children . . . I can still see our happy family gathered before the blazing fire on winter evenings . . . those years have never been erased from my memory."[40]

AFTERWORD

In present historical research, we are often advised to look between the lines to see what is missing. Smith was more than what vanity histories present him as. This man was smart, talented, risky, stubborn, and somewhat rigid. He was humble about the inevitability of his political involvements, despite going back into politics—"something he hated." Reading between the lines becomes necessary when one observes that Smith's daughter Ione wrote that he helped those who wanted out of the cove by buying their property from them. What is not articulated is Smith's possible gain by providing this kind of help.

Reading between the lines, one sees a shrewd, exacting, absorbed, smart businessman who pinpointed the exact location of the Smith Cove railroad site and obstinately kept the railroad development idea alive for the years it took to make a fortune from it. Yet at the same time, equally clear, is the father who cared about his children and loved them while accepting the responsibility of raising them alone.

SMITH COVE PARK

The 1974 Treaty of Magnolia created an underwater extension south of Smith Cove Park. This very significant document limits the Port's future activities and defines a local public process in management of Terminal 90/91.

This Park prevents further westward expansion of Port activities while providing underwater habitat. Originally at 25-acres, some of this Park was traded, permitting the Elliott Bay Marina to move eastward while enlarging the westerly underwater habitat.

During his time, he was the richest man in Seattle who paid the most taxes. In Ione's kind interpretation, he was a man who "helped" all those who had acreage to sell. This assistance cannot be viewed as all too altruistic. The real Smith is more complex than his daughter's single perspective.

This Magnolia pioneer was an unusual man filled with odd energy and curiosity, whose interesting story is never really told in-depth in existing histories. He had an unusual well-to-do life in his time in history. As the first Magnolia settler he becomes most important in our study of Magnolia's beginnings and in the glimpse of Seattle developing as a city. Like peeling one of Smith's homegrown onions, we must seek all of the layers of this interesting man. We should avoid historical stereotypes, over-simplified family admiration, or histories that tell us about Smith by omitting more of his life than recording it. This is exactly what historians are asking of us as we take a look back from our day and age!

This shows the area of the underwater park. Photo by Monica Wooton, 2000.

Monica Wooton thought that a look at the first permanent resident of Magnolia was important for this historical volume. She had heard of Dr. Henry Allen Smith, but when the research said he paddled a canoe from Olympia to Magnolia when he was 22, she became intrigued. In researching his life, she found the biographical material to be sketchy at best. Perseverance paid off and more study revealed the fuller character of Magnolia's first pioneer. The discovery of a document written by one of Smith's daughters, Ione Smith Graff, when she was in her 50s, was a great find and added a dimension to the story that had been missing all along. Thanks go to Paul Dorpat for sharing this fascinating document and reiterating that history is more than one person's story, more than what is already written down, and that what isn't always articulated is as important in figuring out past historical figures as that which makes it into the history books.

Si·?at, (Seattle) Chief of the Suquamish and Duwamish Tribes, 1865

Chief Seattle was a generous and friendly neighbor to the immigrants who began settling on his tribes' land in 1851, several years before treaties made it legal for them to do so. He was also a political realist, foreseeing that the numbers and armed might of the spreading European-American culture made hostility useless. The 1854 speech attributed to him appears to be an accurate reflection of the Indian leader's views on the "change of worlds."

However, in the century and a half since the speech is said to have been made, it has become the stuff of legend. The speech did not appear in print until more than three decades after the treaty negotiations with the American Government. It appeared in the October 29th, 1887 edition of the Seattle Sunday Star as a reminiscence of Dr. Henry Smith. Smith, after whom Smith's Cove in Seattle is named, was one of the area's earliest white residents. He was present at the first meeting with Territorial Governor Isaac Stevens in 1854, where he took notes of Chief Seattle's oratory as it was translated into English for the Governor and his party:

"Your religion was written on tablets of stone by the iron finger of an angry God lest you forget. The red man could never comprehend nor remember it. Our religion is the tradition of our ancestors, the dreams of our old men given to them in the solemn hours of the night by the great spirit, and the visions of the leaders, and it is written in the hearts of our people.

IONE SMITH GRAFF WROTE ABOUT HOW SHE CHOSE TO WRITE *Dr. Henry Allen Smith and Family:*

The Daughters of the Pioneers of Washington has {sic} asked me to write something about my parents and myself. I shall endeavor as far as possible to limit this article to points of interest about my father, not to be found in the many sketches of him in the following and other works:

History of the United States *by George Bancroft*
Blazing the Way *by Inez Denny*
A Chronological History of Seattle, 1850-1897 *by Thomas Prosch*
4 Wagons West *by Roberta Frye Watt*
Various articles by Chronicler C. T. Conover in The Seattle Times *and* Post-Intelligencer
Comprehensive History of Seattle *by Clarence Bagley*
Great Son *by Edna Ferber*

Your dead cease to love you and the land of their nativity as soon as they pass the portals of the tomb; they wander far away and are soon forgotten and never return. Our dead never forget this beautiful world that gave them being. They always love its winding rivers, its sacred mountains, and its sequestered vales, and they ever yearn in tenderest affection over the lonely-hearted living and often return to visit, guide, and comfort them.

We will ponder your proposition, and when we decide we will tell you. But should we accept it, I here and now make this the first condition that we will not be denied the privilege, without molestation, of visiting at will the graves where we have buried our ancestors, and our friends, and our children.

Every part of this country is sacred to my people. Every hillside, every valley, every plain and grove has been hallowed by some fond memory or some sad experience of my tribe. Even the rocks which seem to lie dumb as they swelter in the sun along the silent seashore in solemn grandeur thrill with memories of past events connected to the lives of my people.

Opposite: In 1978, The Yukon Club and Propeller Club erected this monument to Dr. Henry Smith. This land eventually became the link to the transcontinental railroad, The Great Northern, piers 38 and 39, were loading docks for shipping to the Orient. In 1921, it was here " . . . the 2530 foot {40 and 41} piers . . . were recognized as the longest earth-filled piers in the world." The monument can be viewed at the entrance of Smith Cove Park below the Magnolia Bridge. Photo Monica Wooton, 2000.

And when the last red man shall have perished from the earth and his memory among the white men shall become a myth, these shores will swarm with the invisible dead of my tribe; and when your children's children shall think themselves alone in the fields, the store, the shop, upon the highway, or in the silence of the pathless woods, they will not be alone. In all the earth there is no place dedicated to solitude. At night when the streets of your cities and villages will be silent and you think them deserted, they will throng with returning hosts that once filled and still love this beautiful land.

The white man will never be alone. Let him be just and deal kindly with my people, for the dead are not powerless. Dead, did I say? There is no death, only a change of worlds."

While Smith understood both Lushootseed and Chinook Jargon, many have wondered how well he could have remembered the speech after thirty years, while others have been puzzled by Smith's waiting three decades to share such an important text with the world. Still other critics have pointed out how conveniently Chief Seattle's poetic words seem to match with popular nineteenth century notions of Indians as a "vanishing race."

"Authentic" or not, Seattle's speech has become perhaps the most famous example of Native American oratory, and has become a powerful text for environmentalists, Native American activists, and others over the years. In achieving mythic status, though, the speech has often gone through strange transformations. A version of the speech penned for a 1970s film, for example, included references to buffalo, which Seattle never saw in his life-time, and to railroads, which did not appear in Puget Sound until after his death. Illustrated versions of the speech have even mysteriously transformed the Northwest Coast leader into a Plains Indian!

Luckily, in addition to Smith's "original" text, we also have the oral tradition of the Puget Sound Indian people descended from those who participated in the treaty council. Suquamish elder Amelia Sneatlum share another part of the speech as she learned it:

"This is what Chief Seattle said when they were having the treaty at Mukilteo . . .

You folks observe the changers who have come to this land. And our progeny will watch and learn from them now, those who will come after us, our children. And they will become just the same as the changers who have come here to us on this land. You folks observe them well."

We can never know for sure exactly what words were spoken at the meeting in 1854. But we do know that the words of Seattle, passed down in various forms over the genera-tions, have become one of the most important passages in Pacific Northwest, and indeed American, history.

*The common pronunciation "Seattle" is a close approximation of the Chief's name in Lushootseed if pronounced as two syllables (see-AHTL). The often-heard "Sealth," ryhming with "wealth", is completely inaccurate. Courtesy of the Museum of History and Industry Exhibit – "Change of Worlds" - Curated by Greg Watson and Coll Peter Thrush

SMITH COVE

The cove is named after Dr. Henry A. Smith, pioneer who settled here in 1853. Early shipping began here in 1887 when the Northern Pacific Coal Bunker Pier was completed. At that time it was not uncommon to see steamers and sailing vessels berthed on either side of this 2500 foot trestle running over tidal railroad flats. That came to an end in 1899 when the adjacent Great Northern docks and a fleet of fishermen in the Transcontinental Railroad to the west. In 1912 the Port of Seattle purchased the land presently known as Piers 90 and 91 for $750,000. A project of filling and docks and waterfront was completed in 1921, at which time they were the largest earth-filled piers in the world. The Port of Seattle operated them as general cargo facilities until 1942 when, as a result of the U. S. Navy, they remained under Navy control until 1976 when they were returned to the Port.

Erected Memorial Day by May 1976

Fort Lawton: Constant Place of Change

INTRODUCTION TO THE KIEHL COLLECTION GRANT
KING COUNTY LANDMARKS AND HERITAGE COMMISSION
by Sara W. Smith, Bainbridge Island, Washington, December 1997

In 1993, I had a conversation with my grandfather, Frederick Mann, about the work that he and my grandmother, Mia Mann, had done to create a collection of historic photographs documenting the natural and human history of what is now Discovery Park. Frederick Mann was involved in the movement to turn Fort Lawton into a park in the 1960s. Most of the images they collected came one by one from libraries, museums, magazines, newspapers and private collections.

One collection that came to their attention was quite large and of special interest. It became known as the Kiehl Collection. H. Ambrose Kiehl, CE (civil engineer), had been engaged by the US Army in the 1890s to assist in the development of Fort Lawton. Kiehl was also an able and avid early-day photo enthusiast and while doing engineering work for the Army amassed some 1,000 photographs that he took between 1890 and 1917. During this period Kiehl and his family lived on the grounds that much later became Discovery Park but which at the time was a forested wilderness on the outskirts of the city. These images document the clearing of the West Point area, the development of the Fort, family life in the Northwest, gold rush activities in Seattle and many images of Kiehl's engineering work at forts, dams and bridges throughout the Northwest and Alaska. This collection, accompanied by excellent records, was clearly a great boon in the effort to document the park.

The collection was made known to the Manns in the late 1970s. Since that time, Mann had been making copy negatives and prints of those images from the collection that he found particularly interesting and pertinent to the park. In conversations with Laura Kiehl, he had suggested that, after suitable duplication and preservation for the purposes of Discovery Park, the original collection should be placed in the Special Collections Division of the University of Washington Libraries where it would receive proper care and also be available for public study and enjoyment. Laura Kiehl enthusiastically endorsed this idea.

Collage of H. Ambrose Keihl memorabilia and pictures, many of which you can spot in the next pages. Collage assembled by Mrs. Helen Gunn, Laura Kiehl and F. M. Mann. N section, Kiehl Collection, UW Special Collections.

Kiehl beginning his survey of Fort Lawton in 1900. UW Special Collections #Kiehl 3x3-294.

By 1993, when I spoke to my grandfather and grandmother about the photographs, much work had already been done but much remained to be done. It was at this point that a few of us decided that King County might be willing to support this documentary effort in order to help get the fragile and deteriorating negatives into the care of a library as soon as possible.

In 1994, I wrote for a Special Projects Grant from the King County Landmarks and Heritage Commission, a fund supported by hotel/motel tax revenues. We were fortunate enough to receive $7,500 to preserve the collection. The grant was intended to cover the costs of making prints that would be available at the Discovery Park Visitor Center, copy negatives that would be available at the City Archivist's negative collection, and written historical documentation to accompany images where available. Because not all of the Kiehl photos were pertinent to Discovery Park, we selected approximately 500.

Over the last few years we have been working to do this. Between November 1995 and May 1996, I worked in photographer Rod Slemmons' dark room to make 8x10 prints from the original negatives and then 4x5 negatives from those prints. When I moved out of town in May 1996, Rod and Fred Mann continued the work to make the 8x10 prints and negatives. It was then decided, because of the requirements of a hanging-file system that had already been planned to house the Discovery Park photo collection, that 4x5 prints of the Kiehl images were better suited to the needs of the Visitors Center at Discovery Park.

What we have ended up with at the end of these few years of work is: 1) 4x5 prints for the Discovery Park Visitor Center; 2) 4x5 negatives of these prints for the City Archivist; 3) written documentation for many of these images and reference to Kiehl's journals for further information; and 4) 8x10 prints that will accompany the original collection of negatives, photo albums, jour-nals, and equipment to Suzallo Library.

The public now has access to an amazing collection of images documenting one history of the Pacific Northwest. It is accessible in three locations: Allen Library, Special Collections at the University of Washington, Discovery Park, and the City of Seattle Archives. Those approximately 400 images that were not covered under the grant (i.e., did not feature content directly related to Discovery Park) are still accessible in print form through Kiehl's photo albums at Allen Library. Allen will house the entire Kiehl collection, including all original negatives and photo albums.

The Kiehl survey crew (above) and logging crew (below). UW Special Collections #Kiehl M101, #Kiehl 5x7-30.

Aside from the historical value, and perhaps most important to me, the grant has given me the opportunity to work with my grandfather and grandmother, two people whose interest in the history of Washington State and the City of Seattle has affected me deeply and helped determine the shape of my own career and interests. It has been an invaluable experience.

Inside of first Kiehl Fort House, Kiehl office.
UW Special Collections
#Kiehl M189b.

H. AMBROSE KIEHL AND FAMILY
Text courtesy of Discovery Park Archive and Fred/Mia Mann

All of the photographs in this section were taken by Mr. H. Ambrose Kiehl between 1890 and 1917. The Collection contains many images that primarily illustrate everyday family life at the beginning of the twentieth century, and might be typical of those found in many family albums of that period, except that these were taken on the grounds that became Discovery Park. Kiehl was perhaps more prolific than most early-day photo enthusiasts. His Collection contains some 1,000 images, most of which he processed himself. Many were taken using the newly-introduced Eastman Flexible roll film, although he also used the same gelatin dry plates (glass) that he used to more seriously record the engineering projects he was engaged in. Fortunately for us, he kept a detailed photo notebook in which he meticulously recorded the subject, the location and the date of each of some 950 of the photographs he took.

Kiehl was born in Dayton, Ohio, in 1865. He received his training as a civil engineer at Ohio State University in the 1880s. After graduating he "went West," first to San Francisco and then to Puget Sound, where he opened an engineering office called Kiehl and Hogg

H. Ambrose Kiehl, prolific reader, planner and designer of Fort Lawton.
UW Special Collections
#Kiehl 4x5-153.

New barracks. The timber from the Fort was never sold or milled but used as fuel at the Fort.
UW Special Collections #Kiehl 6x8-10.

in Port Townsend. Port Townsend probably appealed to him because, at that time, it held promise of becoming one of the major cities on the Sound. There he met and married Louisa Jean Stockland, whose parents had emigrated from the Shetland Islands in 1857 and had taken out a Donation Claim in the Chimacum Valley, where they farmed. They later established a residence in Port Townsend. The first of the two Kiehl children, Laura Adele Kiehl, was born in Port Townsend in 1892. The second, Lorena Miriam Kiehl, was born in Seattle in 1895.

A decision had been made as part of a plan for national defense to construct a military post on Magnolia Bluff near Seattle. The Quartermaster General of the US Army sent Captain W. W. Robinson ,Jr. to Seattle to serve as the constructing quartermaster to work with the City in assembling the land and start the process of constructing the post. One of his first moves was to employ Kiehl to survey the land, supervise clearing and grading, lay out road and building locations and, with Robinson, supervise construction of the new post later to be named Fort Lawton.

Kiehl's field office.
UW Special Collections #Kiehl 3x3-418.

The first building to be built was a temporary office and residence for the engineer. The Kiehls, not so fondly, called it "the shack." They lived there for only two or three years until the first officers' quarters were completed in 1899. Even though a civilian, Kiehl was able to move his family into the new quarters until it was needed by the Army. This was grand living for the Kiehls. Although lighted by kerosene lamps, it actually had a bathroom, running water, a kitchen and central heating. Kiehl also started building a new house at 421 West Galer Street that became the family home in 1905.

Camping in tents by soldiers as Fort is completed. UW Special Collections #Kiehl 6x8-15.

The first indication that the Kiehls might be a source of early photographs came in 1972. Mrs. Frederick Mann was, at that time, voluntarily searching photo records of museums, libraries and newspapers for early glimpses of the land that was to become Discovery Park. During her search she came across the December 9, 1942, edition of the "Seattle Album" in the *Seattle Post Intelligencer.* It featured a picture of the Kiehl family in 1901, seated in a buggy in front of the first officers' quarters completed at Fort Lawton. Mr. H. Ambrose Kiehl was holding the reins and one of the two children in the buggy was Laura Kiehl who, it was said, furnished the photograph (N-58). The name "H. Ambrose Kiehl, CE QM Corps" was also found on the earliest drawings in Army files that were being reviewed by the Parks Department in the land transfer process. A brief search indicated that there were no Kiehl relatives remaining in Seattle.

Photographic collections so often become scattered and lost after a generation or two. It was undoubtedly the forethought and care of Helen Gunn of Port Townsend that saved the Kiehl Collection from such a fate. Gunn took the trouble in 1976 to write a letter to then Mayor Wes Uhlman saying that she had read that Fort Lawton might become a city park and that a very elderly lady, Laura Kiehl, was living with her. She also relayed that Kiehl had much information and many photographs taken by her father that might be of interest to the City. Gunn is also due much gratitude for her assistance in pulling together the already

Girls from the Fort take a cool break in the tidal waters off South Beach. UW Special Collections #Kiehl 5x7-40.

There were lots of family pictures, all posed for humor, by Ambrose Kiehl. UW Special Collections #Kiehl 4x5-189.

scattered Collection. By that time, Laura Kiehl was confined to a wheel chair and was too weak to rummage through basements and attics to find her father's records and plate negatives.

Laura's own story is of interest. She graduated from the University of Washington in 1916 with the intention of becoming a stockbroker. She may have been Seattle's first female stockbroker, because, as she said, "None of the male-dominated brokerage firms in Seattle would have anything to do with a woman, so I opened my own office—in Smith Tower." She was proud to report that, "I got all my clients out of the stock market before the crash of 1929."

Laura Kiehl begins rifle practice in the remote area of the Fort. UW Special Collections #Kiehl 3x3-275.

Before she died, Laura very generously loaned her father's collection to the Manns with the understanding that it would be made available to the public at Discovery Park for enjoyment and study. She was also very pleased, and in full agreement with the plan that, after suitable duplication for Park purposes, the original collection would be placed in the Special Collections Division of the University of Washington Libraries where it would also be available for public study.

Parcels deeded to the US Government for Fort Lawton

The deeds are as follows:

1. John Sullivan, 14 October 1896, 160 acres.
2. State of Washington, 2 June 1897, tideland.
3. Christian Scheuerman and wife, 14 June 1897, 1.51 acres.
4. Anna Sophia Brygger, 26 June 1897, roadway.
5. Ole Schillestad, 26 June 1927, roadway.
6. Gustaf Anderson, 26 June 1897, roadway.
7. C. F. Anderson and wife, 29 June 1897, roadway.
8. Thomas W. Prosch and wife, 29 June 1897, 310.87 acres.
9. Thomas W. Prosch and wife, 29 June 1897, 20.1 acres.
10. Smith Cove Land Co., 15 July 1897, roadway
11. State of Washington, 17 July 1897, tidelands.
12. Albert T. Bornan, 26 July 1897, 2.50 acres.
13. King County, 29 July 1897, 150.40 acres.
14. Lena Graham, 28 July 1897, 2.41 acres.
15. Lena Graham, 28 July 1897, 3.05 acres.
16. Susanne Scheuerman, 28 July 1897, 10.73 acres.
17. Anna Ellicott, 31 July 1897, 31.18 acres.
18. Catherine Scheuerman, 31 July 1897, 10.97 acres.
19. Mary Jenott, 3 August 1897, 7.68 acres.
20. Thomas W. Prosch, 4 August 1897, lots.
21. Bertha Brodowich and husband, 5 August 1897, 5.45 acres.
22. Horace D. Chapin, 19 August 1897, roadway.
23. Joseph Brodowich and wife, 4 September 1897, 0.25 acres.
24. Christian Scheuerman and wife, 7 September 1897, 1.41 acres.
25. John B. Allen and wife, 11 September 1897, 20 acres.
26. Christian Scheuerman, 28 January 1898, 1.51 acres.
27. King County, 17 February 1898.

Opposite: The Band Building remains today as one of the Fort Lawton Historic District buildings. Only 12 buildings at the Fort have such designation Most of these buildings face the parade grounds. Photo by Monica Wooton, 2000.

Below: Copy of original title of first land given away to the Fort by John Sullivan heirs. Army Reserves, 70th Command Archive.

Bottom: Plan for quartermaster stables, 1907. Army Reserves, 70th Command Archives.

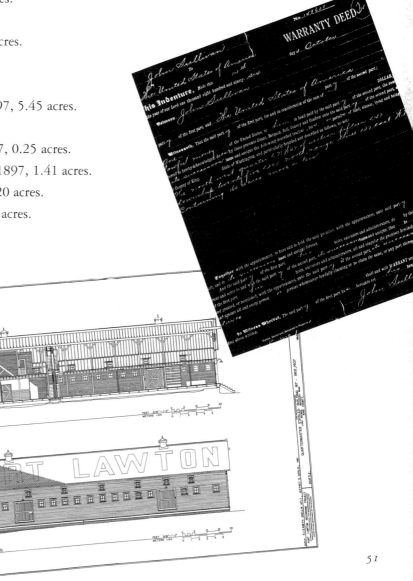

UW Special Collections
#UW 4792.

GENERAL INFORMATION

• W. W. Robinson was sent here to design and build Fort Lawton. He and Kiehl designed the place.

• At Fort Lawton, they used to fire a small cannon during the flag ceremony.

• The buildings were originally painted rust-red and brown.

• There are about 12 different spindle styles on the porch railings of the buildings.

• Original street lamps (1900) were kerosene lamps placed on wooden posts.

• The Kiehls' batten shack was moved and became one of the Non-Commissioned Officers' quarters around World War II in the (present day) Montana Circle area; it was torn down by the Army.

• A woodpile went almost all the way around the Fort in the early 1900's. Wood had been collected from the clearing of the parade grounds.

The Fort Lawton trolley provided public transportation in early 1900s. Washington State Historical Society, Tacoma #Fort/Law 2.

View from South Meadow over Puget Sound.
Discovery Park Archive.

Captain George Vancouver, May 1792

"To describe the beauties of this region will, on some future occasion, be a very greatful task to the pen of a skillful panegyrist. The serenity of the climate, the innumerable pleasing landscapes, and the abundant fertility that unassisted nature puts forth require only to be enriched by the industry of man with villages, mansions, cottages, and other buildings, to render it the most lovely country that can be imagined; whilst the labour of the inhabitants would be amply rewarded, in the bounties which nature seems ready to bestow on cultivation."

Copied from scribbled notes written in Discovery Park/Fort Lawton on July 26, 1999, by Larry A. Shepherd who was last stationed at Fort Lawton in December 1958:

The coolness of the mid-morning fog and the stillness bring an eerie and surreal quality to the area. The southwest gentle breeze has, riding upon it, many stories. It carries an early morning bugle, shouted military commands as the raising of the flag ceremony gets under way. The sound of platoons marching, perhaps to breakfast or to a work detail. There are sergeants barking out names directing soldiers to pick up shipping orders to travel to the big war, to hell, to death so far from this serene place with its water and mountain view, its serenity, its safety.

In that sad time one million strong they came, served here but for a while, and went onto an eternal fate. So many did not return and now lie in marked and unmarked resting places across the silent ocean. But, for just a while they were here in this place. We pay them no homage here. We do not honor them. Yet their deeds have earned them honor beyond what we are able to bestow and that higher honor rests with their spirit in a place reserved only for heroes.

Turning your best ear to the breeze, you will hear a great military assembly from far away. "Present Arms" is the loud command. Marching in review are the kindred spirits of those who will never again touch the shores of home. But here, in this beautiful place, their laughter, their tears, their joy, their anticipation, and their fears are forever written on the wind.

You have only to arrive early, be quiet, and listen.

Fort Lawton Cemetery. Photo by Ken Baxter. Courtesy of Virginia Baxter. Circa 1970s.

THE BLUFF

Conceived from ideas of protecting the Sound,
The shipyards, coal mines, and cities around,
Magnolia Bluff was picked as the site
For building a fort, to Seattle's delight.

Born from the people who gave up their land,
By transferring deeds to the government's hand;
With civic pride the landscape was cleared.
High on the Bluff, Fort Lawton was reared.

It nurtured on wondrous views that abound,
Snow caps on mountains, whitecaps on sound;
Its brawn and its beauty give interest groups chills
At the thought of acquiring a part of the frills.

Terry Solomon
July 1970

MAJOR GENERAL HENRY WARE LAWTON

- Fort Lawton was named after Major General Henry Ware Lawton, who was commissioned a second lieutenant, July 28, 1867.

- His first assignment was with the 41st Colored Infantry, and in 1871 he was transferred to the 4th Cavalry and served in the Indian Wars in the Southwest.

- In 1886, he commanded a column sent in pursuit of Geronimo and received Geronimo's surrender late in that year.

- In September 1888, he was transferred to the Inspector General's Department, and in 1898, as a Major General, he took command of the Second Division, First Corps, in Cuba.

- In 1899, he was transferred to the Philippines, where he commanded the First Division, Eighth Army Corps.

- He was killed in action on December 12, 1899.

Fort Lawton was named for Major General H. W. Lawton. Discovery Park Archives #0-7 and US Army.

FORT LAWTON LANDMARK DISTRICT

Located today within Discovery Park in the Magnolia neighborhood, Fort Lawton was the only permanent U. S. Army garrison post in Seattle and King County. Established as a preservation district by the Seattle City Council in 1988, the Fort Lawton Landmark District includes original Army structures built between 1898 and 1908 and important site features, most of which are owned by the City of Seattle. The District was created to identify and protect significant components of Seattle's history, to assure compatibility between the District and the Discovery Park Revised Master Plan, and to develop review procedures for possible retention, relocation, alteration or addition of structures within the District that could affect its historical or architectural integrity.

Chapel on the Hill. Photo by Monica Wooton, 2000.

The designating ordinance specifies that alterations within the District require a Certificate of Approval from the Seattle Landmarks Preservation Board.

Lawton, Wash. 1914.

THE FORT YEARS

Fort Lawton's military history dates back to the United States' concerns for national defense requiring action beyond our country's borders, beginning with Cuba in 1898 in the Spanish-American War. The post was named after Major General Henry Ware Lawton, who served in Cuba and was killed in the Philippines. In 1910, the famous landscape architect, John C. Olmsted, reported 500 horses at Fort Lawton awaiting shipment for peaceful work overseas. The Fort provided training for infantry soldiers enroute to World War I, which ended on Armistice Day in November 1918.

Baseball players, part of two teams formed of Fort Divisions for tournaments. Courtesy of Dan Kerlee.

The Fort's significant role in history began in 1941 when World War II required a total effort by the United States in defense of freedom and democracy. Emergency construction of buildings covered Fort Lawton, to create a major military base for a Port of Embarkation and returning soldiers. Over a million soldiers were processed through Fort Lawton in World War II, followed by post-war occupation troops and their families. Again in the Korean War, 1950-1953, the Fort was busy as a major Port of Embarkation and base for returning soldiers. Through all of the war years, Fort Lawton also served as a command post for air defense, until 1974 when the 49th Air Artillery Group was inactivated. Until 1968, the Fort was also headquarters of the Tenth US Army Corps, which commanded Army Reserve and ROTC units in the region.

Residents turned out for Saturday and Sunday games on the parade grounds as well as concerts and parades. Discovery Park Archive.

In 1964, the Secretary of Defense announced that 85% of the Fort Lawton site would be declared surplus. Citizens of Seattle wanted their exceptionally beautiful Fort Lawton to become a public park. Our senators and congressmen accomplished legislation that transferred the land from the Army to the City of Seattle at no cost. The City of Seattle received large portions of land in 1972 and 1974.

When the Tenth Corps was inactivated in 1968, a new 124th Army Reserve Command under the Sixth Army was created, with headquarters at Fort Lawton. This headquarters is now located in the northeast corner of the Fort, on land that is still "Fort Lawton." The 124th commands Army Reserve units in Washington, Oregon, California and Nevada.

In 1978, the parade ground and early Fort buildings (1898-1908) were listed in on the National Register of Historic Places. The US Navy, which presently manages the former Fort Lawton housing area for active military personnel, has restored the historic housing to National Register standards. The City of Seattle has retained several buildings to be preserved.

The forgoing brief outline of Fort Lawton's history was prepared by persons with military experience and knowledge of Seattle's beautiful Army Post. The authors carefully sought historic documents with accurate facts. As the work progressed, the significance of Fort Lawton's history was magnified by the call for democracy and freedom heard around the world in November 1989.

Prepared by Resources Committee:

Michael Citrak (Colonel, USA, Ret.)
Paul Purvine (Lieutenant Colonel, USA Ret.)
Bryce T. Wilson (Lieutenant Commander, US Navy WWII)
A. C. Hitchings (Major, USA Ret.)
W. E. Nuetzmann, Lawton School Principal, 1946-54
Major Wanda A. Arceneaux, HQ 124th ARCOM
Margaret Coughlin, Magnolia community planner and historian

"Taps for Fort Lawton." (photo named by Shirley Hitchings). Final military ceremony and gun salute held before the Fort is turned over to the City. Photo by Ken Baxter, November 1964. Courtesy of Viginia Baxter.

Rural Magnolia: A Pastoral Place

By Monica Wooton

MEMORIES STILL SURVIVE . . .

Many Magnolians have fond memories of dairies and farms on Magnolia. While these memories have endured time, sometimes they seem to have been exaggerated in the quest for pastoral scenes and days of the Bluff as a smaller, simpler place. With the advent of the Depression and War, these memories offered some solace. The rural life did exist in this community for about forty-years, but Magnolia was always destined for the city life as its history has proved.

BEGINNING HERE . . .

By 1856, Magnolia was established by Dr. Henry Smith and four other men who were all interesting and singular. Osmine Frost settled in Pleasant Valley, sharing Smith's vision for a railroad to be built and bring fortune to the area. Edmund Carr co-existed with the Native Peoples on the Ballard side of a slim stretch of the Salmon Bay waterway. Erasmus M. Smithers selected land south of Smith's, also sharing his motives for future land development. And David Stanley settled just north of what would eventually become Fort Lawton. To survive, all had to keep subsistence farms established in the area for many more years then they expected.[1]

Frost never made it in that isolated land and was reported to have "gone crazy" by Smith in a published account. Carr moved to Olympia, joined forces with three others, tried to get logs to Yesler's mill for profit to prove his claim, and failed. Then, he began a mill with his partners and secured government permission to keep up the planked City streets. The Indian War interrupted this venture when the entire settlement moved into two blockhouses to fight off Eastern Washington Tribe Indians in 1856. The mill caught fire. Carr's final fate was not reported. Smithers married in 1857 and moved to his wife's land claim and founded Renton. His heirs finally disposed of his Magnolia property in the late 1800s. Stanley became a wanderer from claim to claim, eccentric and unable to function in the territory, relying on the kindness of the other settlers.[2]

After the Indian War, Seattle's population quickly reduced. Land claims were for sale and many of the original settlers, who had no intention of leaving, profited by buying up the land. Many new settlers just wanted off Magnolia.[3]

At the Magnolia Garden Center manure comes in ten pound bags and other assorted weights, sterilized and ready for use. This system lacks contact with live cows though! Photo Monica Wooton, 2000.

An oddity, a stump house outside of Discovery Park. Photo by O. T. Frasch. Courtesy of Dan Kerlee.

Two panorama photos of Pleasant Valley early 1900s. Grand Boulevard is barely cut out as a road, right picture. The type of land in the "valley" for farms. Courtesy of Neil Smith. Photo by Asahel Curtis

John Ross, another early settler and one of Carr's future partners, was bothered by Indians close to the south side of Salmon Bay. He went back to Portland, found a wife and came back to reclaim his land. With much patience and fortitude he was able to establish a fruit orchard on his property, but it required that he not live there for safety reasons. He had to commute to the land on foot or by canoe daily. He had to replant many times as Indians continued to disturb his property. Finally, he was successful and proved his claim. He received another parcel of land for help in building the Territorial University Building—the area's first university.[4]

As most of the pioneer settlers of Seattle stayed together and created a business and social network, those on Magnolia did so slowly. They were isolated for nearly fifty-years by the lack of safe and easy access to the Bluff and the lack of other settlers. Yet, by Smith's land, on what is now 15th Avenue West and Grand Boulevard (now West Dravus Street), a small business center called Boulevard sprang up. The beer of the Claussen Brewing Company was a big seller as the soldiers at the Fort enjoyed wetting their whistles often. There was also a wicker furniture factory/match company, a grocery, a diesel engine shop and foundry, and The Portland Cordage Company (the Rope Walk building) that made mountains of rope. A plant nursery existed and the dump at Interbay was already in use.[5]

Dravus Street, with its many growing pains, became a neighborhood slowly but surely. Side by side, the rural and the urban existed. Even after the train finally did come through following Smith's plan somewhat, transportation off and on Magnolia remained problematic. The addition of the Fort and its trolley helped inter-community travel and provided a good distraction for settlers and soldiers. Soldiers were good consumers, especially of some of the Boulevard businesses. But it wasn't until the Magnolia Bridge was built, cast in concrete in 1930, that Magnolia finally began to open up to population growth. Unfortunately, for the little Boulevard commercial district, the new bridge completely by-passed the Interbay businesses. But one year later the concrete Dravus Bridge opened, enhancing access to the Boulevard business district and adding easier access to the Bluff.[6]

Smith spent some of his time on his Magnolia claim as a practicing doctor, and a serious hobby gardener. He planted an orchard of specially grafted apple trees—the first of the kind in King County and reaped his first crop three years later. He was an avid experimental gardener who produced many varieties of fruits and vegetables to support the diets of his family of ten.[7]

While living at the Tulalip Reservation with his family in tow, and treating the Indians as their doctor, he experimented with the use of tidelands as growing fields. He had some success: onions, rhubarb, apples, and potatoes to name a few.[8]

INTERESTING GOINGS ON . . .

As to agriculture becoming a vocation on Magnolia, interestingly, some of its property was already being platted out as traditional residential neighborhood lots before it was ever settled or barely even seen. Magnolia was already being envisioned as part of a city planning process similar to that of a suburban neighborhood in the 1990s. Some sections were platted as early as 1888 by out-of-state owners, most probably speculators, from as far as New York.[9]

"East Coasters" found the West Coast a good investment. The Emersons were one such couple. A very detailed plat of what appears to be similar to a quite modern suburb was completed for them by a Mr. Barrett. The purpose of the platting was to eventually divide Northwest land into many lots for re-sale with single-family houses, suburban style—a replication of the development of eastern city developments.

Magnolia was annexed into Seattle during 1907, before Ballard, which was a much larger and thriving community, already declaring itself a city on its own. Signs were evident regarding the slow-to-develop Magnolia and its future role in Seattle's residential and commercial development in the long-range plans of Seattle's urbanization. The early developers, the Dennys, Yeslers, and Terrys, had all given up the idea of farming this land, and utilized the region's resources in more profitable ways.

Smith's Cove, with its railroad and proximity to deep water, made shipping a lucrative possibility. This made it highly probable that Magnolia land would grow in value, as Smith had envisioned, and become a shipping center since lumber, fish, and other natural resources existed in abundance. It looked like Magnolia would play some role as a spectacular speculative piece of property in the coming years, and farming would be a transitional stage in the community's growth. However, this evolution would take longer than initially expected.

The plat map of Pleasant Valley Addition, 32nd Avenue West (east) to 36th Avenue West (west), Barrett Street (south), and Bertona Street (north). These lots were laid out as single family residences as early as 1888. In the 1900 three diary farms were here. Courtesy of King County Assessor's Office.

Forget Me Nots, 1917. Leed & Company. Courtesy of Bett Samuelson.

To the sessions of sweet silent thought,
Summon up remembrance of things past.
Shakespeare.

FOR THE TIME BEING . . .

When Congress passed the Oregon Land Law of 1850, it motivated many farm families to risk the long and hazardous journey to the Washington Territory. Land in the early cities in the Puget Sound area was ultimately subdivided. These land parcels were generally livestock farms with small clearings devoted to hay, grain, small orchards and gardens for subsistence.[10]

Many settlers taking these types of claims became the founding fathers of our City. The well-known Denny family began as farmers, but soon began selling piling, rough lumber, and fish. Land and forest resources were used through the clearing of trees for lumber sales that created industrial jobs.[11]

On Magnolia, the landowners who had struggled mightily to farm and prove their claims, seldom profited much as farmers. Seattle's weather and geography made it very hard. Many were anxious to get rid of their land and move, as Seattle wasn't what they had expected. Many settlers who stayed were willing and able to buy up the claims of those leaving.

According to Polk's City Directory from 1900 to 1936 these were the farms listed as Dairy Businesses on Magnolia. Map courtesy of John LaRussa.

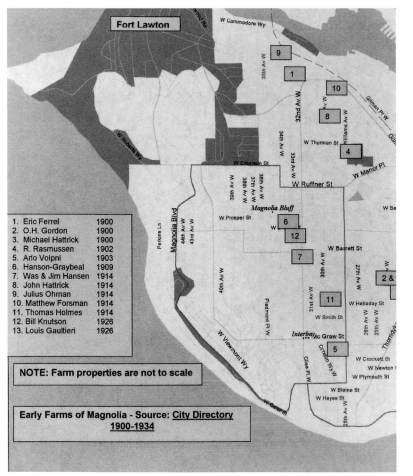

1. Eric Ferrel 1900
2. O.H. Gordon 1900
3. Michael Hattrick 1900
4. R. Rasmussen 1902
5. Arlo Volpni 1903
6. Hanson-Graybeal 1909
7. Was & Jim Hansen 1914
8. John Hattrick 1914
9. Julius Ohman 1914
10. Matthew Forsman 1914
11. Thomas Holmes 1914
12. Bill Knutson 1926
13. Louis Gaultieri 1926

NOTE: Farm properties are not to scale

Early Farms of Magnolia - Source: <u>City Directory 1900-1934</u>

However, with the establishment of Fort Lawton, the Locks, Fishermen's Terminal the development of the railroad and shipping piers, industrialization was truly born on the Bluff. The population grew and the land was now worth more, but not for farming.

REALITIES OF FARMING . . .

In order for large-scale dairying to succeed financially, pastureland—lots of it—was crucial. Fertile lands, and a labor force have always been the secret to profitable farming. It was possible to buy up several small land parcels and build an agricultural commerce, as Ezra Meeker did in 1855 with his hop farm in Tacoma. But, the venture took money and wits. If land was not naturally fertile, feed was expensive, and dairying or vegetable farming for profit was less likely to be a break-even enterprise for landowners.[12]

FINALLY, IT HAPPENS . . .

Fifty years after his arrival, Smith's expectation that a railroad would come to Magnolia, became a reality. In 1887, the Seattle Lake Shore and Eastern Railway finally came along and bought his land except for fifty-acres which he kept in reserve for the Fishermen's Terminal project. The land was filled and graded, and over the years a large railroad developed along

Smith Cove. After several buy-outs, railroad magnate J. J. Hill became the owner. Those trains supported trade from Smith's Cove to as far away as the Orient.[13]

This was the beginning of Magnolia's transition from subsistence farming on barely survivable land to the beginning of true urban development. Before the change however, Magnolia was involved in a period of rural land development.

Bird's eye view of Magnolia, an artist's rendering of a well-planned out future, as real estate developer David Eastman pitched it in his sales and promotion for the sale of lots and construction of homes. Courtesy of Neil Smith.

Magnolia, Agricultural Land: "Have and Have Not . . ."

Magnolia did have some natural pastureland running along Pleasant Valley. Arthur Denny tells a story about his first trip to Magnolia that explains the importance of pasture for livestock and the most obvious geography of Magnolia:

"When we selected our claims we had fears that the range for our stock would not afford them sufficient feed in the winter. . . which caused us a great deal of anxiety. From statements made by the Indians . . . we were led to believe there was prairie or grasslands to the northwest. . . In 1853, when Bell, my brother and myself determined to look for the prairie, it was slow and laborious traveling through unbroken forest . . . in the afternoon we unexpectedly came to a body of water . . . on examination found it to be tidewater. This was our first knowledge of Shilshole Bay."[14]

Unbroken forest and saltwater beaches, not prairie, were the geographic landmarks of Magnolia, although the Pleasant Valley area, from 32nd Avenue West to 34th Avenue West running north to south in the valley of the Bluff, did have pasture. A long thin strip of cleared land on West Commodore Way, and an area on Gilman (Avenue) Road to Grand Boulevard, worked as fine farmland as well.[15]

Early surveyors in an 1890 highway plat book show the Pleasant Valley area drawn as a pastureland where David Frost settled. The leeward hills on the western side of Magnolia provided some sunnier, dry land for orchards and gardens, but not necessarily pastureland. . . ."[16]

The main secret to growing foods on Magnolia lay in the peat bog soil sometimes referred to as "black gold," which was a great feature of Pleasant Valley. But, when it burned, "it burned and burned and was a never-ending headache." Here and there, this fertile soil produced amazing amounts of flowers and foods (and fires) always having to be tended with hard work by the owner.[17]

One or two cows (or goats), homegrown vegetables—enough for family tables, a fruit tree or two, a patch of cutting flowers, and sometimes some poultry for eggs were common for a Magnolia family to own. Having more than one cow provided some with enough milk to share or to sell. Magnolia resident, Shirley Allen Young, said that her brother had a small dairy route on 44th Avenue West for the neighborhood.[18]

The Wilburn's stand amongst their beautiful flower garden, one of the areas planted and tended by the couple on their extra lot. Courtesy of the Miner Family.

Rural times on Magnolia, a boy and his calf and land to roam. Most likely Hanson Farm property. Courtesy of Bett Samuelson.

On 34th Avenue West in Pleasant Valley, there was a small horse stable that housed about six horses for rent by Sylvester Wyse. They provided help in land clearing, plowing or travel. Wyse was an expert in horse problems such as shoe fittings and sprains, and was consulted by his Magnolia neighbors. His horses were used to secure the blackout of World War II, as the civil servants did the rounds on horseback and usually ended up at the Green Light when all was blacked out and locked up.[19]

MAGNOLIA'S BALL FIELDS: A DAIRYLAND OF SORTS BACK THEN . . .

Johan (John) August Hanson arrived in the United States in 1905, set about to make money in logging, and then purchased his Magnolia Merrymount Farm which today is the ball field at 32nd Avenue West and 29th Avenue West, bordered by Barrett and Raye streets. Four brothers and sisters from Sweden arrived to work with him shortly afterwards. Pictures which are no longer publishable, show a huge, meticulously-painted barn, and a well-kept farm. John's workers and siblings herded the cows on foot. The Pleasant Valley land provided a good water supply from Wolfe Creek and pasture enough for the milk herd and two oxen to survive. Ralph and Jack Chambers, sons of the Magnolia Hardware owner, Roy Chambers, remember cows poking their noses into the back door of the hardware store in their pasturing travels quite often. Magnolia was fairly lax about cattle roaming the land, an image that is still cherished by many Magnolians today. Hanson's brother, Swen, was famous on his Queen Anne Merrymount milk route for fine service and personable customer relations. According to Emery Gustafson, "Swen Hansen was well-known for community service, and many acts of kindness on an individual basis. Stories still emerge from people who were unable to pay their bills on time during the Depression, yet Swen kept delivering their milk anyway . . . 'Milk' Hansen also left memories of lifting spirits of the heavy in heart, letting light into dark corners, and scattering a little happiness wherever his container of milk bottles could be heard rattling."[20]

Harry Auckland's daughter, Helen, would walk up the street to get her family a pail of milk from the Hanson dairy. That is how she met Swen, who was two years older than she. They were married in 1917. From then on the Aucklands and Hansens played, planted, and picnicked together, and from this marriage a large and strong family grew. The Aucklands had three blocks of amazingly successful planted gardens which provided a second income for their family.

Merrymount Dairy, under Hanson's direction, joined a small Darigold co-op called Hi-Grade. This helped to keep business going, providing by-products to produce milk. The enterprise not only produced milk, it gave us three life-long Magnolia residents: Bett Samuelson (who passed away October, 2000), Swen (Bob) Hansen, and their brother, Harold Henry Hansen (Barney), who died in 1952.

For all those who remember Magnolia as a dairy land, there were a total of thirteen working dairies between 1900 and 1936 as advertised in the Seattle City Directories.[21]

The Auckland family portrait, the lower left inset shows Harry, owner of a great truck farm, at 32nd Avenue West and Barrett. Courtesy Bett Samuelson. Circa late 1800s.

Only three had enough cows to produce enough milk to function as dairies for long (and two operated off of the same property owned by Johan Hanson). Property in Pleasant Valley (where Albertson's stands today) produced milk enough for milk routes, and that is where the Pleasant Valley Dairy was located.

Merrymount Dairy was very successful under the direction of owners Hanson and Arthur Greybeal (a partner who later left the business).

"In 1926 John Hanson moved to Bothell to begin a new farm venture. Who stayed at Merrymount is questionable, but it was kept as Hanson property. Swen drove daily to the new farm to get the milk for his Queen Anne route, much to the delight of his customers! John's property was eventually sold off in lots, in 1939, after another dairyman took it over as a dairy until 1936.

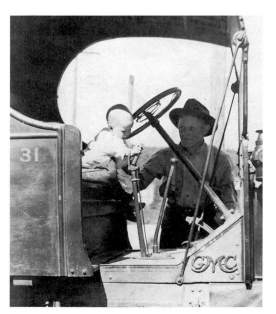

Left: *Swen Hansen, became the milkman for the Merrymount Farm, serving the Queen Anne Area. Here he gives daughter Bett an early career lesson. Courtesy of Bett Samuelson.*

Eventually, the Mayflower Dairy Downtown, became the place Swen picked up his supplies. It was at this time that he and 14 other milk route operators formed the Hi-Grade Co-op for local city farmers in the Darigold building (now Westfarm Foods). This was a bottling plant more than a dairy, where milk by-products were brought and processed for routes. Swen soon was promoted to work inside the operation, sold his route, and retired in 1965. After World War II, Hi-Grade was sold to Darigold, according to Bob Hansen, son of Swen." They have kept no records of the co-op.

The Hi-Grade Dairy co-op was a group of small farmers who joined together to keep their dairies going. Outside the old Darigold Building, now West Farm Foods, the Hensen's Swen and son Barney, second and third in the second row from the right, kept Merrymount in business with this cooperative.
Courtesy of Bett Samuelson.

Tenant Knut Knutsen, later took over the property in 1926. The property by this time is described by ex-Magnolian Ray Peterson:

> *The driveway going down into the farmstead was very deep . . . undoubtedly from much use and constant erosion . . . there was also an unoccupied house that was obviously beyond repair. The milkhouse, where the milk was cooled and the bottles washed and refilled, was also quite old and the wood fired boiler that generated the hot water and steam was a real relic.*
>
> *As you might imagine the roads were not laid plainly and were not at all proper roads as we know them today. They were mainly just dirt ruts with little or no gravel . . . meandering lanes by today's standards . . . south of the dairy barn. Knutsons' had a live-in hand-milker, named Paul Muralt (he really liked onion sandwiches). They milked by hand and did their own bottling right on the farm.*[24]

Swen poses with his milk truck on Queen Anne. He was well-liked and his customers found him to be a gentle giving man. Emory Gustafson devoted a column to those remembrances.
Queen Anne News, July 2, 1987.

Knutsen's trademark for success at Merrymount, now called West Point Dairy, was knowledge of the business and personalized service with loyalty to the customers. Even after being forced out of Magnolia by land development in 1936, he delivered milk to his Magnolia customers until the 1960s, when his son Bill and his grandsons ceased selling by routes, and sold from a dairy stand by the new Bothell farm.[25]

As documented by *The Seattle Times*, the West Point Dairy was the last surviving dairy in the Magnolia area.[26]

In 1936 when the City, Magnolia neighbors and Bill Knutsen realized residential planning did not include a section for cows, the West Point Dairy relocated to Bothell—seemingly a "true" dairy land—and became Bill's Dairy. By 1990, Bill (Knut died suddenly) was smack dab in the middle of urbanization again, owning the only chunk of rural land around![27]

FARMING—IT WAS HERE . . .

There is really no doubt that livestock, chickens, goats, cows and medium-sized truck gardens were a part of Magnolia's past. Much subsistence farming went on during both World Wars. Families ate what they produced and were lucky to sell off the extras. Many members of this community were, by now, successful subsistence farmers, and many grew vegetables and flowers simply because of their familiarity with the land, the seasons, and because they enjoyed it. Some grew fruits or vegetables to sell at the Pike Place Market downtown or at other outlets and stands.

SUBSISTENCE FARMING AT ITS BEST— THE "INDUSTRY" WITHIN

Longtime Magnolia resident Hal Will remembers six lots of combined family land on the corner of Clise Place and Wolfe Creek where the Elder family tended to an impressive garden. "They were hard-working folks with few conveniences, raising two young children and much of their food."[28]

The Merrymount Farm was rented to Knut Knutson, displaced from his Queen Anne location near the present Seattle Pacific University. He ran a fine operation with skill and knowledge of the latest in the milk industry. Many Magnolians became long time customers of his dairy products. Knutson sits on running board, son Bill to his left. Unknown Occupant. Courtesy of The Seattle Times.

Surrounded by hundreds of daffodils, berry vines, rows of potatoes, corn, radishes— "name it, we had it"—Phyllis Elder speaks of her fine family garden of the late 1930s and early 1940s.

"Beans: green, red and white sold well. We gobbled all our own grapes—they grew in the best dark black soil, so rich we never fertilized it. We had chickens and eggs for a short time," said Phyllis, who at 92, remembered those old Magnolia days with a special feeling and exactness in her enduring voice. "Why, we were so poor in those days it was . . . well, plain pitiful." She kind of chuckled as she remembered the differences of then and now, but no self-pity crept through the tone of her words.[29]

Phyllis told of making money setting up a vegetable stand. Her hand-painted wooden sign was often up at the corner of Clise Place and Wolfe Creek (now Clise Place and 32nd Avenue West) with the week's specialty. "I sold big, juicy, perfect strawberries for what you could get at the Pike Place Market, and I would never, never sneak in any poor quality ones in the bottom of the box like some merchants did. Twenty-five cents a pint, for the best berries!"[30]

The Elders lived in a two-car garage. Neatly and cleverly laid out so as not to waste any room; curtains provided privacy and the illusion of rooms. Sixty years later, Phyllis can describe perfectly the little place, down to the tissue paper curtains she made for her windows by stitching the thin crisp paper with tiny sewn stitches. They had no hot water, so washday and baths were a chore. She warmed water on the back of the wooden stove and carried full buckets to the washtub. They could not afford a refrigerator, so the icebox had to do. The Elders made extra money selling the rich black loam from their yard and the surrounding streets under an agreement with the City, as they had proven with their own crops that the soil was excellent.[31]

While her husband worked, Phyllis kept their farm running. She preserved and canned foods for the winter season with her sons, Phillip ("Magnolia's Friendly Mailman" recently retiring after 40 years service to the neighborhood[28]) and Robert, and with her husband's help when he was home. They lived on their corner farm from 1937 to 1946, when the lots first began to sell on Magnolia for residential properties. They finally sold three lots of their property and bought a home of their own a few blocks away. The growing boys could finally get more room. Their schoolmates would often ask if they were poor children. She assured them they were rich in their hearts and souls, and material things didn't matter unless they were wasted.[32]

Everyone has chores when it came to keeping food on the table, young and old. This most probably is young Harry Auckland Courtesy of Bett Samuelson.

Phyllis remembers that her father had given her a radio and it often provided entertainment and sanity. She heard a poem she can no longer remember, but its inspirational nature kept her going when the going was rough. She remembers pinning the poem to the kitchen wall, reading it often and how it raised her spirits so during hard times! In recounting her life of back then, Phyllis has no regrets or bitterness in her voice. She loves to garden, and to this day at 92 years of age, she takes care of her lawn and the landscaping that she designed. The Depression was a time to work hard and survive; no complaining from the Elders!

"SUBSIDIZING THE PLATE" . . .

Monty Holmes told the story of the land his family was asked to tend in 1928 at 3050 West Commodore Way. It was more a handshake deal than a rental agreement. Ole Shillestad's place was a grand 1880s home. Fifteen acres came with the house—more than the usual few lots many subsistence farmers had in those days. The house was built with care and attention to detail. Shillestad had a penchant for architectural flourishes and artistic touches: painted and molded plaster around the lights, fancy moulding, and quality materials of the day were built in the home.[33]

On Pearl Harbor Day, December 7, 1941, Monty and his dad were putting their few cows out to pasture when they noticed soldiers and sailors running frantically from the direction of the Locks toward their nearby bases at Fort Lawton or the Coast Guard Base on West Commodore Way. The Hiram Chittenden Locks provided the fastest route across the canal from the northern part of Seattle for a soldier or sailor to get back to base. This was not just a few men, but many: stumbling, frantic, with no leisure in their step. To this day, Monty remembers how frightening it was to watch; it was not the usual parade of laid-back military he saw cross the Locks daily. He asked his father with alarm what was happening. His father turned to him and announced: "We are at war." Frenzy and fear overtook him, and Monty cried on the spot—a moment he says he will never forget.[34]

Ole Shillestad's farm land and very fancy home on 3050 West Commodore Way. It is rumored that one season the water was so high they had to harvest apples from row-boats. This became the home of Monty Holmes and his family as they became the *caretakers of the property, house, and a small boat moorage inside the Locks.* Discovery Park Archive. Seattle Department of Parks and Recreation. Courtesy of Gladyes Shillestad Keysner.

Monty and his sister crossed the Locks to attend Adams School when the large lock gates had no railings. They clung close to each other and walked as straight a line as they could. They were always quite relieved when they got to the small lock, which did have a railing on one side of the walkway across the gates.

During the World War II years, the schools involved the children in farming by teaching the "principles of your victory garden," Monty remembers. Teachers came out to their students' homes to award ribbons to those children who produced a decent vegetable patch to help the war effort.[35]

Monty, at nine, bought a couple of rabbits at 50 cents apiece, just to raise for fun. It wasn't long before the rabbits did what rabbits do—multiply (after an initial mix-up of and realization of owning two females, and going back to the original owner, trying to give the rabbit back and then having to stack 12 cords of wood—$5 dollars worth—to earn another rabbit, a beloved male that he promptly named Thumper). Monty had nearly 100 rabbits on his hands in no time; and it took three wheelbarrows of grass clippings to feed them every day! Monty figured it out fast: he was in trouble at that point. Rabbits were not a commerce item. "Nobody wanted to buy rabbits!" That night, Thumper went into the family pot.

Magnolia School children experience what many Magnolia and City children throughout the school system experienced during World War II. For many the times of "victory gardens" made home a much more serious place.

"Anything to subsidize the plate, " was Monty's response. Thumper's kin met the same fate.

Fishing near the Locks provided added fare to the table also. Monty says his mother always announced the "table was set" when the tide went out—and Monty and his sister went out to gather the bounty: clams, mussels, and fish.[36]

Coal-burning steamboats were a free source of "clinkers" which were little scraps of coal ash used to spread on the steep driveway to keep it from being slippery. Monty and his dad filled a little skiff they had with fir bark peeled from the logs on the booms around the Locks. Loggers had no use for the stuff, so the family used it to keep their fire extra hot and burning during the nights.[37]

Monty's family was lucky to have the 15 acres to work. They had 24 fruit trees which included Black Bing and a smaller variety of pie cherries, yellow and Italian prunes, Bartlett pears, Gravenstein, Red Delicious and Crab apples. The garden had just about everything, including cabbage, corn, spinach, tomatoes, and "the best radishes!" The huge garden that provided enough food for four perhaps could have been more productive with farm hands around. They simply could not afford it. His father was often gone, whenever he could obtain outside work. It was up to Monty, his mom and sister to tend their land.

They had 100 Rhode Island Reds ("fancy chickens!") that produced a business—all by word of mouth—selling a dozen eggs for 15 cents to those who came by the property. Their livestock included two cows and two goats (bought because Monty could tolerate goat's milk better than cow's milk).[38]

Monty and his sister had a commercial farming enterprise of their own. Their property produced enough raw milk to feed Works Progress Administration (WPA) workers along Commodore Way. Every morning the children loaded their wagon with ice, milked the cows and filled clean bottles, traveled the gravel lane, cream swimming at the top of each bottle, and had a regular milk route at 10 cents a quart. They served the men in the morning or around lunchtime, and on the return route coming home, they knew where the men left their hidden milk bottles for the next day's delivery. They collected and sterilized them so they could be filled for the next milk run. Of those days, Monty recalled that the work was so non-stop, "that literally a swim in the canal or just sitting eating cherries was a thrill."[39]

During early fall when the pears and apples were fully ripe and falling on the ground, they would send off an irresistible aroma. One morning, when Monty was putting Daisy, one of their cows, out to pasture with halter and tether line, the enticing smell of overripe fruit got to the cow. She bolted and ran toward the orchard. Monty hung on to the tether line with all his 10-year-old strength and snubbed it off around a cedar stump. The line went taut. At least Monty had succeeded in stopping Daisy from further antics. He was relieved. It was just then the stump, rotten to the core, pulled out of the ground releasing thousands of angry wasps. They immediately landed all over Monty's body—in his hair, eyes, ears, and neck. His struggle with Daisy was immediately forgotten. To save his life from the stinging, he ran and jumped into the Ship Canal. He swam under one of the mooring docks and got away from the wasps. He ended up with 25 stings. His mother applied two pounds of moist baking soda over his body. From that time on, Monty kept a very tight rein on old Daisy.

The lease agreement also came with a commitment to take care of a small moorage below the property. Monty learned how to roll logs under houseboats to keep them afloat, and this provided a good income eventually. For painting a houseboat, Monty earned his first Rollfast bike which he still has today.[40]

When Monty's dad went to work as a fisherman and was gone from home full time, the rest of the family had to keep things running smoothly and get in the winter stocks. Monty remembers fondly that "in a good summer of a good year my mom set a goal of canning 500 jars of food for the coming winter and it was all done over a hot wood stove."[41]

There remains a persistent story (that may be plain folklore) that in the summer after a heavy snowfall, the water rose so high near the house, apples were picked by standing in a rowboat.

Lorraine and Monty Holmes with Daisy their cow. Between the three of them, they ran a successful milk route for the Work Progress Administration workers at the Locks and in the area. Courtesy of Monty Holmes.

Following pages: Pleasant Valley Farm was located where Albertson's is today. Another successful Magnolia farm serving the dairy needs of Magnolia and Queen Anne customers. Courtesy of Neil Smith.

Below: Forget Me Nots, 1917. Leed & Company. Courtesy of Bett Samuelson.

Dreams of the past fill life with delight.
E. Nesbit.

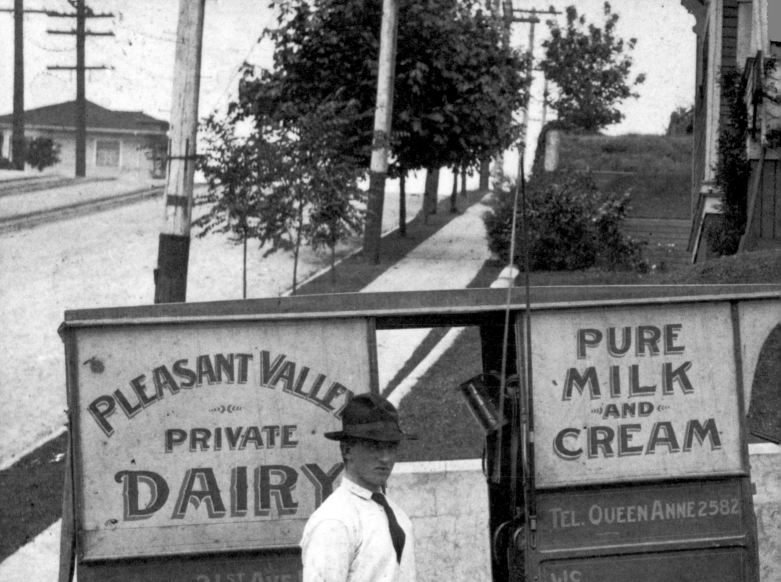

In 1944, Shillestad offered the Holmes the property for $10,000 (about $750 an acre). But, they could not afford it, and the land was broken up into lots and sold. The farming days on the Shillestad property were over, and Monty has spent his life trying to get back to that property and to those rural days of old. The hard work of his childhood was a fair price to pay for the wholesomeness of it all.[43]

Barbara Montaño also lived down on West Commodore Way in one of only nine houses in the area at the time. She and Monty were neighbors. "Magnolia really didn't have many farms. Most everyone grew food to survive the Depression when I was a kid, but little of it was sold commercially." Their "you name it we had it" garden was a significant enterprise. Goats, a horse for a while, chickens and rabbits made up the livestock on the property. Plowing time was a big time of the year for her family. Her father could afford to have the land plowed once a year in the spring for the vegetable garden. From the freshly-tilled soil, and the newly-laid manure came peas, string beans, beets, gooseberries ("Ever have a gooseberry? Mmmm."), horseradish and spinach. Her mom was partial to dahlias and she grew beautiful giant ones. Barbara remembers the fertilizer well. It was chicken manure diluted with water and poured on the garden, or spread at the time of plowing.[44]

For Barbara, the ship canal provided a cool swimming hole and she often took a swim right after school. Barbara fished for her supper many nights—catching mostly bottom fish, and she loved it. On occasion an elusive salmon would take a hook. Fishing was a thrill.

During this time, her dad got a job at Seattle's City Hall, so it was up to her mom to keep the land cared for and productive.[45]

The Auckland truck farm was famous for its huge and beautiful produce. In this picture the young ones of the family are even a bit fearful of such beets and cabbages! Courtesy Bett Samuelson.

THE TRUCK FARMING EXPERIENCE: THE AUCKLAND'S PRODUCE

Out of three city blocks (with the address given as 3009 32nd Avenue West), Harry Auckland and his family produced some of the biggest, most prolific vegetables around Magnolia. Pictures reveal shiny deep orange pumpkins with flawless rinds, corn that was truly as high as an "elephant's eye," and cabbages that were so huge children shied away from them quizzically.[46]

The Aucklands had a large house where family gathered often. Pigs were raised, and venison (hunted on Mercer Island) gutted and butchered. Harry held a regular engineering job as well, so his wife helped out in his absence. They produced such large crops that there was nothing to do but to sell them. This produce was bound for market by truck, or sold off of trucks to the neighborhood population. Five cents could buy a week's-worth of vegetables.[47]

The Auckland's business represented a typical "truck" farm: growing produce for commercial sale, but not for large profits. The father of the family had a regular job as well as helped his wife tend the garden.

When Anna Auckland passed away in 1939, Harry kept up the gardening, his engineering job, and added a worm business to his schedule. He delivered his worms in his Model-T to the Magnolia Hardware for avid fishermen to buy.[34] Magnolians could finally see crops as profitable to grow as the neighborhood population and development expanded. The bridges provided access to other areas of town, and subsistence farming was no longer the only priority.[48]

REALLY A ROAD TO URBANIZATION . . .

In 1936, the last of the farms left Magnolia under the social conventions of urbanization. Yet the memories of the pastoral scenes of wondering cows on undeveloped land, the taste of fresh raw milk, trips for bags of manure for fertilizer from the farms, and the dairies' round cardboard bottle caps used for many childhood games or for individual collections are still vivid for many Magnolians.

Magnolia's early farm history is truly reminiscent of the life described in the book *Little House on the Prairie* by Laura Wilder: The constant struggle, farming to survive, and the small successes are much like many early rural Magnolians' lives.

Whenever it is said that Magnolia was a dairyland, we can remember that there were cows on Magnolia, but not in vast numbers. Farming existed, but for survival through the settlement days and the early twentieth-century World Wars. However, for many Magnolians this is still a romantic notion and favorite memory of a Magnolia past.

Shiny pumpkins large and luscious looking make the growers at the Auckland's proud to pose with their produce. The tall corn crop behind speaks to their talents as small farmers in Magnolia's climate!
Courtesy of Bett Samuelson.

Early in her life, Monica Wooton's family had a piece of rocky barren property on Blewett Pass in the Cascades. The Swauk creek flowed through it. It was an abandoned gold mine. While it was recreational, everything was difficult when they "camped" there. They fetched water from the creek, hunted, waited hours for food to cook on the fire, and slept uncomfortably tossing and turning to howls, strange owl screeches, and imagined bear growls (thought to be right outside the tent). This land was her only exposure to lands similar to those of Northwest settlers. Monica and her family were urban campers.

One Magnolian wrote to her that both her grandfathers farmed and gardened in Magnolia, and that she had lots of pictures. "And, they were grand places to grow up," she added. Pastoral memories of Magnolia are still prevalent. The stories of such memories of Pleasant Valley—the area where Monica grew up on Magnolia—piqued her curiosity.

Author's Note: the "one Magnolian" was Bett Hansen Samuelson, who died the last week-end of October. She never got to see the project she so generously donated, too! May she rest in peace and get a little peek of the book from Heaven! The Forget-me-nots are for you Bett!

Forget Me Nots, 1917. Leed & Company. Courtesy of Bett Samuelson.

United States Army Reserve Center
UNITED STATES ARMY RESERVE

Gateway to War, Guardian for Peace: Fort Lawton

By Rob Hitchings

PREFACE

The Korean War has been known as the "Forgotten War" for as long as I can remember. Many people's perceptions of this war are unfortunately based largely upon the television series *MASH*. One person even told me that she had assumed that the series was really about the Vietnam War, and that the producers had chosen the setting of Korea because it wouldn't bring about any protests or controversy.

To those American men and women who served their country, and to those who are still serving in one of the world's most hostile environments, (temperatures vary from 110 degrees in the summer to 30 degrees below zero in winter), the Korean War is anything but "forgotten." The US Army still maintains a full division on the Demilitarized Zone.

Having grown up in a military family as an "Army brat," the Korean War was very real to me. I saw my father off to Korea from the docks of Tacoma in July 1950 along with the 2nd Infantry Division. I did not see him again for 30 months. Over the years, I came to know many Korean War veterans throughout the Army.

When approached to write this essay, I mistakenly thought that what was first-hand knowledge to me would be readily available in newspaper archives and national vaults. It turns out that specific information on Fort Lawton and its role is almost nonexistent. The sources that a researcher can normally count on, newspaper articles and periodicals, aren't there except in two small columns from *The Seattle Times*. When I contacted the local branch of the National Archives, (NARA Pacific Alaska Region), its response was: "NARA's Pacific Alaska Region does not maintain records created by military units based in area forts. Unit records are maintained by the Textual Reference Branch at the National Archives at College Park, Maryland."[1]

I then contacted the National Archives at College Park and received the following response:

"Twentieth century military records are not maintained by fort but rather by unit. In order to determine what was happening at a particular fort, you would need to know what units were based there and research the individual units. Unfortunately, because of how the army maintained their records, this information does not exist in any one place if at all. In many cases units did not begin to keep records until they arrived in Korea and what has been kept is minimal at best."[2]

Major Desiree Wineland, left; Sergeant Ruben Estrada, middle, and Captain Tonja Williams, right, going about daily business and routines as Reservists at the new Leisy Center. Photo by Monica Wooton, 2000.

The war itself was, of course, well covered in both local newspapers, but as to what was happening here on the home front, there seems to be a singular lack of interest. This is indicated by the two articles I've cited which are written by staff reporters without bylines.

Therefore, I've compiled this essay from bits and pieces and remembered conversations and phone calls to my father who lives in Texas. Keith Penman was nice enough to provide me with his recollections of his time at Fort Lawton while working in the out-processing section. The men I have spoken with who passed through the Fort on their way to Korea, said only that they did not have much time to form any memories of the Fort or Seattle. They were only here on an average of 48 to 72 hours before boarding ship. They were restricted to the post and the processing of their paperwork plus receiving various inoculations that are part of any overseas deployment took up most of their time.

I do hope that I have been able to give an overview of the period, and have shed some light on a bit of the "Forgotten War."

A STRATEGIC LOCATION

Before outlining Seattle and Fort Lawton's role during the Korean War, it is important to understand why a port located more than 100 miles inland would have such a pivotal role in both the Korean War and World War II.

Unlike the low-lying East and Gulf coasts, the ruggedness of the North American West Coast offers only five natural deep water ports: San Diego, Long Beach and San Francisco-Oakland in California; Seattle and Vancouver, British Columbia, in the Pacific Northwest. In addition, the area offers geographic factors such as Elliott Bay where convoys could be assembled within its confines relatively free from delays due to foul weather and storms.

Seattle, while not garnering the glamour or "mystique" of San Francisco, was itself a major transportation hub. It was the northern and western terminus for the Union and Northern Pacific railroads respectively, as well as being the southern end to the Alaska-Canada Highway, or as it became known, the "ALCAN" highway. Seattle's shipyards could repair or maintain both the Navy and Merchant Marine ships. There was also the proximity of other ports such as Tacoma, Everett, Bellingham and some smaller satellite ports used as fueling depots and degaussing facilities, (where the magnetic field built up by a metal-hulled ship traveling through salt water was removed), as well as a berthing for convoy escorts. Bremerton had the only dry dock on the West Coast capable of handling carriers and capital ships. All but three of the ships sunk or badly damaged at Pearl Harbor underwent repair at the Bremerton Naval Shipyard.

Aerial view of Fort Lawton showing massive expansion from WW-II and Korea. Courtesy of US Army Reserve, 70th Regional Support Command. Circa 1950.

Add to all of this the need for a facility to quarter, feed, and process the thousands of troops needed to man and fight in a theater of operations that was, if nothing else, characterized by the shear vastness of the Pacific Ocean. Seattle had just such a facility, within a few miles of the piers from

Mess Hall #1 shows in an out-processing of troops. Courtesy of Discovery Park Archives. Circa 1950.

which those thousands of men were to depart: Fort Lawton. The post had room to expand so it could handle division-sized elements (about 25,000 men during World War II), plus the logistical support troops carrying out the process.

On May 22, 1941, Fort Lawton was placed under the command of the San Francisco Port of Embarkation Commanding General. Its principal function was to support troop embarkation at Seattle. On June 24, 1941, an expansion of the barracks took place at a cost of $826,000.[3]

WORLD WAR II

Feeling the momentum of World War II, Fort Lawton underwent further expansion and transformation as a staging area capable of processing a full division of troops at one time. In addition, many transportation, quartermaster, and engineer units were formed and trained there during that same time.

At the height of the war, 20,000 troops were stationed at the Fort. By the close of the war, 1.1-million troops processed through Fort Lawton. During the War, 5,000 Italian prisoners of war were processed there on their way to Hawaii, and at the close of the war, 1,150 German prisoners of war were confined at the Fort.[4]

With the end of World War II in September 1945, the demobilization of the military began. The catch phrase of the day was "Bring Our Boys Home." Now the US military figured out that if these men had processed into the Pacific Theater (known at this time as the Far East Command), they had to process out the same way. Therefore, beginning in September 1945, Fort Lawton became the debarkation and out-processing center for the men returning from the Pacific, Far East, and Alaska, which was a territory at this time and as such considered "foreign soil."

DEMOBILIZATION

This period of demobilization lasted from September 1945 to June 1947. During that time, the Army was reduced from more than eight-million to a strength of 684,000 by July 1, 1947. The number of divisions fell from 89 in 1945, to 16 in June 1946 to 12 in June 1947. By June 1948, there were ten divisions. During the four months from September 1945 to January 1946, the Army discharged an average of 1.2-million soldiers per month. There are no records available through the military or the National Archives on how many men out-processed through Fort Lawton. It seems that there was not much interest in keeping statistics, only to returning the men to their homes of record.[5]

It was at this time that it became clear that in order to maintain the congressionally-authorized strength of the Far East Command Army of Occupation at 120,500, replacements for the returning troops needed to be processed as well. Therefore, it fell upon Fort Lawton to shift gears and become once again an embarkation station on the one hand and a debarkation station on the other. By 1947, it became possible for military families to join the migration to the Far East. The Military Sea Transport Service had been formed and this became the method by which replacements and their family members left to join their units or loved ones, usually on board converted troop ships.[6]

Piers 90-91, men and material ready to embark for Korea. Courtesy of Discovery Park Archive. Circa 1950.

PASSING THROUGH

Here I speak from experience. In early 1947, my mother and I arrived at Fort Lawton, on our way to join my father in Japan. We were poked, prodded and immunized until we felt like pin cushions. There were all sorts of wonderful names for these shots: DPT, TRIP T, Plague, and the ever-popular J-B Encephalitis. Then we were paper-processed with the efficiency borne of countless repetitions.

We were then transported by military bus to the former Washington Hotel near Pier 36, to await the pending departure of the *USNS Bundy* bound for the port city of Yokohama. From there we went by train to the southern most Island of Kyushu, to the town of Kumamoto, and to the adjoining military base of Camp Woods, which would be my home for the next three years.

Late in February 1950, we reversed course and sailed "stateside." Once more I returned to Fort Lawton—this time, during one of Seattle's biggest snows. As a six-year-old, I remember seeing from the ship while arriving in Elliott Bay, a flashing red neon sign for the Mobil Oil tank farm on Harbor Island. I had never seen neon before. We in-processed and proceeded to our next duty station: Fort Lewis, Washington. As fate would have it, on June 25, 1950, the North Korean People's Army invaded the Republic of South Korea. By mid-July 1950, the 2nd Infantry Division from Fort Lewis embarked from the ports of Seattle and Tacoma bound for Pusan, South Korea.

Military transport with Magnolia in the background, heading for Korea. Photo courtesy of Sargent First Class Keith Penman (USA Ret.). Circa 1950.

From processing troops for overseas occupation, Fort Lawton went without much shifting of gears back into the job of sending men to war in Korea. In July 1951 alone, the equivalent of three divisions or 75,000 men were processed and sent on their way.

The Fort also supplied technical and transportation support to the Auburn General Depot, and to the Seattle Port of Embarkation.

This was the source of the material needed to supply the Army fighting in Korea with the munitions, food, and medical supplies as well as the other logistical support that an army needs while in combat. An article from *The Seattle Times*, dated August 13, 1950, can attest to this:

Men of the 21st Infantry Regiments, 24th Infantry Division passing in review prior to embarking for Korea, June, 1950. Courtesy of Rob Hitchings.

"As a result of the Korean War, the Seattle Port of Embarkation has expanded its facilities and experienced a sharp increase in out-bound cargo and passenger traffic.

The port dispatched twice as much cargo from Seattle as it did last month than it did in June. Out-bound passenger volume tripled. Commercial vessels loaded by the Port received large infraclasses in military cargo. More than three times as much tonnage was carried commercially in July as in June. Exact figures are withheld for security reasons." [7]

Following pages: Fort Lawton Military Cemetery where many Korean War veterans are laid to rest. Photo by Sam Sutherland, 2000.

These increases in the shipping of men and material necessitated the addition of about 1,400 personnel. The Military Sea Transport Service increased from 6 to 18 passenger ships, and from four to seven cargo vessels. It also arranged for the chartering of private ships to carry military cargo. [8]

Facilities used by the Port during World War ll were quickly put back into use, including a terminal at Mukilteo and a storage area at Tulalip, which provided 600 jobs. The Port also entered into agreement with the ports of Tacoma, Olympia and Portland, Oregon, for more pier space and other storage areas in Seattle. The Port also rented five floors of office space in the Smith Tower annex. The Port began operating on an around-the-clock basis seven-days a week. All military and civilian leaves were restricted to emergency only. [9]

At Fort Lawton, men spent an average of seven days between train and ship, so the old World War ll barracks were opened and the second consolidated mess hall was refurbished and staffed. During the war, military families going to Japan, Formosa, and Okinawa were still being processed. The need for troops for Korea did not lessen the numbers needed to maintain the Army of Occupation in the Far East. [10]

While no actual military units processed through the Fort during the Korean War, the numbers of replacement troops being processed were impressive at the height of the War in 1952, as 10,000 men a day were being fed, housed and medically readied for transport overseas. [11]

Fort Lawton became the first step in the "replacement pool," or as it was known to soldiers of the era and later by those sent to Vietnam, "The Repel Depel." The Pentagon had decided that the units already in Korea, which included the 2nd, 3rd, 7th, 24th and 25th

Robert B. Leisy Army Reserve Center is named for Magnolia born and 1963 Queen Anne graduate, Congressional Medal of Honor recipient for action in Vietnam. Courtesy of US Army Reserve, 70th Regional Support Command. Photo by Monica Wooton, 2000.

infantry divisions along with the 1st Cavalry and several separate regimental combat teams and Ranger battalions, and two Marine divisions, were sufficient for the United States' contribution to the United Nations' effort.

Casualties mounted, reaching horrendous proportions early in the war. Some of the units suffered 50% to 75% casualty rates—numbers of killed and wounded not seen since the Civil War. Replacements were the most needed commodity. No matter one's Military Occupation Specialty, infantrymen were the most needed. So cooks, photographers and clerk typists went to the front lines. As the war dragged on, a system was developed whereby soldiers earned rotation points that determined when they would leave foreign soil.

With the end of the Korean War in 1953, the flow of men did not abate. In fact, contrary to what one might expect, the numbers for 1954 were occasionally higher than during the World War II or the Korean War. Half-a-million men passed through the Fort from overseas or Alaska in the three years between the summer of 1951 and the summer of 1954.[12]

A NEW MISSION

In July 1954, the Fort became the headquarters for the Washington Military District which was responsible for the training and inspection of all reserve units in the state. Artillery went back to the Fort when the headquarters of the 26th Anti-Aircraft Artillery Group was reassigned there from Fort Lewis. Its mission was to defend Puget Sound. Additionally, an element of the 25th Air Division North American Air Defense Command (NORAD) was located at the Fort to better coordinate the air defenses of Puget Sound, linking the Air Force fighter interceptors based at McChord Air Force Base, Paine Field, Whidbey Island Naval Air Station, and the NIKE Missile sites being placed around the sound.

In 1957, the Xth US Army Corps was formed and located at Fort Lawton. The Xth Corps was a subordinate headquarters of the Sixth Army Headquarters based at the Presidio in San Francisco. Fort Lawton became the active Army Headquarters to oversee all operations, training, planning, logistics, and finance for all reserve units in Washington, Oregon, Idaho, Montana, Utah as well as part of Northern California. Commanded by a Major General with a full staff and complement of troops, the Xth Corps was to oversee those states' National Guard units and their fixed wing and rotary aircraft as well. It would continue in this role until November 1967 when the 124th Army Reserve Command was formed, and assumed the duties formerly held by the active duty units.[13]

Captain A. C. Hitchings newly home from Korea in 1952. Photo by Shirlie L. Hutchings.

Also, beginning at this time was the operation of the Missile Master complex, a joint-operational facility housing both the 26th Antiaircraft Artillery Group and the 25th Air Division NORAD. The Missile Master, at the Fort, was the command and control for all air defense of Seattle and the Puget Sound region. It was linked to the Distant Early Warning Line on the Arctic Circle, the Mid Canada Line, and to NORAD headquarters in Colorado Springs, Colorado.[14]

If there had been a Soviet air strike, those early warning lines would communicate the number, altitude, heading to the Missile Master complexes throughout the United States and Canada. As each successive line was passed, NORAD headquarters would determine which targets to be struck, and give command over to the complex nearest that target. Once the complex had acquired radar-tracking of the Soviet bombers, fighters would be scrambled to intercept. Any penetration by Soviet bombers of the interceptors would be tracked and firing data passed to the NIKE Ajax and Hercules Missile sites with the command to fire given by the Missile Master. Some of the sites were at Cougar Mountain, Kenmore, and Vashon Island.[15]

My father was assigned to Fort Lawton and the Xth Corps in 1957 following our return from Berlin, Germany. We lived in quarters 703 on Montana Circle from March 1957 until Dad's retirement in 1961, and then continued to live within a few blocks of the Main Gate. I have many fond memories of the Fort: going fishing from the boathouse with my Dad; the Teen Club dances on Saturday nights; boxing groceries for tips at the commissary; firing in rifle competitions on the indoor and outdoor ranges; my first steady girlfriend of five foot two, eyes of blue (or were they green? Memory fades—), blond hair, ponytail and braces.

KOREAN WAR

1950 *June 25:* North Korean forces invade South Korea
June 28: North Korean People's Army (NKPA) forces capture Seoul
July 5: Task Force Smith engages NKPA forces at Osan; first US ground action
July 10-18: 2nd Infantry Division prepares to embark from Seattle
Aug 4: Pusan Perimeter formed
Sept 15: US Xth Corps (later based at Ft. Lawton) conducts amphibious landing at Inchon
Sep 27: US and Republic of Korea forces recapture Seoul
Nov 27: Battle of Chosin Reservoir begins
Nov 29- Dec 1: Chinese forces maul 2nd Infantry Division as it protects the 8th Army withdrawal

1951 *Jan 1-5:* Third phase of Chinese offensive; 500,000 enemy troops push United Nations forces 50 miles south of the 38th Parallel and recapture Seoul
Jan 15: US Army Chief of Staff says, "We are going to stay and fight."
Apr 12: First major air battle
July 10: Truce talks begin
Aug-Oct: Battles of Bloody and Heartbreak Ridges

1952 *Jul 17 - Aug 4:* Battle for Old Baldy (Hill 266)
Aug 29: Largest air raid (1,403 sorties) strikes Pyongyang

1953 *Apr 16-18:* Battle of Pork Chop Hill
Jul 6-10: Second battle of Pork Chop Hill, 7th Infantry Division evacuates after five days of fighting
Jul 24-26: Final US ground combat
Jul 27: Last air combat; armistice is signed

Source: *Fort Lawton, Gateway to Korea.* US Army Reserve 70th Regional Support Command. Fort Lawton Public Affairs Office. June 2000.

Lapel button commemorating the 50th anniversary of the Korean War, June 25, 1950.

Photo by
Rob Hitchings.

Probably the most memorable occurrence for me at Fort Lawton happened on Oct. 31, 1964. I took one step forward, raised my right hand and swore to uphold the Constitution of the United States and to defend it from all enemies foreign and domestic. The officer administering the oath was, my father, Major A. C. Hitchings. Twenty-two years later, I retired from the United States Army.

Rob Hitchings was born in Aberdeen, Washington, March 2, 1944, while his father was serving somewhere in Europe with the 5th Infantry Division preparing for D-Day. His mother was visiting her parents during a trip from Gloucester, Virginia. Rob Hitchings has known the military his entire life. Raised an "Army brat" meant moving approximately every three years, and his "travels" took him and his family through every state in the lower 48 and to Japan and Germany. By the time he graduated from Queen Anne High School in 1962, he had attended 14 different schools. He continued with college and earned a bachelor's degree in history and political science from the University of North Carolina.

Enlisting in the US Army in October 1964, Rob attended basic training and advanced infantry training at Fort Lewis, Washington, "jump school" at Fort Benning, Georgia, and "ranger" training at Fort Bragg, North Carolina. He arrived in Vietnam the last week of December 1965, and served with the Military Advisory Command Vietnam Special Operations Group reconnaissance team. He returned to "The World" November 20, 1968. Rob retired from the Army October 31, 1986, a sergeant first class. Rob then worked for US Plywood and Boeing, and retired in 1999.

Rob's relationship with Fort Lawton began in 1947, when he and his mother processed through the Fort on their way to Japan, returning there in 1950. In 1957, he and his parents returned to Fort Lawton for his father's last tour of duty ending upon his retirement in 1961. He has essentially been a Magnolia resident throughout his life, living on or in the shadow of the Fort.

Replica of the WW-II memorial in Washington, D.C. Photo by Monica Wooton, 2000.

Sergeant Keith Penman

Source: Penman, Keith. Sargent First Class, USA (Ret.). "Re: The role that Fort Lawton played during the Korean War." E-mail to Robert Hitchings. 16 February 2000.

Sergeant First Class Keith Penman USA (Ret.), who served in Korea from August 1951 until May 1952, described the rotation system and process, having been reassigned to Fort Lawton where he served with the Returnee-Reassignment Center 6021 ASU:

Rotation was determined by a point system. As I recall, 2 points for rear area troops (way back), 3 points for support troops in the rear areas (Division HQ) and 4 points for units actually engaged in combat. It took 36 points to get your ticket home. Some spent 18 months, some 12, and some as few as 9 or 10. I arrived at Inchon Harbor in August of 1951 and we sailed under the Golden Gate Bridge on Memorial Day 1952.

Men of the 2nd Infantry Division preparing to return home after returning from Korea. Courtesy of Sargent First Class Keith Penman (USA Ret.).

After reaching the magic number, you were off to the Replacement Depot in Seoul, and then by ship to (at that time) Sasabo, Japan. Sasabo was the shipping point where you had either just missed the last ship or had to wait for enough troops to fill up the next one. I spent 4 days. You finally got called out and placed on a passenger manifest and given a time to be ready to board the bus to the ship. It took 14-days for the trip from Sasabo, Japan to San Francisco.

Shortly after my assignment to Fort Lawton, we received a new Commanding Officer. Lieutenant Colonel Alfred Prahiniski replaced Colonel Thomas Martin. His goal was to receive as many troops as the ships could bring us, and depending on the docking time, send them on their way within 24 hours. Some said it could not be done, but the Colonel proved them wrong. The secret of our success was a lot of hours and time management. The inside story was that the Pentagon had given the Colonel a free hand to develop a system that would speed things up. It all started with the ship being loaded in Japan. As soon as the passenger manifest was completed and the ship loaded, an air courier was dispatched with copies of the orders containing all of the passengers' names and homes of record.

When the courier arrived in Seattle he reported to Building 550, where he signed in and turned the lists over to the Duty Officer or Non-Commissioned Officer (NCO). They then called the Operations NCO and Officer. Time of day was not an issue. When you received the call, you reported in and started the process of preparing for the arrival of 1,500 to 4,000 troops, which depending on the weather, would arrive in 14 days. Going down the lists of passengers to determine where they would be going took several hours. For example, you would go down the list and anyone with a home of record showing Oregon, Washington or Idaho would be marked for Fort Lewis. Camp Atterbury, Indiana had responsibility for troops from the Midwest. The same for all the other camps and forts, many of which are long gone.

As soon as the lists were screened, a count of the number of personnel going to each place was determined. A marked copy with the totals was immediately taken to the Transportation Officer on Fort Lawton, where it was reviewed and a phone call was made to Washington D.C. to order transportation for X number of troops going to Y number of places. Usually, anything over 100 going to any one destination were sent by rail. Smaller groups went by charter out of Boeing Field, or by commercial air out of Sea-Tac. Those headed to Fort Lewis went by Greyhound Bus. At this point, a copy was also sent to Fort Lewis 32nd MRU, where punch cards were produced from the passenger lists. One went to the special orders section to be used for publishing orders; one went to locator for reference and one to the operations section. To make sure that no one was missed on the list, each man was issued a punch card, sort of a boarding pass. The special orders section had about 10 to 12 days to cut stencils, mimeograph and produce orders transferring between 1,500 and 4,000 troops to their next assignment.

Troops passing in review on the Fort Lawton parade grounds. Courtesy of Sargent First Class Keith Penman (USA Ret.). Circa 1950.

Finance is alerted to the ships arrival. Billeting is checking out space requirements. The consolidated mess hall is ordering steaks. Post transportation is preparing for the necessary numbers of buses to bring the men from Pier 36 to Fort Lawton. A team is being picked to process troops aboard ship. Supply is checking to make sure enough uniforms are on hand to take care of however many troops are arriving.

The ship notifies us of its ETA (estimated time of arrival) and the boarding party is sent to Port Angeles to board the ship when the pilot takes over the ship off Port Angeles for the 8-hour trip into Elliott Bay. That gives the boarding party time to process and take care of personnel records and special assignment problems. If there are personnel traveling with dependents, they process them aboard ship as well. The personnel with dependents will be free to leave as soon as the ship docks, unless they need to go to finance to be paid. The rest of the troops will board busses directly off the ship and proceed to Fort Lawton. The busses will unload at the parking lot near the 500 area, (which is still there) and the Colonel or his representative will welcome them home. By this time operations has made up schedules for each group. The troops are broken down into groups of 20 for scheduling for finance, clothing, dining, etc. Each roster has an NCO in charge to guide the group along according to the schedule.

Busses would begin arriving along the street in front of buildings 500, 501, 502 and the shipping building, 503. Post busses were used to shuttle troops to Interbay, just outside the Fort. Trains were sided to take care of all troops leaving by rail. The first busses to leave were usually those for Fort Lewis. Depending on the docking times, most troops were on their way well within the 24 hours. The only exceptions were aircraft delays. The charter carriers were having delays for a while, until the Army decided that the troops would not be brought back to Fort Lawton for the night. If the charters could not meet the scheduling, they would have to provide meals and billeting. They became much more efficient after 60 or more troops were delayed and they had to feed them.

Each bus leaving for the airports or to Interbay was accompanied by an NCO to make sure the troops arrived at the right place, and after a roll call as they boarded the trains or planes, the NCO would stay until the aircraft or train departed. The last of the troops were gone and our work was done. Not quite yet, we had to clean up the barracks, mow lawns and generally straighten up the areas to get ready for the next ship. We sometimes had two ships arrive in the same week, and then sometimes only two or three a month. I would say we averaged about one a week for the most part. Then you also have to take into account that we were also processing troop ships arriving from Alaska.

Major General Clyde R. Cherberg, USA (Ret.)
by Clyde Cherberg

I was born March 1, 1930, to Frank and Ina Cherberg, Magnolia residents. The Cherberg family had resided on Magnolia since the middle "nineteen teens." My parents were the last surname Cherbergs to leave Magnolia, moving to the Grovesnor House at the foot of Queen Anne Hill in 1989. (Other "Cherbergs" with different surnames continue to live on Magnolia.) My father owned and operated a grocery and meat market on Magnolia for many years as did his father before him.

Lieutenant Cherburg on Korea duty. Courtesy of Clyde Cherberg.

I attended Interbay Grade School from the fall of 1935 until the school closed at the end of the school year in 1939 and I was trans-ferred to Lawton Grade School where, among other things, I was Captain of the School Boy Patrol. (As indicated by the name it was all boys in those days.) I attended Lawton through the first half of the eighth grade in 1943 when school population pressure due to wartime increases in Army personnel at Fort Lawton led to the transfer of the eighth grades at Magnolia and Lawton Grade Schools to Queen Anne High School and the hastily created "Queen Anne Eighth Grade Center." Several hundred high school students were transferred from Queen Anne to Lincoln High School to make room.

My father and my uncles John and James Cherberg preceded me in matriculating at Interbay and Queen Anne and I had a number of the same teachers. That started the "Are you related to John (or Jim)?" question that I still hear regularly. I have been asked, "Are you related to John Cherberg?" thousands upon thousands of times. John reported to me, just before he died, that several people had asked him, "Are you related to the general?"

As a mid-year student at Queen Anne High I had the option of graduating in 3 or 4 years. I chose to stay 4 years although many chose 3 years (all girls). While at Queen Anne I was on the baseball team and was a class officer and Boys Club (boys' student body) President.

*Major General Cherberg
handing Korean Service
Medal to Bill Tobin, June
25, 2000.* Photo by
Bruce Savadow.

I entered the University of Washington in 1948 upon graduation from Queen Anne and majored in accounting and military science. I graduated in 1952 receiving a US Army commission as a Second Lieutenant and being designated a Distinguished Military Graduate. I immediately entered the Army serving first in Virginia as a platoon leader in basic training, and then attending school before being transferred to Seattle working at the Seattle Army Terminal on Pier 37 with headquarters at Fort Lawton. Upon my transfer to Seattle, I married Shirley Jean Tyler, a Seattle native and Roosevelt High School graduate whom I met at the University of Washington. We have three daughters, Diana, Teri and Claudia and four grandchildren; all are living in the Seattle area.

I was transferred to Korea in 1953 where I served in the Transportation Corps. I returned in 1954 after declining an assignment to Okinawa. (I had only a two-year active duty obligation but as a "Category 2" (volunteer) officer and a Distinguished Military Graduate I had the option to continue on active duty.) I was separated from the active Army upon my return from Korea. I then joined an Army Reserve unit at Fort Lawton serving subsequently in transportation and artillery units before joining the 124th Army Reserve headquarters staff in 1974. In 1979, I was promoted to Colonel and assumed command of the 1397 Transportation Terminal Unit and its subordinate commands. In 1982, I was selected as Chief of Staff of the 124th, in 1984 as the Deputy Commanding General (Brigadier General) and in 1987 as Commanding General (Major General). I commanded the 124th until June 1991 when I retired. My retirement ceremony was held on the Parade Field at Fort Lawton, the next-to-last military ceremony held on that site.

My civilian employer since I left active duty in 1954 was The Boeing Company. I retired from Boeing in early 1990 and then continued for a time as a consultant to Boeing. At the time I retired I was Manager of the Renton Division Facilities Environmental Engineering and Construction Engineering.

I have often reflected on my almost lifelong association with Fort Lawton which started at least in 1937 when, at age seven, I first ventured on post. I remember pounding a rock on a cannon then placed at the main entrance to the post dislodging a chip of black paint that hit me in the eye sending me screaming home, certain I was blinded. The same cannon now resides in the courtyard of the 70th RSC headquarters building. My subsequent adventure included digging bullets out of the abutment at the end of the rifle range, loading them into my trusty Prince Albert can (large size) and struggling to carry the heavy load home. I remember the thrill of soldiers marching in formation through the neighborhood during World War II. And there was the amazing array of "booty" which I managed to garner by going through the soldiers' and the Army's discards—Japanese helmets, arctic boots, lifeboat rations, flotation belts, even practice bombs and blank mortar shells. Some of these treasures I have retained to this day.

The thousand-to-one chance that I would be stationed at Fort Lawton when on active duty, the even greater odds that I would someday command at Fort Lawton and retire from Fort Lawton in the next to last ceremony held on the "old post" beggars belief. I suppose it would be appropriate that I be buried there, but I have other plans.

My American Dream

by Paull H. Shin, Ph.D.

I, for one, consider it a blessing to be adopted. I was born in Korea, and at the age of four my mother died. Shortly after that my father left me. Having no place to go, my life consisted of standing on the street corners of Seoul begging for food to stay alive. I led the life of a street urchin until the age of fifteen. In 1950, I fled to the southern part of the Korean

State Senator Paull H. Shin giving his "American Dream" address at Korean commemoration. Photo by Corporal Andy Vanderholf.

peninsula. Rumor had it that the US forces were landing in Inchon under the command of General Douglas MacArthur. Having heard that, I decided to walk up to the front and greet the arriving American troops. I proceeded to the front line. It was there I saw a convoy of hundreds of vehicles passing across the bridge so they could continue to advance on the north. I was one of the hundreds of kids standing by the rubber raft bridge waving at the soldiers in the front. "Hallo, chewing gum, Hallo, chocolate," we would shout, hoping that they would throw out candy and things to us. One day, for reasons I don't know why, one of the soldiers lent his hand to me, and as I reached out to him, he picked me up and brought me over to the truck. It was this simple gesture that constituted the beginning of my new life.

The Army took interest in me. There I began my first and new career as a houseboy, polishing their shoes, washing and ironing their clothes, and helping them find some comfort in an otherwise difficult situation. Dr. Ray Paull, an Army dentist, took special interest in me and became my friend. He adopted me. I was sixteen years old then, and after we completed the necessary paperwork, which took nearly two years, I was able to come to the United States at age eighteen. When I arrived in the United States I met my mother and three brothers, who were all Caucasian with blonde hair. Needless to say, I felt extremely out of place. Having been adopted by the Paull family, I was relieved to know that for the first time in my life, there was a place for me. I was given my own room, a bed, new civilian clothes, and they provided me a loving home and an opportunity for an education.

After dinner on my first night, my Dad asked me what I would like to do. "Father, I would like to be educated." He said let's go to the high school tomorrow, to which I replied, "Sorry, Dad, but I have not gone to school in Korea." "Not even grade school?" His question made my complexion turn red with embarrassment. So the next day he took me to elementary school, only to be rejected by the principal, who told us I was too old for that school. I was completely speechless and feeling extremely hurt, but my father was undaunted. He said, "Well in that case, let's go to the junior high school." He took me to junior high school, but there again, the principal looked at me with a smile, but apologetically explained that I was too old. As a last resort, we went to the high school. "You have no grade school education, no junior high school education, how can I possible take you? I'm sorry." When I heard this third and final rejection, I was so disappointed and emotionally hurt that I burst into tears and cried out loud. The principal asked my why I was crying. I said, "Sir, one of the reasons I came here was to get an education, but getting an education has become an impossible dream for me." To that he asked, "Do you really want to study that much?" I said, "Yes Sir." He told me that there was a special program called the GED for boys like me. "Would you like to try that?" I had no idea what the GED was, but the thought of going to school excited me, so without hesitation I said, "Yessir." The principal was kind enough to provide a special tutor for me, Mrs. Evans, who taught me in English, social studies and history during the day. At night my father taught me math, chemistry and physics. My adoptive mother chauffeured me around to school and taught me English. Through this concerted effort and teamwork, I studied for a year and a half. I was able to take the GED test, and I was notified that I passed. I went on to the university, and upon getting a college degree, I continued into graduate school, eventually receiving a Master's and Ph.D. from the University of Washington. As I was walking down the aisle with my diploma in hand, it was my Dad who was emotionally moved. He burst into tears, saying "Son, I want to thank you for what you have accomplished in this country. I said "Dad, how can you thank me? It is I who shall thank you."

Senator Shin, 2nd legislative district, outside legislative chambers in Olympia, Washington. Photo by Dong Huen Lee.

As you can see, I have been very blessed. I consider myself living proof of American blessings and opportunity. I came upon a passage by Benjamin Franklin, who said "A grateful person is one who realizes blessings and reciprocates by serving." Having received so many blessings in this country, I decided to serve. I embarked on a teaching career which has spanned over 31 years, starting with the University of Maryland, Brigham Young University, and Shoreline Community College, teaching Asian history and International Relations to students in the United States.

Because of my interest in paying back the blessing I have received, I was very active in community services, including the PTA, the International Trade Association, and board member of the United Way, the Boy Scouts of America, the YMCA, and the Rotary Club.

I cannot say that my experience is exceptional, indeed, there are many Korean adoptees in the United States who have found successful, meaningful lives, and many ways to contribute to the betterment of their communities. Among my many experiences in the United States, one of the problems and challenges often confronting me was the simple question "Who am I?" They'd ask me if I was Japanese, I'd say no. They'd ask if I was Chinese, I'd day no. Then they'd ask, "Well, what are you then?" To that I told them, I'm an American." But as I tried to assimilate into American life, some situations prevented me from accomplishing this goal. For example, when I attended church I found I was the only Asian in the congregation. Of course the people would act kind and polite toward me, but I couldn't help feeling a sense that I wasn't fully accepted. I don't mind telling you that for years I contemplated whether I really could become an American.

In 1958, I was drafted into the US Army and took basic training in Fort Hood, Texas. Tired of "GI grub" one day, four soldiers and I got on the bus and went to Temple, Texas and found a nice restaurant. So my friends and I decided to treat ourselves. We were ready to walk into the restaurant, but to my dismay I notices a big sign reading "FOR WHITES ONLY." I hesitated, not knowing what to do. My friends said "Come on Paull, you are in the Army, you're one of us," and dragged me into the restaurant. Sure enough, just as we were

sitting down, the proprietor, wearing a tee-shirt and white cap, saw me and rushed over, asking what I was doing there. That evening I cried all night, soaking my entire pillow. The questions racking my mind were "Where do I belong? What should I do? What is my identity? One of the most important lessons I learned from these tragic experiences was transforming negativism into positive affirmation. We all experience negative forces, but we can choose to respond negatively or positively.

The Honor Guard of Chapter 423 Vietnam Veterans of America. Right to left: Robert Weslander (USMC), Jon Naff (USMC), Dan Daniels (USN), Greg DeLosSantos (USN), and Rob Hitchings (USA). Not shown, Steve Brown (USN) and Greg Olson (USA). Photo be Ed Quimby, 2000.

Yes, I'm an adoptee, a Korean-American in an American family, but somehow society often refused to recognize that. But by mingling and association with my students, I taught them the concept that we are all God's children, that we are all brothers and sisters. My belief in the Christian faith helped me to reemphasize this idea and strengthened my conviction that I could be an American just as much as anyone else.

I felt that serving in politics was one of the fastest ways to be integrated into the mainstream. I had a startling revelation in the course of my first campaign. I was afraid to run for public office because of my color. Deep down in my heart I did not believe that I could be fully accepted by the American people. My victory in 1992 proved I was wrong. The fear I had was the fear itself.

In 1998, I ran for a seat in the Washington State Senate, going against a 26-year career politician, and once again being told it was impossible. Once I decided to run, though, I went through 4 pairs of shoes walking 9 hours a day, every day for 9 months, visiting everyone in my district.

One suggestion I would like to make is that everyone must have a dream of some kind. First, a dream and a belief that you are God's child, that you believe in yourself and your capacity to become anything and everything you want to be. The power of positive thinking, and the conviction that you can achieve your dream, cannot be underestimated.

Some people may have experiences similar to mine, while others may even be worse. Be that as it may, we share a common background. There are over 200,000 Korean adoptees throughout the world, though most are located in the United States. Each one of them must go through that cycle, from distinct racial background to social acceptance and integration into the American mainstream.

I went to Yakima, Washington, to give a seminar for the adoption organization KIDS. After the conference, one lady approached me and said "Mr. Shin, until three years ago I didn't even know where Korea was."

Senator Shin was born in 1935 and adopted by an American GI during the Korean War. Brought to the United States by his adoptive family, he began his education with a GED and has earned a Ph.D. in History from the University of Washington. He recently retired from teaching at the college level for 31 years, the last 26 at Shoreline Community College in Seattle. Senator Shin serves on the Higher Education Committee as Vice-Chair; Commerce, Trade, Housing, and Financial Institutions as Vice-Chair; and as a member of the Transportation Committee. Paull and Donna have lived in Edmonds for 31 years and have two children and three grandsons.

Medal Ceremony at Fort Lawton, June 25, 2000
By Rob Hitchings

Fort Lawton ceased to be an active US Army post in November 1967, when the 124th Army Reserve Command (124th ARCOM) was formed to take over the command and control of those Army Reserve units formally assigned to the Xth US Army Corps. This was part of an overall shift in the US military to make the reserve components take a more proactive role.

Monument to the men of the 70th Infantry Division located at "Trailblazer Field" Fort Lawton.
Photo by Corporal Andy Vanderholf.

Within the Army, reserves now make up 51% of the support units.

The bulk of the Fort was turned over to the City of Seattle and became Discovery Park. The Army retained and continues to maintain a section of the northeast corner that contains two reserve buildings: Harvey Hall, a motor pool, and Leisy Center, a maintenance facility. The military cemetery also remains as federal property, even though it is located within the boundaries of the Park.

In 1996 the 124th ARCOM was re-flagged the 70th Reserve Support Command (70th RSC). With the more active role of the reserves came the need for more facilities. A construction project began in 1997 and was completed in June 2000, coinciding with the US Army's 225th birthday and the 57th anniversary of the activation of the 70th Infantry Division, whose patch and designation the 70th RSC had adopted. Also in 1997, the planning for the 50th Commemoration of the beginning of the Korean War (June 25, 1950) began.

On June 24, 2000, the 70th RSC began a weekend of events that Chapter 423 Vietnam Veterans of America had the honor of participating in. Veterans of the 70th Infantry Division attended. Beginning with an open house and the celebration of the Army's 225th birthday, the weekend culminated with the 57th anniversary of the activation of the 70th Infantry Division, the unveiling of the 70th Division monument and dedication of Trailblazer Field. The Honor Guard of Chapter 423 fired the rifle salute followed by echoing Taps played by buglers, remembering those who did not return. This was followed by a staging of a 1950s USO canteen dance that included music of the era played by the 104th Division band.

MAGNOLIA KOREA WAR MEDALISTS

Six Magnolian men were awarded the Korean Medal at Fort Lawton Ceremony June 25 2000: Richard G. Kyle, William Lithgow, Bertil Lundh, Gordon Sierck, Ronald Santucci, and Joseph Smolen, posthumously, to his wife Bea.

June 25, 2000 saw the beginning of a three-year commemoration of the Korean War. The program began with a welcome from the commander of the 70th Reserve Support Command, Major General James M. Collins, Jr., followed by remarks from state Senator Paull Shin, himself a Korean War orphan adopted by an Army doctor. The ceremony culminated in the awarding to more than 100 veterans, or their survivors, the Republic of Korea Service Medal. Many of these veterans had passed through Fort Lawton on their way to Korea or upon their return. Judging by the number of 2nd Infantry Division patches and pins worn by those being honored, it is possible that some of them had served with my father.

Knowing this made my participation all the more special. Joining General Collins in the presentation were Major General David de la Vegene and Major General Clyde Cherberg, both former commanders of the 124th Army Reserve Command and Korean War veterans.

All too often when our Honor Guard is called upon to honor these men and women it is with a Rifle Salute followed by Taps and the words "This flag is presented on behalf of a grateful nation." This was one time we were able to pay our respects to fellow veterans directly. For this privilege I have to thank not only the Army Reserve but the members of this book project.

The Korean War Service Medal awarded by the Republic of Korea to all who served, or their survivors, in Korea between 1950 and 1953. Photo by Ed Quimby.

Opposite: Korean War commemoration collage. Photo by Monica Wooton, 2000.

Fishermen's Terminal: Million-Dollar Industry

By Sam L. Sutherland

PREFACE

Seattle's Fishermen's Terminal has occupied the northeastern edge of the Magnolia community for nearly 100 years. This facility serves as a homeport for hundreds of boats and a multi-million-dollar fishing industry, and its resources have been part of Magnolia's history from early on.

Discovering and researching the history, growth and present-day challenges affecting the fishing industry and the Terminal sent me on many paths. I began with the Terminal. I spoke with fishermen, skippers, suppliers, safety experts, government experts and regulators to learn about what goes on at the Terminal. Conversations with the fishermen occurred in the Bay Restaurant at Fishermen's Center, or on their fishing boats. Family stories came easily from the men who talked about their grandfathers and fathers who fished and in turn taught them. These three generations represent 50 to 95 years of fishing in the Northwest. One of the most interesting men turned out to be deaf. He'd worked 40 years on family-owned fishing boats and on his own boat.

I spent a lot of time walking on the docks and fingers (smaller docks projecting at 90 degrees) to look at and to photograph many of the boats. I pondered the differences in their configurations, sizes, rigging and visible gear. Opportunities occurred for visits with individuals who owned boats, worked on them or supported them. My photography was influenced by the physical size of the Terminal, its many buildings and their arrangement, as well as the daily activities of boats coming and going.

Learning about the history of the Terminal began with a visit to the office at the Fishermen's Center. Jim Serrill offered suggestions, and put me in touch with Bill Anschuetz, Port of Seattle Public Affairs. Two members of Serrill's staff, J. Carl Meyersahm and Gwen Savery, provided guidance, suggestions, and opened the door to the day-to-day actions of the Terminal. Contacts with the Port Commission's Ruth Strawser and Peggy Ellsworth, both of Legal Records, brought me together with bound sets of the port commissioners' records and other valuable data.

Fishing season 2000 takes off to slow start. Photo Sam Suthurland, 2000.

My search also took me to the University of Washington library and School of Fisheries, the International Halibut Commission, the National Oceanic and Atmospheric Administration (NOAA) , the National Marine Fisheries Services (NMFS) , the State of Washington Department of Fish and Wildlife, and the Seattle Public Library. I visited businesses that service the fishing industry. I accumulated a lot of paper, books and publications. The quest for information took me down many paths to many places and people for which I'm grateful. I've gained an appreciation for and some insight into the business of fish.

THE HISTORY:

Salmon Bay Before the Terminal

The earliest fishermen using Salmon Bay were American Indians, specifically the Shilshole-Ahmish, or people of Shilshole, who lived in the settlements at the north end of Salmon Bay and fished for their livelihood.[4]

Kroll Deed Claim Map. Circa 1860s.

The early day residents lived with mature forests likely fir, cedar, hemlocks and spruce. These trees were the resources for their means of existence. As non-Indian settlers moved into the area, a partnership of James and Daniel O'Leary with William Cochran, put loggers to work, and by the early 1900s only a few old-growth trees remained standing. As time passed smaller trees took over, as did the brush and bushes. Vegetation included wild blackberries, ferns, cranberries, nettles, skunk cabbage, and salmonberry.[5]

In time, modest parcels of cleared land supported houses and outbuildings. Subsistence farming made its appearance.

Several creeks emptied into the Salmon Bay from Magnolia and Ballard. At low tides, muddy tidal flats appeared. An 1884 City of Seattle report noted that the beaches near the entrance to the Bay were excellent for clam digging, and that there was an abundant supply of crab, clams, oysters, mussels and shrimp. In early time photographs, the beaches appeared open, with a few snags deposited by the tidal action.[6]

Early non-Indian settlers appeared in the mid-1850s and began filing land claims in the 1860s. A Land Office map revealed Edmond Carr, H. A. Smith, and John Ross filed claims on areas that are the site of today's Fishermen's Terminal.[7] An 1884 Seattle Public Library map, prepared by F. C. Tucker, Civil Engineer and Surveyor, for Eshelman Llewellyn and Company, placed the area for the Fishermen's Terminal in the Pike Addition. This map indicated that a creek flowed through the Terminal area and the water came from the northwest side of Queen Anne. Today, there is no evidence of this stream.[8]

As reported by the *Ballard News-Tribune* July 26, 1902, "A war has broken out between the Puget Sound fish trap owners and the gill net fishermen." The gill netters went into the Salmon Bay traps and fished and the trap owners had them arrested. The gill netters then declared the presence of traps in Puget Sound contrary to federal laws. At the time more than 500 men were engaged in trap fishing. The number of "trappers" at work gives substantial evidence to the presence of large numbers of salmon in Salmon Bay.[9]

After condemnation and land acquisition in 1912, construction began on Fishermen's Terminal in 1913. At that time Magnolia consisted of a few hundred residents, and a small number of subsistence farms. Two wooden bridges provided access to downtown. Construction of the Hiram Chittenden Locks was underway following groundbreaking ceremonies November 10, 1912.[10]

Terminal Creation, Growth and Expansion: 1912 - 1987
The first significant step in the creation of Fisherman's Terminal was when the Port of Seattle Commissioners (General Hiram Chittenden, Judge C. E. Remsberg and Robert Bridges) voted to adopt changes in the harbor lines of Salmon Bay in December 1911, which would result in one of the "districts" becoming Fishermen's Terminal.

A TERMINAL IS BORN: PORT COMMISSION MEETING MINUTES AND REPORTS

"On Friday, January 26, 1912, the Commissioners abandoned its proposed cooperation with King County in the work of improvement of Salmon Bay and lower Duwamish. Instead the Port would provide the entire funds for the Salmon Bay development, $350,000." (Minutes of a special meeting of the Seattle Port Commission, January 26, 1912.)

"On May 31, 1912, by Resolution 53, the Commission of the Port of Seattle provided for the condemnation of land and other property for the purpose of creating, maintaining and operating the Salmon Bay Improvement. This action was a part of a larger action known as the Comprehensive Scheme of Harbor Improvement of the Port of Seattle. The land condemned consisted of approximately 35.4 acres between 15th Avenue West and 20th Avenue West, and between West Emerson and Salmon Bay Waterway." (Port of Seattle Commission Records)

"To acquire for future development a considerable tract of ground on the south side of Salmon Bay in the immediate neighborhood of the Interbay railroad yards and best situated at any point of the bay for future commercial development. As an initial step in this development the commission will make provisions on the east side of the tract for the purse seiners' fleet of Puget Sound. This provision will consist of slips for laying up boats, a marine railway for hauling out for repairs, places for drying out nets, sheds for storage of the paraphernalia of the boats, oil tanks for supplying installation. Plans for this work are completed and bids have been accepted for the dredging and bulkhead work. The plan ought to be ready for use in six months." (Commission's Annual Report, Port of Seattle, December 31, 1912.)

"Actual construction work on the fishermen's dock was begun February 15, 1913." (Commission Records)

The motion of Judge Remsberg carried unanimously. The Counsel was instructed to report on the question of creating one or more improvement districts for the purpose of raising a portion of the necessary funds for such sites and improvements, the remainder to be charged against the entire port.[11]

On January 26, 1912, the commissioners abandoned their proposed cooperation with King County in the work of improvement of Salmon Bay and lower Duwamish, and determined that the Port would provide the $350,000 needed for the Salmon Bay development.[12]

Four months later, the Commission of the Port of Seattle approved land and other property provided for "the purpose of creating, maintaining and operating the Salmon Bay Improvement. This action was a part of a larger action known as the Comprehensive Scheme of Harbor Improvement for the Port of Seattle." The land allocated for the new terminal consisted of approximately 35.4-acres between 15th Avenue West and 20th Avenue West, and between West Emerson and Salmon Bay Waterway.[13]

By the end of 1912, the Port of Seattle Commission's first annual report called the project "snug harbor" and proposed acquiring more land in the Interbay railroad yards for future commercial development.[14]

The construction work on the fishermen's dock began February 15, 1913, according to the Commission records. At the time the Commission reported the fishing fleet of Puget Sound "as a large one, there being about 250 purse seiners, together with gill netters, trollers {sic}, cannery tenders, etc." The boats were dispersed up and down the Sound. With facilities at Salmon Bay, the fleet would be concentrated at the "snug harbor." Revenue projections estimated $150,000 per boat for outfitting, and provisioning.[15]

The Commission's plan called for timber bulkheads with the area behind them to be filled to a height of 12 feet above the present high tide level. The cost of fill at that time was 15 cents per cubic yard. This provided a 4-foot height above the water line when the Hiram Chittenden Locks became operational. On the west side of the property, the development included a wide slip nearly 1,000 feet long with a wharf and large merchandise shed on each side. The facility design supported transfer of freight to and from large ocean steamers to

Opening day at the Terminal, 1913. Courtesy of Gordon Strand, Nordic Heritage Museum.

meet the needs of US Army operations at Fort Lawton. As work proceeded problems developed in dredging out the former tideway swamp. *"The blue clay muck, when dredged up, prevented the fill from being consummated in 1913,"* and delayed the net warehouse and the marine railway, according to Port of Seattle records.[16]

In 1913 Fishermen's Terminal became a functioning, identifiable facility on the edge of Salmon Bay alongside the Northern Pacific Railroad trestle, a wooden structure that connected Magnolia, Queen Anne and Ballard. At this time, the Salmon Bay waterway connected directly to Shilshole Bay and was subjected to the daily tides and the salt water of Puget Sound. This condition would change when the Hiram Chittenden Locks began operation in 1917, and fresh water flowed from Lake Washington and Lake Union and surrounded the Terminal's piers and docks. Fresh water eliminates the barnacles, which in salt water, attach themselves to the hull and increase vessel drag.

In late 1914, the Port of Seattle exchanged title to a portion of Smith's Cove Waterway Commission with the Great Northern Railway Company, receiving in return title to the property consisting of the Salmon Bay Terminal property and what was called "Tract B" which included approximately 7.67-acres south and .83-acres north of West Emerson Street.[17]

While the Hiram Chittenden Locks were under construction, the Port of Seattle completed a permanent bulkhead and a new pier to expand Fishermen's Terminal. Completion of the $500,000 facility heralded a new era in the fishing industry, according to the *Seattle Post-Intelligencer*. A parade of nearly 200 boats led by the *F/V Inga* opened the celebration. General H. M. Chittenden, president of the Port Commission, formally dedicated it on this date. H. J. Hemen of the Salmon Bay Improvement Committee read the General's prepared address. Cavanaugh's Band provided music and the Norwegian Singing Society sang.[18]

The water's depth in Salmon Bay alongside the wharf was reported to be 25 feet, sufficient without further dredging for ordinary fishing vessels. In 1932, the *Ballard News-Tribune* reported the need to dredge the Canal from Salmon Bay to Lake Washington. Shippers claimed the canal inadequate to handle large, loaded vessels as the average depth at the time ranged from 25 to 26 feet. The Port of Seattle engineers recommended a depth of 30 feet.[19]

In 1934, Port Commissioner J. A. Early conceived an overall expansion program for the Terminal to keep up with the growth of the fishing industry, but five years passed before construction began in 1939. The changes included one new net shed and installation of saw-tooth mooring piers of a unique design by the Port of Seattle engineering staff. These were later duplicated by other facilities.[20]

The Terminal site grew slowly until the 1940s. During this era new net sheds, four new docks, and an extension to an existing dock increased the facility's size. The United States entered World War II December 7, 1941. A photograph taken in 1942 shows a large ship under construction in an area now occupied by the north ends of docks 3 and 4.[21]

On July 14, 1945, the Port of Seattle bought 15.73-acres of additional property from the Union Pacific Railroad for $25,130. The property was west of the Salmon Bay Terminal.[22]

On February 5, 1946, the Port Commission bought an additional piece of property from the Great Northern Railway Company to include Block 97, Gilman's Addition: Lots 1,2, and 3 and a portion of lots 4, 5, 6, 7, 46, 47, and 48 for $703. Additional land acquired at Salmon Bay Terminal was Lot 10, Block 100. Gilman's Addition would provide a level entrance to the eastside of the Terminal.[23]

A voter-approved bond issue in 1948 provided $1-million in financing for the Fishermen's Terminal. Charles Regal wrote in the September 9, 1949, issue of the *Seattle Post-Intelligencer*, "They're letting out the seams." Regal reported that the Port of Seattle officials intended to better San Francisco. The Great Northern Railway participated in the plans for future expansion. The new access to the facility was greatly improved with the completion of the Emerson Street Viaduct. The Northern Pacific Railway, the Port of Seattle

Above: Look at the Terminal facility on opening day. Courtesy of Gordon Strand, Nordic Heritage Museum.

Below: F/V Inga leads the parade from the Terminal. Courtesy of Gordon Strand, Nordic Heritage Museum and relative of boat owner.

Fishermen's terminal.
Courtesy of Paul
Dorpat. Circa 1985

and the City of Seattle shared the cost of the elevated roadway. Part of the modernization included 150-feet of concrete bulkhead, 1,650-feet of sheet pile bulkhead, a 270-foot drain line, 38,000 cubic-yards of dredging, 154,000-feet of fill, and 8,500 cubic-yards of grading. Two new net sheds, 60 by 200 feet were constructed, as were two 625-foot saw-tooth piers. A new office building completed the planned improvements.[24]

The formal dedication of the remodeled Fishermen's Terminal occurred May 17, 1953. The $1-million remodel modernized and expanded the facility to provide improved moorage, dry-docking (300-ton and 100-ton facilities), boat and engine repair and maintenance, and supply facilities. A new restaurant, The Wharf, and an adjacent Valhalla Room, offered diners colorful and ever-changing views of the moored fleet. The Wharf Coffee Shop and the Moby Dick Tap Room occupied space in the Fishermen's Terminal Administration Building.

In 1979 and 1980, Port of Seattle construction projects added larger piers and increased the capacity for handling the fishing boats; however, in time the facility proved inadequate and a plan providing preliminary cost data was prepared for extensive renovations. On October 1, 1981, the Port of Seattle Commissioners raised the moorage rates an average of 12% with individual boat owner's costs based upon boat length. From 1980 to 1985, the Fishermen's Terminal operated at a loss. In 1980 the total terminal loss approximated $97,000. By 1985, the loss had increased to $345,000.[25]

In 1986, a plan providing preliminary estimate included widening the northwest dock, dredging, bulkhead repairs, a new commercial building and restaurant, and revision to parking areas, lighting and access. The estimated costs ranged from $9.97-million to $10.4 million. Potential add-ons for additional structural revisions and improvements totaled $4.8-million to $5.9-million.[26]

In 1987, the Port of Seattle adopted a $13-million plan, financed by the Port's general fund and an increase in moorage rates, to improve and further expand the terminal. This included dock enlargements, a two-story commercial complex and parking, additional net sheds and upgrading of existing commercial buildings. At this time, the northwest dock at the northern edge of the Terminal was remodeled into a 50-foot wide, 900-foot long pier to accommodate factory trawlers and other large vessels. The pier strength allowed trucks and equipment to be moved alongside the ships to repair and supply them.[27]

A memorial honoring those fishermen lost at sea since 1900 was erected and dedicated in 1988 after the Seattle Fishermen's Memorial Committee, a non-profit organization of industry volunteers was established in 1985. At that time, there were 120 names listed. By 2000, the names of 627 men and women were listed.[28]

FISHERMEN'S MEMORIAL

In the mid-1980s, a listing of names began for area fishermen and women lost at sea. By October 1985, the tragic list included 120 names and listed those individuals lost at sea since 1900. At the October 1985 Fishing Exposition held at the Seattle Center, John Krueger continued the task of identifying names, and began an effort to raise money for a memorial planned for Fishermen's Terminal.

The Seattle Fishermen's Memorial Committee, a non-profit organization of industry volunteers was established in 1985. In 1999, the board had 12 volunteers, and each participant serves for three years.

The Memorial Committee had the goal of raising $100,000 for the memorial. By 1988, money obtained from fishermen's families, boat owners, the fishing industry, and individuals allowed the memorial to be completed. It was dedicated October 8, 1988.

The memorial consists of two parts: a 27-foot high bronze and granite monument and a separate cast wall with bronze name plaques.

The sculpture created by Ron Petty is magnificent. The base has a 6-foot high, bronze ring, which in bas-relief depicts the fish and shellfish harvested by the Seattle Fishing Industry. This hands-on display attracts the casual visitor and the children. A granite column supports a bronze sculpture of a fisherman landing a halibut.

The fishing industry publication *Tradewinds* carried these words, "When fishermen die at sea, they just disappear. There's no body to bury, no graves to visit. There's no place for the loved one to go to remember."

Fishermen's memorial at the terminal. Photo by Monica Wooton, 2000.

Now the sculptured memorial serves as a residence for memories and a place to reflect and heal, where one can leave flowers, tears, and prayers. A rededication of the memorial takes place the first Sunday in May of each year. Afterwards ministers from different churches participate in a blessing of the fleet.

Since completion of the memorial, the Memorial Committee has expanded its mission, and increased fund raising efforts so that grief support and safety-training programs are included. The service of a grief support professional is available at no charge to assist any bereaved families with home visits and counseling.

The safety training sponsored by the Memorial Committee is accomplished using local facilities. Matching-grant funding supports hands-on training with US Coast Guard approved courses. Included in the training are first aid and cardiac pulmonary resuscitation, firefighting, and vessel stability. Scholarships have provided safety drill instructor training for more than 500 people. These individuals put their skills at work training members on their own boats. In 2000, the Memorial Committee added a new program by establishing a scholarship fund (college or trade school) for the family members of those who have lost their lives in fishing and are identified on the Memorial's plaques.

The added responsibilities taken on by the Memorial Committee require money. One way of raising funds is through the annual Fishermen's Fall Festival in September, and the Fishermen's Terminal Tenants' Association annual banquet and auction in November. Substantial funds come from corporate donation programs that pledge for a three-year period to assure a sustained budget. Other gifts of money come from individuals.

The 1999 Fishermen's Fall Festival, hosted by Terminal tenants and attended by thousands, offered a variety of demonstrations, exhibits, music, performances, and contests. The salmon bake fed over 6,000 individuals at the 1998 festival. The Chinook Restaurant supplied the recipe and provided oversight of the fish donated by Northwest Sea Food to insure safety. Volunteers assembled from the companies serving the fishing industry did the cooking and serving.

Top: Survival gear and immersion suits for safety on the boats. Photo Frank Gieske, 2000.

Middle: US Coast Guard ship Cutty Hunk. Photo Sam Sutherland, 2000.

Bottom: View of the piers and boats moored. Photo Sam Sutherland, 2000.

The southwest area of the Terminal hosted exhibits, demonstrations, boats for viewing, canoe rides, and "hands-on" games like the dunking tank. Large tables covered with ice hosted different fish for the attendees to see and touch the marine products of Puget Sound. Specimens included a variety of fish, squid, an octopus, and the ugly contest winner: a ratfish.

The US Coast Guard cutter *Cutty Hunk* exhibited survival gear and air rescue equipment and allowed the spectators to come aboard. At an adjacent dock, the Seattle Sea Scouts offered free rides in Native American canoes.

Three and four-year-old boys and girls fished in a large circular tank for special fish. In another area other young kids built fishing boats from pre-cut pieces provided by volunteer David Bruce.

Courtesy of The Port of Seattle.

At Dock 7 the dunking tank provided the opportunity to "dunk" a volunteer victim with three throws for a dollar. (Most people demonstrated worse throws than the 1999 Mariners' relief pitchers.) Three hundred feet away in the breezeway of Fishermen's Center, the fish-filleting contest pitted representatives of major Seattle restaurants against one young man from Hawaii. The judges selected Tracy Lawton as the winner scoring him on speed, quality and least waste. The oyster-shucking contest followed with each contestant receiving 15 oysters to open and consume. Three individuals competed at a time, and the winner, John Durand, finished in 57.4 seconds. And he didn't even like oysters! Many challengers left with a cut nose or lip, bleeding fingers and hands.

The biggest and final competition of the day was the Immersion Suit Races. Teams of four competed with the US Coast Guard which competed first, setting a time of 3 minutes, 28 seconds as a target for the others. Out on the west-wall of the Terminal, the two competing teams laid out their suits and awaited the starting signal. At the starter's command, they dressed rapidly, then moved slowly in the bulky suits to the wall's edge and jumped into the water. A 100-foot swim brought each team to a survival raft moored to a dock. Each team member got into the raft without any limbs hanging out. The clock stopped when the fourth individual disappeared inside the raft. Representatives from Trident Foods won the race.

A Glimpse of the Terminal

Generally, Fishermen's Terminal is a quiet neighbor as rows of tethered fishing boats float silently. In the water by Dock 8, geese and ducks circle awaiting visitor handouts. At the Fishermen's Memorial, outside of Fishermen's Center, an honor guard of flowers offers solitary tribute to those fishermen and women who are victims of the seas.

When preparations for fishing begin, the Terminal responds and rumbles with activity. Trucks roll. Machinery is lifted, hoisted, swung aboard, installed. Sounds of work ripple the air and water; drilling, sawing, welding, grinding, and hammering. Painters paint. Boat engines with baritone, bubbling exhausts respond to mechanics' mandates. On the docks, deckhands make preparations—shouting, pointing, laying out lines, measuring, cutting, wrapping and coiling. At Docks 4 and 5, shirtless, muscular young men ready, load and secure 700-pound crab pots for arduous Alaskan voyages. Out on the black asphalt surface of the net repair area, silent weathered net menders twist and turn, pull and tie. Out on the north end of Dock 4, fueling hoses duplicate umbilical cords as boats nourish empty tanks. Food and bait come aboard as the fishing vessels make ready.

Departure time. Goodbyes. Wet cheeks. Hugs and handshakes. Responding to the call, quickly, quietly, one by one, the fleet moves to the Locks and on to the open waters to face chance and challenge. Left behind—families and empty slips.

The Industry:

The Terminal and the Fishermen

The Terminal's past and present story involves people, methods of fishing, and boats of different types, sizes and ages. The Terminal's purpose: fish—many kinds. Some are small in size and others large, some are sleek and fast, lots of them are ugly, and a few live in relatively shallow water while others live in the deep regions of Puget Sound, the Pacific Ocean, and the Gulf of Alaska. Fish are a nutrient in the area's blood stream and contribute to the region's diet, and fishing makes a financial contribution to the Puget Sound economy.

Located on the southeastern edge of Salmon Bay, the Terminal began in 1913 as a small dock and single building. Eighty-seven years later, the facility occupies 76.1-acres, contains 400 berths, provides 2,500 linear feet of loading dock space, and offers 124,000 square-feet of office, retail and restaurant area. Located northwest of Seattle's City center, the Terminal is a component of the mostly residential Magnolia community and not where one would expect to find a multi-million-dollar fishing industry. In 1994, Fishermen's Terminal provided a total of 6,800 jobs, and the economic impact amounted to $403-million.[27]

Fishing can be a family or commercial endeavor, small or large. One way or the other, owning and operating a boat can be expensive, with one major cost element being the license or permit. In September 1999, the cost for a seiner permit for salmon in Alaska varied between areas, but ranged from $25,000 in Prince William Sound to $67,000 in False Pass. These permits must be purchased or transferred from an owner since the State of Alaska ceased issuing

Opposite: Photo Collage of Fall Fishermen's Festival. Photos: Frank Gieske, Sam Sutherland, Monica Wooton, 1999-2000.

Fishermen work the nets. Photo by Sam Sutherland, 1999.

WHAT'S BEING CAUGHT IN PUGET SOUND AND
THE NORTHWEST

*Fishermen from the Terminal catch two types of finned fish in the salt
waters of Puget Sound, and in the Pacific Ocean off the shores of
Washington, Oregon and Alaska. The Demersal live near the bottom or
at mid-depth, and include: cod, lingcod, sablefish, and flat fish such as
sole, rockfish and halibut.*

*The Pelagic live in open seas near the surface, travel in schools, and
usually migrate on a seasonal basis. These fish include: salmon, tuna,
hake, pollock, mackerel, sardine and herring.*

*Salmon are identified as anadromous, meaning they spawn in fresh
water and migrate to the ocean and at maturity return to their home
stream to spawn.*

Crab and shrimp are caught with pots and nets.

*The term "fisheries" identifies the region or area where fish are
pursued, and are classified by being salt water or fresh water, where they
are located, and the type of fish sought. Fisheries also refers to the method
used to catch the fish: trawling, trolling, seining, longlining and the
type gear employed.*

salmon fishing permits in 1974. Other types of fishing require different permits, such as a drift permit in Bristol Bay, Alaska, that could exceed $100,000. Black cod fishing is regulated by federal agency. However, in Alaska, two regions require permits: in Chatham Straits a permit might cost $250,000, and in Clarence Straits, the permit costs approximately $150,000. [28] [29]

From conversations with fishing boat owners, I learned that it's not difficult to lose money in the fishing industry, particularly if one's boat stays tied up to the dock for reasons like no fishing season, and thus no income, as was the case in 1999. There are regular bills to be paid. Insurance is expensive. Liability premiums, costing $1,500 and more, mostly more, are a must for the boat owner. Operating in rough and tumble waters abounds with the possibilities for mishaps and injuries, even death.

A moored boat, inactive and not fishing, still needs maintenance including hull, electronics, engine and hydraulic systems. Nets and gear require care. Other expenditures include moorage and net locker fees. These can exceed $3,600 a month depending upon boat size and equipment carried. Unforeseen expenses come up for incidentals such as rats eating nets, corrosion attacking metal boat parts and gear, and dry rot making mush of wooden structures.

Fishermen and farmers seem to have a lot in common. Both experience and are affected by conditions of nature, the actions of others, and a market that is beyond their control. Many fishermen have expressed concern with the future, and some predict the local commercial fishing industry of small boats will not survive another 20 years. This is evidenced by the many fishing boats that carry "For Sale" signs.

Despite the Terminal's growth during the twentieth century, the economic outlook for Northwest salmon fishermen in Puget Sound is bleak as the twenty-first century begins.

The Present-Day Terminal

By early 2000, the Terminal's 76 acres were valued at about $28-million, and the facility could offer about 400 berths for the fishing fleet and accommodate boats from 30 to 350 feet in length. Loading dock moorage is also available. The 253 net-sheds offer 106,427 square feet of net locker storage, and 82,000 square-feet of fenced storage is provided. [30]

The Terminal hosts substantial numbers of boats. However, many post "For Sale" signs in their pilothouse windows, and others indicate little to no maintenance, demonstrating the economic difficulties of many of the fishermen. After 87 years at Magnolia's north side, Fishermen's Terminal remains the center of the Puget Sound's fishing industry. However, it is wounded, perhaps critically.

Changes In the Industry

The fishing industry and its support services have undergone significant change in the past century, and the Port of Seattle facility at Salmon Bay seen by today's visitor is drastically different from that of 1913. Many factors affect the fishing industry and the Terminal. Size, arrangement, and services reflect the most change. Fishing boats differ in design, construction and size. The Terminal's boats and their crews require a variety of support services from businesses. Hulls need work, as do the engines and the fishing gear. Electronics require maintenance. Safety requires training and special equipment. A variety of supplies, fuel and food are consumed.

Additionally, many levels of governmental regulatory agencies mold the fishing business of today. They are integral to the planning and operations of the fleet and the Terminal.

Conservation and management of living marine resources in the United States is to be carried out by the NOAA's NMFS. The NMFS's responsibilities originate from legislation passed by the US Congress, and from treaties. Five statutes establish NMFS responsibilities: The Magnuson-Stevens Fishery Conservation and Management Act, the Endangered Species Act, the Marine Mammal Protection Act, the Fish and Wildlife Coordination Act, and the Federal Power Act.[31]

The NMFS regulates fisheries in the three to 200 nautical-mile Federal Exclusive Economic Zone seaward of the 48 contiguous states, Alaska, Hawaii, and the US-affiliated islands. Within the 0 to 3 nautical-mile territorial sea, management belongs to the coastal states and the multi-state fisheries commissions. International waters fisheries are regulated by international laws and multilateral agreements between sovereign governments, such as

Seagulls check out the fleet.
Photo by Frank Gieske, 1999.

the International Pacific Halibut Commission established by treaty executed by Canada and the United States. Other regulatory agencies include: the International North Pacific Fisheries Commission, the North Pacific Anadromous Fish Commission, the Pacific Fisheries Management Council, the US-Canada Pacific Salmon Commission. Other agencies include the Washington Department of Fish and Wildlife, the Alaska Department of Fish and Game, and the Oregon Department of Fish and Wildlife.[32]

Net work by fishermen ready getting gear to go. Photo by Sam Sutherland, 1999.

Challenges to the Industry

Fishermen at the Terminal face a future of great uncertainty due to sharp declines in marine stocks. Causes cited include overfishing, and high levels of bycatch which is indiscriminate catching of fish of the wrong species, sex, size, and quality. Bycatch is estimated to be some 18 to 40 million tons on a worldwide basis.[33][34]

Other major factors in this decline include pollution, loss of habitat by stream destruction by logging and commercial development, placement of dams, and chemical dumping. Climatic effects such as El Niño/La Niña, the Pacific decadal oscillation, and global warming have also had a heavy impact according to sources at the NOAA, the Halibut Commission and the University of Washington School of Fisheries. El Niño conditions are good for Alaskan salmon but bad for Washington salmon. La Niña reverses this. As a result, of these declines, cuts in allowable catches of salmon, sockeye, chinook, coho, halibut, species of Pacific cod and other ground fish, and shell fish like the Tanner and King crab (these catches have fallen 94% since 1980) have occurred.[34]

Depletion of the salmon has caused the Federal and State government agencies to take action. In May 1974, Washington State initiated a license moratorium, and began a program of limited entry licenses including charter boat operators. Active, commercial fishermen, to qualify for a 1974 license on a renewal basis, must have landed fish in 1973 and documented the catch. The new law and rules did allow individuals to purchase and transfer a license from another qualified individual.[35]

Another major impact on commercial fishing came from the decision of US District Judge George H. Boldt in 1974. He ruled that treaty Indians have rights to 50% of the harvestable salmon. The impact of this decision viewed from the commercial fishermen standpoint: catastrophic. Boldt mandated reductions in the allowable catches by non-Indian fishermen. This came at a time when salmon stocks were experiencing sharp declines and catch limits had been greatly reduced. Severe economic impact resulted.[36]

To reduce the number of persons/boats engaged in commercial salmon fishing and to provide financial assistance to impacted fishermen including those at Fishermen's Terminal, Washington State began a federally-funded "license buyback" program (Revised Code of Washington, RCW 75.28.510) intended to remove one-third of the licenses during a five-year period. A "boat buyback program" (Washington Administrative Code, WAC 220-95) was introduced. Experience proved the license limitations/buyback more cost effective in reaching the reduction objectives. In 1975, the State issued 6,261 salmon licenses. In 1981 that number had fallen to 5,648.[37]

In 1981, a new program was funded by a grant from the NOAA, NMFS. Each year for four years, the Washington Department of Fish and Wildlife received $2.5 million for commercial and charter salmon license buybacks and 10-year vessel use restrictions. Total salmon licenses reduced from 5,648 in 1981 to 4,562 in 1984. By 1987, the number of salmon licenses fell to 3,857.[38]

Under the sponsorship of the NMFS the Northwest Emergency Assistance Plan, formed by Canada and the United States, continued the license buy back program. In May 1994, the Secretary of Commerce declared a fishery disaster and provided emergency economic aid for Washington, Oregon, and northern California. In 1995 and 1996 the total number of licenses purchased was 438. The 1995-1996 programs affected only coastal salmon fishers. Continuation of the program in 1998 included both coastal and Puget Sound salmon licenses and reduced them from 2,111 to 1,720.[39]

In 1999, the United States and Canada agreed to modifications of the Pacific Salmon Treaty annexes that included coast-wide conservation actions for Chinook and Coho salmon. The agreement also reduced the allocation of Fraser River salmon to the US non-Indian fishermen. The US Government agreed to provide up to $30 million to buy back the licenses of fishers affected by this amended treaty. Congress appropriated $4.625 million for fiscal year 2000. The Washington Legislature appropriated $2.34-million. The moneys appropriated for use in the 2000-2001 were designated predominantly for Puget Sound.[40]

1998 Catch Results

The Washington State 1998 Salmon season bordered on dismal. Climate conditions, habitat loss, and environmental factors impacted the catch.

Washington Salmon Landings - 1998
Source: Washington Dept. of Fish and Wildlife

Gear Type	Chinook	Coho	Sockeye	Pink
Troll	7,275	0	0	0
Gillnet	20,334	24,984	96,812	9
Seine	296	2,130	123,323	343
Tribal	95,074	186,367	312,281	515
Other	2	545	9,178	0
Total	122,981	214,026	542,594	867

In 1974, Judge G. H. Boldt rendered a decision on Native American fishing rights under the existing treaties. After appeals, on January 26, 1976, the US Supreme Court upheld Boldt's decision. The treaty drawn up in the nineteenth century granted Native Americans the right to fish "in common with" other citizens entitling them to 50% of the harvestable salmon and steelhead from Traditional Fishing Waters.

1998 season results:

Percent of the Catch by Fishing Group

	Chinook	Coho	Sockeye	Pink
Commercial %	22.3	12.7	40.6	40.6
Tribal %	77.3	87.1	57.7	59.4
Other %	0.0001	0.0025	0.0169	0.0

The commercial fishing results in 1999 were varied. Salmon fishing in Alaskan waters proved to be bountiful while sockeye fishing in Puget Sound didn't occur. A brief, one-day chum fishing season in Puget Sound for commercial boats yielded minimal results. In contrast to the salmon harvest, crab fishing in Alaska collapsed.
(Source: Washington State Department of Fish and Wildlife)

The license buyback program is scheduled to continue to 2002. The Federal portion of the money ($4.625-million) is designated for purchase of Puget Sound licenses affected by the Pacific Salmon Treaty negotiations with Canada. This Treaty, negotiated in 1930, provided for equal sharing of the Fraser River salmon harvest between the two countries. After the Boldt decision in 1974 on Indian fishing rights, the treaty agreement established the US non-tribal share as 32.3%. In 1985, the treaty terms established the US non-tribal

Typical halibut gear ready for fishing. Photo by Sam Sutherland, 1999.

share of the Fraser River sockeye harvest at 26%. Under revised treaty terms, the US non-tribal share will be 16.5% by 2002.[41]

In 1999, the Federal Government declared nine salmon subspecies in Washington and Oregon as threatened and in need of protective actions under the Endangered Species Act. California and Idaho received similar declarations. Public hearings are underway, and actions under consideration include: limiting development near streams, government acquisition of land abutting streams to prevent development, and strict control of runoff from streets and parking lots.[42]

In early 2000, the Washington's 12-member Forest Practices Board agreed to new logging rules to impose 50-years of tough restrictions on timber harvests near streams and on steep slopes. As compensation the loggers and landowners will receive timber excise tax-credits and compensation for lost timber. The rules are expected to be in temporary effect until June 2001 to permit statewide hearings to assess the environmental and economic impact.[43]

Salmon weren't the only fishery to receive drastic restrictions. Based upon scientists' beliefs that these fish populations have been greatly depleted as the result of natural and man-made factors such as overfishing, the federal government took action. In January 2000, limits were placed on the catches of ground fish taken off the Washington and Oregon coasts. The bottom fish species affected are lingcod, rockfish and bocaccio. Catches were reduced 30% to 50%.[44]

Overfishing in the late 1800s and the early 1900s led to the depletion of the Pacific Halibut also. In 1923, Canada and the United States signed a convention to manage the halibut fisheries. Actual management by the Halibut Commission began in 1924 with a three-month winter closure. Control proved difficult and resulted in shorter and shorter seasons. In 1953, a convention was signed establishing separate seasons by area. Industry established eight-day lay-up periods. Ever increasing fleet size created additional problems. Short multiple seasons for individual areas didn't prove to be the solution.[45, 46]

Legislation by both governments in 1977 extended each country's fishery jurisdiction to 200 miles from shore. In 1979, a protocol to the convention ended US fishing in Canadian waters and vice versa. By 1987, the Halibut Commission used fishing period limits for the first time restricting the maximum pounds landed per vessel during a fishing period. The 1994 halibut season was as short as 24 hours in the Gulf of Alaska, 12 hours in parts of the Bering Sea, and 10 hours on the US West Coast. In 1995, the US Government implemented an individual quota system for catches and seasons in Alaska. The season in 1999 was established from March 15 to November 15.[47]

Because overfishing in the first half of the twentieth century destroyed the fish population, there is no commercial halibut fishing in Puget Sound today, according to the Halibut Commission. However, fishermen at the Terminal fish for halibut in waters off the Washington coast and Alaska. The boats that are used for commercial halibut fishing are called longliners. Many reside in Fishermen's Terminal and they fish in Alaskan waters.

According to the US Department of Commerce, some fish species depleted by overfishing cannot be rebuilt in 10 years under average environmental conditions even under a complete moratorium on fishing for that stock.[48]

Another problem encountered in the fishing industry is fish populations vary from region to region and from year to year. Commercial fishing productivity operates on a cyclic basis, experiencing yields that reflect the high or low conditions of the stock. A good illustration is what happened in 1999. The NMFS closed the sockeye salmon fishing in Puget Sound to preserve the returning population. Estimates placed the expected fish count at 7 to 8-million. The actual number proved to be slightly more than 3 million, and the NMFS closed the season. In contrast, the Alaska salmon catch in the fall of 1999, placed at 25.6-million sockeye, exceeded the capability of the packers. Apparently they ran out of cans.

Alaska now has a "limited entry" permit program for crab, King and Opilio, based upon past participation in this fishery during the period 1988 to 1995. Quotas or limits are imposed by state and federal government regulatory agencies.[49]

In Puget Sound, licenses must be renewed yearly. A license for purse seiners and gill-netters to fish for sockeye in Puget Sound is $630. Limited entry permits exist for Puget Sound crabbing and the market price was placed at $15,000 in the fourth quarter of 1999. Halibut fishing isn't licensed in Puget Sound, however in Alaska, the Halibut Commission establishes quotas.

AND, DESPITE IT ALL . . .

Today's commercial fisherman engage in one of the most dangerous occupations. They face challenges and uncertainties often beyond their control. Their trade demands of these individuals courage, skill, tenacity and hope tempered with a sense of humor. Often their catches come at great risk to the crews and boats, and to the families of those men and women that pursue this industry.

Sam Sutherland, who lived in Magnolia for 34 years, graduated from the University of New Mexico. He served as an engineering officer in the US Navy in the Pacific Theater during World War II and in the Naval Research Reserve. Sam joined the Boeing Engineering Department in 1948. He retired as a Program Manager in 1985. Sam has served as the president of the Magnolia Ecumenical Housing Council, as a member of the Board of Trustees for the Pacific Northwest Ballet, as chairman of Sculptors Northwest and is a member of the Seattle Photographic Society. Sam and his wife Judy have three children, and celebrated their 54th wedding anniversary in June 2000.

The Fishing Boats

The casual visitor should take a walk along the docks and see firsthand the variety of fishing boats that belong to the Terminal's fishing fleet. The principal types are: trollers, gillnetters, seiners, longliners, crabbers and trawlers.

These boats have interesting names not necessarily reflective of their use. To name a few from the fleet: *Dream Girl, Tradewinds, Constellation, Chaparrita, Lady Grace, China B, Tender Retriever, McKinley, Antarctic, Alaskan Beauty, Blue North, Paragon, Last Word, Rover, Miss Mary, Tamarra, Josephine, Fierce Packer, Centaraus, Stanley, Trinket, Black Beauty and St. Nicholas*—named such by its previous owner before being purchased by the present owner's father. Noticeably absent are names of Hollywood stars and politicians.

Many types of fishing vessels are to be found at Fishermen's Terminal, and each type of boat uses a different approach to making a "catch."

TROLLERS require the fishermen to use poles hung at 45-degree angles from their boats to "troll" stainless steel lines and attached lures to catch salmon. The lures are rubber, plastic, or chrome-plated lead and serve as "sinker" to weigh down and sink the line. A "troller" is generally a small boat from 20 to 50 feet in length.

GILLNETTERS use a woven net to catch salmon and herring. The net is draped in the water and fish swim into the mesh structure and become trapped in the small openings. The nets generally drift with the boat, or they may be anchored at or near the bottom. Gillnetters found at the Terminal vary in length, from 25 to 40 feet.

SEINERS, the name derived from the type of net used, deploy a webbed net from massive reels located at their sterns. In deployment, the end of the net is held in position by a skiff (a small, open, powered boat) while the seiner plays out the net from the reel as it moves away from the skiff. The net's top is buoyed by a continuous row of white-plastic floats, or cork floats. The bottom of the "seine" includes a large line that incorporates lead weights and keeps the seine vertical. This heavy line, when taken in, closes the bottom of the net and prevents fish from escaping by diving down. When closed, the net resembles an old-fashioned cloth purse, hence, the name "purse seiner." A typical seine can be 130 to 140 feet deep and 1,800 feet long.

After 30 minutes to an hour, the boat maneuvers back toward the skiff and brings the net's ends together in a circle. This surrounds and traps the fish. About 45 to 60 minutes are required to close the seine and reel in the "bunt" (the purse, a pocket formed at the end of the net). Depending upon the run, the catch may weigh from a few thousand to 25,000 pounds. However, with today's salmon runs, the latter is not likely.

Current regulations require the fishermen to use a brailer, a conical shaped net with a 36 to 38-inch opening, to scoop out and separate the fish trapped in the "purse." A loaded brailer may contain 200 fish. Fishermen remove and return all King, Silver, and Chum to the water. Sockeye and Pinks are kept and stored on the boat. A typical seiner crew may have four members aboard the boat which can range in size from 50 to 75 feet.

LONGLINERS use baited hooks attached to long lines to catch halibut, Black cod, and Ling cod. A "skate" is the term applied to a line and hook combination used by the fishermen. A skate may be 600-feet in length and hooks placed every 40 inches for taking Black cod. Hook placement for halibut is every 9-feet. To deploy a skate, a flag and "bag" (buoy) are attached to an anchor and one end of the skate. The length of line between the flag and the anchor equals the water depth in fathoms plus 25%. At the other end of the skate an anchor, bag, and flag are used. Depending upon the fishing conditions several skates may be attached end to end. The skates with the baited hooks remain in the water for about eight hours, or longer, before retrieval.

Hydraulic-operated winches pull the lines into the boat. Fish and bait are removed as the line is reeled in and coiled. Longliners may employ a four-man crew and vary in length from 50 to 80 feet.

CRABBERS (POTTERS) use specially constructed traps to capture crabs called pots. The trap, essentially a steel-frame covered with mesh, has at one or both ends of the box-like structure openings shaped like funnels. These admit and trap crabs attracted by bait, usually chopped herring placed in bait boxes suspended within the "pot." The boxes are plastic containers, pierced with many holes. They are hung from the upper surface of the trap by a metal clip and line two bait boxes per pot. Pieces of cod may also be placed in the trap. Herring, frozen in 40-pound blocks, are chopped by a powered-machine into small pieces for placement in the boxes.

Ball-shaped buoys, usually orange in color, attached by line to the traps mark locations. A small trap is about 60 inches in length, 30 inches in width, and 24 inches in depth. A few small boats employ circular-shaped, 7 feet by 7 feet by 3.5 feet traps that weigh up to 700-pounds.

Crab fishing in Alaska waters has two seasons: the Opilio crab in mid-January and the King crab in mid-October. The smaller crabs are fished for in water depths from 70 to 90 fathoms and King crab in depths of about 25 fathoms. "Crabbers" may carry up to an eight-man crew, and range in length from 75 to 120 feet.

TRAWLERS employ bag-shaped nets called "trawls" that are dragged behind the boat in mid-water or on the bottom. Trawls are used to catch cod, pollock, rockfish and sole. Raising the trawl to the surface traps the fish. Shrimp are also harvested by this method. Most trawls are launched and recovered from the boat's stern. Some small boats lift the trawls aboard with hoists while larger boats winch them over a ramp onto the boat's deck. Trawlers range in size from 50 to 300 feet.

Photos by Sam
Sutherland, 1999/2000.

Beaches, Berries and Baseball

By Patricia Collins Small

In the years before World War II, to be a girl growing up on Magnolia Bluff was to feel safe and secure despite the Depression and gathering war clouds. At least, that is the picture painted by the women who spent their early years in the Magnolia neighborhood. As they reflect now on those years, memories emerge of a time when girls felt safe and satisfied regardless of the economic status of their family. Dads were breadwinners and moms or grandmothers were home all day. Neighbors were close friends who would help if necessary. Magnolia was a close-knit community.

Girls played softball in dresses in the dusty streets and vacant lots with neighborhood friends, regardless of age or gender. They dug tunnels in the dirt of vacant lots and made forts in the woods with their friends and brothers.[1] They picked enormous quantities of blackberries and the more enterprising girls sold them to the neighbors, even though the neighbors probably had a vacant lot next door with its own treasure of berry bushes.

There was plenty to keep Magnolia girls busy. The trip to and from school was an adventure in itself. There were always friends to walk with and talk over the day's happenings. For those living farther away, and many did, the bus driver was a familiar face. Alvara Forbus Deal remembers the regular bus driver whose name was Ruggles. He knew every child's name and who lived where.[2]

Rather than have a special school bus, Magnolia grade school students received free "tokens" enabling them to ride the City bus that circled Magnolia. When it came time to go to Queen Anne High School, early Magnolia students rode that bus to 15th Avenue West, transferred to the downtown streetcar, changed again at First Avenue North and Denny Way to catch the No. 2 West Queen Anne streetcar to ride up the counterbalance, and then walked four more blocks to Queen Anne.[3] The streetcar on 15th Avenue West also took people downtown to shop at the Public Market or out to Ballard.

While Magnolia is considered one community today, there were several distinct neighborhoods within Magnolia in the early days. On northeastern Magnolia was the area near the east entrance to Fort Lawton. These folks had the luxury of early streetcar access. Children near the Fort went to Lawton School and their parents shopped at Corrigan's Grocery on 32nd Avenue West and West Government Way.[4]

Magnolia Purple takes a mid-game breather after an aggressive first half. Photo by Monica Wooton, 2000.

The Interbay School stood near the old, wooden Dravus Street Bridge at 16th Avenue West and West Dravus Street. Interbay School served many east Magnolia families as well as those from Queen Anne Park on the northeast area of Queen Anne Hill.

Families near 34th Avenue West and West Emerson Street shopped at Burleigh Thompson's Red & White Grocery where children could purchase penny candy such as Tootsie Rolls, jawbreakers and all-day suckers. Parents bought meat that the butcher cut to their specifications from huge carcasses hanging on hooks.[5]

Up on the southeast hill of the Bluff stood Magnolia School where portable buildings served as classrooms while the large red brick building was being built. The Magnolia bus gathered children from all along the south side of the Bluff and Carleton Park to transport them to school. The school and the Village stores helped make that area the most densely populated community on Magnolia. The Woolfolks, Sutloviches and some other Magnolia families sent their children to St. Margaret's Grade School in Interbay. This entailed rides from dad on his way to work, or a streetcar plus bus trip each way.[6]

The subdivisions of the Bluff were important to the girls growing up on Magnolia in the 1930s because, while they had plenty of freedom, they were still restricted a little more than their male counterparts. Most of the time, they played with neighborhood kids. It was a marvelous freedom that the children enjoyed in the years before World War II. The fact that girls could walk through the woods to their friends' homes made even ordinary visits special. They could dawdle along, enjoying the sights, smells and sounds of the changing seasons. School memories were happy ones as most girls were good students. Caroline Heiser, who was Gerry Heiser Cannon's mother, helped get the kindergarten started at Magnolia School. Because there were not enough eligible children, she recruited some nearby four-year-olds to fill the number requirement.[7]

The students at Magnolia School lined the wide halls at Christmas time to sing Christmas carols. Mary McGovern recalls May Day events on the lush green lawn of the lower level playground at Magnolia School. Girls dressed in gauzy dresses danced around the Maypole. There were spelling bees and talent shows where Mary Anne McLeod performed her Scottish dance.[8]

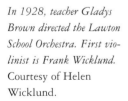

In 1928, teacher Gladys Brown directed the Lawton School Orchestra. First violinist is Frank Wicklund. Courtesy of Helen Wicklund.

Many of the girls' educations included music, and harmonicas were often the instrument of choice. They were inexpensive and easy to learn. Interbay School fostered talent by developing a school harmonica band. Mrs. Atherton taught Magnolia School girls how to play the instrument and they performed for their schoolmates in assemblies.[9]

Lawton School, where several students began a lifelong interest in orchestral instruments, offered free music lessons. Audrey Clarke Carlson learned to play the trumpet and, along with 15 other Lawton students, rode the streetcar up to Summit School to perform with the All-City Grade School Band. Audrey played French horn in the All-City High School Band with several Lawton friends and three of that group, including Audrey, continued to play in the University of Washington band.[10]

Pianos were prominent features in many living rooms at a time when families made their own music and piano teachers lived all around Magnolia. Pupils experienced the agony and ecstasy of public performance as they gave recitals in their teachers' living rooms. Universally, piano practice was regarded with distaste, even by Iris Fribrock Ewing, who later enjoyed a career as an opera singer in Europe and New York. While piano teachers were plentiful, the girls who wanted to be dancers had to travel across town by streetcar to the Cornish School or the Mary Ann Wells School of Dance.[11]

Mary and Louise Sutlovich play cowgirls in 1938. Courtesy of Mary Bishop.

Lawton School was progressive in another area, that of teaching the children about banking. Fathers made "tellers cages" and the students from the 7th and 8th grades were the "tellers," accepting money from each child and posting it in the child's bankbook. Washington Mutual Savings Bank served as the sponsoring institution.[12]

During the school year, the classroom day and the travel involved in getting there took up a good share of the day. But most girls found time to roller skate, ride their bikes or play baseball for an hour before it was time to go home and set the table or help prepare dinner. Mary Sutlovich Bishop was proud when she was allowed to light the coal and wood range when she was eight. She was able to fix simple dinners for the family at age nine. A few homes had grandmothers who lived with the family and were terrific cooks. Although the moms did most of the cooking, many girls learned how to bake cookies and make meatloaf, even if they dreamed of careers in the years ahead.

At least two Magnolia mothers were career women at the time. One was Lady Willie Forbus, the first woman lawyer to practice in the State and a prominent member of the Washington State Legislature.[13] When Gerry Heiser Cannon's father died at a young age, her mother took over running the family business. Her success is evident in the continued existence of the Heiser Body Company.[14]

Shirley Young Allen helped with chores on her family's subsistence farm at 44th Avenue West and West Dravus Street after moving there in 1929. Besides watering the two-acre garden, Shirley helped care for the animals including: rabbits, chickens, three calves, two pheasants and a milk cow named Katie. Shirley considered herself lucky because her brother, Donald, had to deliver Katie's milk to several customers on his bicycle before going off to school. Customers included Dr. Walrath, the dentist, the Rommes who lived by the water tower and the Fords who lived on Magnolia Boulevard.[15]

Weekends provided for more time-consuming activities/trips down to the Wolfe Creek beach below Magnolia Park to play follow the leader on the logs or to just enjoy digging

Mary Pat and Jayne Woolfolk in front of a playhouse Daddy built on the vacant lot next door in 1937. Courtesy of Mary Pat Axley.

in the sand. Of course, when the weather became warmer, there was lots of swimming. Occasionally, the girls took the City transit to Green Lake where they could rent bicycles and circle the lake on a narrow footpath.[16]

Rainy-day activities in the house were numerous before TV and computer games came into being. Girls played with their dolls, made their clothes and made paper dolls from magazine pictures. Vernice Monsey Brown experimented with making her own dolls. Anticipating the Barbie doll of later years, she tried to make dolls with a figure.[17] Monopoly games sometimes carried on for days with the board left standing on a card table in the corner. Old Maid, rummy, pick-up sticks, and Parcheesi were popular indoor games.

Out of doors, bikes and baseball were the old standbys. But when a number of neighbor children got together, it was fun to play kick-the-can, hopscotch, hide-and-seek and whatever games

Charland Family sculpted an ice statue of Uncle Sam and an American Eagle after a big snowfall in 1916. Photo courtesy of Shirley Allen.

their young imaginations created in the woods and fields. Girls rode "girl's" bikes that had a lower center bar allowing their skirts to hang modestly down. Baseball was usually softball, played with a wooden bat and a rubber-covered ball.

Children went to the movies for 10 cents at Fort Lawton or at the Uptown at the bottom of Queen Anne Hill.[18] Some on the north side of Magnolia walked across the Ballard Locks to watch cliff-hanging matinees on Saturdays at the Roxy Theatre that was later named the Bay Theatre, and was subsequently rebuilt in 2000.

Winters in the early part of the twentieth century seemed to have brought more snow than Seattle has seen in the latter part of the century. When it fell on Magnolia the children had wonderful fields and steep hills to sled on before the advent of automobiles and dangerous traffic. A few owned skis, but most families had sleds that were much the same as children's sleds today. Store-bought sleds had metal runners, but many families made their own from wood and boxes. After a heavy snowfall in 1916, the Charland family sculpted a lifelike statue of Uncle Sam and an American eagle that drew visitors from all over Magnolia.[19]

When summer arrived, the beaches of Magnolia came alive, and the children were able to fully enjoy the interesting, almost rural, advantages of the Bluff. Bike rides became all-day treks with baloney or peanut-butter-and-jelly sandwich lunches packed by moms. Mary Pat Woolfolk Axley and her sister, Jayne, preferred 2-cent, raw hot dogs that they purchased at the store. Unlike the plastic-wrapped wieners of today, the local butchers then carried hot dogs that were long strings of sausages. These were cut apart in whatever number the customer requested.

Mary Sutlovich, with her mother, Bertha Sutlovich, poses in 1933 in front of The Lemis II, the fishing boat her Dad fished from in Alaska for six months every year. The Ballard Bridge is in the background. Courtesy of Mary Bishop.

One sunny, summer day, Mary and Louise Sutlovich walked far down the beach from Wolfe Creek to take advantage of a tidal pool full of warm water. Blissfully unconscious of the time, they became trapped by the rapidly rising water and had to scramble over barnacle-covered rocks to get safely back to the park.[20]

As August arrived, the wild blackberries ripened and girls helped their mothers make jam and pies. Other fruits and vegetables were canned for the winter in many homes, and girls often helped by peeling and prepping the ingredients.[21] The produce was washed, packed in glass jars and cooked in large kettles on the stove. A rack inside the kettle kept the jars off the bottom of the pot and prevented them from hitting each other in the rapidly boiling water. More progressive women processed their foods in pressure cookers, which occasionally misbehaved, causing food to be blown all over the kitchen. When pressure-cooked, the food was then packed in sterile jars.

But it was living so near the beach that was the greatest joy for many Magnolia girls. The beach at Wolfe Creek, with its long pier and rowboats, attracted everyone on the south part of Magnolia. Other children would sit on the warm sand just east of present-day Commodore Park and wait for the Locks to release warm lake water for swimming.

Shirley Allen Young's father had a unique refrigeration system devised for when they picnicked on the West Point Beach. After everything else was consumed, he would dig in the sand to surprise the family with ice cream, kept cold in a deep hole he had made earlier.

Mary Pat and Jayne Woolfolk play with girl-friends in front of the vacant lot next door in 1937. Courtesy of Mary Pat Axley.

The Horn children lived on Fort Street and they would walk with their cousins down to visit the lockkeeper in the glass tower. One day, while playing on top of the Locks, four-year-old Helen fell into the water. Their friend the lockkeeper averted tragedy by climbing down onto the pilings to rescue her.[22]

Book lovers read Nancy Drew mysteries and participated in the summer reading programs at the Queen Anne Library before the first Magnolia Library opened on 34th Avenue West and West McGraw Street.[23]

Mary Louise Mitchell models an ermine cape made by her Swedish uncle, Al Raymond, from animals he shot while mining gold in Alaska. Courtesy of Mary Louise Pennington.

Audrey Clarke Carlson liked to help her father in his beautiful garden on 34th Avenue West and West Emerson Street, and later went about selling vegetables to the neighbors.[24] Many households purchased their produce from "the vegetable man" who brought his truck full of fresh fruits and vegetables every week. The "iceman" also came round in the summer to deliver 50-pound cakes of ice that kept the neighborhood iceboxes cold and the milk and butter fresh.[25]

The annual Magnolia Community Club picnic in Magnolia Park was eagerly anticipated and fondly remembered by the families of the area. Games, races, friends and food filled the day. The close-knit community carefully planned the summer picnic, and families joined forces to make it the social event of the year.[26]

Girls rolled in the fall leaves at Magnolia Park and slid in boxes down the big bank above Clise Place West.[27] One young girl enjoyed dreamily watching the dappled waters of Puget Sound as the ferries and ships slipped silently past. Mary Sutlovich Bishop and her sister Louise Sutlovich Major visited the cow that was tethered on 23rd Avenue West and West Raye Street as they walked to the beach.[28] Mary Louise Mitchell Pennington enjoyed the frog pond on the dairy farm in Pleasant Valley.[29] One time, Mary Louise and her girlfriends rowed out to a US Navy ship, bringing apples and oranges to the sailors. When their parents heard about the girls' adventure, such supply trips were cut short.[30]

In 1941, when Pearl Harbor awakened America to peril, the climate in Magnolia changed. Fort Lawton, which had been a friendly neighbor to the nearby residents, became off limits to all but members of the armed services and their families. Wartime measures went into effect and several families remember having "blackout curtains" that were required by the City.[31] These were shutters or heavy draperies that covered windows after sunset so there was no glare in the sky to mark Seattle as a possible target for enemy bombs. Gone was West Point Beach for swimming and picnicking, the Sunday band concerts on the parade ground, and the smooth Fort roads for bike riding and roller-skating. No doubt the Heiser family still heard afternoon Tattoo and evening Taps played over Fort Lawton loud-speakers.[32] But the children were changed too, grown beyond the age where they listened carefully for the bugle calls to know when it was time to come home from playing on the beach.

The sudden presence of thousands of soldiers at Fort Lawton and aboard the City buses struck a note of fear in the hearts of the young women who had grown up in the bucolic atmosphere of Magnolia.[33] Cautious mothers warned their daughters to be careful with whom they spoke when riding buses and walking to neighborhood stores. It was many years before Fort Lawton became Discovery Park and returned to being a tranquil place for people to enjoy the spectacular views and peaceful quiet in the meadows and forests of Fort Lawton.

Sixty or more years later, these girls who grew up on Magnolia Bluff bring their grand-children to play in the parks that have replaced the more rustic areas of their youth. While the grandmothers enjoy watching their young descendants climb on bars, slide down imaginative slides and swing on age-sized swings, in their hearts they remember the "good old days" and treasure the privileges of yesteryear.

The "Girls" who grew up on Magnolia

Shirley Young Allen continued the family music tradition, playing accordion and piano and singing. After marrying Clyde, the couple moved to Texas for six months in 1947. They returned to Seattle to raise their son and daughter in the Young family house on 44th Avenue West. She remembers, as a child, watching her father carry timbers from the road a block away in order to build the house where there were no streets or sidewalks.

Mary Pat Woolfolk (Thorson) Axley was widowed when her son and daughter were very small. This woman, the little girl who loved to play school, became a teacher at Our Lady of Fatima School and West Queen Anne Grade School. Later, she married Don Axley. They still live on Magnolia and enjoy watching their grandchildren attend Our Lady of Fatima School where Mary Pat taught for many years.

Mary Sutlovich Bishop married Homer Bishop and they have two children, Laurie and Mark, who attended Fatima School. Mary had a long career as executive director of the Northwest Apparel Association and is now retired, still living on Magnolia Bluff.

Vernice Monsey Brown developed her childhood love of sewing and craft work to design costumes and provide fashionable hats for her three daughters and three sons. She and her husband, Gavin, live on Magnolia, a few blocks from her childhood home.

Audrey Clark Carlson married Theo Carlson from Queen Anne Hill and they moved to Salt Lake City, Utah. During World War II Audrey worked for the US Army in Los Angeles. Following the war, the couple returned to Seattle where their son and daughter

Below: Alfred and Josephine Charland and their daughter Olive Young, mother and grand-parents of Shirley Young Allen, performed live music at early Magnolia Community Club Saturday night dances. Courtesy of Shirley Allen.

Bottom: Mary Pat and Jayne Woolfolk on a swing Daddy built on the vacant lot next door in 1937. Courtesy of Mary Pat Axley.

Alvara and Dale Forbus pose on skis in 1933. Courtesy of Alvara Forbus Deal.

Right: Mary Lou Mitchell and Naides McCormick pose with friends Herby Vitt and Weldon Andrews in 1937. Courtesy of Mary Louise Pennington.

graduated from Queen Anne High School and the University of Washington. Having grown up in a house her father built at 34th Avenue West and West Emerson Street, Audrey now lives on 31st Avenue West just three houses from West Emerson.

Gerry Cannon Heiser lives next door to the home she grew up in, still enjoying the proximity to the beach and the 300-degree view of Puget Sound. She and her husband, Boyce, raised their two daughters on Viewmont Way West and moved back to the family neighborhood in 1982.

Alvara Forbus Deal lived abroad for 40 years as her petroleum geologist husband, Clyde, explored for oil. Two of their three children were born in Brazil. Alvara broadened her early music and dance interests by attending opera and dance in the many places they lived: Venezuela, Brazil, Uruguay, Argentina, Chicago, Connecticut, Texas and Pakistan. Retired now, the couple has been living on Magnolia Bluff for 13 years.

Mary McGovern Denney lived in Aurora, Illinois, with her husband Robert and their two sons and two daughters. In 1978, she returned to Seattle and began a career with Holland America Cruise Lines, setting up shore greeting programs all over the world. After living in Fairbanks, Alaska, for four years, she returned to Seattle and currently lives on Condon Way West.

Iris Fribrock Ewing sang at the Met as Northwest regional winner of the Metropolitan Opera Auditions. Her singing career took her to Europe and New York City as well as to the Seattle Symphony. Iris retired to raise their two sons and two daughters as she and Walter were transferred from Seattle to Pittsburgh, Pennsylvania; Menlo Park, California, and Bernardsville, New Jersey. Returning to the Northwest, Iris and Walter enjoyed retirement on Camano Island and in their condo on Queen Anne Hill. Walter died in 1999.

Connie Collins Gilkerson was an important figure in the development of the Magnolia Village as the owner and operator of the Small Fry Shop and Kathleen's Gifts for 20 years. Retired now, she and her husband Ray enjoy watching the continuous boat traffic from their condo overlooking the Locks.

The Horn family members in their 1917 Ford in front of their new home. Helen's father worked all day, then built this home at night and on weekends. Courtesy of Helen Wicklund.

Mary Louise Mitchell Pennington lived in New York, Rio de Janeiro and London before returning to the home her family had lived in since 1940 on Magnolia Bluff. She worked for the National Bank of Commerce before it became Rainier Bank, and raised her two daughters in Magnolia.

Helen Horn Wicklund married Frank Wicklund, who was the boy down the block when she was growing up on West Gay Street. Frank and Helen had three daughters and one son who also grew up on Magnolia.

Patricia Collins Small feels an affinity for girls growing up on Magnolia Bluff in the 1930s and 1940s as she was doing the same thing on nearby Queen Anne Hill during that era. Magnolia was "way out in the country." Patty married Al Small before graduating from Seattle University. Their first house was one that they moved across Pleasant Valley from the area where Catherine Blaine School was to be built. They raised five daughters and three sons, which left little time for any activities beyond untold Mothers' Club meetings and carpools to youth activities. They acquired a summer cabin on Miller Bay where Patty gloried in the freedom for her children and herself while husband Al commuted to teaching summer school in Seattle. Since retiring from child rearing, Patty has enjoyed lots of travel, especially to Ireland, the birthplace of all of her grandparents. A real dilettante, she has taken classes in writing, studied genealogy, learned the rudiments of playing the Irish harp, and participates in many lay activities at her parish in Magnolia, Our Lady of Fatima.

New Feminism: The Forbus Family

PERSONALITY OF THE WEEK—By Joan Pritchard
This article ran in the Queen Anne/Magnolia News *October 2, 1963.*

The Forbus home, a neat grey, two-story building, sits high above Magnolia Boulevard. Its windows give a sweeping view of Puget Sound, and also disclose an imposing stretch of lawn.

"The yard work takes my entire week-end." Lady Willie Forbus complained, "but I wouldn't have it any other way. It keeps me in condition."

This is typical of the determination of this Seattle lawyer, for she battled many traditions of the South in securing an education.

"Most Southern women who received a degree were expected to become teachers," she said. "I was always interested in law and civil rights, so I guess that's the answer to why I became a lawyer." It also shows her strength of will.

Lady Willie Forbus was born in Zeiglerville, Mississippi in 1892. A town with a present day population of 50, Zeiglerville is geographically located in Yazoo County between the Yazoo and Big Black Rivers. Here, in the heart of the cotton country, Lady Willie and her two sisters and three brothers were born. (The name Lady was used by all young ladies who were named for their fathers—Mrs. Forbus' father was named William. Hence, Willie Forbus with Lady in front.)

In 1900, the family moved to the Delta where her father became a plantation manager. "Father had the supervision of 90 families, but it was Mother who was responsible for any success we children had." The teaching staff of the Delta schools consisted of one woman. As soon as the students had absorbed everything she could teach them, they were expected to go to work.

"When we reached fourteen, Mother kicked us out of the nest. She bought a two room house in Laurel—now people would call it a shanty—installed a stove and two beds. She took one of my brothers and me there, enrolled us in school, and as soon as we were settled she returned to the plantation. My brother had the money and I did the cooking."

Mrs. Forbus graduated from high school and spent the next two years working so she might continue her education. Equipped with a three-week course in stenography, she found employment with a judge.

"After I had saved enough money to become a risk potential, the judge loaned me substantial funds to go to college," she said smiling. "As soon as I received my B.A. degree from the University of Mississippi I went back to work and paid off my debt. I even worked as a court reporter.

Lady Willie Forbus begins her law career in the only city that would give her a favorable welcome, Seattle. She became known for her sense of fashion, and a strong liberal activism before that practice was fashionable. Courtesy of Forbus Family. Circa 1950s.

Below left: Lady Willie "stumps it" in Walla-Walla for a candidate she supports. Her now famous hats and unique stylishness drew attention to her as well as her brand of feminism in the 30s and 40s, before the word was ever coined! Courtesy Forbus Family.

Below right: A letter from the Senate floor lets Magnolia Community Club members know that Forbus has more on her mind with state legislation. After two terms, she returned to neighborhood politics and eventually took the reins of the Club as its first woman president. Magnolia Community Club History Committee Archives.

"I then applied for entrance to Harvard Law School, but they informed me that they wouldn't accept me—they didn't take women. I decided I'd show them and I picked the number two law school in the country, the University of Michigan. They accepted me."

"I arrived in Seattle with $10," she reminisced." "I stayed at the YWCA for two days until I found a rooming house I could afford. I paid $1 a day. I found work immediately, for World War I was on. I got a job as a law clerk in the office of Judge Donworth (the father of the present Judge Donworth). I took his son's place while he was overseas, and at the end of the year when he returned, I opened my own office. It was hard—I suffered the struggle of all beginning lawyers—and the $25 a month office rent seemed like an awful lot of money."

Mrs. Forbus met her husband Alvero C. Shoemaker, writer and *Post-Intelligencer* editorialist, when they were both members of the Mountaineers. After a year of courtship they were married in 1924. When she had her first child, a daughter, she saw her Mother for the first time in nine years. "I had both my girls at night," she chuckled, "so it wouldn't interfere with my work. My Mother came out for both events and stayed with me for about 8 months each time. After she left I depended on housekeepers." (Mrs. Forbus, who reared her two girls herself, is now a proud grandmother of several grandchildren.)

Mrs. Forbus had the honor of being the first person from the Magnolia area to serve in the State Senate. She served from 1942 until 1946 and was the Chairman of the Judicial Committee and Chairman of the Cities First Class during this term.

"Politics is frustrating," she mused, "for you must compromise with your principles."

Among her many other achievements is her outstanding work as head of the Board of the Florence Crittenton Home of Seattle. She was president of the Community Club for one year and takes great pride in her work with this organization.

"We had to fight for sewers, extensions of the lighting and water systems, paving and sidewalks," she said. "We even had to watch for violators of the building rules."

The Forbus home was built in 1924, a manufactured model home kit, and was the 20th house in the Carleton Park Addition. Lady Willie Forbus has not only watched the area grow, but is responsible for many of the improvements all Magnolians now enjoy. There is no question that the day this sharp, attractive Magnolian was pushed from the nest was a great day for Seattle.

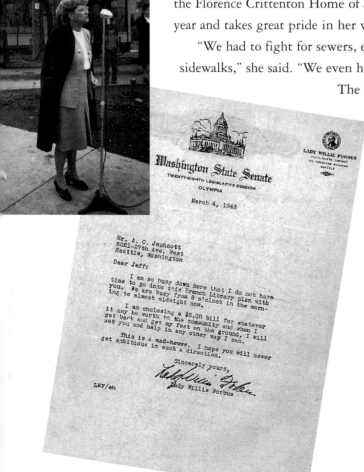

LADY WILLIE FORBUS AND HER DAUGHTERS DEFINE TRADITION DIFFERENTLY—
By Monica Wooton

Author's note: The information for this piece came from original Senate and Magnolia Community Club correspondence belonging to Lady Willie Forbus. She served as the first female president of the Club in 1949-1950, nearly 20 years before another woman was elected to that office, and in many committee capacities before her presidential term. Several conversations with daughters Dale and Alvara regarding their home life provided insight. An article in the Magnolia News *naming Lady Willie "Personality of the Week" for Magnolia, and Anne Ellington's piece for* The Bar Review, *revealed Lady Willie as newsworthy in the business world and for her family life as well.*

"Lady Willie chose law. Her choice was probably dictated by the sharp sense of social justice which has been the fundamental principle of her life. She remembers the commitment of her mother to education, and the extra hardship for girls—all her brothers won college scholarships, while Lady Willie and her sisters had to work, borrow and pay their tuition. Girls didn't get scholarships then in 1910. Girls didn't get into most law schools either . . . she finally got into the University of Michigan (a very good law school) which had one of the few open door policies . . . and remembers law school as nothing 'but starvation and hard work.' . . . Just before graduation the dean told her she would make a good stenographer for some lawyer some day. Her early experience of such attitudes helped to form a life long commitment to civil liberties."—Anne Ellington The Bar Review[1]

Dale Forbus-Shoemaker and her sister Alvara were two of the few girls with a hyphenated last name in the 1920s. Their politically active, liberal mother, Lady Willie Forbus, was ahead of her time.[2]

Determined to pursue the career she had selected in college, law, Lady Willie left behind all family in Mississippi. Seattle became her permanent home, Magnolia was her neighborhood from 1924 until 1993 when she died at 100. Seattle was the City that finally gave Lady Willie a break in the field of law.[3]

Raising two daughters as a single parent after a divorce was also something that was a rarity back then, but Lady Willie Forbus did it. According to Dale, her mother never shirked her duties as a homemaker or mother, despite being the only woman in early Seattle building a law career and political life.

Dale remembers Magnolia Boulevard, where she grew up with her mother and sister, as being full of vacant lots, madrone, dogwood, thimbleberry, and huge maples. Her mother and neighbors adopted Seattle park properties and kept them mowed and neat. Alvara reminds Dale the house they lived in was a pre-packaged design kit. There were only a very few children scattered around with whom to play in the neighborhood.[4]

Dale Forbus-Shoemaker is ready for first day of school. No matter their financial situation, her mother always saw to it they had a few new things to wear, making it a special time of year. Living on the Boulevard in the 20s meant classes at Magnolia School. Courtesy of Forbus Family.

In grade school, Valentine's Day was big to Dale, and she always hoped to get that special valentine. She remembers Halloween as fun too. Her kindergarten teacher, Mrs. Ruby Entz, was round and jolly and always smiling. "I remember she was my very favorite." Dale also mentioned that one thing about grade school she liked was looking forward to the next year, since students knew who their teacher at the next grade would be. The principal knew each child's name and was a happy presence in the halls.

As "a latch-key kid," Dale remembers hurrying home from school to visit a kindly neighbor, Mrs. Knight, who always had a glass of root-beer flavored milk and graham crackers on hand as Dale unwound from the school day. Dale knew that her mother, on a tight budget in the early days of her career, considered graham crackers to be a "treat" food.[5]

When she could, Dale tagged along with her sister, who was three years older. But mostly she remembers her childhood as one of solitary imagination and play. She roller-skated on Mrs. Knight's porch a long concrete affair that was great for such activity. And, she remembers, "If I got an inkling to take my bike apart and scrub down the pieces, I disassembled my bike. We had no board games, and I loved the outdoors more."[6]

Birthdays were favorite days of the year. Her mother would decorate their dining room and keep the party hidden from sight by the French doors. When they were opened, Dale remembers how beautiful and special it all was, with prizes, games, a cake and ice cream. The words "ice cream" are said in an awed, breathless tone even today, revealing its take-your-breath-away specialness back then. This was the ultimate splurge, on money her mother made struggling in a non-traditional role. Dale said she appreciated the gesture tremendously.

When Lady Willie was twice elected to represent the 36th District in the State Senate in Olympia, the girls went to an Olympia hotel with her, got jobs as pages or legislative assistants, and ate all their meals in the cafeteria. But, Dale is quick to add, her mother was a marvelous cook; goulash was her specialty and soon a trademark at any event Lady Willie attended. "I've just mastered that art myself," Dale says proudly. And that traditional Magnolia pastime, blackberry picking and making pies and jams, endures today.[7]

"Hide and seek," and tag were fun for Dale. She was at Magnolia School when the lower grass field was added, and softball was one of her favorite sports. "I wasn't particularly great at it, but I still remember when the crack of the bat connected to the ball, how proud I was. My claim to fame, though, was I got hit in the head with a ball and passed out!"[8]

Dinner-time was also different at their house. Lady Willie cooked weekends, refrigerated the entrees, and Alvara would heat up the food while Dale helped with the table setting. Their Mom would be home at around 5:30 in the evening, and they ate dinner together.

Lady Willie made sure her girls had their "proper" musical training on the piano in grade school. By high school, extra special activities for her girls were ski train trips to Snoqualmie, and dancing lessons at Mary Anne Wells' Studio.[9] About this time, Alvara began her own business. August Lilliquist, a neighbor and friend as well as a Magnolia builder, was an avid ski buff. He made skis, wax, and lent equipment to any interested beginner. He offered Alvara, according to Dale—"really the most enterprising of the two of us"—his ski wax recipe. Alvara took the recipe, worked long hours making the concoction, packaging it, and marketing it. (Mostly Queen Anne classmates became customers!)

Dale recalls that they lived in a home with no religious affiliation, while hardly anyone around them lived without it. Lady Willie chose not to participate in organized religion. While never a huge topic within the family, Dale remembers her mother thought that the traditions of any formal religion were anti-intellectual. This was another traditional area of socialization that did not exist, and Dale remembers it as just another difference in their lives —nothing of great significance at the time.[10]

Her mother's home was a place of study for law journals and case precedents, but not a place where pleasure reading or sports were revered. Dale herself enjoyed the Nancy Drew books, and intimated that she would have been interested in professional sports had she been exposed to them.

"Boys? I didn't grow up with any; they were foreign territory."

Despite the family structure differences, Dale says of her family, "We were a tight-knit unit that endured. We were all the family she had here, she was all we had."[11]

Author's Note: Dale Hogle, retired after many years of teaching foreign language at Nathan Hale High School, has written a book: Birdie: Mississippi Grit *about her grandmother on her mother's side. It is the true story of her mother's plantation, working family, and how Birdie provided a way to get her 6 children all to college in a most heartrending, yet creative story.*

Dale while attending Queen Anne High; by that time, her mother had earned a respected place as a lawyer and amongst some of Seattle's Democratics. Dale is still concentrating on her days of high school, fashions and typical 1940s teen times. Courtesy of Forbus Family.

Dumb Stunts and Grade-School Memories

By Hal Will

COLLECTING MEMORIES

This is a collection of grade-school memories, my own, and those of childhood friends and new acquaintances who grew up on Magnolia Bluff. Although not guaranteed to be accurate "history" in all cases, these memories do reveal a slice of life on Magnolia during the Depression and early World War II years. When recalling memorable childhood happenings of 60 years ago, many events are pretty vivid, but a specific date estimate is not always so easy. While many memories are shared amongst us, there are some details which are hazy or remembered differently, such as when the streets were paved or where certain businesses were located in what is today called "the Village" on West McGraw Street.

THE ERA OF OUR CHILDHOOD

Most of the people whom I have interviewed for this collection of memories are my age or older. I was born in October 1926, attended Magnolia School during 1932-1940 and graduated from Queen Anne High School in June 1944.

We grew up during a simpler and more innocent period with fewer influences from the world at large. We learned about sensational breaking news from the "Extra" edition of daily newspapers such as *The Seattle Times*, *Seattle Post-Intelligencer*, or *The Seattle Star*.

News vendors would be heard shouting, "EXTRA, EXTRA, READ ALL ABOUT IT!" —mostly in heavily populated areas where there were newsvendors on street corners. Paperboys were given 'Extras' covering the Lindbergh baby kidnapping and the plane crash in Alaska that killed Will Rogers and Wiley Post. During the early 1920s, radios did not exist in many households and more than one radio in a family was considered a luxury. Car radios were rare and a quick way to run down a six-volt car battery.

I remember the early 1930s as the worst years during the Depression. Many people in the country were unemployed, and many who did work had to change their lifestyle and do a lot of belt tightening. As children, we knew about Hooverville and other shack towns just as most of us know about homelessness today. However, very few families that I knew personally were without work, although they were all very thrifty. Most families consisted of a father as the wage earner and a mother as the homemaker. Single-parent families did not seem prevalent before World War II.

The latest in scooter technology is enjoyed by J. J. Heinrich, Max Barr and Charley Barr as they coast down Magnolia's West Armour Street. Photo by Roy Scully, 2000.

Magnolia School as it appeared from 1932 to 1940. Seattle Public Schools Archives, #250-282.

MAGNOLIA SCHOOL DAYS

In 1927, Magnolia School was a brand new, nine-room, brick building on the crown of the hill bordered by 26th Avenue West and 28th Avenue West, and West McGraw and West Smith streets. Robert "Bob" Hansen told me of starting school there when it first opened with 159 students enrolled.[1] At that time, the street in front of the school and his home was not yet paved.

His family moved into their new brick home at 1958 28th Avenue West at the corner of West Newton Street one month after school started. His parents Swen G. Hansen and Helen W. Auckland drove him to school from their home on Queen Anne Hill for that first month before moving. Both his father and mother were related to the Hansons and Aucklands of the Merrymont Dairy in Pleasant Valley. Swen Hansen was the only Hanson sibling to adopt the Norwegian spelling "Hansen," which he assumed during his schooling in Norway.

Bob remembers that some kids from Fort Lawton were bused to Magnolia School in an old Army bus. An addition to the school was added to the north end of the central structure while Bob was a student there.

Albert L. "Al" Jones moved with his family to 2654 Dravus Street in 1928 and started attending Magnolia School in the second grade.[2] His father, John Owen Jones of Welsh descent, was a salesman for C & H Sugar Company. His mother was Ruby MacFarlane, of Irish descent, and a homemaker for her husband and two sons.

Al remembers Zella E. Allen as Magnolia School's strict principal who was very serious about penmanship. Al specifically recalled a Miss McManus, who traveled from school to school emphasizing good penmanship for the Seattle School District. He also remembers multiple portable classrooms on the playground behind the school, possibly needed during construction on the main building. Al recalls the lower playground to the east of the school was used for "pick-up" sports like football. It was grass or dirt, while the upper field was gravel.

Sherman L. "Sherm" Sloan Jr. started attending Magnolia School in 1928 also.[3] His family lived about five blocks away at 2435 West Boston Street. His father grew up one block south at 2435 West Crockett Street, and attended Interbay School near 17th Avenue

West and West Dravus Street starting in 1906. It was the closest school until Magnolia School opened its doors 21 years later. Mr. Sloan worked as an import agent for American Mail Line at nearby Pier 41 in Smith Cove during Sherm's grade school years.

Sherm recalls the lunchroom/auditorium wing being added to the north end of the building in 1931 while he was a student there. According to his father, the small house at the northeast corner of 28th Avenue West and West Boston Street had been a school. The house still exists today as a private home.

Robert H. "Bob" Clark and his younger brother Doug lived with their parents, Dr. Earnest M. Clark and Ruth McRostie Clark, at 3020 27th Avenue West.[4] "Doc" Clark, as he was affectionately known to young and old, was very active in Post 123 of the American Legion and other community activities, as was Mrs. Clark, who was known as "Rosebud" by her family and friends. Her sons called her "Sergeant Rosebud" for her drill sergeant approach to getting them up in the mornings. Rosebud and my mother were inseparable friends, so I saw her often.

Bob Clark graduated from Magnolia School in 1935 and was a close friend of Al Jones. Doug Clark graduated in 1939 and shared many childhood experiences with Bob Shrewsbury and my brother, Ed Will. Doug died in 1996, but stories of his experiences and antics by some of his friends are very much a part of our story.

Bob Shrewsbury started attending Magnolia School in 1931 when he, his two sisters and parents moved to 2926 28th Avenue West. He had an insatiable interest in boats.[5] During the summer, he was sent to bible school. Instead of going to the church, he would either head to Hiram Chittenden Locks to watch the boat traffic or to Fishermen's Terminal to climb over old vessels laid up by the Depression. He timed his return home to coincide with the end of the bible-school class. This activity was somewhat curtailed when one of his sisters tattled on him.

My third grade class at Magnolia. Nine of my classmates mentioned in this essay are in this 1935 photo. Courtesy of Hal Will.

Bob's father was Roland "Bonnie" Shrewsbury. Of British descent, he was a trust officer for Seattle First National Bank. Bob's mother was Mary Philippine Redmond, of German descent. None of Bob's relatives know the significance of her unusual middle name.

My older brother, Edward A. "Eddy" Will Jr., started attending Magnolia School in September 1930.[6] We lived in a rental house at Condon Way and West Newton Street at that time, so he had to walk about seven blocks to and from school. Ed was named after our father, of German descent, who was a manufacturer's representative of electrical equipment. Our mother was Jennie May Young, of Scotch-Irish descent, a homemaker for our family of four.

Ed recalls the shiny, smooth new floors in the school hallways and how much fun it was to run and belly-flop for a nice slide, until caught by the custodian. Both Ed and I remember staying at home during our kindergarten year, as there was no kindergarten class at Magnolia until 1934 when Miss Entz was hired to start one.

I started attending Magnolia School in 1932, and I believe my first grade teacher was Miss Dorsey. Ed and I can recall the names of many of our grade-school teachers and remember most of them fondly. I will never forget Mrs. Anderson's insistence that our forearms be on the desk for proper support when we wrote. She added emphasis by a tap on the knuckles with a ruler. Miss Leckey is memorable to me as the teacher who realized how badly I needed glasses and alerted my parents. I have worn glasses ever since.

Other Magnolia School teachers whom I recall were Miss Bergstrom, Miss Bjorn, Miss Carstairs, Miss Erickson, Miss Galbraith, Mrs. Grenell, and Mr. Nelson. During my years there, I distinctly remember just one portable classroom building on the playground behind the main school building, so some had probably been removed before my time there. Enrollment had exceeded 600 by the time I graduated in 1940.

Mothers worked hard to make these costumes for some long forgotten function at Magnolia School. Hal Will is at far left and Jimmy Baird at far right. Courtesy of Hal Will.

There was a good view of parts of Elliott Bay, Elliott Avenue West and Smith Cove from the school and its play fields east of the school building. Sounds from the railroad yard in Interbay and the Smith Cove area were loud and clear. I'll never forget the unusual panorama one sunny morning when a low dense blanket of fog covered Elliott Bay and the railroad yard. It must have been about 50 feet thick, for the ships' masts could be seen above it, and the steam locomotives' exhaust plumes spouted above the fog like geysers. The forlorn wail of steam whistles from trains and many boats in the bay added industrial music to the scene. It was fascinating and beautiful to me. I really miss the sound of steam whistles in daily life today.

My buddy, Clyde F. Holcomb, Jr., arrived in our neighborhood in 1931 when his family bought a house at 2920 West Howe Street. It was across a vacant lot from our rental house at 2917 West Newton. We were the same age, so we quickly became playmates and started school together the following year.

Clyde's father was a salesman for the Edison Storage Battery Company, so he called on customers in interesting places such as lumber mills, boatyards and mines. When we were old enough to sit patiently in customers' waiting rooms, we sometimes accompanied Mr. Holcomb on sales calls during summer vacation. Clyde's mother was Alice Whalley Holcomb.[7] Whalley Place (pronounced "Wally") was named after her father, who was a business associate and friend of David P. Eastman, the Magnolia real-estate promoter during the early 1900s.

Clyde Jr. died in 1985, ending our lifetime friendship, but his name appears frequently as I recall some of the activities and adventures we shared as boys.

Thomas "Tom" Fraser lived at 2526 29th Avenue West, just a block west of the school and about three blocks from Wolfe Creek, a swamp that became our playground.[8] He commented eloquently, "I didn't like the playground project. It ruined a perfectly good swamp!" He recalls collecting crawdads or tadpoles in a jar, and how patient his mother was about the critters he brought home. Tom started attending Magnolia School with me in 1932.

Tom's father was George Fraser, of Scottish descent. He was selling cars for Nelson Chevrolet in Ballard when Tom was born in 1926. His mother was Ethel Lalanne, of French and German ancestry. She was mother to Tom and to his younger sister Virginia.

Lawrence "Laury" Minard was another 1932 Magnolia first grader.[9] His father was Everett Minard, an apple broker. His mother is Gretchen Frank Minard, of German descent, and homemaker for the family of four that lived at 2844 29th Avenue West. Laury must have always had strong feelings for our classmate, Nancy Jane Norton, for they were married after a long childhood friendship that continued throughout their college years.

Nancy Jane Norton Minard started attending grade school with us and lived on 40th Avenue West at a time when their house was surrounded by many vacant lots or woods.[10] Her mother was Ruth Wallis Norton, a homemaker for their family of four. Nancy's older brother Larry was classmate and friend of Bob Shrewsbury and Doug Clark. Their father, Lawrence Norton, of English ancestry, was a car dealer. He brought an old worn-out car home, and parked it on one of the vacant lots for the children to play in. It was inoperable, but the neighborhood kids put many imaginary miles on that old Chevy.

Jean Allyn Thomas lived at 3002 28th Avenue West and was another 1932 first-grader.[11] She lived in the same neighborhood as Bob Shrewsbury and Frankie Pollard. She said that

The main entrance to Lawton School as it appeared in the 1930s. Seattle Public Schools Archives, #243-1.

Frankie, her next-door neighbor, was her real special pal when they were seven and eight years old. Frankie did not have the chance to grow up with the rest of us. He died of leukemia when he was about 16, so his friends still fondly remember him today as young Frankie.

Jean's father was Marvin S. Allyn, a comptroller with Washington Cooperative Farmer's Association located on Elliott Avenue West. Her mother was Esther Allyn. They were a boating family, and Mr. Allyn was commodore of the Seattle Yacht Club at one time.

Russ Langstaff's second grade class on the Lawton School steps. Courtesy of Russ Langstaff.

LAWTON SCHOOL

A new eight-room brick building replaced the old South Salmon Bay School in 1908, and was renamed Lawton School. However, major geographic changes were underway in the area in preparation for the Hiram Chittenden Locks, the Lake Washington Ship Canal and the resulting maritime traffic. The Great Northern Railway's main-line trestle near 14th Avenue West had to be modified to allow boat traffic, so a more favorable location for a new bridge was chosen west of the new locks site; this required a long cut through the Lawton Park neighborhood and the rerouting of Gilman Avenue West from West Thurman Street to West Government Way. The four-year-old school was in the middle of the new Gilman Avenue route, so it was condemned in 1912. A new Lawton School was erected in 1913 on the block bordered by West Elmore and West Thurman streets, and 26th and 27th avenues. It has since had additions and remodels, and was then completely rebuilt at that same location.

Russell O. "Russ" Langstaff attended Lawton School from 1930 to 1938.[12] His family lived at 32nd Avenue West and West Elmore Street in the home his father and uncle built in 1906. Russ was born in 1923 and was brought home in the family's 1916 Model-T Ford. His father was Otto Langstaff, of English ancestry, and a glazier for W. P. Fuller Company. His mother was Bessie whose family was from Kentucky. She was a homemaker for the family of five that included Russ's younger brothers, Lee and Eugene.

Nature hikes in Miss LaRue's sixth-grade class, a tour of the Seattle Cedar Mill, "Pet Days," "Field Days" and Halsey Taylor, the janitor, are what Russ remembers best about Lawton School. Russ has a thick scrapbook illustrating his years there.

Russ also remembers the whole family getting involved on cold winter mornings helping Mr. Langstaff get the family Model-T Ford going. They didn't have antifreeze so the car was drained on cold nights. Water was heated on the wood cook stove the next morning to refill the car's cooling system, and then the family would get out and push the car down West Elmore Street to get Dad started off to work.

FAMILY ENTERTAINMENT: RADIO PROGRAMS AND MOVIES

One of the few activities entertaining enough to lure kids in from play before dinner was listening to the radio. We'd sit on the floor in front of a radio with playmates and listen to Jack Armstrong, The All American Boy, sponsored by Wheaties, The Breakfast of Champions; Jimmy Allen, a World War I flying hero; Sky King; and Little Orphan Annie, sponsored by Ovaltine. Orphan Annie offered some spooky mystery content and I think it was preferred by the girls. Some programs offered prizes such as secret decoder rings or badges that enabled us to decode messages broadcast during a program. The prizes were won by mailing in a number of cereal box tops plus a nickel. A stamp cost 3 cents. In the evenings, the whole family often listened to radio shows such as One Man's Family, Fred Allen, Fibber McGee and Molly, Jack Benny, and Amos-'N-Andy.

By the late 1930s, a few homes had floor model console radios in nice mahogany cabinets with a big speaker and a large impressive tuning dial. Some even had a short-wave band. The new "Electric Tuning Eye" was one of the latest radio technologies. It resembled a greenish cat's eye about an inch in diameter that changed shape to help dial in a station. A nearby friend's family had one of these deluxe radios so the neighborhood kids usually congregated there at program time.

For many parents, evening recreation was limited to playing cards. Bridge and pinochle were popular games among neighbors and organized bridge clubs were numerous. Many adults, including our parents, belonged to social groups that organized card parties, dances or other functions for members, such as the Pleasant Valley Neighbors Club or the Magnolians. The American Legion and other service groups also provided activities for adults and families. Parents and grandparents were active with the PTA, Cub Scouts, Boy Scouts and Sea Scouts.

Families had to leave the Bluff to see a movie, and it was considered a special occasion. The theaters nearest to Magnolia were on Queen Anne Hill and in Ballard. Al Jones remembers walking across the Locks to Ballard for Saturday matinees at the Bay Theater. The price for a movie ticket was 5 cents, but there was always a drawing for a bag of groceries—a worthwhile prize during the Depression.

Television didn't even exist in our vocabularies in the 1930s. We were still excited about the radios. Television was first available in Seattle on Thanksgiving Day in 1948, and quite a few years passed before many families owned a TV set.

Following pages: This 1935 aerial shows the extent of development, vacant lots and thick woods existing on the south end of Magnolia. The wooded areas across the center of the photo were considered "our woods" as we were growing up. Magnolia Beach, the boat house and dock at the bottom of the photo were our summer playground. Photo copyright by Walker and Associates, negative # 692.

PLAYING IN OUR NEIGHBORHOOD

Every neighborhood on Magnolia Bluff had woods or at least numerous vacant lots for kids to play in during the 1920s and 1930s. My neighborhood was blessed with a very generous expanse of unspoiled woods near the three different houses my family rented on Condon Way West from 1929 to 1943. Land in the valley to the west of Condon Way and 30th Avenue West was mostly thick woods for about four blocks over to 34th Avenue West. In a north-south direction, these woods extended for five blocks north from West Howe Street to the south wall of the businesses on West McGraw Street. This area was at the south end of Pleasant Valley where the two hills that form Magnolia Bluff converged to form a narrower valley. What was our Wolfe Creek Road, is now 32nd Avenue West which runs along the low point to Puget Sound. I, my buddy Clyde Holcomb, my brother Ed, and other neighborhood kids considered this area "our" woods.

"Our" Wolfe Creek

I feel sorry for young boys who never had a creek in which to play. My friends and I had Wolfe Creek. It originally drained much of Pleasant Valley, emptying into Puget Sound at the south end of Magnolia Bluff. The floor of the valley a few blocks north of McGraw Street was partly peat bog and swamp.

The creek was quite noticeable where it drained from the north and dumped into a sump on the west side of Roy Chambers' Magnolia Hardware store on West McGraw Street. A pipe carried the creek under McGraw Street, under the stores on the south side of the street and beyond. By the mid-1930s, my buddy Clyde Holcomb and I discovered the outlet of the pipe in a large wooded depression two blocks south at the intersection of Clise Place West, 32nd Avenue West and Wolfe Creek Road.

Bob Hansen posed for a Darigold photo contest, and won. Courtesy of Bett Hansen.

This low area was triangular in shape, stretching about 100 feet along Clise Place West and Wolfe Creek Road, and was about 50 feet wide between the roads at its south end. This spot would keep Clyde, me and numerous other friends occupied for hours in warm weather. The creek flowed more slowly through there, over a sandy area with cattails and skunk cabbage growing around the edges. Fortunately, the creek exited this area into a fairly narrow ditch along the east side of Wolfe Creek Road. That made it possible to build a dam across the outlet by working fast.

If we succeeded in stopping the flow, a large shallow pond would start forming that could grow to 25 feet in diameter. It could get as deep as our dirt-and-mud dam. We literally "worked like beavers" to keep ahead of the rising water. It was a constant battle to plug the many leaks in the muddy barrier, but the creek always won and washed out our dams. The bigger the dam was before it washed out, the more spectacular the flood that overflowed the ditch down Wolfe Creek Road. Such were the rewards of our frantic dam building.

The triangular hollow, where numerous schoolmates spent so many hours in a contest with the creek, has been filled in. It is now an elevated yard and carport site for the house at 1957 Clise Place West. Our creek flows through a pipe several feet below the present road grade, and has become just part of the storm sewer system that dumps out on the beach at the end of the road.

Sherm Sloan's dad told him about salmon spawning up Wolfe Creek at one time. Apparently, salmon fishing used to be good in the area, possibly when Wolfe Creek had a more natural outlet than a storm sewer pipe.

Despite the maps and street signs that call the road to Magnolia Beach 32nd Avenue West, many of us will always know it as Wolfe Creek Road. Personally, I'd like to see it renamed as such.

LOCAL TRANSPORTATION

During my early grade school years, I did a lot of walking and rarely rode the bus. This is probably typical of most of my generation. I did not own a bicycle until my first year in high school. Typically, families who had cars had just one which was used by the wage earner. I remember a few women had cars, but they were the exception—although this changed rapidly during World War II.

When I did leave the Bluff on a bus, it was usually with my mother. If my mother had to shop downtown, she had to take my brother Ed and me in tow because sitters were not part of our routine. Trips off Magnolia Bluff were infrequent and usually with my parents or those of a friend. A trip downtown to the family doctor's office in the Medical Dental Building was a big excursion.

In the early 1930s, the 28th Avenue West or Carleton Park buses went only to the foot of the West Garfield Street Bridge that is known today as the Magnolia Bridge. From there, we transferred to the buses from Ballard to get downtown. Sometimes, we just walked from the bottom of the bridge south one block to the Piggly Wiggly Market for fresh produce. I am still reminded of the Piggly Wiggly when I see the building that now houses the Builder's Hardware at 1516 15th Avenue West since the structure and parking lot have changed very little. I still remember the friendly driver of the Carleton Park bus was Mr. Ruggles. He knew most of his passengers by name.

The only streetcar line on Magnolia went from 15th Avenue West and West Dravus Street to Fort Lawton's east gate and uphill a considerable distance inside the Fort. Lawton School students living more than a mile from school received free tokens. We understand the streetcars were rough riding. They had hard seats, no springs and the roadbed was bumpy. The old buses that replaced them were not much better.

Fageol built the earliest Magnolia buses that I remember, with the old-fashioned hood out front. They really struggled up the West Garfield Street Bridge, as well as other slopes on their routes. I remember new buses showed up on the Bluff in 1939 or 1940 when I was in the seventh or eighth grade. I was on the safety patrol assigned the crossing-guard duties at 28th Avenue West and West Blaine Street, about eight blocks south of Magnolia School.

One morning, instead of the usual old Fageol gas bus wheezing up the hill from the West Garfield Street Bridge, a new Twin Coach bus came along, engine racing in a low gear. It struggled up the hill like the Fageol, but with a new sound and a new look. It resembled an upside-down bathtub, sort of wide and squat. When I got to school, we boys talked about the new Twin Coach gas job without a hood and with the engine cross-wise in the rear, over the wheels. The girls just considered it another bus. How dull could they be?

Early buses serving Carleton Park and Magnolia Bluff. These and later models used to struggle up the West Garfield Street Bridge. Washington State Historical Society, Curtis # 38871.

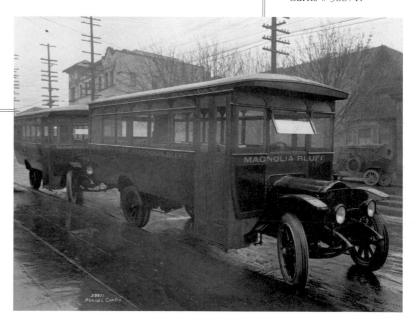

The Elders and Their Creek

On the east side of Clise Place, across from the Wolfe Creek damming area, there was a small dwelling. This was the home of the Elder family. They were hardworking folks who had few conveniences while raising two young children. I had always compared Mr. Elder to President Abraham Lincoln because of his obvious industrious nature and his grace while chopping wood.

During recent phone conversations with Robert Elder and his mother, Phyllis Paul Elder, I learned that Robert and his younger brother, Phil, had a creek of their own that I never knew about. It was south of their home in the woods across West Crockett Street. They also built dams to create a pond, even if fragile and temporary.[13]

Robert spoke of fashioning bows and arrows from local tree cuttings. The two brothers would use leaves floating on their pond for targets, apparently becoming quite proficient at hitting them from perches in surrounding trees. Although they were nine years younger than I, they too enjoyed extensive woods and a creek in our neighborhood!

A neighborhood group paused for this 1931 photo on the Hansen family's front steps. Left to right in the top row are Bob Hansen and Wes McCormick, holding his dog Spot. Jack Wilson and Barney Hansen are in the middle row and Dean Mitchell is on the lowest step. Compare the scooter in this photo with those in the "now" photo at the beginning of this chapter. Courtesy of Bett Hansen.

Horses

In the early 1930s, horses were not uncommon on Magnolia. Al Jones was paid to take care of two for a brief period, and he liked to ride. His friend, Elsworth "Snicks" Sunde, had two horses so the two boys could ride together around Pleasant Valley. Al remembers galloping along 34th Avenue and believes it was unpaved at that time. Al also frequented the cavalry stables at Fort Lawton in 1932 when he was about 12. The soldiers welcomed kids who could ride, for they would help exercise the horses. Al recalls his favorite horse named Martina whom he used to ride to West Point and gallop along the sandy beach.

The Greens' Stable

The woods directly west of Wolfe Creek Road and our dam building area attracted the attention of a few of my classmates when workmen started clearing out underbrush in the late 1930s. When we learned they were going to build a stable there, our attention really focused on their progress. The property belonged to a Magnolia resident, Mr. Green, who was the owner of Green's Fine Furs in downtown Seattle. He was building a stable and riding paths there for his two sons, John and Bobby. The Greens lived about six blocks away from the stable location at 36th Avenue West and West Constance Drive. The boys were younger than I, and may have gone to a private school because I don't remember them attending Magnolia School or Queen Anne High School.

The stable was a simple structure just sufficient to hold two ponies and supplies of hay, straw and oats. When it was finished and the ponies arrived, we started going to the stable frequently. The bigger pony was named Tempter. He was brown and white and belonged to John. His younger brother Bobby had a dark brown Shetland named Skippy. Neither pony had a very good disposition, but we all liked them and wanted to be able to go into their stalls, brush them and feed them oats. Of course, we also wanted a turn at riding them, so we were willing to do many menial chores to earn riding time.

My brother Ed earned a little spending money by cleaning stalls and feeding the ponies for a short period. Our house was less than two blocks away, so Ed could go there daily before school. A caretaker was eventually hired and lived in a tiny house that was moved onto the property near the stable.

Visiting Ponies

John and Bobby Green would sometimes ride the ponies up to our house on Condon Way West, possibly to show my mom. I remember John riding Tempter up a step or two to our front door and ringing the doorbell. When Mom answered the door, she was startled to find Tempter's nose there in front of her, but she quickly recovered to pet him. She loved animals but "drew the line" when John tried to ride him into our living room. On another occasion, Bobby rode Skippy, the Shetland, up our wooden back steps to the kitchen door. I don't recall how he backed him down all of those steps to solid ground again.

At some point, the Greens moved and the stable ceased to exist. A house at 2010 Wolfe Place now occupies the stable site. The caretaker's little house was eventually moved about a block away to 1919 32nd Avenue West on "our" Wolfe Creek Road, where it stands today.

Wishing With the Point of a Slice of Pie

For years prior to the Greens' stable being built, I always made a wish by saving the point of a piece of pie to eat last and make a wish. Most of the time, my wish had been for a pony. I probably reasoned that my wishes had something to do with the reality of two ponies coming to live less than two blocks from our house. As I grew older, my "pie wishes" changed to wanting kayaks, canoes, rowboats and outboards, since my desire for a pony had been somewhat satisfied by Tempter and Skippy.

Camps and Tree Houses

Home building and street improvements were accelerating on Magnolia in the last half of the 1930s. Most of my friends remember projects in or near our neighborhoods that were the source of building materials for kids' camps and tree houses. We built little camps in any convenient clearing. There were many large maple trees suitable for tree houses and lots of vacant lots, some wooded, on which to build small camps. Most of the materials came from scrap piles at the projects, while some were pilfered from better stock after hours.

This picture interrupted a game of "Cowboys and Indians." Left to right: Raymond Petrich, Hal Will, Eddy Will, Dick Dawson and Eugene Petrich. Courtesy of Hal Will.

Laury Minard recalls a dark Sunday morning when his dad, still in a tuxedo after a Magnolians dance, was kindly driving him around his paper route. The car's headlights illuminated one of the neighborhood boys struggling away from a construction site with a bundle of shingles. Mr. Minard asked Laury if he knew the name of the shingle thief. Laury pretended he didn't. That is how another kids' camp enjoyed the luxury of a shingled roof and a father in a tuxedo didn't turn in the young shingle thief.

Bob Hansen is proud of the fact that he was a designer and builder in his grade school years. He said that his brother Barney and their friend Dean Mitchell were "the salesmen type" and good at acquiring building materials, but that he was the one who designed and constructed their camps and tree houses.

Trench Camps

Bob Shrewsbury remembers that he, along with his buddies Doug Clark and Frankie Pollard, plus others, built things of various types in the vacant lots just south of Doug's family home at 3020 27th Avenue West. They even had enough ambition to dig trenches, cover them first with boards, and then with dirt and sod for an out-of-sight camp or clubhouse. This vacant area was also the scene of a rock-throwing exchange where Doug was hit on the head and ended up with a metal plate in his skull. This, however, did not prevent his service aboard a Navy destroyer in the South Pacific during World War II.

"Allentown"

Somewhat classier camps did exist, and were described by Nancy Norton Minard. Some kids in her neighborhood learned to be entrepreneurs with multiple, little kid-built structures in an area they called Allentown. It was named for Allen Morgan, whose father was a banker. Allen's camp building became the bank, complete with play money. Participants in Allentown operated imaginary businesses. Nancy's had a grocery store stocked with empty food containers such as cans, cereal boxes and milk bottles. Nancy, Geri Marty Andrew and Jean Martin Bell remember playing in wooded areas wearing "mother-sewn" costumes depicting Peter Pan and other fictional characters.[14][15][16]

The "Cool Dry Place"

Houses were being built on vacant lots near my neighborhood so kids were able to scrounge a board here and there, and stash them on a vacant lot about 200 feet south of our house. Our project was to build a camp. It would consist of any scrap material acquired from construction sites, the woods, the beach or discarded wooden crates. Shiplap boards (plywood's predecessor)—dirty and damaged from use in concrete forms—were the main component. The design depended on the available materials and the talent of the participants.

Artist: Hal Will.

I don't remember the names of everyone who built this camp, but I'm sure that my brother Ed was involved as well as my buddy Clyde. We did finish a modest one-room, dirt-floor, leaky-roof camp. We were quite proud of it. It sat beneath a huge maple tree and faced Condon Way. A scrap of packing-crate wood found among the scavenged building material had "KEEP IN A COOL DRY PLACE" printed on it. We sawed off the first part and nailed the last three words "COOL DRY PLACE" over the door. It was located at what is today 2029 Condon Way West. The site is now occupied by a far more imposing structure. Sixty years later, the phrase "cool dry place" still revives a mental picture of that camp for both Ed and myself.

The 1936 Magnolia baseball team coached by eighth grade teacher, Ethel Galbreath. Front row l to r: Dean Mitchell, Dave Grauberger, Donald Young, Henry Pederson and Fred Grauberger. Back row l to r: Dave Hassel, Dave Pollard, Harold 'Barney' Hansen, Upton Fitzgerald, Bill Rattray and Harold Lundin. Courtesy of Shirley Young Allen.

The Langstaff Place

Russ Langstaff had a different "camp" situation. His father was a great collector of lumber and always seemed to have a supply stacked around the family yard. Russ built a small building of his own in his back yard. It was, therefore, a more private and permanent structure, but grew from the same urge "to build something" as the other camps had.

The "Beach"

The "Beach" describes the south side of Magnolia Bluff from Four Mile Rock on the west to Smith Cove on the east. Almost everyone I knew who lived on Magnolia Bluff spent part of the summer at the beach. The most common access to the beach was either through Magnolia Park or down Wolfe Creek Road (32nd Avenue West). There, on the beach at the foot of the road, was Tom Connley's boathouse and dock. Mr. Connley was a fairly heavy-set man, who was always in blue coveralls and an old felt hat. His wife, in contrast, was thin and weathered. Their boathouse was a "has-been" from the decade earlier. There were virtually no customers renting the old rowboats. The beach at that location was not very attractive to swimmers, so the Connleys' little lunch-counter area was a virtual ghost town.

Discovery

By the time Clyde Holcomb and I discovered the boathouse, the dock was decrepit to the point of being dangerous. The big heavy rental rowboats were pretty beat up, and the covered boat storage area was decorated in thick dust and large cobwebs. The Connleys allowed us to fish from the dock and to use the changing rooms free of charge. We occasionally bought a bottle of pop or a can of shoestring potatoes from Mrs. Connley. Their living quarters were part of the boathouse structure, otherwise they probably would have boarded up the place.

Top: Clyde Holcomb pretending to pull in a big fish at the dock on Magnolia Beach. Courtesy of Hal Will.

Bottom: Clyde Holcomb showing a small perch he caught. Courtesy of Hal Will.

We Fished for Hours

Clyde and I, plus numerous other friends, spent many hours fishing for perch from the dock when the tide was in. We could see the fish feeding around the piling by looking through cracks or holes in the planks. We used pile worms for bait so we had to visit the beach at low tide to dig for them. Bullheads were ugly little fish that looked like a baby cod or a catfish, but they were too easy to catch and useless to eat. We rarely saw any other fish under the dock except perch. The small perch were called shiners. They nibbled at our bait while we would try to place our hook and worm close to the bigger perch. There was great excitement when any of us caught a good-sized perch. Since we fished through holes or cracks in the pier's decking, we sometimes caught a fish too fat to fit through the opening. We would try everything to get it up on the dock but sometimes we had to let it go. Our mothers dreaded seeing us trudging up the dusty road home with one or more perch dangling on a string. However, they were very understanding, so we ate some of the larger ones for dinner and the others became fertilizer in the garden.

Changing Rooms

Although we were usually engrossed in our fishing, we kept an eye peeled for any girls approaching the boathouse. Their only purpose for coming there would be to use a changing room in the boat storage shed. There were only two rooms empty enough to be used for changing. We would quickly and quietly hide in the dark storage rooms on either side of the two changing rooms and remain absolutely silent. It was a 50-50 gamble whether a girl would use the room next to one of our chosen hiding places. We sometimes jammed one of the doors to limit the number of available rooms to one. We knew every knothole in the old board partitions and we knew how to keep our eye far enough away to be unseen. As the old saying goes, "Boys will be boys."

The "Mazong Temple"

Virtually everyone I interviewed was familiar with Magnolia Beach as a place to go and spend time in the summer. Sherm Sloan, with his buddy Dean Mitchell, used to go across West Boston Street, through the woods below 30th Avenue West, to the beach via Magnolia Park. When asked about memories of the beach, Sherm and Al Jones both recalled an enclosure that occupied a part of the beach near the high tide line about four blocks west of Wolfe Creek Road. It was commonly known as the "Mazong Temple." Neither of them knew how to spell it, but that is the way it sounded. It looked like the foundation of a beach house of bygone years. It was formed by bleached pilings forming a rectangle of about 20 by 30 feet. It was open to the sky as well as the bluff above. It was frequented by a group of men who Sherm thinks were wrestlers. The guys were muscular and deeply tanned all over. They sunbathed in the buff within their "temple," so they were a topic of discussion and some mystery.

Above: The 1939 Lawton Safety Patrol members. This was a relatively new activity at that time. Four that I recognize are Marvin Durham, Roy McClure, Ted Gardlin and Don Peterson.
Seattle Public Schools Archives, #243-54.

Left: Certificate issued to Junior Safety Patrol participants at grade school graduation. The four signatures at the bottom are of interest. Arthur B. Langlie was Mayor of Seattle and went on to be Governor of Washington. Worth McClure was Superintendent of Schools, William H Sears was Chief of Police and George W. Kimball was Director of Junior Safety and organizer of the Safety Patrol in Seattle.
Courtesy of Hal Will.

Too Shallow

At high tide there could be about 8 to 10 feet of water at the seaward end of the Connleys' boathouse dock. A sewer pipe that served a lot of Magnolia extended, half buried, parallel with the dock and out into deeper water. Sherm recalls Jimmy Ranken showing off by diving from the dock railing. He didn't clear the pipe enough to avoid bad barnacle scrapes as a reward. It still hurts me to visualize that dive.

"Fleet Week Crawl"

The sewage from that pipe was untreated in those days, so the swimming conditions would be considered unacceptable now, but we swam there and survived. I used to think the floating sewage was the Navy's fault when the fleet was in and ships were anchored off the Bluff. I coined the name "Fleet Week Crawl" for the swimming style that cleared floating debris away before each stroke. It wasn't the Navy after all. It was our own Magnolia Bluff sewer.

Russ Langstaff at Magnolia Beach with the boathouse dock behind him. Courtesy of Russ Langstaff.

The Yearning for Boats

Things that float fascinate many boys. We were no exception. Logs were worked off the beach at high tide and rafts were assembled from driftwood just to ride them and possibly paddle a short distance before abandoning them. But what we really wanted was a boat.

Al Jones used to go to Smith Cove to row around in Mitchell Dearman's skiff even though Al's father had declared Smith Cove off limits to Al at that time, for safety reasons. Mr. Jones, on his way home, somehow spotted Al from the trestle, resulting in tighter restrictions when Al arrived home.

Al later found an old rowboat for $5 and arranged to keep it at Tom Connley's boathouse for a minimal monthly fee. Over time, that fee became too much of a burden on Al, so he just left his boat with Tom, who didn't need another old boat.

Bob Shrewsbury was attracted to the water and to boats at an early age. He was fascinated by the Washington Tug & Barge Company tugs when they moored at Smith Cove between Piers 40 and 41. He would later own two of them.

Ship Aground

Bob's friend, Emerson Matson, lived on Perkins Lane near Four Mile Rock. Early one morning a ship ran aground in the fog near his house. He called Bob who called Doug Clark, Frankie Pollard and Allen Morgan. They all played hooky from school to go to the beach. Wading up to their knees, they investigated the ship. The fun ended when "Emmy's" mother discovered them and sent them back to school.

The "Borrowed" Boat

Bob Shrewsbury and Doug Clark "found" an old boat on the beach at the high tide mark. It was loaded with rocks, probably to keep it from floating away at high tide. It didn't occur to them that it probably belonged to someone. They unloaded the rocks and "found" some oars and launched it for a ride. The tide was carrying them toward West Point, so they struggled to row against it to get back. Doug lost his oar, so they could only row in circles. He jumped overboard to retrieve it, but he wasn't doing so well with all of his clothes on, so Bob threw him the other oar. Fortunately for the intrepid pair, two men in an outboard boat came along. Bob yelled, "Save my friend!" which the two men did. They then took the wayward boat in tow. "You stole my boat and I've been looking for it," said one of the men, Jack Scherenzel, who owned a nice summer home on the beach just west of the Mazong Temple. Mr. Scherenzel did not press charges against Bob and Doug.

Russ Langstaff's First Boat

Like Bob, Russ frequented Fishermen's Terminal to be near boats. Russ and his friend, Claude Whitman, became a familiar sight to the customers and employees during 1935. One day the Terminal superintendent offered the boys an old decrepit dory. Of course they accepted it, even though it wouldn't float. They were boys!

They got busy with tar and any other caulking material they could scrounge. When they finally launched their new vessel, it would only float for short periods. Fortunately for them, Salmon Bay was the floating storage for many booms of logs. That minimized the stretches of open water. They could frequently step out onto a log boom to bail their sinking craft. They could even venture to the Ballard waterfront in short trips with frequent bailing. The important thing was, they had a boat!

My Boat

In the late 1930s, a neighbor a few blocks away from our house was building a pleasure boat in a shed behind his house at 2421 31st Avenue West. His name was Burton W. Sawyer, but to everyone on Magnolia who knew him he was "Doc." My Dad would help him by doing the electrical wiring. When my Dad worked on Mr. Sawyer's boat, I went along to soak up the wonderful smell of oak and cedar shavings

My first boat ready to launch. It was built in the basement during the spring of 1940. Courtesy of Hal Will.

and sawdust. I also enjoyed Mr. Sawyer's thick Maine accent as he told stories, described boat-building steps, and patiently answered my endless questions about boats.

Mr. Sawyer was the one who suggested I build a boat of my own. Dad and I listened as he described where the materials could be acquired either for free or for a reasonable price. My Dad warmed up to the idea and encouraged me to seriously consider it. He said that he would help me, which he did. I have always been so thankful for that encouraging nudge.

We selected a design that met with Mr. Sawyer's approval and my boat-building lessons began in earnest. We all went to the Magnolia and West Point beaches where I learned how to select oak dunnage lumber suitable for frames in my boat. Dunnage was crating or bracing material used to contain cargo in a ship's hold during an ocean voyage. It was

Dad and I carried the boat into the water. What a thrill it was to have my own boat! Courtesy of Hal Will.

plentiful since freighters from hardwood regions of the globe would often throw the dunnage lumber over the side as they passed Magnolia Bluff when entering or leaving Elliott Bay. The oak frames, knees, stem and oarlock blocks for my boat were cut to shape on Doc Sawyer's band saw. All other sawing was done by hand.

I think my source of earnings at this time came from delivering magazines and ice cream for the ice creamery on West McGraw Street. I didn't have a bike so I could only deliver to customers within running distance. I really had to save up to buy the wood that I couldn't find on the beach. The hardware and other items had to come from a ship chandlery on the downtown waterfront.

The boat was finished in time for summer vacation in 1940. A neighbor's trailer we borrowed for the trip down to the beach at the foot of Wolfe Creek Road. Dad and I carried the boat across the rocky beach and into the water far enough for it to float. It was such a thrill to get aboard that beautiful boat, of my own creation. A couple of years later, the boat was smashed in a winter storm. I cried.

Outdoor Games

There were various children's games involving running, hiding, falling down and yelling. Most neighborhood streets were unpaved dirt roads, some oiled to keep the dust down at the option and expense of local residents. Homebuilders often paved the sidewalks, while streets were still dirt. However, many sidewalks only consisted of two 2 x 12 planks laid side by side. Tom Fraser recalled the nasty spills caused when scooter or bicycle wheels dropped between the planks. Of course, roller-skating was limited to paved areas. When we were at the sand box age, we just used a dirt side street. Russ Langstaff remembers a lot of road grading in his neighborhood from 1928 through 1932 that uncovered nice sandy soil to play in.

Some kids had cap pistols, but most just pointed a finger or stick and yelled, "Bang, bang, you're dead." This game was typically called "Cowboys and Indians" or "Cops and Robbers." Of course, there were other games to use up our youthful energy.

Kick-the-Can

Kick-the-Can was one of the few pastimes that included girls. Bob Shrewsbury, Patricia Jephcott Timberlake and Jean Allyn Thomas remember playing the game in their neighborhood. It was usually played after school before dinnertime. It was a form of hide-and-seek with variations involving a tin-can. The game involved coming out of hiding to kick-the-can being guarded by the unfortunate person whose turn it was to be "it." I can still visualize a shiny tin-can sitting under the street light on the southwest corner of 29th Avenue West and West Crockett Street. Allowable hiding places were only within the yards on the four corners of the intersection. As we grew older, we sometimes tried to hide with a preferred girl, but that was not an important part of the game yet.[17]

Time to Come Home

Many of my generation remember the motherly instruction, "Come home when the street lights come on." Streetlights at the time were clear, unprotected bulbs protruding down from fluted metal disks that served as reflectors. There seemed to be one at each intersection. There were no photoelectric sensors to turn them on automatically, so an electrical worker would throw a switch from some central location to turn all the streetlights on. I wonder if that worker realized how many kids' games were thus terminated.

"Eenie Einie Over"

We used to play a game called "Eenie Einie Over." (And, I have no idea how it should be spelled.) It involved throwing a ball over the portable building on the schoolyard to unseen players on the other side. We would yell "Eenie, Einie Over" as we threw the ball so they could watch for it. Their reward for catching it allowed them to sneak around the building and throw the ball at us instead of back over the roof. It sounds rather silly and dull now, but it was good exercise and very entertaining to us then. The name has stuck with me for 60 years without ever hearing anyone else mention it.

The Yo-yo

The yo-yo craze hit town when I was about 11 or 12. Yo-yo peddlers were young men who were very talented yo-yo experts. They would demonstrate the most fascinating tricks at any location where young boys congregated. Naturally, the sidewalk in front of the Magnolia Pharmacy was frequently the scene of yo-yo sales pitches and demonstrations. That is where I first learned about them. Of course, I had to have one. I became fairly proficient with it, but not flashy. The few tricks I accomplished were "Walk the Dog," "Round the World," and "Rock the Cradle." I still enviously admire yo-yo experts.

Al Jones, Norm Jones and Bob Clark about 1925. Courtesy of Al Jones.

Swings

I imagine that every neighborhood had a swing of some sort. All that was required for a good "rope swing" was a husky tree limb with 15 to 30 feet of clear space below it and a strong piece of old rope. A high place was required from which to jump or drop such as a dirt bank or a crude platform of some sort. Thus, the term

The "Bootlegger's" House

Across the street from Doug and Bob Clark's house on 27th Avenue West was a two-story, brick mystery house where the shades were always drawn. Nobody seemed to live there, but a shiny bakery delivery truck seemed to make a lot of trips to and from the address. If one of the owners found the neighborhood kids too close to the house, he told them, "Scram, there's nothing here for you!"

There was much excitement one night when there was a resounding boom from the house. Bob recalls watching the police and fire department activity from across the street at 2 a.m. He believes that the police were aware of the bootlegging operation there, for they "rescued" many jugs from the basement before the firemen arrived on the scene. Bob Shrewsbury remembers his father and neighbors "rescuing" jugs from neighboring lots the next morning.

Neighbors not surprised . . .

Bob Clark had heard that there were two large vats in the basement where something went awry causing a fire. The next day, a newspaper photo showed a police officer standing by a ruptured still in the house's basement. He remembers that the kids in the neighborhood sensed something strange at that house because there was a definite odor from the mash by-product that was dumped brazenly in the vacant lot next door. Bob Shrewsbury said that there was another house in the neighborhood that he and his buddies thought was somewhat suspicious as well. Laury Minard lived more than two blocks away and said that he found a perfectly good rocking chair in a vacant lot near his house that had come from the bootlegger's house. He added it to his family's furniture.

"drop-swing" was identical with "rope-swing." They were affordable during the Depression as long as an old piece of rope strong enough to hold a kid or two could be scrounged. Sometimes pieces could be found on the beach, but knowing someone in the maritime industry helped. A simple knot at the bottom would suffice to brace the feet against, but they could be more elaborate. Bob Shrewsbury recalls that the swing he and his friends built consisted of an old tire to sit on, with the lower end for hooking their feet.

My brother Ed brags about using a swing some of his crazy friends hung in a madrone tree along Magnolia Boulevard. It swung out into free space over the edge of a 200-foot bluff. Some of Bob Hansen's neighborhood friends had a rope swing fastened to the branch of a tree hanging over the street. They found sport in swinging across the road as close to an approaching bus as they dared. He said that one kid fashioned a dummy like a scarecrow, and then dropped it from the swing in front of a bus, terrifying the occupants.

The swing in my neighborhood hung from a big madrone at the northwest corner of Condon Way West and West Howe Street. There was a perfect dirt bank to launch from and a vacant lot to swing over. I'd guess the rope was about 20 feet long, and the knot at the end cleared the ground by about two feet. I remember enjoying many hours taking turns on the swing with neighbor friends. The only bad thing I remember was losing my grip on the rope at the high end of the arc and landing on my back with a thud. That was my first experience of having the wind knocked out of me. I thought I was dying for a few moments.

Skating

Al Jones and Tom Fraser both recalled playing hockey (on roller skates) at the tennis courts at West Howe Street and Magnolia Boulevard West. The skates were crude with steel wheels and clamps to fasten them to the soles of our shoes. Russ Langstaff remembers setting out for the University District on skates with his friend, Jimmy Dodson. Those old steel wheeled skates didn't survive the trip. Jean Allyn Thomas remembers beating all the boys in her neighborhood at skating around the block. She claims her slim build presented less aerodynamic drag. She said it was a bad move. The boys wanted to win!

Several of us remember ice skating on ponds down at Smith Cove near the Rope Walk, a long narrow factory that manufactured rope, or the Great Northern round house, a semicircular building where locomotives were serviced in Interbay. The ponds were shallow, so bits of grass or weeds protruding from the ice caused frequent spills.

Bicycles

At varying ages, most of us eventually had bikes. Russ Langstaff had a bike as early as the third or fourth grade. Bikes turned out to be an important part of his life in subsequent years, as a bike club member and bike repairman. In contrast, I didn't get a bike until high school when my 1942 paper route required and financed a used one. Geri Marty told of receiving a bike as a gift from a relative in the East. It turned out to be a boy's bike, but that didn't keep her from putting many miles on that bike.

Ping-Pong

My dad bought a Ping-Pong table in the early 1930s and put it on sawhorses in our basement. It was the first piece of plywood I ever saw. It was also the only Ping-Pong table in the neighborhood, so it was well used by young and old alike, especially during winter months. I think I was knee-high to a grasshopper at the time, so I was too short to do well at the game.

Jack Reedassle, Bill McElroy and Hal Will with airplane models on Bow Lake (now SeaTac) airport runway before airport completion. Courtesy of Hal Will.

Model Airplanes

After 1938, when our family moved to 2109 Condon Way West at the foot of West Boston Street, we built airplane models with balsa frames and tissue-paper coverings. Some were gliders and others had rubber-band-powered propellers. Bill McElroy was the model-plane expert in our crowd. He would bring some of his models to our neighborhood to fly. The steep West Boston Street hill in front of our house was a good gliding spot, as was our back porch.

Sometimes, when models became banged up or fell from favor for any reason, the destructive side of our personalities surfaced. We would light the nose on fire and launch the plane where it would glide to a fiery end. If we could find a firecracker, we'd glue it to a wing root so the fire also ended with a bang and a collapsed wing. Of course, we always imagined the planes were German or Japanese. (The Germans had started their aggression in Europe as well as the Holocaust, and were at war with Great Britain and our other allies. And even before the Pearl Harbor attack in December 1941, many Americans despised the Japanese war machine for its atrocities against the Chinese.)

Fly-powered Airplanes

We went through a phase of model building when we discovered how to make tiny gliders with a wingspan of about 2 inches and a stick body of about 1 inch long. We cut bamboo slivers and glued them in the outline of the wing. We then poured glue on the surface of some water in a basin. The glue formed a very thin film on the water that would stick on the wing when the glider was raised from the water under the film. The glider was useless without a motor, however.

So, we would very carefully put our tiny gliders in matchboxes for protection and head for the drugstore with a tube of quick-drying glue. The drugstore was a good source of flies, and always provided an audience. We'd sit at the soda fountain and look for big flies. If they would land, we knew how to catch them without hurting them. It then took two people to get the glider ready and attach the "motor." A drop of glue had to be placed on the front end of the fuselage stick then the glue drop had to be touched quickly to the back of the fly between its wings. With a lot of luck and a strong fly, the glider would buzz to the ceiling area until the fly was pooped. The novel aircraft would then glide while the fly rested, then buzz away again. This fad was quite labor intensive and full of failures, so it didn't last very long. Dick Werttemberger, the drugstore proprietor, was happy it didn't catch on for any extended period of time.

Artist: Hal Will.

The "Quicksilver" Bonanza

One of our acquaintances who lived near the water tower discovered a puddle of mercury beneath the tower. He told us about it and the "rush" was on. For some reason, boys are fascinated by mercury, which we knew as "quicksilver." Needless to say, there was an immediate "quicksilver rush." We invented all sorts of ways to play with the shiny liquid metal. We tried to pick it up, we made little channels in the dirt to let it flow to another area, and we coated metal objects with it. We turned every penny we could acquire into slippery, dime-like silver coins. This sport was brief because someone captured all of the quicksilver and took it home.

We hear of the dangers of mercury poisoning now, but then we just blissfully enjoyed its unique properties and lived through it. Neither my brother Ed nor I know to this day why it was there, where it came from, or where it went.

Plays for the Playfield

I remember that some amateur theatrical productions were staged to raise money in 1939 to build the playfield between 32nd and 34th avenues, just north of the business district on West McGraw Street. Frances Atherton, a music teacher, local voluntary talent scout and musical director, recruited performers from all age groups, from grandmothers to grandchildren, for these musical extravaganzas. There were magic acts, minstrel acts, young dancing groups, various other skits, and of course, "The Mother Singers." Many of our moms participated despite teasing by their families. The dignified title quickly eroded to "The Momma Singers" and that is how they were known all over Magnolia.

Harmonica and Trumpet Lessons

Mrs. Atherton lived in our neighborhood and tried very hard to form a kids' harmonica band, or at least to teach some of us to play some tunes on the harmonica. She didn't charge for lessons, but we had to buy a harmonica of modest value.

The Dawsons were neighbors on Condon Way West and were good friends of my folks. Their son Dick was a buddy of my brother Ed. Mr. "Gene" Dawson played the trumpet and insisted that I had the lips of a trumpet player. I couldn't see anything unusual about my lips by looking in the mirror, but I did go to their house for a couple of lessons. I don't think I lasted for more than five sessions. I'm sure the Dawson family—the entire neighborhood, in fact—was glad the lessons didn't continue.

Bob Hansen played First Trumpet in the Queen Anne High School Band and orchestra from 1937 through 1939. Courtesy of Bob Hansen.

Bob Hansen Could *Play*

On the brighter side, Bob Hansen played the trumpet, and played it quite well. He played in grade school and while attending Queen Anne High School where he was in the All-City High School Band. He said that Mrs. Atherton wanted him to play in one of the plays she directed in the Magnolia School auditorium, but that he declined.

And, So Could Russ Langstaff

Russ Langstaff studied violin during his youth and played in the Queen Anne High School Orchestra. He continued to play thereafter, but not professionally.

Girls

I don't remember at what age girls became interesting *as girls* instead of being there simply to tease, avoid, or treat just like other guys. I do remember a small part of my very first situation that was thought of as a date. It was with Geri Marty, who lived just two blocks away and who I was beginning to think of *as a girl*. That was my problem. Neither Geri nor I remember what the occasion was, but I was to go to her house and walk with her three blocks up to Magnolia School for some function. I set out from home hearing Mom's last words about gentlemanly behavior. By the time I arrived at Geri's house, all I could remember was that I should walk on the side of the girl toward the street to protect her from danger. I wasn't told how far toward the street to place myself, so, while she was walking on the sidewalk, I was about 5 feet way—almost in the gutter. Neither of us remembers any more about the episode.

Jean Allyn still remembers the time Bob Jeffery threw her hat in the bushes on the way to school. If he'd been walking five feet from her, that would not have happened![18]

I think it was probably in the seventh or eighth grades that girls started being a distraction to us. And, they still are.

MISCHIEF, MISTAKES AND DUMB STUNTS

Too Young to Drive

Kids, especially boys, can't wait until they reach 16 to be licensed to drive a car. It might have been easier to drive without a license on Magnolia in the 1930s than it would be today. Many of the dirt roads and trails hardly qualified as "official" streets. A motorcycle policeman named Rogge tried to discourage such activity on Magnolia, with only occasional success.

Bob Walker was an older resident who always seemed to have interesting cars. Most of us remember he had a Cord sports car. We all remember that the cowboy actor Tom Mix was killed driving a similar Cord. Bob also had a Model-T Ford that Tom Fraser wanted to try out at Mel Bedall's Gilmore service station on West McGraw Street and 32nd Avenue West. The trouble was, Tommy hadn't mastered the unique Model-T transmission pedals and almost drove through the building. He found the correct pedal needed to stop just in time.

Mr. Walker also had an old open roadster that he was trying to run on kerosene. He rigged up valves on the dashboard to switch from gasoline to kerosene after the engine was hot. I witnessed one of his tests when he switched to kerosene going down the West

Tom Fraser in his new Cub Scout uniform.
Courtesy of Tom Fraser.

McGraw Street hill from 28th Avenue West. White smoke spewed from the exhaust pipe as he sputtered past the stores only to come to a wheezing stop before he reached 34th Avenue West. That was probably the end of the kerosene fuel experiment.

Larry Woods delivered goods in his Model-A Ford for his employer, the Magnolia Pharmacy, so it was often parked on 33rd Avenue West facing the west side of the store. My brother Ed liked to sit in cars and pretend that he was driving. One day while "pretending" in Larry's car, Ed somehow got it started and hit the drugstore wall, emptying the shelves of merchandise. Somehow, Ed survived the displeasure of Larry and storeowner, Dick Werttemberger.

To work off his resulting debt, Ed did janitorial chores in the drugstore. This involved sweeping the floors with a sawdust compound. Dick carefully directed Ed to the box of compound he was to use for the job. Dipping his hands into the sawdust mixture, Ed discovered too late that he had put his hands into the resident cat's private bathroom. Dick was always joking around like that.

BB Guns

Daisy Air Rifles, more commonly known as "BB" guns, became more common as boys earned enough spending money to afford them. Bob Shrewsbury remembers the sport of shooting at streetlights, while Patty Jephcott reports that Doug Clark used her family's porch light for target practice from his house across the street. There were some BB gun wars and there were accidents. One local youngster permanently lost the sight in one eye from a stray BB.

Dodging Cars

Tom Fraser and his neighborhood friends invented an even more dangerous sport than shooting BB guns. They had a contest to see who could be last to dash across the street in front of an approaching car. Tom reports that he was the champion, until his father caught him in the act and used a length of rubber hose on his bottom to influence his behavior.

Tanning Sherm and Shirley

"Seat-of-the-pants" punishment was experienced by Sherm Sloan and his younger sister Shirley after the two of them decided to pick on passing neighbor girls by calling them names and throwing clumps of dirt at them. Unfortunately, their targets were daughters of a customs agent. Sherm's father was an import agent whose job depended upon working very closely with customs. Mr. Sloan gave the two aggressors "pants down" punishment in the house.

Preschool portrait of Sherman Sloan Jr. Courtesy of Sherman Sloan Jr.

Construction Train Runaway

Among the more dangerous and stupid activities in which I was involved was fooling around with a string of narrow-gauge railroad cars. They were being used to move dirt at the playfield site. It was between 33rd and 34th avenues just north of the West McGraw Street business district. The cars were on a track about two blocks long running from a little engine shack at the low end to high ground at the north end. The construction crew made the mistake of leaving the string of cars at the high end of the track when they quit for the day. They should have known better! There were probably about 10 boys involved in this stunt. Most of them were older than I. All we had to do was take the blocks out from under the wheels of the lead car and give the string a healthy push to get it started. Once it was moving, nobody could stop it. It went down the hill for two blocks hitting the engine shack. I don't remember the outcome of the runaway rail cars because I was probably running for home as fast as I could.

Free Fireworks

Bob Clark told me of Hitt Fireworks Company, located near Interbay, that had a fire. I learned mainly of the aftermath when the soggy inventory, ruined by water from the fire fighting, was thrown out at the Interbay landfill. Some of Bob's friends had retrieved a bountiful supply for themselves. He recalls an open steel barrel with a fire burning in it at the top of the West Dravus Street hill. The kids would stand around and lob fireworks into the barrel and wait for the result. This apparently entertained them for some time.

Alphabetized name list for Magnolia School 1940 graduation: Jean Allyn, Bob Arnett, Gudmund Berg, Chuck Burkland, Virginia Burns, Darcy Clawson, Joyce Cutter, Wally Dash, Petra Debuque, Hugh Degler, Don Douglas, Dorothy Flakstad, Tom Fraser, Barbara Graben, Trava House, Robert Jeffery, Patricia Jephcott, Betty Johnson, Robert Johnson, Carol A. Jones, Jimmy Lee, Milton LeJune, Rayjean Marshall, Jean Martin, Geri Marty, Bill McElroy, Laurence Minard, Carl Molander, Vivian Monsey, Margery Montgomery, Nancy Jane Norton, Dorothy Ohde, Elizabeth Owen, Shirley Peck, Patty Punett, Gloryann Rishel, Alice Jean Robson, Bud Sandvigen, Georgia Schwartz, Iris Sharton, Louis Sheldahl, Hal Will, Robert Winder.

Horse On the Balcony

Bob Clark and my brother Ed each recalled a Halloween prank at the large house on the southwest corner of 28th Avenue West and West Dravus Street. Several people had lived in the house, but it eventually belonged to the Magnolia Presbyterian Church. It was probably vacant on that Halloween. Some boys led an old horse into the house, up the stairs to the second floor, then out on a balcony at the front of the house. There are conflicting accounts of how the horse was returned to solid ground, but it obviously would have caused quite a stir in the neighborhood.

Homing Pigeons

Laury Minard and a Magnolia School classmate, Carl Molander, had an interesting experience with pigeons. Carl's dad built a screened aviary at his house so that Carl could keep some birds. Mr. Molander was an engineer for the Great Northern Railway, so Carl was familiar with the railroad yard at Interbay, and he knew the pigeon population there. Laury and Carl set out to "acquire" some pigeons for the new aviary. They purchased a box of chicken feed, then located an empty boxcar on a siding. A trail of feed was sown leading to the open door of the car and a tempting supply was scattered on the floor inside. The pigeons took the bait and a fair number congregated inside the car. The boys then went into action. Carl climbed into the car with an empty potato sack then Laury pushed the door shut. There was a lot of commotion inside the car as Carl worked at filling the sack with unwilling birds. Finally, he signaled Laury to open the door and he emerged with the sack of unhappy pigeons. The boys took the birds to the aviary and pondered how to make them into homing pigeons. They eventually released them to see if they would "home." They did. They went "home" to the railroad yard.

Courtesy of Hall Will.

Glider

Al Jones remembers that an officer at Fort Lawton had a glider that he wanted to launch from the top of the hill by Officers' Row down over the large parade ground below. The officer picked 15 to 20 husky volunteers from the group that had assembled to man the towrope for the downhill run. He picked young Al and another kid as the likely lads to pull down on a rope at the tail to hold the nose of the glider up for takeoff. The pilot boarded his glider and gave the signal for the men to run down the hill with the towrope. Nobody told Al when to let go, so he didn't. He almost had his first in a long career of flights, but instead he was dragged down the hill and the glider stalled, then crashed. The pilot was very unhappy, so Al made a hasty departure.

Brothers Norm and Al Jones in Scout uniforms about 1930. Courtesy of Al Jones.

Fire-Fighting

The Magnolia Firehouse, Station 41, was built about 1933, and is still located near the intersection of 34th Avenue West and West McGraw Street. As any normal kids would be, we were attracted to the station when the truck was out in front. It was very shiny, very red and very impressive. The only fireman I remember at Station 41 was the one who always seemed to drive the truck. He was nicknamed Tiny, undoubtedly for his build. He must have weighed 250 pounds or more. I am thankful that we had a fire station so close to our play area.

Smudge Pots and Torches

Shortly after our family moved two blocks to a different rental house at 2109 Condon Way in 1938, there was a period of major water and sewer-line work all around the Bluff in preparation for concrete paving. Several of my neighbor friends and I became interested in the work centered around the intersection at 29th Avenue West and West Boston Street. This was one block up the steep Boston Street hill from our house. There were deep trenches down the middle of the streets radiating from this intersection, with piles of dirt everywhere. These trenches and dirt piles were an attractive playground for the neighborhood boys.

Five or six of us were there one evening. We had to wait until the workmen left at quitting time. It must have been winter because it was already dark when they departed. The workers left burning "smudge pots" around the ditches and on the dirt piles to warn people away from the hazards. These smudge pots were round, black metal containers of kerosene about 8 inches in diameter with a burning wick sticking out of the top. They looked just like comic-strip bombs. We found that it was fun to carry torches as we crawled through the ditches. We found old newspapers, rolled them up, then lit them from any smudge pot. However, they didn't burn very brightly or stay lit very well.

The Ditch Digger

The gasoline ditch digger that dug the trenches was parked at the southwest corner of the intersection, near the Woodruff family's house. Some of us discovered that the ditch digger's gas tank was dripping into a puddle on a metal pan below. Newspapers dipped in the puddle made a much better torch. Most of us were pretty careful with our new discovery. However, the youngest participant, Jimmy McGovern, went back to the gasoline puddle with a torch that was still glowing. The puddle ignited, enveloping the gas tank above it.

That Ended Our Play!

We could sense that something terrible was going to happen, so we each ran toward the security of our respective homes. I can still see Mrs. Woodruff standing on her back porch in the orange glow less than 30 feet away from the fire yelling something at us. Her house and her family were in real danger. It was inevitable that the gas tank would blow. I ran down the hill and into the front door of our house as fast as I could, probably yelling for Mom. Ed and Mom were home, but I don't think Pop was home from work yet. I don't know who phoned the fire department, but fortunately someone did. It wasn't as simple as dialing "911" in those days. A less memorable number was looked up and dialed on a slow rotary dial phone. Mom came out of the kitchen to see what I was yelling about as I cowered behind the living room window. She was horrified to see the neighborhood bathed in the orange glow. I think she got to the front door in time to see the gas tank erupt. Fortunately the flames went upward more than sideways, so the Woodruffs' house didn't ignite. It was more of a "Whoom" than a "Boom." I can still hear myself saying, "Jimmy did it. Jimmy did it."

Hal Will about 1938 when the ditch digger episode unfolded. Courtesy of Hall Will.

The Aftermath

We could hear the fire truck's siren from the time it left the station, which fortunately was only six or seven blocks away. It seems that the fire department extinguished the fire quickly, but my recollection of the aftermath is really quite incomplete. I don't remember punishment, but I sure deserved to be grounded or under house arrest or something. Although Mrs. Woodruff knew all of us involved, she either didn't name us or the fire department didn't choose to follow up with us. I don't think any official ever came to our house to interrogate me. I sure was ready to say, "Jimmy did it!" I think I avoided that intersection, and the possible wrath of the Woodruffs, for a long time afterward.

"THE DRUG STORE"

What is now Tully's Coffee at the southeast corner of 33rd Avenue West and West McGraw Street occupies the space we knew as "the Drug Store," which was originally Craigen's Pharmacy, one of the first businesses in the area. The owner's daughter, Janice Craigen, was in my third grade class but moved off the Bluff when her parents sold the store during the mid-1930s.

When Dick Werttemberger became the new owner, he renamed the business the Magnolia Pharmacy. It was like a good old-fashioned drug store and soda fountain that Norman Rockwell might have featured in one of his Saturday Evening Post *cover illustrations. Many of us remember Rosie, Fern, Larry Woods, and Art Harding who worked there in the late 1930s.*

"The Drug Store" was the place to meet friends or pass the time. Mr. Werttemberger was an outgoing person with a great sense of humor and a gift for tolerating, yet controlling, the kids that frequented his establishment. His hearty laugh could be heard throughout the store. Although none of us had a lot of loose change, his soda fountain managed to separate us from much of it. Ice-cream cones, sodas, floats and malts were popular fare. Bob Hansen fondly remembers pineapple shakes as one his favorites. Bob Jeffery recalls an ice-cream sundae called "Lucky Mondays" which was served with a doily that, when moistened, revealed if the sundae was free. Dick Werttemberger had a special talent with ice-cream cones. When a customer was innocently reaching to take a cone from his outstretched hand, it might be suddenly lowered just enough for the customer's hand to grab the ice-cream instead of the cone. The timing was usually perfect. He caught all of the regular cone buyers at one time or another when they least expected it. This trick always ended with much loud laughter.

The front door opening onto McGraw Street used to be dead center, with magazine racks below the large windows on each side of the door. Comic books consumed the east side while anything more serious was neatly displayed on the west side. There wasn't much floor space between the comic books and the end of the soda fountain, but it was often filled with kids reading the comics, while buying very few. When the kids became too loud or too numerous, Dick would suggest they go outside and play in the street so that his "paying" customers could have some peace and quiet.

Displayed amongst the more serious magazines was Esquire. *We boys would often sidle over and sneak a peek at the pin-up-girl painting in each monthly issue. These were created by artists Petty and Vargas and were very pleasing to our young eyes. "Put the magazine down or I'll call your mother!" Mr. Werttemberger would sometimes yell from the back of the store if he noticed us looking at* Esquire. *He knew all of us by name, as well as our mothers, so we believed his threat.*

Repeat Offender

Unfortunately, I was involved in an earlier incident requiring the fire truck. Brother Ed, Clyde Holcomb, Dick Dawson, Ray and Eugene Petrich and I, plus others, often played in "our" two-block square area of woods that we entered at the west end of Newton Street. I think a few of us were trying to cook potatoes in a rock-lined pit that we had already heated with a small campfire. It may have been something we heard about in Cubs or Scouts. I only remember two things about the incident: my potato was burned on one side and raw on the other, and after we left the woods there was a fire where we had been. Again, someone called the fire department and we could hear the siren as it left the station in the Valley. The firemen saved our woods for us and we learned a fire safety lesson. We kept out of sight until the fire truck left.

The Smokehouse

Russ Langstaff and his friends used to swim down under the Great Northern Railway Bridge near the Locks. He recalls an incident when he was swimming from Mr. Mike Bergen's smokehouse float with the Peterson boys. The boys' antics tipped the float sufficiently to topple the smokehouse into the bay. Russ can still see the long-bearded and very angry Mr. Bergen attempting to chase them. Youth was in their favor, so they escaped his wrath that day.

EARNING MONEY

All of us boys had experiences earning money during our grade school years and on into high school. Virtually all of us had paper routes and some had some unusual ways of earning money.

Bob Hansen had *Seattle Post-Intelligencer* paper routes from 1936 to 1939. Sherm Sloan had one route which was two blocks wide from 34th to 36th Avenue West, extending from Thompson's Grocery at 34th Avenue West and West Emerson Street all of the way to Salmon Bay. He served houseboats inside the Locks and remembers they were faithful payers. His second route was from 27th Avenue West to 32nd, extending from West Blaine Street to West Armour Street. Sherm also worked at Mel Bedall's Gilmore service station.

This canvas magazine delivery bag identified me as an official representative of these magazines even though I was only knee high to a grasshopper at this stage of my business career. Photo by Monica Wooton, 2000.

One of my first jobs was selling the *Saturday Evening Post, Ladies Home Journal, Country Gentleman*, and *Liberty* magazines. I still have my canvas shoulder bag.

In 1941, I had a *Seattle Times* route that covered 34th Avenue West to Montavista Place West and West McGraw Street to West Armour Street. Home building was progressing at a rapid pace so I easily won prizes for signing up new customers. I recall a "carrier special" train trip to Vancouver, B. C., and a boat trip to Victoria on the *Princess Alice* that I won from the *Times*. My buddy Clyde took over that route in 1942 when I created a new route on the emerging Navy Base at Smith Cove.

Bob's Unique Business

Bob Shrewsbury also sold the *Post* and *Journal* at an early age. Bob's *Seattle Times* paper route included the area from 28th Avenue West to Thorndyke Avenue West and West Blaine Street to West Armour Street. He remembers that it included just 40 customers although it covered many square blocks.

That job was clean compared to an earlier endeavor selling cow manure for fertilizer. Bob and Frankie Pollard would fill potato sacks with dry cow droppings at the dairies and sell a bag for 50 cents to neighborhood customers. Delivery was made with a rickety wooden wagon that had to be nursed along the rough unpaved roads in the area at that time. This business faltered when they were attempting to fill a special order for "wet" droppings at 75 cents a bag, requested by Bob Hansen's mother.

The destination was many blocks from the dairy, so they attempted to deliver two bags in one trip. They put two empty bags in the wagon, and wheeled it around the pasture collecting wet ones. By the time they struggled uphill out of the dairy in the vicinity of West Armour Street, the heavy cargo was taking its toll on the boys as well as on the wagon. Before they reached 28th Avenue West, where they would have an eight-block downhill run to West Newton Street, the wooden bottom broke out of the wagon and the bracing collapsed. The final disposition of Mrs. Hansen's order is not clear, but they went out of business on the spot.

Bob Shrewsbury during grade school years. Courtesy of Bob Shrewsbury.

Baggage Smashers

Sherm Sloan's father was an import agent for the American Mail Line whose ships to the Orient operated out of Pier 41 at Smith Cove. Sherm visited the area frequently with his dad. Mr. Chappell, the janitor at the company office on the pier, hired the people who assisted passengers with their luggage from the ships, through customs, and then to waiting cars, taxis or buses. For some reason, these people were called "baggage smashers" and for some reason Mr. Chappell hired Sherm. It was an interesting experience, for the job entailed opening each piece of luggage for customs and then re-packing it after the inspectors had done their work. During this time period, many people were returning to the US from China to flee Japanese aggression on the mainland, so some had all of their possessions to take through the inspection process. Sherm recalls spending six hours helping one party and receiving a sizable tip for his efforts.

Sherm also told of going to Smith Cove with friends Chuck Osborn, Dean Mitchell, Fred Grauberger and Fred's brother Dave. They sometimes walked down the 23rd Avenue trestle and then slid down a supporting timber as a shortcut to ground level. On one such descent, Chuck's pants got hung up on a nail in a place that he couldn't reach to untangle himself. The other boys had to climb back up to lift him to freedom.

This group sometimes went to the salmon terminal on Pier 40 where they had watched workers putting labels on cans of salmon often enough to perform the job themselves. The boys were allowed to do so while the workers went outside for a smoke break. They were given some cans of salmon in return. This was a worthwhile reward during the Depression.

Russ Langstaff Remembers

Russ Langstaff had a *Seattle Times* paper route that covered a large but sparsely-settled area. It encompassed 28th Avenue West to 34th, from West Barrett Street to West Government Way. He remembers selling an "Extra" edition on the street as well as door-to-door when Will Rogers and Wiley Post were killed in an Alaska plane crash.

Russ remembers helping his father deliver coal during the Depression. Mr. Langstaff was a glazier for W. P. Fuller Company. His company retained its employees during the tough times by having them work one week on and one week off. Mr. Langstaff acquired two surplus white trucks from his employer. One was a 1.5-ton and the other a 4-ton, of about

American Mail Line's *passenger ship President Grant arriving at Smith Cove's Pier 41 from the Orient in the late 1930s. "Baggage smashers" were hired to assist passengers through customs with their luggage.* Seattle Post-Intelligencer Collection, Museum of History and Industry, #124021.

1923 vintage. On his off weeks, he would go to various local coal mines such as Newcastle, Tiger Mountain and Cedar Mountain, where he could buy their product for $2 a ton. He would then bag and sell it on Magnolia for $4 a ton.

Russ used to accompany his father to the Fort Lawton rifle range when he was about 10. He remembers "pulling targets" in the pits. Sometimes the shooters would pay for the service. Russ also participated as a shooter. The rifle range area is now a parking lot at Discovery Park.

Bottle deposits

Our wooded areas had all been logged and probably had at least 20 years of new growth of mostly alder, maple, madrone and assorted brush. The City had roughly graded many of the future streets through the woods, but brush had almost hidden them again. These overgrown roads were often used as lovers' lanes. Those in the know could drive in far enough to be hidden by the brush and consider themselves all alone. As Clyde and I became "worldly wise" about the acres of woods within our range of exploration, we learned the location of the lovers' lanes. We could depend on finding discarded beer bottles and other things. Some of the most popular spots were around the stable and along Clise Place West. These spots were within a few blocks of the grocery and drug stores. There was a deposit on beer bottles so they were worth money when returned to the grocery stores. "Stubbies" (the short 12-ounce beer bottles at that time) were worth 2 cents and the rarer quart bottles were worth a whole nickel. The bottles were usually dirty or sticky and contained dead bugs. It was obvious that beetles loved beer, and at least they died happy. The grocers weren't thrilled to see us coming in with our bounty, but they always gave us the appropriate refund. A bag full of bottles could buy a few sodas, cones or comic books.

Al and Horses, a Lawn Roller and Goat's Milk

Al Jones recalled taking care of some horses in partnership with Bob Clark. They arranged grazing and stable space at a dairy in Pleasant Valley. The business failed when the horses got loose and ruined somebody's lawn, and Al's father had to pay for some repairs. On another occasion, Al got in trouble at home when he sold his father's water-filled lawn roller to Roy Chambers at Magnolia Hardware for $5, thinking his father didn't use it anymore. He was badly mistaken. His father said, in no uncertain terms, "Get it back!" So Al had to buy it back from Roy Chambers. Mr. Chamber's son Jack ran the Gilmore service station for a while and Al worked there for him at that time. Al and Sherm Sloan told how Johnny Gorman raised goats and sold goat milk from his mother's home between 27th Avenue West and Whalley Place.

Epilogue

Al Jones learned to fly out of Boeing Field in 1938. He joined the Royal Canadian Air Force in 1939 and flew 40 missions as a bomber pilot over Europe and then transferred to the US Air Force and flew 48 missions as a night-fighter pilot, also over Europe. Al retired from the Army Air Corps as a colonel and command pilot. Following World War II, he flew for several non-scheduled airlines for about 10 years before going to Boeing as a test pilot, then instructor for customer airline pilots. He retired from Boeing in 1981 after 25 years of service with the company.

After World War II Coast Guard service, *Bob Shrewsbury* worked on tugs and then bought one himself. Two of the tugs that Bob used to observe as a kid at the Washington Tug & Barge Company moorage at Smith Cove were the Bee and the Triumph. Early on, Bob bought both of those boats. He created Western Towboat Company that has grown into a significant and respected part of the Puget Sound, West Coast and Alaska towboat fleet later managed by his two sons.

After graduation from Queen Anne in 1944 and serving in the US Navy, *Tom Fraser* followed in his father's footsteps operating a successful used-car business most of his working life.

Sherm Sloan graduated from Queen Anne High in 1940 and entered the US Marine Corps the same year. He was in a tank company most of the time serving in the Atlantic then South Pacific areas. Sherm was discharged in 1945 after five years of service. After several temporary jobs, he joined the Kroll Map Company where he worked for 47 years, retiring as President.

Most of these happy boys are unidentified but they are friends and neighbors of Al Jones about 1927. Courtesy of Al Jones.

Bob Hansen studied the sheet-metal trade at Edison Technical School for two years following his 1938 graduation from Queen Anne High. He then worked for Puget Sound Sheet Metal Company on war-related production for four years. He then entered the US Navy for two years, after which he became "Mr. Sheet Metal," instructing at Edison until retirement.

Russ Langstaff served on Navy minesweepers from 1944 to 1946, after which he worked as engineer for Puget Sound Tug & Barge. He barely survived the sinking of the tug Neptune off the Columbia River Bar. He then worked for the City of Seattle's Parks Department for 30 years until retirement in 1983.

After graduating from Queen Anne High School in 1944, Hal Will served on US Army tugs in the South Pacific, then pursued photography schooling and work after discharge. Polio in 1949 changed his occupation to electronics with the John Fluke Manufacturing Company. He retired from Fluke in 1998 after 43 of years service.

Museum of History and Industry, #86.5.12.754

Hal's family moved to Magnolia from the University District in 1929, when he was about three years of age. With the exception of military-service years, he remained a Magnolia resident until 1967 when, with his wife Shirley, he moved to their present home in the Ballard district overlooking Shilshole Bay and the north end of Magnolia Bluff.

The Boettigers of Lawton Wood

By Hal Will

Hal Will writes of friendships with President Franklin Roosevelt's grandchildren from the perspective of contemporary grade-school classmates. Wayne Gray writes of his friendship during the same period but from the perspective of a slightly older, next-door neighbor.

Playmates

President Franklin D. Roosevelt's daughter, Anna moved into the Grant House in Lawton Wood, at the northernmost point of Magnolia Bluff. It was, and still is, on a bluff facing north on Shilshole Bay. Her husband John Boettiger had taken over as publisher of the *Seattle Post-Intelligencer,* and Anna was the Women's Editor. She had two children from a former marriage to a man by the name of Dall. In 1937, the children were enrolled in Magnolia School. The daughter Eleanor, nicknamed Sisty, was about 10 at the time, while her younger brother Curtis, nicknamed Buzzy, was about eight. Their presence at school added considerable activity since they were escorted, chaperoned, chauffeured and watched over constantly by two or three Secret Service men. Of course, grade-school kids were in awe of the company of "G-men" at recess and lunch. I don't recall seeing them in the classrooms, however.

"FDR" visited Seattle in 1937. His motorcade visited Magnolia School, since his grandchildren were students there. The whole school lined up out in front to wave as he passed. Sisty and Buzzy may have been in the car with him, but I don't remember.

Patty Jephcott Timberlake remembers inviting Sisty to her Halloween party. Sisty's grandmother, Eleanor Roosevelt, was in town, so she attended with Sisty and the appropriate number of Secret Service agents to keep the Jephcott residence at 3021 27th Avenue West secure.

My good friend, Dean Phelps, and I were invited to Lawton Wood to play with Buzzy, so periodically we would walk there together. I'm not sure if Buzzy or the G-men selected Dean and me as acceptable playmates, and I don't recall any other boys at the house when we were there. While our "play" at Buzzy's house isn't too memorable, I do remember his standard-gauge Lionel train. He had all of the accessories such as crossing gates that worked, remote-controlled switches, a depot with a man who waved a lantern when the train passed and more. We could spend a lot of time with that train. Buzzy's family had two beautiful Irish setters that were fun to play with and there was a large lawn where they could run. However, we couldn't leave the yard to play in the nearby creek or woods.

Nancy Norton Minard remembers attending Sisty's birthday party in Lawton Wood and Mrs. Roosevelt was at the party. Dean and I went to one of Buzzy's birthday parties, and Mrs. Roosevelt was also there. When I got home, my folks asked all about the party. When I told them I sat next to Mrs. Roosevelt while we had ice cream and cake, they quizzed me about her. "She's not very good looking, but she was real nice," I replied. My dad was not a Roosevelt fan by any means, but he was glad to hear that she was "real nice."

The 1937 Christmas at the Boettiger house in Lawton Wood with Eleanor Roosevelt handing out gifts to her grandchildren, Curtis 'Buzzy' Dall on her left and Eleanor 'Sisty' Dall on her right. Neighbor youngsters were included and given gifts.

Author Wayne Gray is the tallest boy at the back. His younger brother Paul is at the back behind Mrs. Roosevelt. Seattle Post-Intelligencer Collection, Museum of History and Industry, #25027.

A Glimpse of Eleanor and Franklin

By Wayne Gray

During the Depression years of the 1930s, Franklin D. Roosevelt was President. In the fall of 1936, his daughter Anna and her new husband moved from Washington, D.C. to Seattle where he operated the *Seattle Post-Intelligencer*. The house they leased in Lawton Wood, near Fort Lawton, was across the road from where my brother and I grew up. He was 13 at the time, and I was a year older.

On nice days, Anna's two children Sisty and Buzzy would be outdoors playing— always under the close watch of a Secret Serviceman. As we gradually got acquainted we were allowed to join them in games of baseball, tag and roller skating on their sidewalk. When it rained and the children couldn't come outdoors, we sometimes would be invited to sit in one of the "G-man's" car with him while he watched over the household. Tom Carmody was his name and he would spin us yarns about his experiences.

In May 1937, the President's wife Eleanor made a trip by plane to Seattle to visit her daughter and her family. She also visited our home and gardens and wrote of it in her daily newspaper column, "My Day," which appeared in all Hearst newspapers including the *Seattle Post-Intelligencer*.

At Christmas of the same year, Mrs. Roosevelt returned to Seattle. On that Christmas day, in the evening, the neighborhood playmates were invited to a party. We met this gracious and pleasant lady who later was on her knees handing out gifts to each of us. Her manner of speech was something very new to us. However, she and her family were under close guard at all times, and we were not around long enough to do more than meet her, have a couple of pictures taken, enjoy some refreshments, and say our goodbyes.

A month later, in late January 1938, while she and the President were on a train trip of the country, they visited their Seattle family. This was written about in another "My Day" column. This trip was extremely well-guarded by several Secret Servicemen and Seattle police officers. We did not get to meet the President, but did manage to see them all ride by on an outing with Buzzy riding on his grandfather's lap in the front seat of the open touring car, and Sisty in a jump-seat, while their mother and grandmother were in the back seat. They were all looking and smiling at the camera, but no one was waving. A day or so later Mrs. Roosevelt was on a plane for New York and the presidential party returned to Washington, D.C. by train.

The Lawton Wood house occupied by the Boettigers in 1937 and now owned by the Abendroth family. In my memory, it hasn't changed much in 63 years. Photo by Hal Will, 2000.

The Village

By Joan Santucci

The businessmen who bought lots on West McGraw Street before it was even paved surely knew what they were doing. Since it was first developed after 1923, the area known as "the Village" has been home to about 400 businesses or services. At first, the half dozen or so of them were centered on McGraw Street. By 2000, the Village expanded on the south to West Lynn Street, north to West Ray Street, west to 35th Avenue West and east to 31st Avenue West.

At the time Seattle's original zoning ordinance was adopted, some lots on West McGraw Street were zoned for business. By 1925, there were four stores open for business: Craigen's Magnolia Pharmacy, Jorgenson's Market, Howard T. Lewis Real Estate and Scott's Service Station on McGraw Street.[1] On April 1, 1927, Magnolia Hardware opened and joined the new business district. Roy Chambers erected the two-story building that housed the hardware store on the street level and his family's living quarters on the second floor.

According to his sons, Ralph and Jack, Roy's business was so poor during the Depression years that he had to go to work for Ernst Hardware, leaving his wife Ruth to run the store. Roy also built the Magnolia Lumber Store across the street that he both leased out and operated himself at various times.[2]

Denton and Delorez Rossell bought the building in 1980 and remodeled it to house Eleganza Ltd. which sells reproductions of sculptural masterpieces. Denton remembers the day when a distinguished looking gentleman came in and he thought to himself, "Here's someone who will appreciate what we're doing." Denton showed him around the new shop. On leaving, the man remarked, "I sure wish we had the old lumber yard back."[3]

Magnolians have always had to eat, so it is not surprising that the first business on the newly-platted West McGraw Street was Jorgensen's Carleton Park Grocery, which opened in 1925. Thompson's Grocery had existed since 1909, but it was located at 34th Avenue West and West Emerson Street, well north of what evolved into the Village.[4]

By 1933, Magnolia's shopping district had grown to include two grocery stores, a dry cleaner and a barbershop.[5] Despite economic hard times, Magnolia's business district continued to expand.

The first of a number of CAFFÈ Appasionatos in the Seattle area, the Magnolia store is nestled in the heart of the Village on West McGraw Street. Photo: Monica Wooton, 2000.

This aerial view featuring West McGraw Street was taken sometime in the 1930s. Note the start of Village businesses in lower left corner. Courtesy of UW Special Collections Archives.

Joseph and Laura Jacobson moved with their sons Russell and Ray from South Dakota. They opened Jacobson Brothers Grocery in 1936. After eighteen years in business, they sold it and it was renamed Blue Ribbon Foods. Safeway moved into Magnolia in the late 1930s to the site at 34th West and West McGraw where the library and several banks would at some point settle. It is now home to Key Bank.

Magnolia's first public house, beloved to many, was the Green Light Tavern, which moved into the Village in the 1930s. It evolved into the Leprechaun, then Ernie's, and then into the Blackthorne Village Pub, and is now simply The Pub—located on West McGraw Street in half of the space formerly occupied by the Magnolia Pharmacy.

During the 1940s, the Village flourished, even as Magnolia men and women marched off to war. It was during this time that the first businesses with "Village" in their names appeared. It seems that references to Magnolia's shopping area as "the Village" or "Magnolia Village" developed casually. By 1948 we had Village Auto Service, Village Beauty Salon, Village Cleaners, Village Grill and Village Variety Store to name a few.

After it opened in 1943, the Magnolia Library skipped around the Village for many years in a constant quest for more space. The present branch located at 34th Avenue West and West Armour Street is not now in the Village proper, but its previous locations were all in the heart of the business district. It first opened on a part-time basis at 3200 West McGraw Street, thanks to a contribution of $300 from the Magnolia Community Club. Within three years the library moved to larger quarters at 3416 West McGraw Street. In 1959 the library relocated once again because of space considerations to the old Safeway building at 34th Avenue West and West McGraw Street. Finally, in 1963 the Seattle Public Library purchased the land at the present site and construction began in February 1964.[6] In 1966 The American Institute of Architects, in cooperation with The American Library Association and the National Book Committee, presented its First Honor award to Kirk, Wallace, McKinley, AIA Associates and the Seattle Public Library for the design of the new branch.[7]

One-day Watch Repair Service

One year Guarantee!

MAGNOLIA VILLAGE JEWELER
3209 W. McGraw AT 2-8510

Magnolia News, April 27, 1967.

The Magnolia Theatre opening in 1948 was cause for great excitement, especially among the youngsters who finally had a movie house in their own neighborhood. Those attending the first showing saw the hit move *Mr. Blandings Builds His Dream Home* starring Cary Grant and Myrna Loy.[8] Before Our Lady of Fatima Church was built, parish members attended Mass at the theater on Sunday mornings. Longtime Magnolia resident and parishioner Gloria LaRussa remembers falling asleep during Mass while sitting in one of those comfortable loge seats.[9]

The opening of the theater combined with the Magnolia Bowl, the Magnolia Ice Creamery, and Evelyn's Ice Creamery increased the area's entertainment opportunities. Alas, juvenile patronage was not enough to keep things going and all of these businesses eventually closed in the late 1960s. Washington Mutual built its Magnolia Branch on the old theater site, yet many Magnolians miss having a movie theater nearby for some Hollywood-style entertainment and easy parking.

Next to the Fire Station on 34th Avenue West, the theater which showed kids matinees on the weekends, was a haven for Magnolia youngsters. Photo by Ken Baxter. Courtesy Virginia Baxter. Circa 1960s.

The types of businesses in the Village have varied greatly with the times. By the late 1940s construction was booming and so were the seven real estate offices located in the Village. The increase in population also brought with it seven gas stations. Doctors, dentists, barbers and beauticians soon arrived to take care of the residents' personal needs. The 1940s also brought the money-men. In 1948 the Magnolia State Bank was the first to open on the Bluff. It eventually became the People's Bank Magnolia Branch. Since then, banks have come and gone, and/or changed their names. By 2000 it leveled off at three commercial banks to include Bank of America, Key Bank and US Bank. The Village is now home to two savings and loans banks: Washington Mutual and Washington Federal Savings.

There were not many eating establishments in the Village during its first forty years. The first on the scene were Tenny's and the Magnolia Bowl Snack Shop that opened in the 1940s.[10] Tenny's became GG's some time in the 1960s and in its present reincarnation is Szmania's opened in 1990. The boomer kids loved Cherrie's

Popular with many during its heyday, the Magnolia Bowl, before it closed, also featured slot car racing to the delight of Magnolia boys. Photo by Ken Baxter. Courtesy Virginia Baxter. Circa 1960s.

Delicatessen, and going with Mom to the Hickory Hut on 33rd Avenue West between West Wheeler Street and West McGraw Street as it was the only cafeteria-style restaurant ever located in the Village. It went out of business when the building complex was developed into medical and business offices in the 1980s.

Born in 1928, Bob Smith was raised in Magnolia and recalls delivering ice cream on his bicycle for the Magnolia Ice Creamery during the late 1930s. An enterprising young man, he also collected dried "cow pies" from the West Point Dairy to sell by the gunnysack to local gardeners. Bob also recalls that in 1938 he won a contest to name the new dry cleaners going in on West McGraw Street. Bob thought that since this business was going to be located

Magnolia Hardware is the oldest existing business in the Village. This photo was taken when it was located on West McGraw Street, but without its second story which had housed the original owner and his family. Photo by Ken Baxter. Courtesy Virginia Baxter. Circa 1960s.

Right: Magnolia News, April 27, 1967.

Honey, WE'VE GOT TO DO SOMETHING ABOUT THE HOUSE!

It's no problem — our one-stop paint-up, fix-up store is

MAGNOLIA LUMBER
Al Munro
3216 W. Wheeler   AT 2-2443

178

west of 34th Avenue West, in the area known as Carleton Park, a combination of names might work. That business thrived for many years as Carnolia Cleaners. In the late 1990s it merged with another well-known Seattle-area dry cleaners and is now known as Madison-Carnolia Cleaners. Smith has fond memories of swimming in Wolfe Creek and spending time at the Magnolia Pharmacy during his boyhood. He still remembers an item served at the fountain called a "Lucky Monday"—a chocolate soda topped off with a chocolate sundae with all the trimmings.[11]

In April 1946, the *Seattle Times* described the Village as resembling:

". . . a bustling Western town. The wide street has stores of every description to take care of the needs and desires of the residents. Bakeries, ice cream parlors, drug stores, variety shops, beauty salons, cleaner's establishments, hardware stores, radio repair stores, a branch of the public library, real estate offices and "super-markets" line McGraw Street in the section referred to by Magnolians as "The Village . . ."[12]

FOR RENT

NEW SOUNDPROOF OFFICES
In center of Magnolia Village. Rentals low as $37.50 per mo. Heat, light, water included.
Call AT 3-4560 Days
AT 2-7194 Eves.

Magnolia News,
April 27, 1967.

Magnolia Pharmacy got its first competition in 1946 when John Johnson opened J & J Pharmacy at the corner of West McGraw Street and 32nd Avenue West. In the 1950s, the two pharmacies were joined by Drug Fair around the corner on 32nd Avenue West. The latter changed to Thrifty Drugs, but it closed in the late 1970s. Bartell Drugs, a Seattle drug store chain, joined the community in the 1980s, initially at 32nd Avenue West and West Smith Street, the site of the old IGA Grocery and formerly the Big Bear Store. Bartell's business increased to the point that a new store was built at the site of the old Tradewell grocery store on 32nd Avenue West and West Lynn Street. By the end of the twentieth century, Bartell's was the only drug store remaining in the Village.

Located on 34th Avenue West, Thrifty Drugs was popular for its soda fountain. Photo by Ken Baxter. Courtesy Virginia Baxter. Circa 1960s.

Long time Magnolia resident, Patricia Forhan Taft, recalls a brief time when the Village extended to Magnolia Boulevard. According to Pat, one summer in the early 1940s, two of her sisters and a friend of theirs, all teenagers, decided to go into business for themselves by opening a concession stand. Somehow the girls, Kathleen "Tot" Forhan, Peggy Forhan, and Mary Ellen Currid, decided on Magnolia Boulevard as their business location. They applied for a business license and were issued a permit. Builder Pat Currid helped them construct a stand and hauled it to Magnolia Boulevard where they set it up right above Magnolia Park. They stocked their concession stand with pop, candy, ice cream, and dry ice. Local youngsters became their customers. Word got around about the three young entrepreneurs and eventually there was a newspaper article written about them. This brought them to the attention of a Magnolia resident who complained to the City of Seattle.

Arnold Rusch of Village Bakery putting the finishing touches on one of his wedding cakes. Courtesy of Hedy Rusch. Circa 1950s.

An inspector was sent out who then ordered the stand be moved into the park. No signs were allowed to advertise the change of location. This spelled the death knell for the fledgling business. The Forhan and Currid families then had a party to celebrate the girls' business venture and topped it off by eating all the leftovers from the stand.[13]

From 1949 to 1979, the Village Bakery, like a number of other Magnolia businesses, enjoyed a great reputation that went far beyond the boundaries of its neighborhood. It was owned and operated by Arnold and Hedy Rusch, Swiss immigrants who had both worked in New York at the 1940 World's Fair. They were brought to the Northwest to run the Swiss Bakery on Fifth Avenue in downtown Seattle. By 1949, they had saved enough to buy Binick's Electric Bakery at 3207 West McGraw Street. According to Hedy, Arnold was a gifted baker who could really stretch his ingredients if necessary and still turn out superior products. Besides serving Magnolia, they also did specialty baking for the Rainier Club, the Harbor Club, and a number of local golf and country clubs. Many a Magnolia bride fed a piece of Village Bakery cake to her groom on her wedding day.[14]

Magnolia's first post office was located in the back of Thompson's Grocery at 34th Avenue West and West Emerson Street. By 1933, the neighborhood had a post office that it shared with West Queen Anne, but it was located in Interbay. This meant a trip across the bridge just to buy some stamps. After much pressure was applied to "the other Washington," Magnolia's very own post office was put in the heart of the Village on the McGraw corridor in 1954.[15]

Over the years the Village has seen many specialty stores come and go. Some could not be supported, and others, such as Magnolia Hi-Fi, outgrew the neighborhood. One of the longtime stores, LeRoux's Men and Boys Wear, was opened in 1948 by Bud LeRoux. In 1955, Bud sold the store to Russ Jacobson of Jacobson's Grocery.

Jacobson went on to open the Magnolia Bowl which, like the grocery store, did not survive to do business in the twenty-first century. LeRoux's, however, is thriving and still doing business at the same location with the addition of a women's line of clothing as LeRoux Magnolia. (The boys' wear was dropped many years ago.)[16]

The business opening in the Village that seemed to have caused the biggest community uproar was the Washington State Liquor Store. There did not appear to be any middle ground; residents were either for it or against it. The Magnolia Community Club mounted a drive to oppose the Liquor Store based on what seems to be the fact that the existing tenant of the proposed store had lost his lease in a peremptory manner. The MCC felt that the tenant, Magnolia TV Service, was an ideal member of the business community that provided a valuable service to area residents.[17] The MCC received a lot of flak on this issue, both pro and con. In October 1959, one irate member wrote to the club president:

"Why should we have to drive all the way to Ballard or Queen Anne when we want to buy liquor? You're not going to dry up the world, so why not stop trying? Anyone who knows anything at all about alcoholics also knows they will get something to drink if they have crawl on their hands and knees to Oregon for it. Keeping a store out of Magnolia isn't helping anyone or anything excepting your conceit."

By 1978, Magnolia's Liquor Store reported receipts of $1.2-million—not bad for a community of approximately 20,000 persons.[18]

Any discussion of the history of the Village usually includes sharing fond memories of businesses such as Meredith's 5 and 10 Cent Store, (usually just referred to as "the Dime Store" or as "I. Meredith's" by some of the ladies), Cherrie's Delicatessen, Blue Ribbon Foods, and Magnolia Hi-Fi which started out as Magnolia Stationers and Camera. The baby boomers who grew up in Magnolia remember the Magnolia Theater, the Magnolia Bowling Alley, the Big Scoop, and the Magnolia Library at its second location at the corner of 34th Avenue West and West McGraw Street. Moms of the boomers shopped for the tots at Small Fry Shop and purchased outfits for themselves at Celia Jeanne and Miss Walker's Dress Shop. Dads, of course, did their local clothes shopping at Le Roux's Apparel for Men and Boys.

By the beginning of 2000, the Village was home to no less than 10 restaurants, not counting coffeehouses. Perhaps the biggest change in the make-up of Village eateries has been Seattle's growing addiction to espresso and dark roast coffee. The Village had a street espresso vendor, yet what really sets it apart is the location of three major coffee shops within one block of each other on West McGraw Street: Starbucks Coffee, Tully's Coffee, and CAFFÉ Appassionato. The Upper Crust Bakery, also on McGraw Street, caters to sit-down coffee drinkers as well. Together these

We Specialize in

LANDSCAPING & PRUNING

Do It Now!!

MAGNOLIA GARDEN CENTER

Hugo Berg

3213 W. SMITH
AT 4-1161

Top: Magnolia News, February 11, 1970.

Bottom: This Shell station was one of seven different stations that existed at one time in the Village. Photo by Ken Baxter. Courtesy Virginia Baxter. Circa 1960s.

establishments make the Village a real meeting place. Young mothers, with infants and toddlers in tow, visit with friends and their children, while seniors on their walks in Magnolia, like a place to stop and chat with neighbors and friends.

Today's Village is definitely not just somewhere to do business, but rather a dynamic gathering spot where Magnolians can meet and greet, and enjoy themselves while running necessary errands.

While it is true that not every business may be able to make it long term in the Village, there appears to be a sizeable field of shoppers—enough to keep 80 to 90 establishments going at any one time. The Village is alive and well, upbeat, sometimes upscale, and always looking to serve its neighborhood.

Joan Santucci and her husband Ron moved to Magnolia on June 1, 1956. Ten days later they welcomed their first child. Joan had no car, but had a household to run, so baby, buggy and Mom went shopping in the Village nearly every day. Who needed to venture downtown or out to Northgate Mall? Within close distance were grocery stores, live butchers, pharmacies, a hardware store, and Rudy's Shoe Store. (Plenty of shoes were purchased as eventually five other babies arrived in the Santucci home.) There were clothing stores, doctors' and dentists' offices, and the Hickory Hut for lunch.

Joan's favorite of all was the Dime Store, actually Meredith's 10¢ Store. What a treasure trove was found in there! Toys, party favors, patterns, fabrics and notions for sewing, yarn and needles for knitting and crochet work, glassware, pots and pans. One could buy tools, cosmetics, jigsaw puzzles, chewing gum, bobby pins, mops, brooms—you name it—and Meredith's likely had it!

There was something for everyone at the Dime Store. Photo by Ken Baxter. Courtesy Virginia Baxter. Circa 1960s.

Joan has celebrated 44 years living with her family in Magnolia and still loves the Village. A few old-timers are still with us, but many stores and businesses have come and gone. The make-up of the Village is ever changing, but it is still Joan's favorite place to shop even if the Dime Store is no more.

A Big Splash!

By Joan Santucci

As the twentieth century drew to a close, one of the more controversial issues to effect the Magnolia community ultimately impacted the Village. The neighborhood was to receive funds as mitigation for Metro's work on the sewage treatment plant upgrade at West

Fun in the sun at Magnolia's pool. Photo by Monica Wooton, 2000.

Point. In the spring of 1991, $3 million was deposited into the Community Improvement Fund and a steering committee was formed to solicit ideas for capital projects.

It seems everyone had thoughts on how the funds should be spent. Some wanted more tennis courts, others opted for additional play fields, there was a demand for upgrading the Magnolia Recreation Center, golfers wanted a course, and a large contingent was in favor of an indoor swimming pool.

The issue was put to a community vote in May 1992. According to the Magnolia Community Club, a pool was first choice by a wide majority. The site chosen was Parks Department property behind the Blaine School gym on 32nd Avenue West across the street from Albertson's.

There were many setbacks on the way to getting the pool, primarily the lack of sufficient money. Swimming pools are costly to build. The community started its own drive to add to the fund. Finally, the plans for an indoor pool were scrapped in favor of a less expensive outdoor pool.

Following pages: The Seattle Fire Department gives Magnolia kids a chance to see the fire engine up close and personal. The venue: Magnolia Village! Photo Ken Baxter, courtesy of Virginia Baxter. Circa 1950's.

Making a splash. Photo by Roy Scully, 2000.

The pool opened June 16, 1998 and is named for Lowery C. "Pop" Mounger, a longtime Magnolia resident who strongly supported youth recreation programs. Pop was an outstanding example of the virtues of hard work, honesty and athletics to Seattle youth. The Mounger family's generous contribution to the pool fund was instrumental in ensuring that the pool would have all the necessary amenities to make it a true community asset.

The pool operates from Memorial Day to Labor Day, seven days a week, for activities such as lap swimming, competitive training, swim instruction, water fitness, recreational swimming, water safety training, special events and rentals.

According to Bill Bottenberg, city-wide Aquatic Coordinator for the Seattle Parks and Recreation, the pool cost more than $2 million to build and serves between 600 to 800 persons per day during the summer.

A success since the day it opened, the Pop Mounger's pool is a welcome addition to our Village family.

My Navy Base Paper Route

By Hal Will

NAVY PRESENCE AT PIER 41 NOTICED

In the early spring of 1942, just a couple of months after the Japanese sneak attack on Pearl Harbor, I noticed a few US Navy vessels at Pier 41 (which is now Pier 91) in Smith Cove as I was riding the bus up the Garfield Street Bridge (now called the Magnolia Bridge) heading home from Queen Anne High School.

I was 15 and a half years old, a sophomore, and had just bought a second-hand bike from an acquaintance so I was now mobile enough to ride down to Smith Cove after my paper route on Magnolia Bluff. A Marine sentry stood guard at a new wire gate on the west side of Pier 41. Several former purse-seine fishing vessels, in Navy gray paint, were moored there. They had been converted to minesweepers.

I still had my *Seattle Times* paper bag over my shoulders with just one paper remaining that was for my folks. Some sailors spotted me and talked me into selling them that paper. They suggested I bring more papers the next day, and every day after that. They were starved for the news.

I started ordering extras each day and returned to the pier after my regular route. The crews of the sweepers grew to expect me so I felt a responsibility to repeat my daily visit to their moorage area. Navy activity at Pier 41 increased rapidly, and bigger ships and more of them started appearing.

My daily "extra" paper order was becoming so significant that the circulation manager for our area suggested I find someone to take the Magnolia Bluff route off my hands. It was obvious I couldn't do both routes justice. I talked my buddy, Clyde Holcomb, into taking that route. This enabled me to get to the Navy base earlier and find more customers. Some shore-based personnel on the base even became steady subscription customers.

Within a few months the Navy had taken over all of Piers 40, 41 and much land north of the bridge. The security gate at the head of Pier 41 moved to the bottom of the ramp in the center of the Garfield Street Bridge. This was the main access to the new base. I had to get a security pass to get on the base, but then I was allowed to go anyplace I could find customers.

When more papers were needed to supply many, or unusually large ships, I called Times Circulation and ordered more. They were delivered by truck to the porch of the little cafe

Pier 91 and the adjacent Port of Seattle land now serves the importing of Japanese cars. This is quite a contrast from serving as a US Navy Base during World War II. Photo by Monica Wooton, 2000.

187

at the foot of the Garfield Street Bridge. It was officially listed as the Terminal Cafe in *Polk's City Directory*, but everyone seemed to call it "The Greek's." The congenial owner's name was Gust Diamond.

Times circulation was very accommodating and dependable about leaving the requested papers and identified the bundle with my route number. And there were numerous incidents when large ships would leave between my early afternoon assessment as I rode up the bridge on a bus, and when I came back down the bridge on my bike with my papers around 4 p.m. A Navy cruiser could generate sales of 50 papers, but it could sail away while I was ordering those 50 extras. I might end up with a bundle of 100 papers at The Greek's that I couldn't sell. I viewed these occasions as "disasters" but the newspaper picked them up at night without charging me, as long as I called promptly and confessed my predicament.

There were times when I sold out my regular supply plus the extras waiting for me at The Greek's. I can remember running out of papers at the seaward end of one of the piers then trying to sneak past a line of ships full of sailors wanting papers that I couldn't supply. It seemed life threatening! I'd take off my canvas paper bag and try to fold it into an inconspicuous wad under my arm or inside my coat or shirt. I'd then ride my bike north as quickly as possible to the safety of the civilian world. It usually didn't work, however. The waiting customers impatiently watched my progress from ship to ship. They were mighty

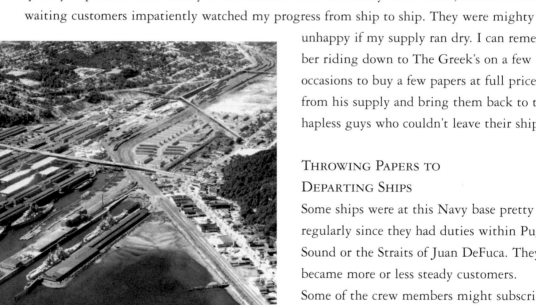

By the end of WW-II, the Naval Base had occupied all of the vacant land at Smith Cove. This post-war photo shows four aircraft carriers, two battleships and two cruisers awaiting lay-up. UW Special Collection #14461.

unhappy if my supply ran dry. I can remember riding down to The Greek's on a few occasions to buy a few papers at full price from his supply and bring them back to the hapless guys who couldn't leave their ships.

THROWING PAPERS TO DEPARTING SHIPS

Some ships were at this Navy base pretty regularly since they had duties within Puget Sound or the Straits of Juan DeFuca. They became more or less steady customers. Some of the crew members might subscribe by the month expecting a paper if they were in port during my delivery rounds.

Sometimes, the ship itself was the customer. Occasionally these vessels would be casting off lines to leave for patrol or sweeping operations as I was coasting down the Garfield Street Bridge. Their whistle signal could cause a spurt of adrenaline in me and I'd pump my bike as hard as I could toward the pier.

Most of the Marine guards knew me and saw the "situation" so they'd wave me through the checkpoint at the foot of the ramp without slowing down. I'd peddle out to the appropriate pier as far as necessary to get seaward of the ship backing out, and then stop to fold up a few papers for throwing. As I threw papers at the waist of the ship (a convenient open-deck area amidships), there were many willing "wide receivers" trying to catch them to keep them from bouncing overboard.

*USS Pintail backing
away from Pier 41. Papers
were often thrown to
departing ships this far
away from the pier.*
Puget Sound Maritime
Historical Society
#3169.

On windy days or when the span of water between ship and pier was too great, a lot of papers went in the water. The cheering section often spanned the ranks from the skipper on down. The papers that got aboard might be the last ones for a number of days and had to serve the whole crew.

Of course, a good number of the tossed papers might splash short of the ship while some sailed clear over. Some skippers would stop engines or otherwise maneuver to give me a better chance to get papers aboard. I didn't worry about collecting for papers "airmailed" aboard. My customers were always fair to me and some even tipped!

Sunday Morning Routine

My favorite part of Sunday morning delivery was the chance to eat bacon, eggs and the works, with *real* butter, aboard one, two or even three of the minesweepers. These were the days of strict rationing of butter and many other commodities. Three breakfasts was my limit. I had to pump back up the bridge towing my trailer after my deliveries, sometimes with heavy leftover Sunday papers.

I felt a closer association with the small minesweepers. These were the converted purse-seiners that first attracted me to Pier 41 when the Navy base consisted of just a wire gate at the head of the west side of the pier with a Marine guard and one or two sweepers. The Sunday breakfasts, galley handouts and relative small size, made them "friendly" vessels to this 15-year-old.

The Navy classed these vessels as "Auxiliary Minesweepers, coastal," thus the letter designation AMc. Names I remember well are *Pintail* (AMc 17), *Nightingale* (AMc 18), *Crow* (AMc 27), *Pheobe*, and *Frigate Bird*, whose hull numbers I don't recall. *Goshawk* (AMc 79) was another, slightly larger steel North Sea trawler type.

Along with my buddy Clyde, and his dad, I was to later spend many hours in the Coast Guard Reserve "riding herd" on the sweeping gear towed by these minesweepers up and down the Sound.

Paper Trailer for My Bike

I picked up my steady daily supply of papers at the Times paper shack at 3311 West McGraw Street. It was an old garage, next to the Union 76 station, waiting for "progress" to knock it down. The number of papers delivered there for my route was about 75. There were days when I couldn't sell all of them, and also many days when I needed more.

At any rate, I had to carry them in my canvas bag, half in the back and half in the front, and I had to ride one and a half miles from the paper shack to the piers. The first half-mile was uphill then the rest was a fast coast from 28th Avenue West and West Blaine Street. I always hoped to be traveling light on the steep uphill mile heading home.

I couldn't carry all the Sunday papers on my back in one trip, and I didn't want to make two trips, so I built a little trailer to tow behind my bike. It was made of plywood on a wooden frame and was just big enough to hold a stack of papers about 20 inches high. It had a canvas tarp to keep the papers dry during the Seattle winter. A tongue, formed from a piece of conduit, was fastened to a pivot on the little cargo rack over the back fender of my bike. My dad was a helpful participant on the project.

There were railroad tracks along all faces of the piers with some pretty large gaps in the timbers adjacent to the rails. In spite of riding cautiously near the rails, I did have a couple of scary spills. Luckily, I didn't pitch over the side into the water, or worse.

I had to invest in a pair of fat balloon tires, about 10 inches in diameter, for the trailer. Tagging along behind the bike, the trailer was hard to keep out of the ruts on the piers but the fat balloon tires spanned the ruts and wide gaps around railroad tracks pretty well. The tires were made of inferior rubber and seemed to lose air from week to week. I had to remember to get them pumped up every Saturday night before the load of Sunday papers flattened them. The trailer served its purpose but it still wasn't pleasant to tow on the uphill mile going home, especially if it wasn't empty.

Destroyer that Wouldn't Stop

One summer afternoon the pier was pretty deserted so I had papers left over. I was thinking of leaving for home when one of the old flush-deck destroyers rounded Magnolia inbound to the pier. I remember the names of three flush-deckers that I sold papers on frequently, but I'm not sure which one this was. I think it was the *Williamson*. It had only two of the original four stacks and it was classed as a seaplane tender.

As it approached I could see it was heading for the west side of Pier 41 so I peddled over there and headed to where a couple of line handlers were waiting. It was the last berth at the shoreward end of the pier by the Garfield Street Bridge. A Navy Captain and one or two other officers were also waiting, but the area was otherwise deserted.

I always enjoyed watching steam-powered Navy ships maneuver. Their engines were silent so the other sounds like the ring of the engine room telegraph and the rush of swirling water at the stern were vivid.

As the destroyer coasted close along the pier where we were waiting, heaving lines tossed from the ship arced up and thumped on the timber pier decking. These were light lines with a weight on the end used to pull heavier mooring lines from the ship to the pier. At about the same time, the clang of the engine room telegraph could be heard signaling for reverse. I watched for the rush of water at the stern when the propellers reversed. Nothing happened! The telegraph rang again. Again, no swirl at the stern as the ship continued its glide toward the end of the waterway!

USS Williamson as it appeared in light gray paint before Pearl Harbor. It was this destroyer, or one of her sisters, that failed to stop when landing at pier 41. Puget Sound Maritime Historical Society #2771.

Now it was apparent on the ship's bridge and elsewhere that there was a problem. Orders were shouted to get lines ashore and snubbed down. But the two-line handlers on the pier were being towed by the hawser and were not able to get the eye at the end of the large mooring line near a mooring bit on the pier. The ship kept gliding toward the dead end of the berth.

It seemed to get quiet again when it became obvious the ship was not going to be stopped. For those not familiar with destroyers, I should point out that they have very sharp bows. It was a pretty high tide so the fore deck was above the pier. The ship knifed into the heavy timbers at the north end of the waterway like a slow motion ax swing. The old-fashioned anchor and its chain made a raucous clatter as it was peeled away from its stowage area at the bow. The pier's huge timbers were wedged up into the air with terrible cracking sounds as the destroyer made a wedge-shaped hole about 15 feet into the north end of the berth.

The officers on the pier were calm through it all. After all the crunching noise stopped, the captain made some fitting but humorous remark to ease the tension. It was obvious it would take a long time to restore normalcy enough to announce "Paperboy at the gangway." I was in danger of holding up dinner at home so I folded up about 10 extra papers and tossed them on the deck at the waist of the ship, then headed home. They would be appreciated after the turmoil subsided.

I must have driven my folks crazy talking about exciting happenings at "the piers." I was probably pretty animated at the dinner table that night!

About 40 years later, at a Puget Sound Maritime Historical Society Board meeting, a conversation prompted me to tell this pier-crunching story. My friend and fellow board member, Gordon Brennan, turned to me and said, "I was there!" We compared memories and realized we were both within a few feet of each other. Gordon was a fuel officer at the Naval Base waiting to arrange fueling for the destroyer and I was the paperboy waiting to sell some papers. It was another case of "a small world."

Tows Up the Garfield Street Bridge

The most tiring part of my paper route at the Navy base was the daily climb back up the Garfield Street Bridge and on up to the high point at 28th Avenue West and West Blaine Street. From there I could coast home just four blocks. It was good exercise but not very pleasant, especially in cold rainy weather or when the wind was strong. Bicycle gearshifts were a rarity then and my bike certainly wasn't that well equipped.

The original bridge had a sidewalk on both north and south sides at that time. They were raised above the roadway the height of a very high curb. Pedestrians were protected from a very long—and certainly fatal fall—by a three-foot concrete railing.

Due to my slow hill climb, I would often pump up the sidewalk to keep out of the roadway, especially after dark. Although I used the sidewalk to avoid danger from vehicles, there were numerous times, due to strong winds, when pumping a bike alongside that low railing was just too scary. I'd move to the roadway and take my chances there, under those conditions.

On several occasions, Clyde's dad would spot me as he was driving homeward up the bridge and stop to give me a tow. Those were the days when cars had running boards and door handles one could hold onto. With my right foot on his left running board and his window open to talk to me, he'd give me a welcomed tow up the long uphill route. It's difficult now to visualize the relatively few cars on the road then. There was gas and tire rationing and fewer people commuting, so this was not a dangerous practice.

The Navy Net Tender Boxwood was one of several actively installing anti-submarine nets in 1942 to protect Port Townsend's harbor and the approaches to Bremerton. They were nicknamed "Elephant Boats" for obvious reasons. Puget Sound Maritime Historical Society #523-1.

Four-Stacker Almost Blew onto Beach

One of those very windy winter evenings, as I was walking my bike up the bridge, I watched a four-stack destroyer backing out of the west side of Pier 41. It was pushed broadside by the howling south wind, very close to the shallows west of the pier. The Navy later filled this area for the officers' club and athletic fields.

I thought sure it was going to hit as it struggled full power forward until too close to the pier then full power astern until too close to the shallows. She was "in irons" and struggling to reach deep water and safe maneuvering space, and it was getting dark. The ship finally managed to get its stern headed away from the shoals so it could back out into the safety of Elliott Bay. I went on home with more excitement to discuss at the dinner table.

CLYDE'S SUMMER WATER TAXI

There were times during the summer when Clyde would come down to Pier 41 in his 17-foot open boat to pick me up after my paper route. Of course, civilian boats were not allowed to approach the base very close so we had to be careful. I'd ride my bike over to the western-most part of the base under the Garfield Street Bridge (now the Magnolia Bridge) where no vessels moored. There was a steel ladder there that reached down to the water, at any tide. Clyde would approach cautiously, when he saw me there, and wait for a sign from me that it was OK.

One time, a Marine guard came over to chase Clyde away, but finally let him approach when he was convinced we were not up to any trouble. I would lower my bike down to the boat with a piece of line Clyde would throw up to me, and then I'd climb down the steel ladder and away we'd go, back to Magnolia Beach. I usually pre-arranged with the closest guard to let me be picked up by Clyde. They usually saw no harm in our water taxi arrangement.

I don't recall now why we went to the extra trouble, since I had to get my bike from the boat to dry land on Magnolia Beach, which was not too easy. I remember getting aboard at Pier 41 clearly, but getting the bike ashore at the beach escapes me. It must have been uneventful, and pointless. We probably did the water taxi bit just to prove we could get away with it once in a while. I know it was only done on summer afternoons in calm weather. I couldn't risk losing my bike overboard. The paper route could not be covered without it!

ACEY AND DEUCEY THE HUSKY PUPS

One of the more unique Navy ships that used to call at Pier 41 was the gunboat *Charleston*. There were only two of this class in the Navy, the sister ship being *Erie*. I thought the *Charleston* resembled a miniature heavy cruiser. It had good shear to the hull, turrets, teak-planked decks and even a Marine detachment aboard. Marines manned the watch at the gangplank where I would sell papers on the quarterdeck. I liked the *Charleston*.

And, I fell in love with "Acey" and "Deucey." They were roly-poly Malemute pups and were new mascots aboard the gunboat. I would sometimes overstay my normal time aboard the *Charleston*, rolling on the deck with those pups. They were as wide as they were long the first time I played with them and they had teeth like needles. I'd roughhouse with them whenever their ship was in. They'd meet me at the top of the gangplank, if they were on deck, and I'd play with them while waiting for customers to come to the quarterdeck.

I missed the pups when the ship was gone for an extended period, probably to Alaska. When it finally returned, I was anxious to get out to the southwest end of Pier 41 where it always moored. As I finally got close enough I could see two full-grown dogs on the quarter-deck. Instead of waiting at the top of the gangway like they used to do as pups, they came bounding down and met me while I was still on my bike. They knocked me down and romped all over me, licking my face while standing on my paper bag. They had me pinned so I couldn't get up. The Sailors and Marines got a big kick out of my struggle to get out from under those playful dogs and get on with selling papers. I was very happy they remembered me.

That was the last time I remember seeing Acey and Deucey, or the *Charleston*. I remember reading that her sister, the *Erie*, was sunk by a German sub in the Atlantic or Caribbean.

By the time this photo was taken about 1947, most of the larger fighting ships had been moved to mothballed storage elsewhere. However, one carrier, one battleship, twelve destroyers, and numerous smaller vessels remain from World War II service. Photo source unknown.

FALSE OBITUARY DISCOVERED

One afternoon, when business was poor and I had quite a few papers left, I waited around for an old four-stack destroyer I saw coming around the Bluff. It took quite a while for it to make its approach and get secured, plus get a gangway ashore and secured. Finally, the word was passed that the paperboy was at the gangway. About five or six crewmen bought papers quickly and that seemed to be it.

I hung around hoping to sell more since I still had about 10 more left. Suddenly, a commotion started below decks and guys were shouting about something. Eventually more crewmembers poured up on deck to buy papers. Soon I was sold out.

Evidently, the destroyer had been out on patrol for some time and one of the crewmember's picture was in a news item. One of the early customers spotted it and the word spread quickly through the crew's quarters. It seems the sailor's wife, residing in the Seattle area, had received word that he had been killed. The *Seattle Times* also heard about it and had interviewed her.

The "deceased" sailor was very upset, while the reaction of fellow crewmembers ranged from sympathy to laughter.

HANDLING MONEY AROUND WATER

I became pretty good at handling money out on the piers. Of course, I was dealing with seagoing people who were also good at it. Paper money could fly away in the wind while coins couldn't float worth a darn. The weather decks of ships were crowned to drain water into scuppers then overboard. Coins tended to follow the water route. It was best to assume that money dropped was money lost.

I was constantly making change, since my business was mainly cash sales. I had to be prepared to change bills as high as $20s, but usually no higher than $5s or $10s. Silver 50-cent pieces were commonly used and silver dollars were not as rare as they are now. I carried a deep leather coin purse with two sections in it. Paper bills were in one section and coins were in the other. I called it my "bank" and always knew exactly where it was. It was probably worth $30 to $50 most of the time.

Most of my sales transactions were either on the pier by the gangway or on deck at the head of the gangway in an area called "the quarterdeck." On smaller or more home-based vessels, I could go into the galley or even through the crew's quarters to sell or deliver papers. On larger vessels they would usually announce over the ship's public address system, "Paperboy on the quarterdeck" or "Paperboy at the gangway," often preceded by a whistle signal on the bos'n's pipe. I was always addressed as "Paperboy" or "Mac." Nobody knew me by my real name, Hal.

On one occasion, a ship had pulled in its gangway to depart before I pulled up. Crewmembers at the rail were trying to buy papers from me by reaching across the gap between ship and pier. (There were large logs floating along the face of the pier serving as fenders to hold the ships away a reasonable distance.) As I was also reaching to the ship to pass papers and make change, I lost my grip on my bank. It fell like a rock and hit the log fender. Since the top was open, coins sprayed out in all directions clattering against the steel side of the ship and into the water with many small splashes. The sailors and I looked down at the log where just a few coins remained, but not the bank. I think a couple mumbled, "Sorry." I finished selling and headed home poorer and sadder, but wiser. Considering all the money changing I did around the water, I was fortunate to have only dropped the bank once, but it was a major financial setback for me.

Giving Up My Navy Base Paper Route

There are childhood memories that seem as clear as yesterday, yet there are events that happened that I cannot recall at all. Giving up that paper route is one of those events. At some point before summer vacation of '43, I gave the route up to look for a job on a tug. My Navy-Base paper route was my first real entrepreneurial success and, at 15, I loved it for the access it provided me to ships and to the Navy. It added excitement to a year I will always fondly remember.

Hal Will had a love affair with boats from an early age and a fascination with the US Navy because of a relative who was a Navy officer and role model. Hal was always alert to any maritime activity at Smith Cove as seen from the Garfield Street Bridge, now the Magnolia Bridge, on his daily trips to and from Queen Anne High School. Early Navy activity that he noticed at a Smith Cove pier, soon after the Pearl Harbor bombing, triggered this 1942 adventure.

Magnolia's Wooden Trestles

By Hal Will

TRESTLES, A DEFINITION

For purposes of this discussion, trestles are defined as cross-braced wood structures of timbers or piling to carry pedestrian, railroad or other vehicle traffic. They typically do not span very long open spaces without a bridge truss. Seattle's shorelines were laced with trestles in the late 1800s and early 1900s. Timber was plentiful and trestle construction was a well-known trade. Interchangeable names for trestles described here might be wooden bridge or viaduct.

MAGNOLIA ISLAND, ALMOST

The peninsula now called Magnolia Bluff was very nearly an island when the first white settlers arrived at Alki on the shores of what is now called Elliott Bay. A long shallow cove extended north from Elliott Bay between Magnolia Bluff and the hill named Queen Anne. It was named Smith Cove, or Smith's Cove, after Dr. Henry Smith, an early homesteader in the area. Another shallow saltwater inlet named Salmon Bay separated Magnolia Bluff and Queen Anne Hill from land to the north, and curved into the low land between those hills as if trying to meet Smith Cove. The low-land isthmus separating these two saltwater areas was all that kept Magnolia Bluff from being Magnolia Island. This area was appropriately named Interbay.

TRESTLES TO MAGNOLIA

The earliest settlers on Magnolia had to cross this isthmus to reach the Bluff, so many of the earlier buildings on Magnolia were grouped near Interbay. The first vehicle trestle crossed this isthmus at Grand Boulevard, later named West Dravus Street (No. 1 on the map). It had to carry traffic over the existing railroad lines that were well established through this low area before 1900. They were Seattle Lake Shore & Eastern and Seattle & Montana railroads. This trestle shows on *Baist's 1908 Seattle Real Estate Atlas* and includes the street railway line

The west end of the Magnolia Bridge showing the steel bracing added over the years. Photo by Monica Wooton, 2000.

Dravus Street trestles looking west toward Magnolia. The streetcar trestle is just left of the roadway. Courtesy of Dan Kerlee.

to Fort Lawton.[1] On the 1908 map, no other trestles are evident crossing the isthmus or the tide flats to the south. It is possible that real estate maps might not show all the trestles but dated photographs reveal many clues about trestles. A May 1903 photograph clearly shows that the original wooden trestle on West Garfield Street did not yet exist.[2] This is understandable since only the Great Northern piers 38 and 39 on the east side of Smith Cove near 15th Avenue West were under construction at the time. (Those piers no longer exist.) The only other commercial activity was the Pioneer Glass Works on the Magnolia shore and it was served by a Seattle Lake Shore & Eastern Railroad spur track (sidetrack) from Interbay. The glass works ceased to appear in *Polk's Seattle City Directory* after 1904.

TRESTLES TO
MAGNOLIA
PRIOR TO 1930

1-*West Dravus Street*
2-*West Garfield Street*
3-*23rd Avenue West*
4-*South Shore*
5-*West Wheeler Street*
6-*20th Avenue West*
7-*Lawton Way*
8-*West Halladay Street*
Drawn by Hal Will

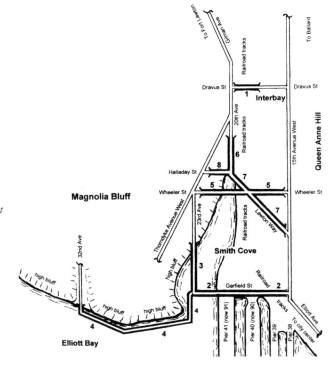

This 1929 photo shows the 23rd Avenue West Trestle from the left (north) and the Garfield Street (wooden) Trestle from the right (east) meeting in mid-photo. This route to Magnolia was about to end when the concrete Garfield Street Bridge replaced the wooden trestle during the next seven months. Seattle Municipal Archives, #29360.

THE GARFIELD STREET TO 23RD AVENUE ROUTE

Baist's maps and photographs dated 1912 clearly show not only the West Garfield Street wooden trestle (No. 2 on the map) extending from 15th Avenue West to 23rd Avenue West, but also a north-south trestle (No. 3 on the map) connecting the Garfield trestle to the Bluff at 23rd Avenue West and West Newton Street. These two structures provided the first vehicular access to the Bluff across the tide flats south of West Dravus Street.[3]

The Wheeler Street Trestle viewed from Thorndyke Avenue West at 23rd Avenue West on Magnolia looking east toward Queen Anne Hill. The intersecting trestle across mid picture is the Lawton Way Trestle. Courtesy of Neil Smith. Museum of History and Industry #1999.67.7.

"THE WHEELER STREET TRESTLE"

Several Seattle Engineering Department photos dated April 17, 1914, were taken from vantage points on Magnolia and Queen Anne Hill to document what was called the West Wheeler Street trestle.[4] It was probably relatively new at this time. The trestle on Wheeler Street was a straight east-west trestle from 15th Avenue West to Thorndyke Avenue West on the Bluff (No. 5 on the map). However, it intersected a long trestle extending from Thorndyke Avenue at 20th Avenue West to 15th Avenue West just a few blocks north of the Garfield Street trestle. This dog-legged structure followed 20th Avenue West a few blocks in a north-south direction (No. 6 on the map), then Lawton Way diagonally to 15th Avenue West (No. 7 on map). Both trestles had wooden trusses spanning the railroad tracks near the center of Smith Cove. This was really a long and involved trestle system. This total structure was possibly referred to as the Wheeler Street Bridge.

The west half of West Wheeler Street Trestle is shown looking west toward Magnolia from the intersection with the Lawton Way Trestle. The bridge truss spans the railroad tracks below.

Courtesy of Neil Smith. Museum of History and Industry #1999.67.6.

The northwest portion of the Lawton Way Trestle where it spans the railroad tracks then meets the 20th Avenue West Trestle.

The photo is taken from the intersection with the West Wheeler Street Trestle. Courtesy of Neil Smith. Museum of History and Industry #1999.67.5.

The Wheeler Street Trestle, as well as most of the Lawton Way Trestle, was destroyed by fire June 30, 1924, when a spark from a steam locomotive ignited a span over the railroad tracks. Photo by Clarence Langstaff.

FATEFUL DAY FOR TRESTLES

The most destructive day for Magnolia trestles was June 30, 1924. The next day *The Seattle Times* reported: "SEATTLE BRIDGES BURN, Replacements Will Cost City $250,000."[5] A fire on the Lawton Way trestle, believed to have been started by sparks from a steam locomotive, was brought under control within an hour but it broke bounds later and spread to the Wheeler Street trestle, virtually destroying it. In all, about 12 or 15 blocks of trestle were destroyed and the remainder of the structures was declared a total loss. Magnolians were again totally dependent on the Dravus Street trestle or the Garfield Street/23rd Avenue West trestles. This situation was to last almost five years.

During the first four of those years, many ideas were proposed for improving access to the Bluff. Possibly the most unusual was the proposal to tunnel from Smith Cove to 30th Avenue West in Pleasant Valley. However, a plan was finally approved. Described by the *Seattle Post-Intelligencer* on June 12, 1928, as a timber trestle virtually replacing the 20th Avenue West-Lawton Way dog-leg that burned.[6] The east-west Wheeler Street trestle would not be rebuilt, but a new ramp from Thorndyke Avenue West at West Halladay Street would connect with the new trestle where 20th Avenue West joined Lawton Way (No. 8 on the map).

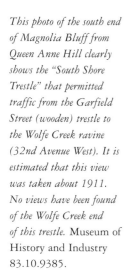

This photo of the south end of Magnolia Bluff from Queen Anne Hill clearly shows the "South Shore Trestle" that permitted traffic from the Garfield Street (wooden) trestle to the Wolfe Creek ravine (32nd Avenue West). It is estimated that this view was taken about 1911. No views have been found of the Wolfe Creek end of this trestle. Museum of History and Industry 83.10.9385.

A series of City Engineering Department photographs taken December 18, 1928 show construction of the trestles well along with the only unfinished section where bridge trusses would span the railroad right-of-way.[7] These photos clearly show the new trestle had concrete piers to hold the trusses. This sign of permanence as part of the wooden structures is a little surprising considering that the new concrete Garfield Street Bridge would be dedicated in two years. Photos taken May 15, 1929 show the new trestle complete and now identified as the Lawton Way Bridge.[8] This trestle was still in use in 1944 when it was showing definite signs of age.

THE SOUTH SHORE TRESTLE

The Magnolia area trestle with the least graphic documentation and no known official name was one that extended from the west end of the Garfield Street trestle at the west side of Smith Cove (No. 4 on the map). It angled around the south end of the Bluff on tideland and came ashore at 32nd Avenue West for a convenient and gradual grade up to the Pleasant Valley area. There is photographic evidence that it definitely existed but the views are from such a distance that it is difficult to ascertain the width of the roadway. In one view it looks broad enough to accommodate automobile traffic of that era. Based on limited photographic evidence, we know that this route to Magnolia existed, at least from 1911 through 1915. The route is now partially covered by the Elliott Bay Marina parking lot.[9]

This May 1929 photo shows the newly completed Lawton Way Trestle looking northwest as viewed from about 12th Avenue West on Queen Anne Hill. This trestle branches west to Thorndyke Avenue on Halladay Street and north to Thorndyke on 20th Avenue West. The concrete Garfield Street Bridge (now Magnolia Bridge) was under construction at this time and would be dedicated in just seven months. Seattle Municipal Archives, #29359.

THE TRESTLE ERA ENDS

Access to Magnolia Bluff will always involve bridges of some sort due to the significant railroad presence in the Smith Cove, Interbay and Salmon Bay areas. Concrete and steel has replaced wood but the trestle era is memorable to some. A trestle brings to mind the many thousands of hammer strokes of pile drivers, the massive size and number of timbers involved, and the spikes, nuts, bolts and washers required to hold them all together. They were a vital part of Seattle's early growth and expansion, but the life of these wooden structures was relatively short due to decay, wear or fire.

Hal Will grew up on Magnolia and was always fascinated by the activities at Smith Cove, as viewed from buses traveling on the Garfield Street Bridge. During World War II, he gained more first-hand knowledge of the area. Subsequent interest in maritime history broadened Hal's interest in Smith Cove's history. He also has a fascination with trestles.

Critical Connection: Bridge to the Bluff

By Joy Carpine

Harry Stimmel may have been the first person to take advantage of the modern West Garfield Street Bridge. He lived on Magnolia Boulevard near the top of the Bridge, and worked for the telephone company downtown. His commute home took him north on Elliott Avenue West and 15th Avenue West onto Magnolia via the West Dravus Street Bridge. Ever since the Wheeler Street trestle burned down in June 1924,[1] and the wooden Garfield Street trestle closed, getting to the south end of Magnolia had been a time-consuming effort. One evening in 1930, before the concrete Garfield Street Bridge was opened, Stimmel just couldn't resist; he sneaked across the Bridge and made it home in what must have been record time. "It was a nice short cut for him," said his daughter Mary Ann Stimmel Hill.[2]

The "short cut" was a major achievement for Magnolia residents who had lobbied for a permanent bridge since the wooden Wheeler Street Bridge burned down. Before 1930, the tide flats of Smith Cove on the south end of Interbay (the lowland that separates Magnolia and Queen Anne Hill) were criss-crossed by three wooden trestles that served both pedestrians and automobiles. These trestles, located at West Wheeler Street, Lawton Way and West Garfield Street, had to be rebuilt nearly every decade due to their inevitable decay or loss by fire. Decay may have been hastened by the seawater they crossed—Interbay was not dry land as it is today; high tide brought shallow water in as far as Armour Street.[3]

The Garfield Street trestle did not make the steep climb up Magnolia Bluff to meet Galer Street as the modern Bridge does. It ran only to the bottom of the Bluff, where one arm of the trestle turned north and connected to 23rd Avenue West, and the other arm turned south to Smith Cove.

How Magnolia Finally Got Its Bridge

The Bridge was a product of a strong community effort. On July 8, 1924, about a week after the West Wheeler Street Bridge burned, the Magnolia Improvement Club and the Carleton Park Improvement Club (which changed its name to the Magnolia Community Club in October 1932[4]) took up the cause of lobbying for a new bridge by writing a letter to J. D. Blackwell, the city engineer.[5] Progress was slow; two years later the club appointed a committee "to push the permanent Garfield Street Bridge with the Planning Committee

The Magnolia Bridge in 2000, looking east toward Queen Anne Hill. Photo by Roy Scully, 2000.

Getting to and from Magnolia wasn't always easy. The license plate of this unfortunate vehicle dates this photo at 1925. Rotted timbers were likely the cause of the trestle's collapse. Museum of History and Industry #83.10, 368.2.

and City Council."[6] The Club minutes show that other groups were also working for a new bridge; members from the Magnolia Improvement Club attended Carleton Park meetings several times and reported their own efforts.

Progress may have been slowed due to the fact that a new wooden trestle was built in 1925. According to a September 1925 article in *The Seattle Times*, "Since this temporary structure has been actually under construction, the talk of a permanent structure that would be a credit to the growing community has been dropped."[7] In early October *The Seattle Times* reported that the City had assured residents that the "unsightly" trestle would only be there for five or six years, after which "they were given to understand that the city, the railroads and the Port Commission would jointly finance a permanent bridge of credible type across Smith Cove."[8]

The Seattle Times suggested that the residents were beginning to think that they may have been lulled into submission by the City's promises, and so the Carleton Park Improvement Club, the Point Club and the Pleasant Valley Club were quietly beginning to work together to lobby for a permanent bridge.[9]

According to *The Seattle Times*, the Carleton Park Improvement Club met on October 13, 1925, and resolved to bring the issue to the voters in the form of a bond issue in the spring election.[10] *The Seattle Times* quoted the president of the Carleton Park Improvement Club, Dr. H. T. Harvey, as saying "Residents of Magnolia Bluff are united in their demand for a permanent steel and concrete span wide enough to accommodate the needs of the Magnolia Bluff district."[11] Later that month the Garfield Bridge Club petitioned the City Council to provide bonds for the Bridge's construction, saying that the costs should be shared between the City, the Port of Seattle and the railroads.[12] One month later, in November, the Garfield Bridge Club was taken aback when City Engineer J. D. Blackwell reported to the City Council that the permanent Bridge would cost an estimated $890,250, and that 6,000 local lots would be assessed $50 in order to raise $300,000 to pay for part of the Bridge.[13] Bridge Club President Mrs. C. B. Coselman responded by saying that "everyone at the City Hall knows the property will not stand this," and that the Club intended to ask for another estimate.[14]

By December 2, 1926, the estimated cost had shrunk to $750,000, and the City Council asked Blackwell to prepare the specifications for the concrete and steel bridge.[15] City Council members E. L. Blaine, John E. Carroll and Otto A. Case favored construction of the Bridge,

206

July 2
~~June 2~~, 1924.

Mr. J. D. Blackwell,
City Engineer,

Dear Sir:

Under date of July 1, 1924 the following quoted letter was
addressed to the Board of Public Works:

"Owing to the destruction of the W. Wheeler Street bridge by
fire and the emergency existing for immediate action to care for the
situation caused thereby, the Board of Public Works is requested to make
such studies and investigations as may be necessary to enable the corporate authorities of the City of Seattle to intelligently determine the
steps to be taken to construct a bridge to take the place of the structure
destroyed, and to communicate to the City Council its recommendations
in regard thereto at the earliest possible date. Yours very truly,
John E. Carroll, Chairman, Streets and Sewers Committee."

The above refers to the West Wheeler Timber trestle, the Lawton Way Timber trestle and the 20th Ave. West Timber trestle, all or
part of which were destroyed by fire Monday afternoon, June 30th, 1924.
The Board of Public Works held a special meeting to consider the above
communication, at which were present Mr. David B. Eastman representing
his own property and the Magnolia Improvement Club and Mr.
Harold A. Phinney representing his own property in Carlton Park and the
Carlton Improvement Club.

Phinney and Eastman made the following recommendations:
speedily as possible the existing roadways and make a
y looking toward the erection of a permanent steel
t Garfield Street from the Roadway in front of the
ck as it now exists to the top of Magnolia Bluff, using
dvisable switch backs to attain the rise without
essrs. Phinney and Eastman expressed themselves as
rary structure of any kind being put in.

er was referred to you to work out a plan along the
ted and to submit a definite recommendation thereon
e Board to be held Monday, July 14, 1924, in order
recommendation may go to the City Council at its
on that date.

Respectfully,

Secretary.

y
stman
Improvement Club

GARFIELD BRIDGE CLUB

2358--28TH AVENUE WEST

SEATTLE, WASHINGTON

August 13, 1926

AN ORGANIZATION CONSISTING OF
RESIDENTS OF
MAGNOLIA BLUFF, CARLTON PARK,
PLEASANT VALLEY AND SURROUNDING
COMMUNITIES TO
"CONSTRUCT A PERMANENT BRIDGE
AT GARFIELD STREET"

Magnolia Bluff Improvement Club,
% Mrs. E. G. Spangler, Secy.,
2638 West Crockett Street,
Seattle, Washington.

Gentlemen:

We understand there is to be a meeting
held in the near future at Steiner's Hall, Interbay, regarding the construction of a viaduct connecting 15th Avenue West with Magnolia Bluff.

As we have received no notification of
such a meeting, and understanding that all clubs
of the district were expected to send representatives, we would appreciate it if you would be so
kind as to advise us of the date and time of this
meeting.

Thanking you in advance for your courtesy, we remain

Very truly yours,

GARFIELD BRIDGE CLUB.

By _____
Secy.

---

*The burning of the West
Wheeler Street trestle in
1924 triggered Magnolia
residents to lobby for a concrete bridge to the Bluff. It
took many years of letters,
meetings and hand wring-
ing before construction
began in 1929. Magnolia
Community Club files.*

while fellow council members Ralph Nicols and Philip Tindall argued for a cheaper structure.[16] Four days later, the City Council voted 6 to 2 to continue with plans to construct a permanent bridge, at the estimated cost of $750,000.[17] By April 1927, the estimated cost dropped again to $660,000, and the streets and sewer committee approved the new Bridge construction and repair of the burned West Wheeler Street Bridge.[18] The cost of the new Bridge was intended to be shared between the City, Magnolia land owners in an enlarged improvement district, the Port Commission and the railroads in Smith Cove.[19]

In 1927, the Carleton Park club considered the possibility that Magnolia property owners, not the City of Seattle, might have to pay for most of the cost of the Bridge. They hoped they would not pay more than $25 per 50-foot lot,[20] but in 1928, City Ordinance 57283 assessed 5,651 properties in Magnolia a total of $358,907. Another ordinance (#61004) in 1931 added an additional assessment of $31,000 to the local improvement district, bringing Magnolia's contribution to the Bridge to $389,907. The City gave $245,000 from the general fund, and the railroads paid $140,000.[21] The total cost of the Bridge came to $774,907.[22] The Carleton Park Club also put up $75 for the opening ceremony, and committee member Mr. W. S. White said he would "have the Police Band out to play for this occasion."[23]

The City ordered the construction company, J. M. Clapp, to begin work on the reinforced concrete and steel viaduct August 12, 1929. Records show that laborers were paid 62.5 or 75 cents per hour. Blacksmiths made 87.5 cents an hour, and foremen brought home $1.125 an hour. Carpenters made $4.50 per day. Sacks of cement were 50 cents each, and renting a Ford truck for ten hours (without driver) cost $10. Gasoline for the truck cost 19 cents per gallon.[24]

The new Bridge was completed December 22, 1930.[25] It connected Magnolia Bluff and 15th Avenue West, crossing the head of Smith Cove and the Great Northern, Northern Pacific and Oregon & Washington railroad tracks. A ramp near the midpoint of the Bridge at 20th Avenue West provided access to the Smith Cove waterfront and the massive docks (now Piers 90-91). A trestle connected the Bridge to 23rd Avenue West; motorists driving onto the Bridge from the trestle used a ramp on the south side of the Bridge to join eastbound traffic, and westbound motorists exiting the Bridge onto the trestle used a ramp on the north side. The trestle was removed by 1942,[26] but its exit and entrance now connect to ramps that provide access to Smith Cove Park and the Elliott Bay Marina.

In 1929, the West Garfield Street Bridge was a wooden trestle. Note that the Bridge does not ascend Magnolia Bluff, but ends at the bottom of the hill, and takes a right turn to 23rd Avenue West. Seattle Municipal Archives #7504, May 15, 1929.

This March 6, 1930, photograph shows the wooden West Garfield Street Bridge and the surrounding tide flats. The hillside has been cleared to make way for the new Bridge's route up onto Magnolia Bluff. Seattle Municipal Archives #3865, Orig. No. 8056.

THE BRIDGE IS IMPROVED AND RENAMED

In 1934, the Magnolia Community Club took up the cause of getting a traffic light installed at the busy intersection of 15th Avenue West and West Garfield Street, where much of the northbound traffic turned left to access the Bridge,[27] and pedestrians got on and off street cars and buses.[28] A stop sign was put up, which was replaced by a traffic signal in 1940. Apparently the stop sign delayed traffic at the intersection of 15th Avenue West and West Galer Street, and "business men of the neighborhood complained."[29]

The new West Garfield Street Bridge opened to vehicles and pedestrians in December 1930. This photo was taken from the west end of the Bridge. Note the connecting trestle on the left, which leads to 23rd Avenue West. Seattle Engineering Department #4582, #8877.

An overpass was added in 1957-1958, which took motorists over 15th Avenue West and onto the Bridge, thus reducing back-ups at the base of the Bridge on 15th Avenue West. Instead of turning left, northbound motorists could now turn right off of Elliott Avenue West and follow a curving road onto the overpass and the Bridge. In order to accommodate the new traffic accessing the Bridge, the bridge deck was widened to add a new lane on the north side. The Tubbs Cordage Company's one-story Rope Walk building had to be shortened in order to accommodate the expanded Bridge.[30] Pedestrians got better access to the Bridge, too. They could now use the newly lit steel stairway on the south side of the Bridge, which was accessed by a walkway that began on the west side of 15th Avenue West and crossed under the Bridge to the stairs.

The Bridge served the Magnolia community well, but by 1959 it was showing definite signs of wear. City inspection found that it displayed "an uneven deck surface, exposed reinforcing steel, spalled and/or separated concrete, pronounced surface cracking, loss of support to suspended spans and an undulating movement of the bridge deck."[31] The City Council passed an ordinance on August 10, 1959, to provide $825,000 to rehabilitate the aging Bridge, and extensive underbracing was done.[32]

In 1960, the Magnolia Community Club petitioned the City to change the name of the Garfield Street Bridge to the Magnolia Bridge. In a 1959 letter from the Magnolia Community Club President to Roy Morse, the City's Chief Engineer, Colonel Walcott Denison wrote that the Garfield Street name failed "to convey the grandeur of this Bridge," or denote the neighborhood which it served.[33] Although the City considered the request to have "little merit,"[34] in March it did agree to change the name to the Magnolia Bridge,[35] and posted new signs shortly thereafter.

THE RENAMING OF THE BRIDGE

In 1959, Magnolia Community Club President Murray Ferguson started the ball rolling to change the name of the West Garfield Street Bridge to the Magnolia Bridge. Ferguson lived near the Bridge at 2641 West Boston Street with his four children and wife Betty. He thought that it was ridiculous that the Bridge was named for a street that didn't access the bridge, or even exist in the vicinity. In addition, Ballard, Fremont, the University District and Montlake had bridges named after their neighborhoods. Ferguson and Colonel Walcott Denison presented the idea of the name change to Seattle City Council member Myrtle Edwards, who said, "I think it's a fine idea." Ferguson was thrilled because other City bureaucrats showed little interest. "She was so instrumental when others might have blocked it," said Ferguson. Years later, Ferguson was pleased that the bike trail that runs through Myrtle Edwards park and connects to Smith Cove Park passes under the Magnolia Bridge.
—Personal interview with Murray Ferguson, September 22, 2000

This overpass eased congestion at the base of the bridge. Museum of History and Industry #86.5, 753.4. Circa 1957.

In 1960, the Bridge also got a bus shelter on the 15th Avenue West on-ramp. Although a bus shelter may seem like a small improvement, getting one took countless meetings and letters, and $274.87 from the Magnolia Community Club reserve fund.[36] Now bus riders could wait for the bus on the Bridge without getting soaked.

In 1991, when the marina, restaurants and shops were built below the Bluff west of Smith Cove, the developer added entrance and exit ramps on the north and south side of the Bridge. The ramps used the same connection points to the Bridge that the 23rd Avennue West trestle once did.[37] These stubs had been blocked off for years, but they were opened again so that the public could access the Smith Cove waterfront from the Bridge. But there is no access directly to or from Magnolia.

This view of the south side of the bridge, looking toward Queen Anne Hill, shows some remaining scaffolding under the bridge and a Texaco smoke stack in the distance, circa 1930. Seattle Engineering Department #8880.

NEW YEAR'S MUDSLIDE

The 1997 New Year brought the most dramatic trouble the Bridge had ever experienced. On January 2, the backyards of six houses perched on the Bluff near the west end of the Bridge slid down, knocking out several reinforcing beams.[38] Those six houses were damaged,[39] and one house lost a back porch.[40] *The Seattle Times* reported that approximately 20,000 cubic yards of earth moved off the Bluff that day, enough to "fill Husky stadium 12 feet deep."[41]

Part of that earth swept under the Bridge between two support columns, taking some cross braces with it before smashing into a house below. More earth came to rest against one of the Bridge's footings, which jeopardized the Bridge's structural integrity. If that footing had moved, the section of the Bridge that it supported could have collapsed.[42]

Officials closed the Bridge to vehicular traffic, leaving only West Emerson Street and West Dravus Street to serve the 17,000 vehicles that used the Magnolia Bridge each day. Gridlock was the result. The Bridge wasn't scheduled to open for months. *The Seattle Times* reported that most businesses in Magnolia Village suffered from a lack of customers, and a paramedic was stationed in now-isolated Magnolia to respond quickly to any medical emergencies.[43]

Colonel David O'Denius, USA, and his wife Nancy, lost nearly everything after the mudslide and part of the Bridge slammed into their house that was property of the US Navy.[44] They lived in what was originally Bachelor Officers' Quarters, located on the south side of the Bridge, below the house occupied by Admiral William Center, USN. The O'Deniuses and Center had an inkling that the bluff was not stable, because a small mud-slide landed in the O'Deniuses' driveway on January 1, the day before the major slide. On January 2, the Admiral brought out the Navy's Construction Battalion, or "SeaBees" to check the hill. According to Nancy O'Denius, at 4:00 p.m. the SeaBees declared the Navy property on the south side of the Bridge safe.

At 4:30 p.m. part of the Bluff on the north side of the Bridge collapsed,[45] sending a wall of mud into the Bridge, and then into the O'Deniuses' home. The muck and debris from the damaged Bridge knocked down walls and filled the kitchen with mud. Furniture hung over the edge of the house above the garage. Nancy said that they weren't home when the slide hit, but the Admiral was, and he knew that the O'Deniuses' dog was probably in the house. He called the police, who rescued Lucky, a black cocker spaniel, before the O'Deniuses came home.

This 2000 photo shows the Port of Seattle Terminals 90 and 91 and the on-ramp from Smith Cove, which was added in 1991 when the Elliot Bay Marina was built. Note the newly stabilized portion of Queen Anne Hill, which lies above the 15th Avenue West on-ramp at the east end of the bridge. Photo by Sam Sutherland, 2000.

After the slide, the O'Deniuses and Lucky stayed in a hotel for a while before they moved into housing at Fort Lawton. "Everything we owned could be done in one load of laundry. I thought that we'd never have anything again," said Nancy. One night a transient called them and told them that he'd been living in their house, and that he had possession of their marriage certificate, bank records, and other important documents. He wanted money in exchange for the papers. "How dare you call us up and do this to us!" David O'Denius said to the man. He refused to give him any money. They alerted the police and handed over their answering machine tape, which had captured the entire conversation. They never caught the man or got their documents back, and the US Navy paid the City to bulldoze the house shortly afterwards.

The O'Deniuses lost almost everything that they owned but they were able to save some unexpected things, such as the brass bed that they were able to locate because the posts stuck out of the muck. Their Kharastan rug that had been buried under a radiator and two feet of mud, looked considerably better after $250 worth of cleaning.

The Bridge, too, looked considerably better after its rehabilitation; it reopened May 8, 1997,[46] almost two months ahead of schedule. Three contractors had worked on the job; the first on the scene was Sverdrup Civil, Inc., which did the initial work to stabilize the hill, constructed access roads into the slide area so that they could remove the slide material, and began to build a stabilizing wall.[47] Atkinson Construction built a "soldier pile" wall to stabilize the Bluff. They made sure to install a drainage system so that the wall wouldn't act as a dam to the water in the hillside above. Mowat Construction repaired the supports under the Bridge.

Frank Yanagimachi, the City's Project Manager for the slide repairs, said that they later found evidence of an underground spring, which contributed to the weight of the hillside. This coupled with the heavy rainfall and snowstorms of late December,

The January 1997 mudslide swept down the hill between two of the bridge's support columns, knocking out cross braces and filling the Navy home below the bridge with debris. Courtesy of The Seattle Times.

along with the weight of the drainage from the houses located in the area, caused the edge of the Bluff to collapse. When the soldier pile wall was constructed, provisions were made for the neighboring houses to connect their drain spouts to the wall's drainage system, so that water would move safely down the hill.[48]

Although the City had estimated the repair costs would total $5.3 million, they came in under budget at roughly $5.2 million.[49] Federal Highway Administration emergency funds covered about 70% of the costs, and the City paid for the remaining 30%.[50] "It was a lot to get done in such a short period of time, and a relief to get it done in such a short period," said Yanagimachi.

THE EAST SLIDE

1997 brought trouble not only for the west end of the Bridge, but for the east end as well, when heavy rains early in the year caused the greenbelt on the hill above the east end of the Bridge to begin sliding. This movement was much less dramatic than the January slide and didn't directly impact the Bridge—yet.

Queen Anne Hill is located above the Magnolia Bridge on-ramp off from Elliott Avenue West. That part of the hill has steep sections at the top and at the bottom. A relatively gentle slope in the middle separates the steep upper and lower portions. In 1997, some earth slid on the hillside above the on-ramp, but it didn't touch it. Because the slide was relatively minor, the City put the problem on the back burner while it attended to Seattle's numerous other trouble spots caused by the winter storms.[51] This was hardly the first time that part of the hillside proved to be in the grip of dynamic forces; in the 1950s part of 12th Avenue West on Queen Anne was lost to a slide, and photos from earlier in the century show landslides and residents' attempts to build retaining walls.

In March 1997, the City hired the geo-technical and environmental consulting firm Shannon & Wilson to assess the hill and recommend what measures should be taken to stabilize the hillside.[52] The hill continued to move in various places, and in early February 1999, a debris slide encroached upon the Magnolia Bridge on-ramp that is accessed from Elliott Avenue West, making damage repair a "number one priority" for the City.[53] The Street Maintenance Division of Seattle Transportation periodically stopped vehicle traffic onto the on-ramp and cleaned up the debris. It placed bales of hay

> ### MUDSLIDES
>
> *Severe mudslides on Queen Anne hill hit the Magnolia Bridge and a Forward Thrust Operation Triangle Park[1] at the Bridge entrance during 1996 and 1997. Continued sloughing of the hillside finally caused the closure of traffic on the bridge on-ramp in February 1999.[2]*
>
> *At first concrete blocks were used to protect the roadway and park. But numerous new slides from March 1997 to 2000 later expanded the slide area to the south and eventually necessitated the ramp closure to traffic. This meant new designs were necessary and more intensive and expensive work to be done.*
>
> *Owners of homes and condominiums above the slumping Queen Anne Hill slope have spent "a staggering $671,000 of their own money so far to put in a series of retaining walls to protect their property."[3] This hillside has had a long history of slides. A 1950s slide took out 12th Avenue West, which no longer exists except for portions on street ends.*

on the ramp to control the silt, and built a series of "ecology block walls" along the sidewalk to keep dirt off of the ramp. The ramp was closed to traffic by the end of February, because the hill continued to slide, and pushed the ecology block walls out into the travel lanes.[54]

It was clear that the entire hill above the ramp had to be stabilized in order to address the continual creep of debris, and so work on the hillside began in July after Shannon & Wilson assessed the problem and developed a plan.[55] CH2M Hill, a sub-contractor of Shannon & Wilson, designed a retaining wall that would go above the on-ramp, and Frank Coluccio Construction Company did the work.[56] Beginning July 23, crews worked seven days a week for 12 to 18 hours a day.[57]

Three soldier pile walls were built to stabilize the hill; one near West Galer Street and 11th Avenue West, one near 12th Avenue West and West Garfield Street, and one along the on-ramp. The hill was further stabilized by a system of drainage trenches, some as deep as 12 feet.[58] These drainage trenches and a piping system bring the water to either Baker

This March 15, 1915 photo was probably taken from a hotel that was perched on pilings in the tide flats of Smith Cove. Now Builders Hardware and a parking lot are found where the hotel once was, and an on-ramp takes vehicles onto the bridge. The houses at the top of the hill remain today. Seattle Municipal Archives #2771.

sedimentation tanks or sedimentation ponds located on the hill. These tanks and detention ponds remove silt from the water. From there the water flows into the storm sewer system, which empties into Puget Sound via a 36-inch outfall near Pier 91.[59]

The on-ramp remained closed until September 3, 1999. The soldier pile wall near the ramp was not quite complete as it still needed a concrete facing. This was finished by late October 1999. In spring of 2000, a coating was applied to protect the wall from graffiti.[60]

Emergency fund money from the Federal Highway Administration paid for most of the work on the hill.[61] The final bill came to approximately $5.5 million.[62] Project Manager, William Anderson, says the federal government will pay $5 million, and 1997 emergency slide appropriation money from the City will pay for the rest. According to Anderson, the project will be finished by the end of October 2000.

Who owns the land on the hill? The heavily wooded greenbelt is a mixture of Seattle Parks Department land, Seattle Transportation street right-of-ways (land that the City could use to build streets), and the private property of the houses on 11th Avenue West that are perched on top of the hill. The private property owners had been grappling with the problem of the sliding hill for some time, and in 1998 and 1999 the 11th Avenue Homeowners' Association built retaining walls in order to preserve the homes at the top of the hill.

Anderson says that the southern part of the hill is continuing to slide, but it's not jeopardizing any homes or buildings. No retaining walls will be added to that part of the hillside, but trench drains will be installed and re-vegetation work will be done.[63] But Anderson doesn't anticipate another major slide in the stabilized area above the on-ramp to the Bridge in the foreseeable future. "If we've done our job we shouldn't," said Anderson.

A COMMUNITY BRIDGE

The fall of 2000 saw the beginning of construction of the West Galer Street flyover, which will connect the Elliott Avenue West on-ramp to a new port access road and the Immunex Corporation complex, which will be located west of 15th Avenue West and Elliott Avenue West.[64]

From the very beginning, the West Garfield Street/Magnolia Bridge has connected not only Magnolia Bluff to a major thoroughfare, but it has connected Magnolia residents to each other. They were the ones who joined forces and lobbied to have the short-lived wooden trestles replaced by an attractive, permanent structure. The Bridge has evolved to suit the changing needs of the community it serves, and it will continue to be altered as the years go by—probably with as much controversy as it has caused in the past.

Queen Anne mudslides threatened the bridge's east on-ramp between 1997 and 1999. Stabilizing the hill was a major undertaking involving three retaining walls and a drainage system. A pedestrian trail allows access to the $5.5 million project. Photo by Joy Carpine, July 12, 2000.

Joy Carpine is a Seattle native who grew up in Magnolia on 36th Avenue West. She graduated from Franklin High School in 1991, and earned her bachelor's degrees in political science and editorial journalism at the University of Washington in 1996. She is currently a producer for Oxygen Media. As a child, she and her neighborhood friends played regularly in the 70th Reserve Support Command property. They were sorely disappointed that increased security during the Gulf War meant new razor wire that prevented them from retrieving lost balls in the equipment lot via a secret gap in the fence. Her mother Heidi sent her to Discovery Park Nature Day Camp for so many years that Joy had to wait until all the other kids tried to name the beach creatures and their habits before she was allowed to jump in with the answers. The Magnolia News *often uses its photo of her high school ballet class to announce the Roseanne's School of Dance annual recital. Joy is inspired by her many family members and neighbors who have devoted years of service to Seattle and the Magnolia community.*

The Twenty-Year Battle for West Point

By Scott L. Smith

Author's Note: This is the story of a beautiful site that could be the Emerald City's crown jewel, except for a sewage treatment plant located at its most prominent point. The story traces the West Point sewage plant debate as seen through my eyes, based on my experiences serving in the Magnolia Community Club (MCC) for more than 20 years. I served on the Board and as President, but mainly on issues related to the Municipality of Metropolitan Seattle, known as Metro. I also served on the Discovery Park Advisory Committee for many years. To give the reader a taste of the emotions that drove the arguments against expanding and upgrading the treatment plant, I have included my opinions on the issues. Although working for various environmental groups and the MCC, my opinions do not necessarily reflect the views of these organizations. Indeed, some Magnolia residents and a few MCC board members held vastly different opinions and there were many heated arguments. However, while testifying at public hearings and in arguments before the hearing examiner and City Council, I strived to consistently support the Club's position.

PREFACE

Various battles pepper Magnolia's history. "NIMBYism" (Not in My Back Yard) is a term often used to describe opposition to change. Most of us lament change, such as the passing of the horse and buggy, which might represent happy childhood memories. Forces outside our community sometimes cause changes that are not necessarily bad. However, the community must seriously question the reasoning of public agencies seeking the "cheapest alternative" and private groups seeking such things as a variance to zoning or building codes.

Change often has at least some adverse impacts. For example, the Burlington Northern Railroad, prodded by Magnolia and Queen Anne residents, recently took some significant measures to quiet its activities at Interbay. The roar of jets has replaced the modest drone of the DC-3 over Magnolia. Now, the Magnolia Community Club is working hard to bring over-flight airplane noise down to a more acceptable level. The Club has a reputation for bringing together local experts and volunteers necessary to win such battles.

Some battles are internal affairs and include such things as beautification projects and spot rezoning. More intensive battles most often involve inappropriate uses of industrial land bordering Magnolia. Few long-time Magnolia residents can forget the stench from burning garbage at Interbay. It took many years, but what was once a garbage dump is now a golf course.

Opposite: Aerial photo of West Point looking northeast into Discovery Park, showing the landscaped berm and beach trail. The USCG lighthouse residences and VTS radar tower are bottom left. Three of the six digesters and two covered rectangular primary sedimentation tanks are center. The other three digesters, offices and the biosolids-handling buildings are right. The open round secondary settling tanks are upper left. The treatment plant's HPO basins are just off the photo, north of the settling tanks. King County (WPsmallaerial.JPG). Circa 1999.

217

In the past, many land-use decisions were a product of smoke-filled rooms. Most of these decisions are now governed by the federal and state Environmental Protection Acts of 1972, which now require a public process and mandate publication of all the facts regarding a project *before* a decision is made.

Some of the most significant battles pitted Magnolia citizens against public agencies. A battle with the US Army eventually brought Discovery Park into the Seattle parks system. A battle against the Port of Seattle resulted in the Treaty of Magnolia.

Magnolia did not win every battle and some battles remain unresolved. The battle over the West Point Sewage Treatment Plant, for example, is in remission. The most recent eruption of this 30-year battle resulted in more than 100 conditions to the secondary treatment construction permit, some of which will forever affect Magnolia and the daily operation of the West Point sewage plant. These conditions also set a precedent for all future construction projects anywhere in the City.

The Settlement Agreement, also a product of this battle, contains the community's "Bill of Rights" with respect to West Point. Community leaders must guard against public officials ignoring the requirements of this and similar documents. The Battle for West Point will probably erupt again sometime in the future. How will the next Magnolia generations react? Will they remember what history has taught us?

Unidentified Seattle resident enjoying the view from West Point. The lighthouse is at the end of a dirt road. The view is much the same today, except the foreground is cluttered with sewage treatment plant structures. A wide paved road now provides public access to the lighthouse, the West Point sewage treatment plant, and handicapped parking for the West Point beach trails. Courtesy of Neil Smith. Museum of History and Industry, #1999.67.21. Circa 1940.

EARLY SEATTLE PARKS

Early Seattle leaders recognized the need for public parks. Graves were relocated in 1884 to create Denny Park. The City bought Volunteer Park in 1876, using it as a cemetery before it became a park in 1892. Alki Beach had a major amusement center called Luna Park in 1889. The City bought Woodland Park in 1900 despite it being outside the city limits at the time. The City Council continued to acquire park properties in the early 1900s, despite the fact that Seattle still had more trees than people.[1]

Completion of the Hiram Chittenden Locks and the Ship Canal in 1916 lowered the water level in Lake Washington about 8.8 feet, creating hundreds of acres of future park land.

The automobile and streetcar brought people to parks and recreation areas in ever-increasing numbers. Golden Gardens became a city park in 1923 and automobile access made it popular as a swimming beach. However, few people knew of the health threat from raw sewage flowing into Puget Sound less than two miles away at West Point.

West Point, at the western tip of Seattle's Magnolia community is one of the very few beaches in the central Puget Sound basin that is accessible at high tide and also near a large urban population. This alone makes West Point beaches valuable as a recreation resource. The bluffs above West Point have magnificent views of Puget Sound and of the Olympic Mountains. Yet its most valuable asset, limited vehicular access, is what makes it unique in an urban area. As automobiles clog our streets and parking lots, future generations will need such a retreat. This is the primary goal of Discovery Park and, someday, Seattle residents will see the removal of the existing sewage treatment facilities to further this goal.

The West Point Lighthouse, constructed in 1881, was accessible by a narrow dirt road down a steep bluff. In 1886, the City of Seattle swapped 700 acres with the owners, and then deeded this land and West Point to the US Army. Fort Lawton was intended to protect the new naval shipyard at Bremerton, but it has never been clear from whom. Thus, West Point became further isolated from the general public, although many Magnolia residents had access to the Fort and West Point beaches.

Aerial photograph of West Point. Metro has filled portions of the North Beach prior to construction of the primary treatment plant. The raw sewage plume from the original outfall reflects the increase in population. Metro King County Archives. Circa 1963.

DILUTION IS THE SOLUTION

While Seattle was ensuring its citizens had access to nature in an urban environment, it was also facing the challenge of dealing with what to do with the sewage generated by an increasing population. The Fort Lawton tunnel is an early element in Seattle's sewage plan. This is an underground, 12-foot diameter, brick structure extending from Interbay to the North Beach, generally following West Emerson Place and West Commodore Way. The tunnel and a collection system brought sewage from most of Seattle's shoreline outfalls to West Point. Construction on this 3.5-mile sewage tunnel began in 1911 and went into service in 1913. The shallow outfall at the end of this tunnel discharged raw sewage just a few hundred feet offshore. Sewage drifted with the wind and tidal currents, while contaminating most of Magnolia's beaches and even Golden Gardens. This situation became worse as Seattle's population grew.

Public concern over pollution in Lake Washington led to a public vote in 1958 creating the Municipality of Metropolitan Seattle, also known as Metro, to solve sewage treatment problems on a regional basis. Metro planned construction of large treatment plants at West Point and Renton and took over management of the existing treatment plants at Alki, Carkeek, and Richmond Beach. Metro closed the other treatment plants, including those discharging into Lake Washington. A new interceptor diverted Eastside sewage to a treatment plant near Longacres. This new plant discharged directly into the Duwamish River. The existing Fort Lawton tunnel already collected sewage from most of Seattle, thus West Point became the site for the other new treatment plant, which used a new deep-water outfall.

The West Point facility became operational in 1966 on beach property leased from the Army. Some shoreline fill along the North Beach buried a new pipeline connecting the Fort Lawton tunnel to the plant located near the Lighthouse. Metro leased an additional 40 acres of North Beach tidelands from the Department of Natural Resources for possible future expansion. Metro also constructed a sludge lagoon with a barrier wall of large rocks called a rip-rap on the South Beach. The new primary treatment plant drastically altered the beauty of West Point, but removed a major source of pollution from local beaches.

Metro obtained a federal grant to test the use of sewage sludge as fill material. The idea included building a road from Pier 91 to West Point by gradually extending the rip-rap from the lagoon all along the shores of Magnolia. However, the sludge soaked up rainwater like a sponge and the test failed.

Originally the West Point plant digested sewage sludge and collected the by-product, methane gas, as fuel. After the sludge test failure, Metro diverted the digested sludge into the outfall where it settled to the bottom of Puget Sound. However, the State Water Quality Act of 1971 put a stop to this practice because sludge is only slightly better than raw sewage. In 1972, Metro opted to dewater the sludge to a mud-like cake and truck it off-site. Metro investigated several disposal options, including soil enhancement to

---

PRIMARY TREATMENT

Primary treatment is a physical process that screens and separates sewage solids from water by slowing the influent velocity at the plant. Some chemicals assist the settling process. The raw sewage coming into the plant is dirty gray and contains several thousand milligrams of suspended solids per liter. Primary treatment has the following steps:

The collected wastewater passes through rotary screens to remove sand and debris from the plant's influent. After washing, this material ends up in a landfill.

The influent enters large rectangular tanks with slow-moving scrapers that collect the settled solids from the tank bottoms for additional treatment (digestion).

Before 1995, the West Point primary effluent got a heavy dose of chlorine to kill coliform bacteria before being discharged into Puget Sound.

After primary treatment, the water is nearly clear, but with suspended solids reduced to a few hundred milligrams per liter. Since 1995, this effluent goes to the new secondary treatment process.

---

grow trees on a University of Washington test site at Pack Forest. The new State Environmental Protection Act required an Environmental Impact Statement (EIS), the first of many. Metro had promised that Magnolia residents would not see, hear, or smell the West Point treatment plant, but its existence suddenly became obvious as the tandem trucks, hauling the smelly sludge, began rumbling through the community.

The real battle for public use of the 32 acres of land at West Point began in 1972 with the passage of Public Law 92-500. This law established the national goal of ". . . protection and propagation of fish, shellfish, and wildlife and provides for recreation in and on the water . . . by 1977." Achieving this goal required a minimum of secondary treatment (see page 221) for all sewage effluent discharged into waters of the United States. This landmark federal legislation came at a time when many communities across the nation were still dumping raw sewage into the nearest body of water. Metro's newly constructed primary sewage treatment facilities at West Point were, supposedly, the long-range solution to all of our water quality problems. PL 92-500 complicated things, requiring upgraded facilities at the West Point sewage treatment plant (Renton already had secondary treatment).

The Department of Defense further complicated things by declaring Fort Lawton surplus property. The City of Seattle took title to 534 acres of the Fort at no cost. The military housing transferred to the US Navy, and the Army Reserve retained some property. No longer buffered and isolated by the Fort, the West Point beaches suddenly became accessible to the general public. Park planners and Discovery Park supporters saw an opportunity to restore West Point to a natural condition and remove the treatment plant in the process. This was the beginning of a long uphill legal and political battle.

Metro held lots of public meetings between 1972 and 1977, but not much changed. Metro had drawings showing 40 acres of shoreline fill at West Point for the facilities required to comply with PL 92-500. Metro also talked about leap-frogging secondary treatment to Best Practicable Treatment (BPT, see page 226). PL 92-500 recognized that some sensitive waters in the nation, such as Lake Tahoe, might require a higher level of treatment to preclude water quality problems. Eventually, it became clear that Metro's definition of BPT was something called "advanced primary," requiring only a few minor modifications to the existing West Point treatment plant. Metro went with this strategy by citing studies of the Central Puget Sound basin that showed no signs of stress from the primary effluent being discharged off West Point. Metro argued it would be better to spend the money solving the region's combined sewer overflows.

Construction photo of pipes from the Fort Lawton tunnel portal being buried along the North Beach. A diversion structure (upper left) will split sewage flows from the large pipe into three smaller pipes near the primary treatment plant area. King County Archives #W1-147. Circa 1964.

There was a steady stream of environmental impact studies, public hearings, and political maneuvering through 1982.

REGIONAL WATER QUALITY PLAN
However, in 1977, Metro issued an EIS that compared various secondary treatment options and combined sewer overflow alternatives. Metro estimated the costs of upgrading to secondary treatment and compared these with using only primary treatment at West Point and various options for correcting the combined sewer overflows in and near Seattle. The most expensive alternative in this study was for a new secondary treatment plant at Interbay and abandoning the facilities at West Point. This would mean that the City would have to pay for demolishing the concrete at West Point and restore the land for recreational use.

This EIS, while still a draft and open for public comment, had presented the environmental community and the Magnolia Community Club with a dilemma. Upgrading the West Point Sewage Treatment Plant to secondary treatment might destroy valuable tidelands with fill and adversely impact adjacent Discovery Park with machinery noise, truck traffic and sewage odor. On the other hand, continued discharge of primary effluent from West Point almost certainly risked long-term damage to Puget Sound. The combined sewer overflows required correction in either case.

Metro studies showed Puget Sound had an abundance of dissolved oxygen and apparently remained unaffected by the biological oxygen demand pollutants in the effluent being discharged at West Point. However, sewage contamination appearing in isolated bays miles from West Point went unexplained. Moreover, pollutants from hundreds of industrial sources also ended up in Seattle's sewage system. Chemicals and heavy metals were accumulating in bottom sediments and impacting bottom fish. Primary treatment removed about half of these industrial pollutants, while secondary treatment promised to remove more than 90%. Secondary treatment was a very expensive solution to a problem that might otherwise have unknown economic impacts if each individual business had to fully treat what it discharged into the sewer.

The environmental community threatened a lawsuit in 1980 to force Metro to remove the sludge lagoon at West Point. Removal of the lagoon had been a condition of the City's original construction permit, but was repeatedly postponed by Metro because of the high cost of hauling the accumulated sludge to a dumpsite. The Seattle Parks Department resolved the issue in the following year by using the sludge in Discovery Park as fill over rubble from demolished buildings. This left a budget surplus with which Metro hired Wolf Bauer, a beach-restoration consultant, to restore the South Beach at West Point.

A PL-92-500 amendment permitted cities near the ocean to apply for a marine waiver from secondary treatment and, if approved, continue discharging primary effluent into the offshore currents. The intent of this waiver was to reduce construction costs faced by coastal cities such as Los Angeles. However, Puget Sound is not the ocean. Most coastal cities decided to use secondary treatment anyway, obtaining federal grants for up to 75% of the cost.

Metro decided to apply for this waiver in 1978 because of high costs of secondary treatment and the documented water quality problems of combined sewer overflows within Seattle. Metro staff argued that Puget Sound flushed quickly and the currents off West Point flowed generally northward. They blamed seals, whales, and passing ships for the pollution detected in nearby bays and inlets, but never funded studies to determine the actual cause. The environmental community strongly opposed the waiver application because it did not protect the long-term health of Puget Sound.

During this debate, some people asserted that the Puget Sound salmon population decline started with primary treatment at West Point. Actually, this decline probably resulted from several factors mostly unrelated to sewage treatment. Destruction of inter-tidal habitat from shoreline fill, a typical cause, began

Aerial view of West Point as the primary treatment plant nears completion. The digesters are complete and a roof covers the primary sedimentation tanks. The rip-rap enclosure on the South Beach is the sludge lagoon and the beach disturbance is from the new outfall construction. The effluent pump house is under construction next to the digesters. King County Archives. Circa 1965.

early in Seattle's history. This allegation added spice to the debate, and in 1999 the Puget Sound salmon would become an endangered species, whatever the causes for its diminished population.

The Metro request for a waiver languished until granted in 1981 by the US Environmental Protection Agency, pending approval by the Washington Department of Ecology (WDOE). The environmental community filed a lawsuit to block the waiver in 1982. The WDOE finally approved the waiver in 1983, but reversed itself in 1984, citing high levels of heavy metals and other pollutants in sewage. Further, the WDOE imposed a 1995 deadline on Metro to achieve secondary treatment or risk a building moratorium in the West Point service area. Metro later cited this deadline as another reason for West Point expansion, claiming acquisition and development of any non-shoreline site prior to the deadline impossible.

The WDOE required Metro to reduce combined sewer overflows (CSO, see page 228) by 75%, but Metro argued it had already reduced them by that amount. The WDOE made it clear that Metro must reduce these overflows by another 75% and eventually have no more than one overflow event per year per outfall. In retrospect, it is strange that Metro tried to avoid secondary treatment by citing the CSO reductions as more important. Then, when forced to upgrade to secondary treatment, Metro considered its previous combined overflow reductions adequate.

By this time, the City of Seattle already had an overflow reduction program underway. This combined with Metro's previous efforts had reduced most of the Lake Washington overflows to one event per year. However, Metro still had major outfalls at Lake Union and Elliott Bay, each with only expensive solutions on the drawing board.

PLAN-LEVEL PERMIT PROCESS

Metro issued a second EIS in 1985 that identified four alternatives to upgrading the facilities at West Point and dealing with the CSO issue. However, this EIS completely ignored the City of Seattle's Shoreline Management Program that stated:

"Expansion of existing sewage treatment plants is prohibited in the Shoreline District unless no feasible alternative to such location exists.

The determination as to feasibility shall be based upon the goals and policies of Resolution 25173, the Shorelines Management Act of 1971, as amended, and a full consideration of the environmental, social, and economic impacts on the community."

SECONDARY TREATMENT

Secondary treatment is a biological treatment process, generally used after primary treatment. Secondary treatment has the following steps:

At West Point, the primary effluent goes into another set of large tanks where it mixes with high purity oxygen (HPO) to stimulate the growth of naturally occurring bacteria

The oxygenated liquid settles in large round tanks where the bacteria consume sewage solids and gradually die.

The settled solids go to the digesters.

The clarified effluent requires much less chlorination (than primary effluent) before discharge.

After secondary treatment, the water is clear, with less-than 30 milligrams (suspended-solids) per liter. This effluent appears drinkable, but still contains large amounts of phosphorus and nitrogen compounds. These compounds can have adverse impacts on some receiving waters, such as Lake Washington.

During a hearing before the City Council, in an effort to communicate that the Draft EIS was inadequate, I told the members that the four shoreline alternatives were not apples and oranges, but lemons. A few days later the City Council declared the Draft EIS inadequate because of the Shoreline Management Program, forcing Metro to issue a supplemental EIS in 1986 proposing three conceptual non-shoreline alternatives:

- *A new treatment plant at Interbay (5I), while retaining a building at West Point for a pumping station to the existing outfall. This proposal had the plant split on both sides of Dravus Street, requiring a new overpass.*
- *A new treatment plant in the Duwamish industrial area (5D), between East Marginal Way and First Avenue South. This alternative required an expensive pipeline from Interbay to get north-end sewage to the Duwamish plant. Another pipe crossed the Duwamish River to take the treated effluent under West Seattle to an outfall near Alki Point.*
- *Smaller plants at both the Interbay and the Duwamish sites (5S). This eliminated the long underground pipeline, but still had major impacts on two communities and carried the highest price tag.*

Although this plan-level document was not site specific, people all over the region took it as such and became upset. Eastside residents did not like the proposed increase in sewer rates. Kenmore residents objected to the proposal for a small treatment plant on their shoreline. Georgetown residents were certain that odors from a Duwamish plant (alternatives 5D or 5S) would invade their neighborhood. Some Queen Anne and Magnolia residents objected to anything resembling a treatment plant at Interbay in lieu of West Point. During public meetings, Metro staff members caused more enmity by disclaiming technology could control sewage odors at any location, but that the winds dispersed the odors at West Point. Their statements inferred that better the West Point raccoons suffer rather than whole neighborhoods. It was the first time Metro admitted its treatment plant smelled.

While arguments raged over the non-shoreline alternatives, Metro published another Draft EIS for construction of additional digesters at West Point. The three existing digesters were gradually filling up with sand because cleaning required taking a digester out of service. Previously, Metro had used the sludge lagoon to dump the sand cleaned from a digester. Rather than cleaning and trucking the sand off-site, Metro had allowed it to accumulate within the digesters. Metro claimed increased sewage flows precluded one digester being removed from service for cleaning. Metro stated that the funds invested in the additional two digesters would not influence the still pending site decision. However, the timing of this event and the lack of documentation on the volume of sand actually removed from the digesters still clouds Metro issues.

DIGESTION

Digestion is a method of treating one of the by-products of primary and secondary treatment. Solids (sludge) collected during the treatment process go to large tanks (digesters) where anaerobic (without oxygen) decomposition takes place. The digesters operate sequentially, each holding solids for several days, while reducing the volume and releasing methane gas. The digested solids are then partially dewatered and transported off-site as bio-solids. The collected methane gas becomes fuel in engines to produce electricity (co-generation) or to drive treatment plant pumps.

The Metro Water Quality Committee recommended the non-shoreline alternative 5D, despite the high cost for the underground conveyance system from Interbay and property acquisition in the Duwamish industrial area. However, the full Metro Council rejected this recommendation July 17, 1986, voting 19 to 16 for the least-expensive alternative, which required the largest physical expansion on the West Point site. Some doubted the proposed facilities could fit on the West Point site without shoreline fill, thus violating the State Shoreline Management Act. Park supporters were certain the site would obliterate public access to the beaches with concrete and sewage odors.

Logically, the Water Quality Committee members had the highest level of technical knowledge and thus made a sound judgment in selecting an alternative. However, the full-council vote was purely political since most of the 38-member Metro Council represented county districts and Eastside cities. Metro eventually came under the control of King County and the Metro Council disbanded, correcting this imbalance in representation.

Meanwhile, the National Oceanic and Atmospheric Administration (NOAA) sued Metro and the City of Seattle, claiming water pollution from combined sewer outfalls had damaged shorelines and inter-tidal areas of the Duwamish River and Elliott Bay shorelines and adversely impacted aquatic life in these areas. NOAA won its lawsuit and the City of Seattle and Metro had to spend several million dollars trying to remedy some of the damage in the Duwamish River. Fish habitat improvements appeared in several areas, but it was a token effort because no amount of money could remedy 100 years of abuse to our inter-tidal areas.

The next conflict came before the City Hearing Examiner late in 1987 to determine if there was a feasible alternative to upgrading the West Point plant. This determination preceded the City Council's consideration of a permit allowing Metro to continue with project-level planning. This three-sided hearing pitted the City and the Puget Sound Water Quality Defense Fund against Metro. The Defense Fund represented several environmental groups and the Magnolia Community Club. The Defense Fund founder, Tom Wimmer, also founded the Washington Environmental Council.

The hearing proceeded with difficulty. Each time the City or Defense Fund found a discrepancy in Metro's arguments, Metro revised its plan, reducing cost or footprint at West Point. Unfortunately, the non-shoreline alternatives did not receive similar improvements. Thus, the differences between expanding West Point and any of the non-shoreline alternatives kept getting larger. Despite Metro's arguments to the contrary, the hearing examiner

Construction photo of North Beach with Shilshole Marina in the background. The concrete retaining walls are visible along the berm prior to landscaping. Vegetation now hides the concrete and most of the treatment plant. King County (9515.2 #31 WestPoint TPcnstrtn.JPG). Circa 1996.

BEST PRACTICABLE TREATMENT

Best Practicable Treatment, also called advanced waste treatment, generally removes specific pollutants from secondary effluent. Effluent discharged from a secondary treatment plant still contains phosphorus and nitrogen compounds. Some receiving waters are sensitive to one or both of these nutrients. Lake Washington was dying from the nutrients in sewage effluent from several small secondary treatment plants that were discharging into the Lake prior to 1966.

ruled there was at least one feasible non-shoreline alternative—a new secondary treatment plant at Duwamish. After several days of arguments before the City Council in early 1988, the Council voted to overrule the hearing examiner's recommendation, citing adverse community impacts and high sewer rates.

In the months before this hearing, Council member Norm Rice chaired a Metro sub-committee called the Mitigation Committee. Among other things, Rice proposed Metro create a $50-million fund to acquire and improve public access to the Seattle shoreline, thus replacing the recreational value lost by upgrading the West Point plant. The proposal probably swayed some votes on the Metro Council. However, the fund had shrunk to $25 million during the arguments on "feasibility" before the hearing examiner. Metro tried reducing the fund to $12 million during the City Council hearings, but the chairperson cut off debate on this issue. In 1991, the City of Seattle got $25 million and King County got $5 million for shoreline procurement and improvement, primarily for salt-water beaches.

Council member Rice's spouse, Constance, had a good job with Metro at this time. It was difficult to not see this as a conflict of interest, as Rice's actions seem to reflect the Metro preference for upgrading West Point, especially since he promoted this position before the EIS and hearing examiner record came before the City Council.

The Defense Fund appealed the City Council's decision to the State Shoreline Hearings Board arguing that least-cost alternatives always endanger shoreline sites. Arguments before the Shoreline Board began in the spring of 1989. After thirty days of hearings, the longest shoreline hearing on record, the Board had a split vote (3 to 3) giving Metro a shaky win. On appeal, the State Appeals Court judges found no reason to reverse the Board's decision.

PROJECT-LEVEL PERMIT PROCESS

Metro issued another EIS in 1989, discussing site-specific construction impacts for the expansion and upgrading of the West Point treatment plant. The MCC decided to proceed independently, but parallel with the environmental community. Forthcoming construction at West Point adversely impacted only Magnolia, while Puget Sound impacts concerned the Defense Fund. The Seattle Department of Construction and Land Use issued a long list of proposed conditions to the permit. These conditions went before the hearing examiner in May 1990. This time the examiner came from out of town to assure neutrality.

This four-sided hearing went on for over a month, with Metro sparing no expense in exhibits and witnesses. The MCC spent only $100 and called only one witness to explain sewage odor. Several Magnolia residents, including some lawyers and engineers, contributed time and critical advice during this hearing.

After the hearing examiner published his findings and recommendations, the parties moved into the City Council chambers. Paul Kraabel, who grew up in Magnolia, chaired these hearings. Metro still argued against many of the nearly 200 recommended conditions, but these efforts were unsuccessful. The hearing examiner's recommendations became the Permit Conditions with only minor changes in language.

At the end of the City Council hearings, I first learned of talks between the environmental community and Metro in an effort to avoid more litigation and construction delays. I represented the MCC in these negotiations. Representatives of the parties signed the resulting Settlement Agreement, with then-President Ursula Judkins signing on February 19, 1991, for the Magnolia Community Club.

The community steeled itself for construction impacts scheduled to start in the spring of 1991. Meanwhile, Magnolia community representatives began meeting to decide how to spend the community mitigation funds set aside by the Permit Conditions and the Settlement Agreement. A community-wide vote easily put a swimming pool at the top of the list.

Magnolia had tried to get a swimming pool since 1921, but each of several efforts failed. This time the City Council threatened to scuttle the effort by refusing to fund the pool's operation and maintenance costs. Discussions with the Council finally ironed out the sticking points and the outdoor Magnolia pool on 32nd Avenue West just south of West Smith Street became a reality in 1998. John Wells led these determined Magnolia citizens.

Mitigation also funded the landscaping along West Government Way, stoplights at several intersections, the new Visitor's Center at Discovery Park, and purchased some property in the Kiwanis Ravine. Part of the $25-million shoreline improvement money is expected to go toward the purchase or development of the surplus Navy property at Terminal 91. Of course, Metro also improved some of the roads within Discovery Park, and paid for the berms and landscaping surrounding the West Point treatment plant, almost hiding it from public view.

The temporary pier at West Point became a key mitigation element. Metro brought in countless barges loaded with sand and gravel. Contractors mixed most concrete on-site with a temporary batch plant. The net effect of barging eliminated hundreds of construction trucks from Magnolia streets on a daily basis.

During the first few months, Metro contractors violated dozens of permit conditions. The first violation occurred when contractors began clearing the unused portions of the West Point site on a weekend in May 1991. A permit condition prohibited weekend work on the site when most visitors use Discovery Park. By the fall, the alleged violations filled several pages. The City Council brought the parties together again for more heated words. Following this meeting, Metro gradually brought their contractors into line and one senior Metro engineer found a new job in California.

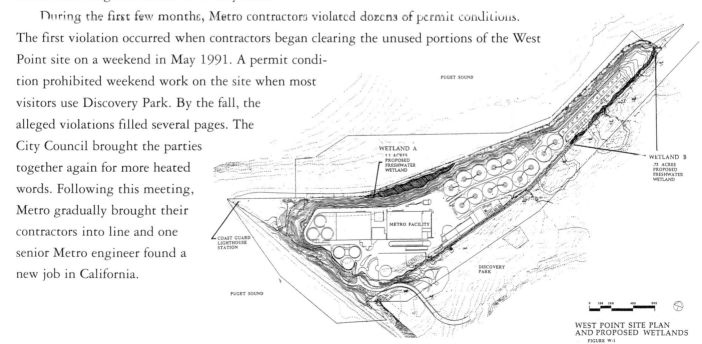

WEST POINT SITE PLAN
AND PROPOSED WETLANDS
FIGURE W-1

The remaining four years of construction saw reasonable compliance with the permit conditions. There are several operational permit conditions, such as noise and odor control at the plant. These conditions require continued compliance and monitoring of plant performance forever.

The upgraded and expanded West Point treatment plant began secondary treatment in December 1995, meeting the state deadline, followed by a formal dedication in July 1996 (when the weather was better). However, a steady stream of odor complaints came from Park visitors during the spring of 1996. The permit conditions required Metro, now a department within King County government, to reduce sewage odors to no more than three odor-units. By definition, 50% of an average population will smell something at one odor-unit, so the three odor-unit limit imposed by the City Council will be noticeable to many park visitors.

COMBINED SEWER OVERFLOW

Combined sewers are pipelines carrying both storm water and raw sewage. Many older cities, including Seattle, have a combined sewer system, while newer communities usually have separate sewer and storm water pipelines. In a combined system, a heavy rain often fills the pipeline and an emergency discharge must occur to prevent property damage. This discharge is mostly surface runoff, but always contains some sewage contaminating the waters near the discharge location.

A site west of Elliott Avenue West at West Mercer Street is slated to become a new storm water facility in late 2000. When completed, this plant is expected to reduce the number and volume of overflows at the Denny Way outfall by storing storm water for later treatment at West Point. Similarly, Metro had already converted the Alki and Carkeek primary treatment plants to serve as storm water treatment plants in the mid 1990s.

However, these separated sewer systems have one major flaw. Whatever goes into the storm sewer goes untreated into the receiving waters, including engine oil, animal wastes, silt, lawn fertilizer, herbicides and pesticides. All of these substances are harmful to the near-shore aquatic community and eventually to us. Effective upstream controls might avoid future construction of expensive storm-water treatment facilities.

Metro staff blamed the sewage odors on the privatized sludge-drying process operated by Reidel/SMI, a steam drying operation that produced a dry product. However, the existing digesters had a long history of odor complaints and might have contributed to the problem. King County promised a full investigation.

Late in 1996, Gary Locke, the outgoing King County executive (and governor-elect) ordered the Reidel/SMI facility shut down. The County Council reversed this order after objections by the parties of the Settlement Agreement. The new County Executive, Ron Sims, and Council member Larry Phillips discussed the Settlement Agreement with party representatives in early 1997. The County then hired a consulting firm to research the process and similar technologies.

The consultant's report concluded the sludge drying process was impractical since no other city used the technology. This conclusion ignored the fact that no other city had permit conditions limiting sludge hauling. Thus, no other city needed to develop a new sludge disposal technology. This argument fell on deaf ears and the County bought out Reidel/SMI's interest in the facility and shut it down in 1998.

One factor in the shutdown order came from language in Metro's union contract that allowed only Metro employees to operate sewage facilities. This means that privatized sewage facilities are illegal in King County. At what point this contract clause was included in the contract without notice is still unclear.

One important permit condition limits the number of bio-solids (sludge) trucks from the plant. The Settlement Agreement also stated a goal for eventual removal of the existing sludge digesters. Had Reidel/SMI eliminated its deficiencies and expanded its sludge-drying process, it might have satisfied both of these requirements. Exactly what will happen to the existing digesters is now an unanswered question. However, without some new technology the number of bio-solids trucks traveling from Magnolia will certainly increase as sewage flows to the plant increase. Almost certainly, increasing the West Point plant's treatment capacity to 159-million gallons per day (mgd) will eventually result in exceeding the permit condition limit without some major changes in handling of bio-solids.

Probably the most important statement in the Settlement Agreement involves the future expansion of the West Point treatment plant to its ultimate 159-mgd capacity. The Agreement limits the discharge of sewage effluent pollutants to the maximum allowed by State law when the plant is operating at its present design limit of 133-mgd. That means that increasing capacity requires, somehow, that the West Point plant get more efficient as it gets older. This statement intentionally puts severe constraints on any future expansion of treatment capacity. These constraints could get even tighter if the legislature ever imposes tighter limits on sewage pollutants.

> ### BIOLOGICAL OXYGEN DEMAND
>
> *Biological Oxygen Demand (BOD) is any organic material that takes up oxygen during decomposition. Treatment plants regularly test samples of treated sewage effluent for BOD. Too much BOD can deplete the receiving waters of the oxygen required for survival of aquatic life forms. State law requires effluent discharged into Washington waters contain no more than 30 milligrams of BOD per liter.*

FUTURE EXPANSION

During 1999, the King County Council discussed whether to expand the West Point treatment plant to its maximum capacity (159-mgd) or to build a more expensive north-end treatment plant. Earlier discussions between the County Executive, Ron Sims, King County Council member Larry Phillips and representatives of the parties to the Settlement Agreement cited several reasons for a new north-end plant:

- *A north-end plant is inevitable regardless of what happens at West Point. It is only a question of when.*
- *Further delays in constructing a north-end plant will only increase costs and compound existing problems complying with the permit conditions and the Settlement Agreement.*
- *Increasing West Point capacity has serious financial and legal risks if the plant cannot meet the Settlement Agreement constraints on effluent pollution.*

Operational photo of unidentified operator in primary treatment plant control room showing mimic board and recording devices. King County Archives. Circa 1966.

In December 1999, the County Council finally adopted a plan to build a new north-end treatment plant, relieving Magnolia from the impacts of any additional West Point construction in the near future. However, the expansion threat remains as long as the West Point plant and politicians exist.

The future of the West Point plant and its relationship to the Magnolia community requires continual review. Those in positions of leadership within the Magnolia community must ensure future compliance with the Permit Conditions and the Settlement Agreement. Promises easily become forgotten or ignored by politicians blinded by the high cost of public works projects required to meet the needs of an ever-increasing regional population. Expanding West Point will always seem a simple solution.

The Battle for West Point will probably continue well into the twenty-first century. Many of the concrete structures at the existing West Point treatment plant will require renewal in 50 years or so. In other cities, treatment plants usually include a large land buffer that provides space for future expansion, upgrading and renewal of facilities. However, the Settlement Agreement prohibits expanding the West Point plant beyond the present 32-acre footprint. This makes any renewal of the West Point facilities extremely difficult using any existing technology. What options might be available in the future are uncertain.

Scott Smith came to Magnolia in 1947 with his mother and stepfather, Lois and Bud LeRoux. Graduating from Queen Anne High School in 1949, he immediately went on active duty with the US Navy. He served as an aviation electronic technician at Naval Air Station Sandpoint before becoming a naval aviation cadet in 1950. Completing flight training in 1951, he flew in several Navy attack squadrons, served as in instructor at Pensacola, Florida, and commanded a carrier attack squadron aboard the USS Ticonderoga *during the Vietnam War. He retired after 25 years in the Navy and returned to Magnolia with his wife, Rosealma, and their children, Jennifer and Bradley.*

Scott joined the MCC Board in 1974 and began working on Metro issues. Appointed to Metro's Citizen's Water Quality Advisory Committee, he served as its first elected chairman in 1975. He became president of the Magnolia Community Club in 1978 and continued to serve as the Club's Metro chairman for several years thereafter. Scott also served on the Discovery Park Advisory Committee for many years and instructed marine-technology subjects at Seattle Central Community College.

With the help and advice of countless others, including several attorneys, Scott represented the Magnolia Community Club on Metro issues before the hearing examiner and City Council. He was also a major witness before the State Shorelines Hearing Board and represented the Magnolia Community Club during the Settlement Agreement negotiations.

The Chronology of West Point

1851 Seattle is first settled. The first water closet is installed in the White House.

1881 US Lighthouse Service erects the West Point Light, the only red beacon for mariners on Puget Sound.

1882 Seattle health officers criticize sewers as inadequate for a town of 4,000.

1889 Seattle voters approve the largest bond issue yet ($190,000) to build a sewerage system.

1892 Seattle city engineer R. H. Thomson proposes West Point as the site for an outfall into Puget Sound.

1904 Study of currents identifies West Point as the best discharge point for untreated wastewater into Puget Sound.

1911 Seattle completes the Fort Lawton tunnel to bring flows to West Point, the Lake Union tunnel for discharge into Elliott Bay, and the Rainier Valley system for discharge into the Duwamish River.

1940 Seattle City Council decides to build its first primary treatment plant near the Duwamish River off Diagonal Way and proceeds to construction.

1952 Seattle City Council decides to expand the Duwamish River plant and build a primary treatment plant at West Point, although only the expansion actually occurred.

1956 King County, Seattle and Washington State fund a comprehensive sewage and drainage plan calling for closing the Duwamish River plant, completing pipes to West Point and building primary treatment plants at West Point and Renton, with regional capacity.

1957 Voters reject a proposal to create the Municipality of Metropolitan Seattle (Metro) to be responsible for sewage, public transportation and comprehensive planning in the Seattle/King County area.

Seattle opens its first primary treatment plant on salt water, at Alki Point.

1958 Voters approve creation of Metro, with responsibilities limited to regional sewage collection and treatment, including clean-up of Lake Washington. The Metro Council is assembled with representatives from major jurisdictions in the region.

West Point terminus of the twelve-foot-diameter Fort Lawton tunnel constructed in 1911. Weir just inside the portal diverted storm water and sewage directly onto North Beach. King County Archives, #W1-153. Circa 1963.

1959 Metro Council adopts the first comprehensive sewer plan for the region, including construction of regional treatment plants at West Point and Renton and closure of the Duwamish River plant.

1960 Washington Supreme Court upholds agreements between Metro and Seattle, clearing the way to implement the comprehensive sewer plan.

1961 Independent engineering study confirms feasibility of the comprehensive sewer plan.

1962 The US Army grants Metro a 99-year easement for approximately 30-acres at West Point for a sewage treatment plant and related facilities.

1963 Metro begins construction of its $12.9-million primary treatment plant at West Point.

1964 Washington State Department of Natural Resources grants Metro an easement for a sewage disposal plant on 40 acres of tidelands at West Point.

US Department of Health, Education and Welfare conveys 2.67 acres of surplus property to Metro at West Point for public health purposes.

1966 Metro dedicates its primary treatment plant at West Point.

1970 President Richard Nixon signs the "Fort Lawton Bill," allowing transfer of surplus federal lands at no cost back to the cities that donated them.

1971 Metro Council reaffirms the comprehensive sewer plan's two-plant concept.

1972   Federal government transfers 391-acres of Fort Lawton to Seattle for development of the largest park in the City's system.

Federal government transfers approximately 40 surplus acres at West Point to Metro, including the same 30 acres granted to Metro by easement in 1962.

Congress passes the Clean Water Act requiring secondary treatment at all municipal wastewater plants by 1977; President Nixon vetoes but Congress overrides.

1973   Metro begins planning to bring its primary treatment facilities on Puget Sound into compliance with the secondary treatment requirement.

1974   Washington State Department of Ecology issues a five-year interim permit for continued discharge at West Point, later extended to remain in effect until secondary treatment is in place.

Newly formed Puget Sound Water Quality Defense Fund sues to stop Metro's plan to pipe solids from Renton to West Point.

1976   Metro begins soliciting public comment on its plan for secondary facilities.

1977   Lobbying by salt water dischargers, including Metro, convinces Congress to amend the Clean Water Act to allow waiver of secondary treatment requirement for existing facilities, as long as marine water quality is protected.

1978   Metro applies for secondary treatment waivers for all four of its wastewater plants with outfalls into Puget Sound.

1981   Metro eliminates its solids test lagoon at West Point and restores the south beach with gravel and grasses.

US Environmental Protection Agency tentatively approves a waiver for West Point, subject to concurrence by the state Department of Ecology.

1982   Metro moves into the final stage of its facilities plan for continued primary treatment, as allowed by the waiver.

A coalition made up of the Puget Sound Water Quality Defense Fund, Friends of Discovery Park, Washington Environmental Council and Legal Advocates of Washington sues to block the Metro waiver.

1983   Metro Council approves facilities plan, including continuance of primary treatment at all four Puget Sound plants.

State Department of Ecology concurs with waiving the secondary treatment requirements for West Point.

1984   State Department of Ecology issues its policy and strategy for municipal wastewater management, noting that secondary treatment will eventually be required for all plants.

Metro issues a study report documenting toxicant problems, including those in Elliott Bay, and compares the ability of primary and secondary treatments to remove toxicants in wastewater.

National Oceanographic and Atmospheric Administration releases its analysis of currents, showing protracted retention—not rapid flushing—of discharge into Puget Sound.

State Department of Ecology reverses its earlier decision and orders Metro to provide secondary treatment for the West Point service area by early 1991.

Metro begins soliciting public input on a program to address toxicants in Elliott Bay and the Duwamish River estuary, including upgrading plants to secondary treatment and increasing control of overflows from combined sanitary/stormwater sewers.

1985   Metro issues a draft environmental impact statement analyzing four alternatives for secondary treatment, all involving continued treatment at West Point. Seattle protests that no inland locations were studied.

1986   Metro Council agrees to consider Seattle's proposal to replace West Point with a major secondary facility in the Duwamish River industrial area or at Interbay, or replace West Point with smaller facilities at both sites.

Seattle City Council withdraws its legal challenge to Metro's draft environmental impact statement and concurs with the mayor's appointment of a Citizens' Technical Advisory Committee.

Photo of primary treatment plant construction activity at West Point, looking west towards Bainbridge Island in the background (February 1964).
King County Archives #W1-146.

Metro issues a supplemental environmental impact statement on inland alternatives to upgrading West Point.

Metro Council rejects its Water Quality Committee's recommendation for a Duwamish-area plant and adopts a plan to upgrade West Point.

Metro applies to the City of Seattle for a plan-level siting permit for West Point.

1987   State extends its deadline for complying with federal discharge water quality standards at West Point to Dec. 31, 1995.

Metro completes construction of two additional solids digesters at West Point to increase capacity.

Seattle's Department of Construction and Land Use recommends against issuing the plan-level siting permit on grounds that other sites are available.

1988   Seattle City Council issues a plan-level siting permit, stating that it sees no feasible alternative to upgrading West Point.

Puget Sound Water Quality Defense Fund and others appeal the siting permit to King County Superior Court and to the State Shoreline Hearings Board.

Metro applies to the City of Seattle for a project-level zoning permit.

1989   Metro staff and consultants complete pre-design of the upgraded plant.

Metro Council authorizes contracting with a private company for a new approach to solids processing at West Point.

Superior Court vacates Seattle's plan-level siting permit and remands the matter to the Seattle City Council.

Metro submits a revised application for a project-level siting permit addressing project changes.

State Shoreline Hearings Board ties 3-3 and fails to overturn Seattle's plan-level shoreline permit for West Point; appeal goes to the Washington Court of Appeals.

Seattle City Council issues a new plan-level siting permit for upgrading West Point.

1990   Superior Court upholds Seattle's new plan-level siting permit.

Washington Court of Appeals upholds the State Shoreline Hearings Board's decision not to overturn Seattle's plan-level shoreline permit.

Metro Council sets West Point budget at $578.5-million, based on cost estimates prepared at 25 percent of design.

1991   Seattle City Council issues a project-level siting permit with conditions.

Court of Appeals denies request to reconsider its decision.

US Corps of Engineers issues permits for West Point, including wetland fill.

Metro and project opponents sign a settlement. Opponents agree to file no further appeals and drop pending appeals; Metro agrees to additional environmental mitigation.

Metro awards the site-preparation contract and construction begins.

1995   Metro, now King County Department of Metropolitan Services, begins secondary treatment at West Point.

1997   Construction, landscaping and certification of West Point complete.

Excerpted from Steward of the Waters, *a King County Water Pollution Control booklet, 1995, 37-40*

Twelve-foot-diameter pipe from the Fort Lawton tunnel portal being buried along North Beach. Workers are connecting sections of pipe. King County Archives #W1-109. Circa 1964.

Pioneer Family: Helped Build Magnolia

By Monica Wooton

THE NEW LAND

Heinrich Meiners, cabinet builder, and his wife Catherine, emigrated in 1880 from Wolfenbuttle, Braunschweig Germany, through Ellis Island, before it was an official immigration station. Washington would not become a state until nine years later. The family name was simplified to Miner in the paperwork. Heinrich had a dream when he arrived, one typical for many immigrants, to farm his own land in America. He and Catherine settled in New York for six years, far, far away from Magnolia, the neighborhood that would eventually reap many benefits from this man's family legacy.

While still in New York, their family grew. German-born daughter Alma was joined by Frederick and Dorathea (Dora). Catherine Miner had contracted consumption and it became clear she could not take the climate and poor air of New York. With the need for a healthier place for Catherine to live and the promise of steady employment for Heinrich in the mining industry, they moved on to Denver, Colorado, in 1886.

While in Colorado, there was news of the Great Seattle Fire of June 6, 1889, which lead Heinrich to believe that he could easily get work in the rebuilding efforts in Seattle. His skills as a cabinet builder were well suited for woodworking.[1] So in 1889, the family decided to move again, this time to Seattle. Although, Heinrich didn't know it at the time, he was right about work to be done in Seattle. According to *Highlights of Seattle's History*, "Most everyone agreed the fire . . . in a way, was a blessing in disguise. Frontier Seattle was re-built as a modern city, ready to face the challenges and opportunities of the 1890s."[2]

The timing of the Great Seattle Fire, the Klondike Gold Rush, and Seattle Mayor Robert Moran's shipyard, had a positive impact on Seattle's economy, and proved somewhat lucrative for Heinrich. He built school desks, bank teller cages and many new wood-crafted items needed by a city that had 30 square blocks to rebuild after an overlooked glue pot bubbled over in a carpenter's shop causing the huge fire.

Magnolia remodels today seem to be of grand scale. Small intimate houses make way for this new building trend. Photo Monica Wooton, 2000.

Original citizenship document of Heinrich and Catherine coming to the US from Germany. Courtesy of Miner Family.

After their arrival in Seattle, the Miners lived on Capitol Hill for a short while. According to Helen Miner McDaniels, Heinrich and Catherine's granddaughter, "They pastured their cow near 15th Avenue East and East Mercer. Grandmother suggested that they buy some land in that vicinity. Grandfather . . . asked why he should buy land there, when they could take out a homestead in Darrington for nothing."[3] (Darrington is located about 60 miles northeast of Seattle.)

THE FIGHT FOR THE LAND OF THEIR OWN

In 1886, Heinrich and Catherine were granted US citizenship qualifying them for a land grant under the Homestead Act of May 20, 1862. While some immigrants could get homesteads by proving that they were working on citizenship status, the Miners' citizenship provided them that legal right automatically. There was land still being granted in Darrington, a small town outside Seattle, that offered less crowded spaces and cleaner air. Catherine needed these amenities as her health continued to decline. Heinrich filed a claim in 1890, and joined the more than 400,000 settlers who claimed acres during a five-year period.[4] He wanted to farm this land and earn it, through his labor, using his own hands, to build a place of their own.

Heinrich settled on a piece of property he thought had potential: 160 acres just southwest of the Darrington town center with Brown Creek flowing through it, and Squire Creek flowing on the eastern boundary of the property. On his newly acquired land he built a simple, rustic primitive cabin. He and Catherine tried diligently to get the farm up and running. He took on additional work wherever and whenever he could and used the earnings to improve his property.

Of that period in their lives, the family history relates:

This is the first claim cabin Heinrich built in which he and Catherine lived. Early 1890s. Courtesy of Miner Family.

*"Life on the Darrington Homestead was filled with hardships. Heinrich worked at many odd jobs to support the family. He worked the boronite mines at Windy Pass, built a house at Oso, worked the mines in the Silverton area, and farmed. The flooding of their potato fields and first cabin, Catherine's chronic illness and subsequent frailness finally forced the family to move back to the City of Seattle in 1897."[5]

The homesteading experience was more a nightmare than a dream, but the Miners persisted long enough to gain ownership of the land. They eventually lost one cabin to a flood of the nearby Squire Creek in 1893. They fought hard to fulfill the five-year residency requirement of the Homestead Act, and hung on two more years, finally procuring the piece of Darrington property as their own by residing on it despite the hardships. After all their struggles of seven years, the paperwork arrived making the property formally theirs.

According to the 1961 *World Book Encyclopedia, Volume 8 H,* "Of the public lands that passed into private hands between 1862 and 1900, not more than one acre in six, possibly nine, was settled by a homesteader. Chief benefactors were speculators, who sold the land, and others who sought control of the natural resources of the West." Despite the dire statistics, the Miners had succeeded, to some degree, just by holding onto the land. However, the Miners could not subsist upon nor make a living on the Darrington land.

When they moved back to Seattle, Heinrich obtained steady work at the Moran Brothers Shipyard. He worked on many interesting ships, including "the mighty Nebraska."[6] He was one of 2,100 men in 1898 who worked on Moran's special project building 12 steam sternwheeler riverboats in less than four months for use in the Yukon Gold Rush. Heinrich was later sent to St. Michael, Alaska, to repair storm damage suffered by the boats in the ocean on the trip north. The boats eventually went to the Yukon River to work the Gold Rush, and the workers on the boats were paid in gold coins.[7] By now, Heinrich accepted that the Darrington land would never fulfill his dream of farming, and it was a great disappointment to him.

Heinrich and Catherine Miner. Heinrich still hearty in his seventies, Catherine is frail looking from consumption and much younger in this picture. Courtesy of Miner Family.

FATEFUL MEETING: MAGNOLIA AND THE MINERS

In 1900, Heinrich eventually settled his family in the "Fort Lawton area," as he referred to it, on a lot where he built his family a home. When the railroad tracks came to Interbay shortly thereafter, the house was bought by the railroad, forcing another move upon the family. In 1906, son Frederick built a home for his father that still stands today at 3641 22nd Avenue West. There, Heinrich and Catherine lived four years. Catherine succumbed to frail health and died in 1910, at age 57. Frederick went back to Darrington to gain more home-building experience there.

Heinrich's life changed once he settled into Magnolia. He finally relaxed and enjoyed life more, gardened with a passion, and became a "market-gardener." He raised raspberries, pears, currants, chickens and eggs, and brought them regularly to the Pike Place Market for sale.

Frederick built a home at 3806 25th Avenue West for his wife Lillian and their six children. "Grandpa Henry" lived close by, and loved to spend times with the family and to pass down family stories and humorous tales. Hienrich gardened until his death in 1936 at age 87. From the time he left Darrington, until he died, he only returned there once in his later life, as it was a painful experience for him.

A DREAM THAT WOULDN'T DIE

Heinrich's son, Frederick, loved the homestead in Darrington. The property had been a special part of his young life. He and his sister Dora drew many sketches of homestead living. His father's dream and talent to build were passed along to Fred. He maintained and improved the property as a much loved and cared for recreational property, while involving the whole Miner clan in the enterprise.

Building boats in the backyard, Frederick builds a business This boat is called The Seabird, which brought the family its first car in a trading deal. Courtesy of the Miner Family.

To make a living, Frederick built commercial boats on speculation. In 1911, he began towing cut timber through the narrow channel from Lake Washington to Puget Sound. "There wasn't any deep water between Ballard and Magnolia really then, except when the tides filled the tidelands, before the Hiram M. Chittenden Locks existed," son Walt explained.[8]

There was enough water to float precious fresh-cut lumber to Puget Sound when the tide was high. Katherine "Bo" Miner House, one of Frederick's daughters, describes her father in his hand-built, 35-foot tug: "Before the locks were finished and the waterway deepened, it took an experienced pilot with his little pilot boat to navigate this channel safely. At low tide it was a mud flat and it was very easy to miss the channel and put your boat aground."[9]

There was usually a buyer or good trade to be had for Frederick's boats. Son Fred, Jr. said, "In 1926, our Dad . . . sold a 34-foot trolling boat, *The Seabird*, to a man from Oregon. The man from Oregon had a 1924 Dodge Brothers touring car that Dad took in trade as part payment for the boat. This was our first car."[10] With special permission, Fred launched his boats at the Coast Guard launch on Commodore Way. Besides building boats, Fred was a respected woodworker at many of the local shipyards, including the Moran Shipyard like his father.

On summer Sundays, the Miner family and friends (often up to 20 people) took a boat ride in one of Fred's boats and picnicked on Lake Washington. They loaded into one of Fred's hand-built boats and traveled to Leschi Beach or Madrona Park. Sometimes they wandered as far as Suquamish beach for supper and to play and relax. Today, Coast Guard standards would never allow the boat occupancy they managed out of one of Fred Miner's boats back then!

THE THIRD GENERATION CUT FROM SIMILAR CLOTH

In 1930, it took three teams of hired horses
to haul one of Frederick's newly-built
salmon trawlers from his backyard where it
was built to the Coast Guard launch site at
West Commodore Way to sell. (Frederick
obtained special permission to use the
launch.) The boat was placed on top of two
6-inch thick planks, and skidded along
West Commodore Way to the launch site on

Salmon Bay. The combination of gravel and newly paved streets took 4 inches of wood off
the planks en route! Hired teamsters drove the horse teams and were in charge of the moving
expedition. Young Walt Miner, 13 at the time and third generation Miner, walked proudly
alongside his father's handiwork. Helen Miner McDaniels, Walt's sister, stood ready to
christen the boat at the launch with the traditional bottle of the champagne.

Walt Miner, thirteen and third generation and son of Frederick, walks proudly beside one of his Father's boats being brought to West Commodore Way to the Coast Guard's Launch. Courtesy of Miner Family.

The Miner children and grandchildren spent hours watching their grandfather and father
dedicate time to building; first at the homestead in Darrington where floodwaters and snows
had ruined the first cabins and required rebuilding, and then on Magnolia building their
own homes and using boat-building skills in their later careers.

A drastic need for naval shipbuilding in Seattle during World War II prevented Walt
from serving in the armed forces on the front. He was made to stay behind to utilize his
skills in the boat yards. He worked for the war effort building minesweepers for the British
and US Navy.

Helen Miner McDaniels does the traditional honors at the launching. Courtesy of the Miner Family.

He then received the opportunity to work as a home-building
apprentice, with various home builders and their programs. He was
awarded an apprenticeship certificate presented to him by Eleanor
Roosevelt.[11] Walt says with a chuckle that one thing he noticed
right away was that the home builders got more money than boat
builders. "Mainly I learned about myself! I *wanted* to learn about the
business of building homes."[12]

In the fall of 1941, while taking ballroom dance lessons,
Walt met Eleanor Toms, a University of Washington student from
Spokane. They were married in 1942 and Walt built their first
Magnolia home, a small two-room house. The family grew, and as
four children (Carol, Bob, Patricia, and Marilyn) began to fill their
home, they remodeled the house and added three more rooms.

It was in 1947 when Walt officially painted "Walter J. Miner, Builder" on the door of his only truck and launched into home building on Magnolia. For two years he worked alone. Rudy Garish joined as his only assistant in 1949, until he went on his own.

Type of new Houses In Pleasant Valley Addition

Lots 50' X 120'
City Water
City Light

DAVID P. EASTMAN
209 COLMAN BUILDING

David Eastman's idea of an ideal Magnolia home. Courtesy of Dan Kerlee. Circa 1909.

Walt knew that there was land enough to make a living building on Magnolia in the 1940-50s. "It seemed there were woods covering half the Bluff, " he reminisced. Walt, a practical man, bought single lots or small groups of lots, and then built affordable, well-built homes, using as much of his own labor as he could.[13]

Other builders on Magnolia included transplanted Magnolian David Eastman, a salesman with clever sales techniques and marketing graphics, who, with partner John A. Whalley, was selling off lots and fancy home designs as early as 1906. His clientele seemed to want more expensive, exclusive, elite and larger homes on the Bluff or in Pleasant Valley. Eastman's home was an extremely fancy house and stands on Magnolia today. Other house builders of note in Magnolia were mostly developers or contractors who bought large parcels of land and built semi-like developments, or had crews build many homes of a similar style in a particular section of Magnolia. August Lilliquist and Ben Dahl, known for brick-fronted houses, and a "Lady-team" consisting of contractor James Paul Jones' mother, and Sally Bostrum, marketed many of Jones' houses. Modern Home Builders ventured onto Magnolia Bluff in early years, as well, offering small homes and duplexes for sale. The most remembered of these homes stand today as duplexes on 33rd and 34th Avenue West, between Ruffner and Barrett streets.[14]

Frederick built this home for his father and mother, Heinrich and Catherine in 1906. It still stands today on Magnolia. Courtesy of Miner Family.

These types of developments and sales pitches were not Walt's style or inclination. He wanted families to be able to afford a home, have a quality place in which to watch their family grow up, and not have to constantly worry about the house payments or the house falling down. He wanted to build as much of that home himself. "Some people worried a lot about how they were going to pay the $35 a month for the house payment! Many customers were GIs just home from the war." Walt set out to build his business reputation on Magnolia on simple, affordable, and well-built homes that were the best quality for the money; homes he built himself.[15]

In 1945, at the beginning of his career, a few very small homes were scaled-down versions of the simple World War II-style homes—were built without basements. Materials were stretched to make up for war shortages and used creatively to make well-built homes. The houses sold.

BUILDING UP THE BLUFF

With Walt's business established in Magnolia, the craft of building was definitely now evident in the third generation of Miners. Fine building skills, persistence, and the conscientious work ethic of the son and grandson of Heinrich and Catherine Miner positively impacted Magnolia's neighborhood homes with Walt's almost single-handed home construction business. The kind of work ethic the Miner grandparents demonstrated in the early Darrington days was not lost on any Miner generation.

Walt remembers that his very first "house plan" was sent to the City of Seattle for permits as a roughly rendered sketch. The permit went through that day! "Things have changed a lot since then!" he commented, chuckling.[16]

The post-war housing market boomed. In the next few years, more home builders moved into Magnolia markets. Walt commented on the growing number of builders coming to the Bluff, stating that "many Swedish builders and companies from Ballard did new or continuing work on Magnolia homes."[17] Competition was increasing, but Walt Miner was in demand.

Watching market trends on Magnolia and understanding the ebb and flow of the US economy resulted in Walt changing his business with the times. He began building tiny, one-story homes without basements, and small one-story houses with basements. He moved onto larger two-story homes with basements, to the newer style of larger ramblers with garages, to fancier architecture and remodels, as money began to come in with new Magnolians and with the booming economy.

Walt kept working, lot by lot. His reputation as a fine Magnolia builder and honest man took him through the decades successfully. Walt kept building. Demands for his homes continued.

After remodeling his own two-room house in 1946, he sold it the following year. He built two larger houses for his family as the four children grew and his business prospered. The year 2000 marked 47 years that Eleanor and Walt have resided at their Magnolia home at 4027 29th Avenue West.

ANOTHER GENERATION STEPS FORWARD

Walt's son, Robert "Bob" Miner graduated from the University of Washington in the late 1960s with a degree in landscape architecture with two years of extra emphasis in architecture. He then worked for the City of Seattle for seven years.

Bob mostly sat behind a desk drawing designs and plans for civic beautification projects and downtown plazas. Tiring of the indoor office work, Bob decided to work in home construction with his father. Walt was pleased to have his son's help and taught him the building business. Heinrich had taught his son, Frederick, who in turn taught his son Walt, beginning at the Mieners Homestead in Darrington, with woodsheds, shake cabins and puncheon bridges on which they practiced the skills they all honed into livelihoods. Bob's father, Walt, was now inducting the fourth generation into the family business.

Frederick built this home for his family at 3806 25th Avenue West. Courtesy of Miner Family.

"By wisdom a house is built, and with understanding it is established." —Proverbs 24:3, RSV. A philosophy of Walt's from early building days. This is the home he built for his family and has resided in 47 years with Eleanor and his growing children. Courtesy of the Miner Family.

Bob Miner spent 18 years at his father's side building and remodeling. Over time, Bob assumed complete responsibility for the business, as Walt partially retired and regularly spent some of each year in Arizona. Bob continued utilizing Walt's principles of good home-building. Lots on Magnolia were now scarce, so father and son adapted and earned great reputations in remodeling on Magnolia. They continued the practice of working alone and with their own skilled hands.

Magnolia homeowner Tami Gillman said of the father-son team:

Walt and Eleanor outside the Darrington rebuilt cabin on one of the days they often visit and maintain the buildings and enjoy the property. Courtesy the Miner Family.

"I first interviewed Bob, early in my project planning. The Miners were known to have a waiting list. Bob came highly recommended, but I talked to other builders. I went and looked at other work he and Walt had done. The thing that really sold me was the guarantee that if he came in 10% over the bid he would not charge for the extra work. That was never done in the building business when I had my work done; now it's somewhat standard. I hired him and his father.

They came in under the time frame and the work was of real quality, when the City inspectors came they knew it was a Miner job, knew the Miners work well, and the inspection went very smoothly. They remarked they never had a problem with Miner contracts. The Miners are very good at what they do."[18]

During this time, Bob, like the three generations before him, built two of his own homes on Magnolia. The Magnolia houses that Bob built, when compared to those built by his great-grandfather, grandfather, and father, in general reflected the Magnolia market trends over the previous 50 years: modern architecture, larger room spaces, and more cost per square foot.

Walt built more than 150 homes, many multiplexes and seven apartment buildings on Magnolia over the years. Together with his son, Bob, they remodeled many, many homes during an 18-year period.

TIMES . . . THEY ARE A CHANGING

With Walt's full retirement at age 77 in 1994, and Bob's interest in a new venture, Walt and Bob ended their father-son business that same year. Bob has taken his skills to Tucson, Arizona, where he and his wife Beth have built a beautiful, modern ivory-colored stucco bed and breakfast called The Jeremiah Inn. The Inn has a beautiful setting in which the building blends nicely with nature. At sunset, the orange reflection of the sun turns the building a deep salmon, and the rolling hills in the background are a stunning match.

When asked if Walt was sad to see the family building business end and his son head for a new part of the country, he says with a sweet smile, "Well, I look at it this way . . . how many fathers and sons have the good fortune of spending 18 years working side by side."[19]

One can't help but think of Bob's son Matthew, and Walt's other three grandsons, the fifth generation of the Miners, and wonder if they too will choose building as careers.

A FAMILY WHO WORKS

Over the years, Frederick, his sisters and brothers, and all of their children and grandchildren, have chosen to spend time at the Darrington Homestead carrying on the up-keep of the buildings there, preserving it for family posterity. While it did not become the place Heinrich and Catherine imagined, it became a great place still!

Frederick's grandson, Gary W. House, son of Frederick's daughter Katherine Miner House, wrote in *Meiners' Homestead Booklet 100th Anniversary of The Darrington Homestead*:

"The Bush," "The Ranch," "The Country" . . . the "The Place" {bring} special "fond memories", including putting in place a waterwheel that really worked! We also built a famous small log house out of poles and a huge, old stump. I also remember Mom, Dad, and I working on the foundation and later the walls of Mom's cabin. I think we started it in 1953 and Walt and a work party framed it up fast . . . it sure helps if you know what you are doing!"

Katherine Miner House and Frances Miner Buchanan, two of Walt's sisters, lived out their lives on Magnolia as well, enjoying Darrington too.

As with each Miner generation, the Meiners' Darrington Homestead became part of the lifetime memories for Bob, his wife Beth, and their family:

"Some of my earliest memories of that Darrington cabin were of the old bear rug on the floor, the mountain goat horns on the wall, and the two old Victrolas in one of the corners. I remember evenings with games at the table by the light of the old Aladdin lamp and when old records were being played on the Victrola, Pa dancing with Aunt Bo or Mom . . . And, in the summer of 1972, Beth made her first

Bob and Beth Miner's new adventure, The Jeremiah Inn in Tucson, a modern building Bob built that melts breathtakingly into the salmon sunsets in the evening and surrounding hills. After his father's retirement, Bob went on to this project with his wife. Courtesy of Miner Family.

The 3rd and 4th generation of Miners gather for Walt and Eleanor Miner's Golden Wedding Anniversary. (center of picture) Family left to right: Larry and Pat DuCharme, Ron and Carol Erickson, Walter DuCharme, Andrew DuCharme, Matt Miner, Mark Miner, Beth and Bob Miner, Marilyn and Ben Nakagawa. Courtesy of the Miner Family.

trip to a family gathering in Darrington. She excused herself to go "down the path" during a break, in the Yahtzee game and didn't return for the longest time. After about 30 minutes, we all were wondering if she was ill and began calling to her from the back porch. We learned that the outside latch had fallen closed and she was locked in the outhouse.[20]

Original Homestead deed for Darrington Meiner's property. Courtesy of Miner Family.

THE END . . . THE CONTINUATION . . . One-hundred twenty years after Heinrich and Catherine arrived in America, their grandson Walt enjoys retired life with his wife Eleanor. This third generation of Miners raised four children, ran a successful business and continues to worship at the Magnolia Presbyterian Church with a close group of friends. They are an "old-fashioned" family—something they cherish and live daily, despite trends in American family life.

In 1990, the Miner family celebrated 100 years at the Meiners Homestead in Darrington. What began as a "dream for land," had become a family retreat for several generations. Members of the extended Miner family wrote and published a book celebrating the family's centennial in Washington state and the land that did become its own. The book provides accounts of fond memories and old photos tracing the family's good times at the homestead. Patty Miner DuCharme, Heinrich's great granddaughter and Walt's daughter, sums it up: "Darrington is our heritage, a reminder of who we are, where we have come from, and what a wonderful legacy we have."[21]

The community of Magnolia is that kind of place as well. The Magnolia pioneer Miner family helped shape our community and left a large legacy of homes—not just houses—for Magnolia families!

Bob Miner's son Matt (fifth generation), at age 11, drew his sketches of the Darrington Homestead, like great aunt Dora and great grandfather Fred. Mark, Matt's younger brother, writes poetry about the Homestead. Walt Miner's grandsons are also pursuing their family's legacy: Andrew DuCharme is doing construction in a junior college program and his younger brother Walter helped build the new woodshed and his own bunkhouse at Darrington.

Monica Wooton lived in a Miner-built home the first four years of her life. Men like Walt Miner inspired her father to build his own home on Magnolia, where a brother from the second LaRussa generation now lives. Bob Miner and Monica, a lifelong resident of Magnolia, shared the same babysitter, Mrs. Cabeen. She often saw the "Walter J. Miner truck" parked around Magnolia, and noticed her father light up with a warmth and respect whenever they ran into Walt around the neighborhood. Monica never knew that Walt, a Magnolian from a family of Magnolian pioneers, had built so many houses!

Walter DuCharmes'
(Walt's daughter Patty's
son) bunkhouse and
garden. Built by himself
on the Darrington
Property. This makes the
fifth generation of builders
in the Miner Family.
Courtesy of Miner
Family.

Discovery Park:
A People's Park In Magnolia

By Bob Kildall

MEMORIAL TO US DISTRICT JUDGE DONALD S. VOORHEES

Authors Note: Before Don died he asked me to say a few words at his memorial service about Discovery Park. After his death July 7, 1989, Anne Voorhees asked me to help in a different capacity. This is the speech I wrote and later used at a Friends of Discovery Park memorial service and in a letter to the editor.

Discovery Park is his park—that we all agree. He felt that Seattle would be known for this Park—like London is known for Hyde Park; Vancouver for Stanley Park; San Francisco for Golden Gate Park and New York for Central Park.

It was a difficult task. The Department of Defense wanted an anti-ballistic missile base and the ABM headquarters for the entire West Coast located here. Native Americans claimed the property. We didn't have enough money to buy the land and no federal law allowed excess property to be given for parks and recreation. A golf initiative proposed an 18-hole course. And Metro had its own plans for the Park's beach.

The missile base was moved. A treaty was signed. A federal law was passed. The golf initiative failed. And even Metro studied an off-site solution first suggested by Don. He named the park "Discovery" partly after Capt. George Vancouver's ship. But even more "because when our children walk this park, discoveries will unfold for them at every turn." History, beauty, nature and the future are melded here.

He has been called "a great gentleman of grace and dignity," a "judge's judge" known for his "unswerving politeness." But when involved in securing Discovery Park you have to add: a determined gentleman, a good judge of the spectacular beauty of this property, its value to us all, and a man who was unswerving in his goal to acquire it and to protect it for all time.

The trail to the South Beach offers a sanctuary where visitors can escape the city crowds and find solitude in the woods. Photo by Roy Scully, 2000.

Judge Donald S. Voorhees
Courtesy of Anne
Voorhees.

Don wrote the central purpose and role of this park for the
Park Master Plan—a purpose we all defend. "That role should be to
provide an open space of quiet and tranquility for the citizens of
this City—a sanctuary where they might escape the turmoil of the
City and enjoy the rejuvenation which quiet and solitude and an
intimate contact with nature can bring."

He is gone. His good work remains. We lost a friend, as many
did. But when we walk these woods in his park and see the birds,
the mountains, Puget Sound and a glorious sunset, we will
remember. And those who live here in the future are sure to ask,
"Who made all this beauty possible?"

THE DISCOVERY PARK STORY

One of our nation's most important park stories describes how local
citizens, against overwhelming odds, turned an old US Army Fort
in the Pacific Northwest into Discovery Park, Seattle's largest open-
space park.

A park at the Fort Lawton site had been a civic dream ever since 1917 when City leaders,
disappointed that less than a major fort had been built on the grounds, sought the return of
the property for a City park.

An opportunity to establish a park arose 47 years later when the Department of Defense
(DOD) announced plans to surplus 85% of Fort Lawton.[1] By 1964, it was clear that Fort
Lawton did not fit the modern military defensive needs of the nation. Responding to the
DOD decision, a citizens' committee planning the major Forward Thrust bond issue in 1965
included $3 million as "seed" money for a park at Fort Lawton. In early 1968, Seattle voters
approved this bond issue.

Later that same year, officials and citizens faced a seemingly impossible task to acquire
the Fort for a park when the DOD announced plans to instead level 330 acres at the Fort
to build an anti-ballistic missile base. The missiles would defend against inter-continental
ballistic missiles, yet to be built. For security reasons, the rest of the Fort would likely be
placed off-limits.

The history section of the 1972 Fort Lawton (Discovery Park) Master Plan notes:
"The threatened loss of the site at first evoked a cry of protest from only a relatively few
individuals. In time, however, that faint cry of protest became a roar of outrage from the
community."[2]

Twenty-five civic and environmental groups, led by US District Judge Donald S.
Voorhees, organized the "Citizens for Fort Lawton Park" (CFLP) in June 1968. They sought
Washington State's congressional delegation's help to not only move the proposed ABM site,
but to obtain excess Fort Lawton property for a City park. The CFLP protest brought action
by US Senator Henry M. Jackson who interceded with Secretary of Defense Clark Clifford to
block the ABM site in the Fort.[3] Finally, in December 1968, Clifford declared that the
ABM plans for Fort Lawton were being abandoned.

However, under the existing surplus laws, the City would have had to pay millions to acquire the Fort, despite the fact that almost 70 years earlier the Seattle Chamber of Commerce, in the City's interests, had deeded title to the property to the US Government at no cost in hopes of seeing a major military fort built there.

Local environmental and civic groups contacted their national offices in Washington D.C. to lobby for a new federal law introduced by Jackson. In Congress, it was referred to as "the Fort Lawton Bill." It was supported by Washington State's entire congressional delegation. For the first time, cities would be able to obtain excess federal property for park and recreation uses for less than 50% of fair market value. To assure that Fort Lawton came free to Seattle, Jackson added to the law, ". . . if the municipality had given the property to the federal government it *shall* be returned without cost."[4]

After abandoning their plans for an ABM installation, the military declared much of Fort Lawton as surplus to its needs. However, Jackson's legislation was only one of several laws covering federal surplus property. Many competing claims for Fort Lawton were made under other existing excess property laws: The US Navy and US Coast Guard wanted housing, school administrators wanted a campus, veterans groups wanted an "Arlington of the West" cemetery, the State wanted a correctional facility, builders wanted high-rises, and a local group, the United Indians of All Tribes Foundation, wanted ownership. Most of these claims were withdrawn after public demands for a park at Fort Lawton grew in intensity. The park proposal prevailed.

Seattle added 15% more acreage to its existing parkland as a result of Jackson's legislation. These additions included Discovery Park, Magnuson Park and the Seattle Tennis Center on Martin Luther King, Jr. Way. More than 700 cities located within all 50 states received thousands of acres of federal property for parks worth nearly $1 billion.[5]

The south meadows command dramatic views of Puget Sound and the snow-covered Olympic Mountains. Photo by Bob Kildall, Summer 2000.

Opposite: The magnificent sea cliffs tell 20,000 years of geologic history in colorfully stratified layers. Photo by Ken Baxter, courtesy of Virginia Baxter.

By early 1971, the Bureau of Indian Affairs asked the City to include a 19-acre site for an Indian Cultural Center in the Park. After negotiations, a lease was drawn up and accepted by both parties in late 1974. It called for the Center to be "Indian in spirit, simple and honest in design, to enrich and be in harmony with the natural setting and uses of a city park at Fort Lawton."[6] As the underlying federal deed allowed only park and recreation uses, the City, through the federally-funded Seattle Model City program, provided funds for a building in downtown Seattle to house needed urban Indian social services.

Earlier, Dan Urban Kiley of Charlotte, Vermont, and his Seattle assistant John Morse were hired to produce the Fort Lawton Park (Discovery Park) Master Plan. In the plan submitted to the City in 1974, Kiley wrote that if the guiding principles were faithfully followed we ". . . cannot fail to create a park which will be one of the great urban parks in the world—and a joy to this City forever."[7] Words from the Master Plan have been used countless times to fend off incompatible uses proposed for the park:

The primary role of this park in the life of the City is dictated by its incomparable site. That role should be to provide an open space of quiet and tranquility for the citizens of this City— a sanctuary where they might escape the turmoil of the City and enjoy the rejuvenation which quiet and solitude and an intimate contact with nature can bring.

The Plan also contained this warning:

In the years to come there will be almost irresistible pressure to carve out areas of the park in order to provide sites for various civic structures or space for special activities without number for which, it will be contended, this park can provide an "ideal site" at no cost. The pressures for those sites may constitute the greatest single threat to the park. They must be resisted with resolution. If they are not, the park will be so fragmented that it can no longer serve its central purpose.

In his 1979 book, *Enjoying Seattle's Parks*, author Brandt Morgan of Santa Fe, New Mexico, wrote:

The spirit of nature thrives in this park, which is gradually reclaiming the old Fort Lawton Army base. Discovery Park encircles generous areas of woodland and beach, and offers mountain views and a variety of natural life zones to explore: meadows with deermice and shrews; forests with wildflowers and ferns; tidal beaches with barnacled rocks and smooth sands; and magnificent sea cliffs that tell 20,000 years of geologic history in colorfully stratified layers.

Wildlife abounds in this nature park. Over 150 species of birds have been seen here and giant squid have been sighted off the beaches. Flying squirrels soar between tree branches. Rabbits hop down hidden pathways. Berries abound in the summer, mushrooms in fall and spring. Discovery Park is a tranquil place away from the stress of the City— at once a wildlife sanctuary and an outdoor classroom for people to learn about the natural world.[8]

In the past three decades there have been more than a hundred proposals for "just a piece" of Discovery Park for "a worthwhile use." If even half had been successful, there would be no park left. Citizens who fought so hard to create our 534-acre Seattle park remain diligent to see that the Park's Master Plan is carefully followed.

The Park has become an escape for city dwellers from the streets, buildings, cars, noise, pollution, crowds and the stress of urban living. The chance to be in contact with the wildlife, view the serenity of the mountains and Puget Sound, and the opportunity for peace and solitude is an invaluable gift that Discovery Park affords local residents and visitors from all over the world. They appreciate and are amazed that within just a few minutes from the center of a city that it is still possible to find a place of wildness, quiet and tranquility.

Artist Ray Collins, courtesy *Seattle Post-Intelligencer*, April 24, 1978

The Battle at Discovery Park

lic horse rental stables, a stadium site and a Seattle version of the Butchart Gardens.

In 1975, voters had to sink a ballot issue that would have turned a large park area over to golfers. More recently, the attack came from the city's Landmarks Preservation Board, intent on preserving 25 old fort buildings as examples of turn-of-the-century government issue.

With the golf course matter resolved and historic preservation in abeyance, park lovers probably are sighing with relief. But it's too

Whitebear now is asking the park board for two more acres (a former Coast Guard antenna site) for a longhouse. Whitebear says it would be used for ceremonial salmon dinners, education gatherings and "possibly, a restaurant." The park board is considering the request.

While the Indians besiege Discovery Park on one side, the cavalry attacks on the other. Much to the dismay of Seattle officials, the federal government is searching for a religious organization to buy the old post chapel.

they'll arrange easy credit terms.

How can federal guidelines be so misguided ? Can nothing be done to prevent this latest carving up of the park property?

It's apparent that constant effort, diplomacy and negotiation will be required for Discovery Park to fulfill the goals worked out by planners, city and citizens to subordinate all development to the environment of the magnificent natural site. The need for continuing vigilance is not unique to Discovery Park, nor to Seattle. Nearly 100 years ago, citizens

"The special difficulty of the park in city administration lies in the ordinary unreadiness to regard it otherwise than as a body of land held for a variety of purposes, vague and variable. Every year in its history some project of ruinous tendency has had the warm support of many men, the advantage to be gained by it seeming to them for the time to stand out with such perfect clearness."

As Olmsted made plain, it is essential to resist pressures to chop up an urban park site into special activities, no matter how

THE BATTLE BEGINS

"The Battle for Fort Lawton" was a hot topic in the years following the decision to establish Discovery Park on the grounds of Fort Lawton. In a "P-I Opinion" dated April 24, 1978, the *Seattle Post-Intelligencer* addressed the number of proposals for the parkland, despite the effort to keep the Park intact as a natural refuge.

Ignoring the deep commitment of many Seattle citizens to the belief that there is no more valuable use of this site than as an open space, the idea that the land can still provide an "ideal site" at no cost for structures and activities without number has persisted in the form of more than 100 additional requests during the more than 20 years following the publication of this editorial:

The City of Seattle may come to regret disarming of Fort Lawton—now known as Discovery Park. Those long-range guns, symbolically at least, might help repel attacks on plans to turn the former army post into an urban wilderness.

Well-meaning people keep devising new ideas for what can be installed at Discovery Park. More than 100 serious proposals have been put forth, including plans to turn it into an anti-ballistic missile base, a national cemetery—'the Arlington of the West,' a residential academy for school dropouts, location for public horse rental stables, a stadium site and a Seattle version of the Butchart Gardens.

In 1975, voters had to sink a ballot issue that would have turned a large park area over to golfers. More recently, the attack came from the City's Landmarks Preservation Board, intent on saving 25 old Fort buildings as examples of the turn-of-the-century government issue.

With the golf matter resolved and the historic preservation in abeyance, park lovers probably are sighing with relief. But it's too soon.

Two new obstacles to wilderness surfaced last week. The first came from the United Indians of All Tribes Foundation. That group leases 22 acres of land inside the park for their cultural center, Daybreak Star Arts Center.

Foundation director Bernie Whitebear now is asking the Park Board for two more acres (a former Coast Guard antenna site) for a longhouse. Whitebear says it would be used for ceremonial salmon dinners, education gatherings and 'possibly, a restaurant.' The Park Board is considering the request.

While the Indians besiege Discovery Park on one side, the cavalry attacks on the other. Much to the dismay of Seattle officials, the federal government is searching for a religious organization to buy the old post chapel.

A General Service Administration (GSA) spokesman said federal guidelines require that religious organizations be given first chance to acquire any surplus federal chapel, memorial or shrine.

GSA's Auburn office is accepting bids through May 22. The price is a firm $67,750, but the feds say they will arrange easy credit terms.

How can federal guidelines be so misguided? Can nothing be done to prevent this latest carving up of park property?

It's apparent that constant effort, diplomacy and negotiation will be required for Discovery Park to fulfill the goals worked out by planners, city and citizens: to subordinate all developments to the environment of the magnificent natural site. The need for continuing vigilance is not unique to Discovery Park, nor to Seattle. Nearly 100 years ago, citizens working to create Central Park in New York City faced similar pressures. More than 35 proposals—from a stadium to the location for Grant's tomb— were offered. The great park designer Frederick Law Olmstead {sic} could have been discussing Discovery Park, instead of Central Park, when he wrote: "The special difficulty of the park in city administration lies in the ordinary unreadiness to regard it otherwise than as a body of land held for a variety of purposes, vague and variable. Every year in its history some project of ruinous tendency has had the warm support of many men, the advantage to be gained by it seeming to them for the time to stand out in perfect clearness."

Wildlife lagoon on North Beach Trail. Photo by Heidi Carpine. Circa 1995.

As Olmstead {sic} made plain, it is essential to resist pressures to chop up an urban park site into special activities, no matter how worthy.

The Park Board, the City and the citizens must keep Discovery Park a sanctuary where people can escape turmoil and enjoy quiet and solitude. There is no more valuable use for Discovery Park than unspoiled beaches and meadows.

COMMANDER CLOSES FORT LAWTON'S NORTH GATE

The front page of the March 20, 1969, edition of the *Magnolia News* featured three articles on Fort Lawton. One posed the question: "If and When . . . Natural Park at Ft. Lawton?" A second article was, "Veterans Group Proposes 'Arlington of the West.'" The third article was titled, "New Commanding Officer Takes Over Ft. Lawton."[2] A distinguished career officer, Colonel Stuart J. Palos was the new Post Commander at Fort Lawton. This is where this story began.

For years, US Army personnel at Fort Lawton and the neighboring communities of Magnolia and Lawton Wood had enjoyed a close and friendly relationship. Many retired soldiers and their families chose to live in the surrounding residential areas after their military careers. In fact, retired Army Colonel John R. Dey, a past Fort Lawton commander (1957- 1959), was the president of the nearby Lawton Wood Community Club.

Palos arrived just three months after *The Seattle Times* headlined: "Fort Lawton Won't Get Missiles; Two Kitsap County Sites Chosen—Army Base May become City Park."[3] The news of the abandonment of Fort Lawton for a missile site was well received—particularly by those who wanted a park. (Kitsap County never received missiles either.)

For a while after Palos assumed command of the Fort, there were few if any changes. The Fort was open and quiet. Residents living in Bay Terrace, Commodore Way and Lawton Wood could drive back and forth between the Fort's east and north gates. The Metro bus stopped just inside the gate as it always had. There was a covered bus shelter for the convenience of the bus riders.

However, by early October, residents were well aware of the "new" security measures at the Fort Lawton gates. According to the October 8, 1969, *Magnolia Journal*, Palos addressed incidents on Fort property involving vandalism, drag racing, improperly licensed vehicles, speeding, drunk driving and illegally-equipped vehicles. He was quoted as saying:

On a clear day, the North Beach Trail includes a majestic view of Mount Baker. Photo by Bob Kildall, Summer 2000.

"Little has really changed. The authority to limit civilian access to the Post has always existed, as has the prerogative to stop and search all vehicles entering or leaving the Post. However a rash of traffic violations, loose dog problems, and an increase in the trafficking in marijuana at the Fort has led to a somewhat more stringent enforcement of existing regulations."[4]

Two days later *The Seattle Times* reported that the Fort was still open, although the covered bus shelter just inside the Fort gate had been moved to an interior housing area. Palos was quoted as saying that he had a responsibility to the people living on the Post and that the shelter was moved to accommodate them. He added that he did not have the money to build a new one for the outside neighbors, nor would he permit private citizens to build a new shelter at the old site.[5]

By October 23, the story became front-page news. *The Seattle Times* reported that Fort Lawton-area residents claimed they were harassed and threatened by military police who were stopping drivers. Residents were apparently unhappy about not being fore-warned of the North Gate closure. Dey was quoted as saying that during his two years as Post Commander he "never found it necessary to close" the Fort. Army Corps of Engineers officials said that there was no written egress agreement for Lawton Wood residents, and that over the years, crossing over into the Fort had been by verbal consent. But Lawton Wood resident Mrs. Neil L. Wells was quoted as saying that provisions were made for egress when Congress accepted the property for a military facility. Her grandfather, Christian Scheuerman, had homesteaded on property that was now part of the Fort.[6]

"Patience—we'll be with you in a few bolt-cutting minutes." October 30, 1969. Courtesy of Alan Pratt and *The Seattle Times.*

Things remained tense through the middle of November. Stories appeared regularly in the community and city newspapers. US Senator Henry Jackson became involved in mediating the issue, as did top ranking Army officials. Palos finally met with the Magnolia Community Club Board in a room full of irate citizens November 13.

Besides the inconvenience the closure created, citizens voiced concerns about delays that might occur for fire trucks and emergency vehicles in an emergency. Palos said that if there were a fire he would see to it that the gate was opened promptly. A resident in the back of the room shouted:

"I am with the fire department. You won't have to come and open the gates for us. We don't wait. We have chain cutters on the trucks. We'll come right through the gate. You may not know it, but the last time we had to use the North Gate on a call it wasn't to get to Lawton Wood. We were coming into the Fort to put out a fire at the NCO club!"

His statement broke the tension. Even Palos relaxed. People laughed. There was agreement to answer the problems. The Army and the residents patched up and resumed their friendly relationships. Today, the Army Reserve headquarters is on a remainder of Fort Lawton just outside the northeast corner of Discovery Park. The reservists and the neighbors work closely together and communicate regularly. Community organization representatives are invited to Army special events.

WHAT'S IN A NAME?

Was Discovery Park named for Captain George Vancouver's ship the HMS *Discovery* that sailed into Puget Sound in 1792? Many authors of travel books and guides seem to think so.

Stephen R. Whitney in *Nature Walks in & Around Seattle* claims the Park was named for Vancouver's ship.[8] This opinion is repeated in *Insight Guides, Seattle; Magnolia: Yesterday and Today; Enjoying Seattle's Parks,* and numerous books and articles.

Colleen Cramer in her book *Romance on a Shoestring* describes Discovery Park as:

". . . meadows are superb open slopes for informal play, kite flying or casual strolling." Kiley Plan 1974. Photo by Roy Scully, Summer 2000.

. . . 534 acres of romantic, out of the way places to explore, Seattle's largest park got its name for obvious reasons. A map from the visitor center will help you navigate through this scenic wonderland of forest, beach and grasslands.

However, none of these opinions is entirely correct. The person who first suggested the name "Discovery Park" was US District Judge Donald S. Voorhees, who had led the effort to create a park at Fort Lawton in 1968. He is known as "the father of Discovery Park." His suggestion was subsequently adopted by the Seattle City Council as the name for Seattle's newest park.

Voorhees was a student of Puget Sound history and Vancouver's exploration. But he was also an avid follower of the philosophy of Frederick Law Olmsted, the famed American landscape architect. Voorhees believed the name combined the history of Vancouver's exploration of Puget Sound on the *HMS Discovery,* with the excitement of visitors when they discover the wonders of nature in the Park. When asked to make a choice between the meanings, Voorhees would choose the experience of "discovery" by citizens, particularly children, visiting the Park for the first time, over the historical connection with the *HMS Discovery.*

Forests, deep ravines, views of Mt. Rainier and Olympic National Parks, make the Park's 2.8 mile loop trail an unforgettable walk. Photo by Bob Kildall, Summer 2000.

Prior to Voorhees' suggestion that the Park be named Discovery Park, the Magnolia Community Club had made ten recommendations if Fort Lawton were to become a park. One regarding the name read, "In appreciation of the many years in which the US Army had been a good neighbor, we recommend the park be named Fort Lawton Park."[9]

Today, the community accepts and embraces the City Council's decision to name Seattle's finest and largest nature park "Discovery Park." But Magnolians still thank the Army for preserving such a fantastic site within the City for so many years.

Cougar lies low in city park

Artist Alan Pratt courtesy of *The Seattle Times*.

WILD COUGAR IN DISCOVERY PARK

For a week during the summer of 1981, Discovery Park was in pandemonium, and for four of those days, the Park was closed after a cougar was reported to have run through the Naval Capehart housing area located in the middle of the Park. (The Capehart housing area is one of the pieces of property in Fort Lawton retained by the US Government.)

The next morning, Saturday, August 23, a park visitor spotted a cougar on the loop trail near the south bluff overlooking Puget Sound and the Olympic Mountains.

Sightings continued throughout the weekend, to include a number from Perkins Lane residents located just south of the Park who said a cougar was seen in their backyards. On Monday, Chief Park Ranger Paul Frandsen announced that the Park was closed.

By Tuesday, the State game officials arrived with trained hunting dogs to search the entire Park and portions of Fort Lawton retained by the US Government. In the meantime, a cougar sighting was recorded in the Park as well as near Smith Cove at the south end of Magnolia at 3 p.m. Finding nothing, the State game officials called off the cougar hunt. The Park remained closed.

On Wednesday, Park Ranger Bob Mindick discovered cougar tracks along the south bluff trail. Plaster casts of the tracks were made. The Burke Museum mammalogist, John Rozdilski, verified that the tracks belonged to a cougar. The State game officials returned with their dogs. That evening at 7 p.m., a resident reported another sighting of a cougar at the Burlington Northern Railroad tracks and Gay Avenue West near the Hiram Chittenden Locks and Commodore Park north of Discovery Park.

At 1 a.m. Thursday, a State game agent spotted a cougar sitting in a Pacific Madrone tree on the edge of the south bluff of Discovery Park. Just as the cat was about to jump from the Madrone, the game agent hit it with a tranquilizer on his first shot. The cougar fell into a ravine. As the story goes, the agent jumped into the ravine only to find the cougar was still conscious. Luckily the agent was unharmed. The 117-pound cougar was then captured and taken to the South Tacoma Game Farm. It was later released into the Cascade Mountain wilds the following week.

With the cougar captured, Frandsen opened the Park again to the public. A few days of excitement were over, but have not been forgotten.

Where did the cougar come from? At first, state game officials thought it took a marathon swim from Bainbridge Island. Later they abandoned that idea. In a 1993 children's book, *J. G. Cougar's Great Adventure*, author Virginia Bishop Tawresey muses that the cougar came to Discovery Park by hitching a ride on an open and vacant train boxcar.[10]

Today, the best guess is that it came down the Burlington Northern Railroad (BN) tracks from the Cascade foothills and then into the Park through the Kiwanis Ravine. Animals are safe on the tracks. They easily avoid the occasional train.

Several animals besides the cougar have likely used this BN wildlife corridor. Bears found their way into Edmonds-area backyards. A deer once ran into and shattered a Ballard store window. They both presumably found their way by coming down the tracks.

The Park staff named the wayward cougar "D. B. Cougar" after the mysterious skyjacker "D. B. Cooper" (who parachuted from a Northwest Airlines Boeing 727 over the Cascades in November 1971 with $200,000 and has never been found by authorities). In the following years, a special "D. B. Cougar Day" celebration was held for the cougar that paid a mysterious visit to Discovery Park.

Opposite: Discovery Park's most impressive tree is a Bigleaf Maple (Acer macrophyllum) found on the Loop Trail. Photo by Penny Rose. Discovery Park Archive. Circa 1990s.

Driftwood on the Puget Sound beaches of Discovery Park attract park visitors. Photo by Roy Scully, Summer 2000.

WEST POINT AND THE HISTORIC LIGHTHOUSE

Listed on the National Register of Historic Places, the West Point Lighthouse opened on November 14, 1881. It was built eight years before Washington Territory was granted statehood on November 11, 1889, and it is the oldest lighthouse in the Seattle area.[11]

The lighthouse tower is 27 feet high. It has a 1000-watt quartz lamp inside with a French lens built in 1860. On a clear night, the flashing white light can be seen up to 19 miles and the red light up to 16 miles.[12] West Point greets ocean commerce going to the Port of Seattle, Tacoma and other Puget Sound ports, as well as naval ships, ferries, cruise ships and smaller craft sailing on Puget Sound.[13]

An officer-in-charge of a sailing expedition named the spit where the lighthouse is located "West Point" in 1841. The 43-year-old Lieutenant Charles Wilkes was in command of the United States Exploring Expedition that sailed from Norfolk, Virginia, on August 18, 1838.[14] Wilkes, who would later serve as an admiral during the

Completed in 1881, the historic West Point Lighthouse is the earliest Coast Guard lighthouse built in the lower Puget Sound region. Photo by Bob Kildall, 2000.

Civil War (and was involved in the "Trent" affair in which he intercepted a British ship during the war), commanded a squadron consisting of six vessels. His instructions were to visit Rio de Janeiro, Tierra del Fuego, Valparaiso, the Fiji Islands, the Hawaiian Islands, Japan, China and the northwest coast of America. Besides naming West Point, he named many other places in the Puget Sound area.

In 1907, people came to the lighthouse to salute the "Great White Fleet"—16 US Naval ships—as they steamed past West Point. President Theodore Roosevelt sent them on a worldwide "goodwill" tour to express the strength of American sea power to other nations. The ships were painted white to emphasize this point.

In 1910, well-known landscape architect John Olmsted sketched a plan for Fort Lawton. The sketch shows West Point and the existing pristine beach with an adjacent salt-water marsh.[15] (Olmsted, the stepson and nephew of Frederick Law Olmsted, known as the "father of landscape architecture," developed the 1903 plan on which Seattle's park system is based with his stepbrother Fredrick Law Olmsted, Jr. The Olmsted brothers also designed the landscape plans for the Alaska-Yukon-Pacific Exposition in 1909 on what is now the University of Washington campus.[16])

It wasn't long afterwards that Seattle engineer Reginald H. Thomson completed the 12-foot diameter, brick-lined Fort Lawton sewage tunnel in 1911. It was designed to bring wastewater from central Seattle to an outfall off West Point. Sewage collected throughout Seattle was sent through sewer pipes and collected into Thomson's tunnel. The untreated sewage was dumped off the West Point beach.[17] Fear of a cholera epidemic caused the City to stop dumping in the lakes and to ship the sewage to be diluted and disposed of in Puget Sound instead.

It was 55 years before simple primary treatment of sewage was provided at the West Point Treatment Plant in 1966. It was another 29 years before compliance with the National Clean Water Act and additional State requirements was achieved when secondary treatment of wastewater was added at the West Point treatment plant.[18]

Since that time, and as part of the mitigation for the use of shorelines, the Municipality of Metropolitan Seattle (Metro)—now Metropolitan King County—has worked to hide the plant and to restore public use to the shorelines. Additions to the area include a path north of the plant that complies with the American Disabilities Act, a lagoon for nature studies, and a restoration of the beach for enjoyment.[19]

West Point has been the scene of many proposed developments. In March 1968, even before Fort Lawton became a park, the Washington State Oceanographic Commission's Puget Sound Oceanographic Study Committee chose West Point as the "logical place to have a major aquarium and research facility combined with an educational facility."[20] The same month, a column in *The Seattle Times* proposed "a research-and-recreation aquarium, a public park at Fort Lawton, and a bay-level waterfront parkway linking Smith Cove and West Point."[21] The Oceanographic Commission would ". . . operate the aquarium complex on a revenue-producing basis from admissions, concessions, a restaurant and cocktail lounge."[22] Dixy Lee Ray, then director of the Pacific Science Center and a member of the Oceanographic Commission, and later Governor of Washington State, called for the parkway to "open up the possibility for use by the aquarium complex on the south of the point, (to) . . . enable more people to reach the aquarium more easily, and would provide needed parking space."[23] They expected to get unlimited fresh water from Metro's sewage treatment plant and 12.4 acres of unused Metro land at no cost from Metro.

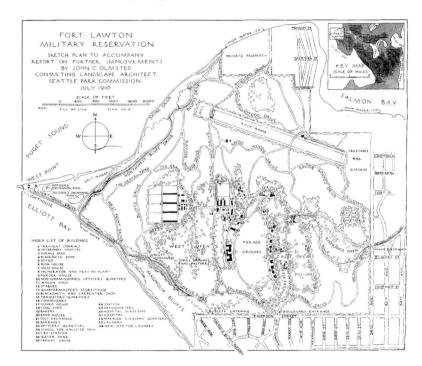

July 1910 map of Fort Lawton by John C. Olmsted for the Seattle Park Commission. (Olmsted, stepson of famous American landscape architect, Frederick Law Olmsted, planned the Seattle Park and boulevard systems. Discovery Park Archives.

Called into action, Sierra Club leader Mike Ruby led an initiative signature gathering to protect both West Point and Golden Garden beaches from the proposal. The City Council agreed with the initiative and adopted it without a vote, so the research and recreation and the shoreline roadway proposals failed.

In 1972, the Seattle Department of Community Development provided a permit to Metro to build a sludge dewatering facility on the south beach of West Point. It was application No. 20 and provided for a five-year use of a "rock-diked" sludge fill.[24] The test was to see if sludge could be used to fill 400 feet out into Puget Sound for a roadway. Public pressure later was

Left: The South Beach is broad and spacious at low tide and its charm and mystery come from its isolation and its great expanse. Photo by Ken Baxter, courtesy of Virginia Baxter. Circa 1960s.

successful in removing the sludge basin, which was a failure. Tests showed that sludge absorbs water too easily to support a roadway. Beach expert Wolf Bauer was hired by Metro to restore the beach. That carried out the goal of citizens who preferred a "natural and open" beach.

There were other proposals that never made it. The US Corps of Engineers listed West Point as a possible location for a wet moorage for private yachts. It conducted a test in 1971 to see if a "floating breakwater" could be constructed there. In 1980, Marine Animal Resource Center director Tag Gornall asked for a seal resource center to be built on Coast Guard Lighthouse property at West Point.[25]

Because of the strong support by citizens for the guidelines laid down by the Discovery Park Master Plan, these proposals failed from overwhelming public opposition. Proposals that brought cars and buildings to the interior of the Park or to the shoreline were rejected by the Master Plan.

Somehow, West Point has survived. Harvey Manning, founder of the Issaquah Alps Trails Club and author on hiking in Western Washington, calls West Point the greatest beach in King County.[26] There will be new challenges to leaving the beach in a natural condition, but there will also be a strong defense by citizens to preserve this superb shoreline for wildlife and human recreation. What eventually happens will depend on the resolve of future generations.

Artist: Susan Welch.

FRIENDS OF DISCOVERY PARK

Speaking before the Seattle City Council in 1974, US District Judge Donald S. Voorhees recommended that an organization such as the Friends of Central Park in New York be formed to support Seattle's Discovery Park. Voorhees told Council members that it was important to monitor the actions proposed for the Park and to defend the principles and philosophy found in the 1974 Discovery Park Master Plan.

Having led the CFLP in a successful effort to secure Fort Lawton from the US Government for a park in 1968, Voorhees' experience and credibility led to the establishment of a supporting organization six years later.

As a result of Voorhees' address to the City Council, members of the CFLP met December 4, 1974, to form the Friends of Discovery Park. Charter Board Members elected at that meeting were: Bob Kildall, President, Gerry Lamphier, Frankie Piper, Mike Ruby, Robert Sotnik, Bernie Whitebear, and Thomas O. Wimmer.

The purposes of the Friends of Discovery Park (Friends) are found in their by-laws:

The purposes of this corporation (FRIENDS OF DISCOVERY PARK) shall be to defend the integrity of Discovery Park; to create and protect there an open space of quiet and tranquility, a sanctuary where the works of man are minimized, appearing to be affected primarily by the forces of nature, a place which emphasizes its natural environment, broad vista and unspoiled shorelines; and to promote the development of the park according to a master plan responsive to these goals.[27]

More than 750 Seattle citizens are members of the Friends. Nearly three-quarters of the members live outside the Magnolia community. The Friends have been in the forefront of nearly 100 issues where the integrity of the plan for the Park was in jeopardy.

In 1989, the Friends asked the City to create the Discovery Park Memorial Fund and raised more than $34,800 for the Discovery Park's new Visitor Center, dedicated in 1998. To protect the nesting Great Blue Herons and other natural qualities of the Kiwanis Ravine, the Friends obtained $775,000 in State, Metropolitan King County, Shoreline Park Improvement Funds and Metro mitigation funds to purchase property in the ravine, which is adjacent to Discovery Park. This purchase protected a wildlife corridor through the ravine. The group also gives financial support to the Discovery Park day camp programs and to other Park programs.

Bald Eagles nesting in Discovery Park. Photo by Martin Muller. Circa 1980.

While the Friends work closely with the park staff, the group stays independent of the Seattle Parks and Recreation Department by deliberate choice. It values its freedom to defend the Park by opposing or creating initiatives and referendum, to oppose issues considered harmful to the Park when the City has not or cannot take political action, or when there is concern for a City action deemed contrary to the Master Plan, and to lobby State, County and City governments.

Sunset at Discovery Park from the south meadow. Photo by Paul Frandsen. Discovery Park Archive.

Following pages: Mount Rainier from Discovery Park, looking southeast over Perkins Lane and Elliott Bay with an infrared process. Photo by Ken Baxter. Courtesy of Virginia Baxter. Circa 1970.

Bob Kildall, a Seattle native, grew up on Queen Anne Hill and has lived on Magnolia with his wife Ruth since 1965. They met at the 1962 World's Fair in Seattle. He was active in creating Commodore Park across from the Chittenden Locks, and was chairman of the 50th Anniversary Celebration of the Locks. He is a former Chairman of the Seattle Board of Parks Commissioners, past President of the Magnolia Community Club, and the founding President of the Friends of Discovery Park. His work on Discovery Park spans more than three decades. On April 21, 1988, he received the first State of Washington "Thomas O. Wimmer Award for continuous, long-term, dedicated service to maintain and enhance environmental quality in the State of Washington." Bob has three children: Katie, Maria and Kristian.

Fort Lawton/Discovery Park 1896—1999

From author's personal records and newspaper clippings.

1896 Secretary of War chooses Magnolia Bluff as fort site.

1897 Seattle Chamber of Commerce deeds property, at no cost, to the United States for fort.

1900 Fort Lawton established.

1910 Olmsted Brothers present plans for Seattle's park system.

1911 Tunnel built under Fort Lawton to discharge sewage into Puget Sound.

1908-1941 Fort Lawton has little military use.

1917 Civic leaders and editors call for return of Fort Lawton for a park.

1938 Seattle refuses offer of Fort Lawton for $1 during the Great Depression.

March 31, 1968.
The Seattle Times.

1941 Fort Lawton is major shipping point for troops during World War II.

1944 Italian prisoner-of-war is hanged at Fort Lawton by troops angered over special treatment of prisoners not given to U.S. black troops.

1950 Fort Lawton is major shipping point for troops during Korean War.

1957 Capehart military housing units built.

1962 Metro receives 99-year lease for 30 acres for the West Point treatment plant from Army.

1966 West Point primary treatment plant completed.

1968 Forward Thrust Park Bond Issue includes $3 million to purchase Fort Lawton for a park.

West Point is named as site for Aquarium-Research center. Initiative prevents that location.

Tideland parkway from Smith Cove to West Point is proposed for Aquarium, but denied.

The Department of Defense proposes an anti-ballistic missile system to defend against inter-continental nuclear missiles.

Citizens for Fort Lawton Park organize to oppose ABM plans.

UW Chapter of the Federation of American Scientists opposes the ABM.

DOD abandons Fort Lawton ABM site in December.

1969 Senator Henry M. Jackson introduces Federal Lands for Park & Recreation Purposes Act "the Fort Lawton Bill." It allows cities to acquire surplus federal property for park uses at little or no cost.

After a community survey, the Magnolia Community Club (MCC) supports a Fort Lawton Park.

Veterans' groups seek to site a national military cemetery on the south bluff, but are denied.

The Post Commander closes the Fort gates, citing security concerns.

Park Superintendent Hans Thompson requests planning proposals for Fort Lawton Park. Dan Urban Kiley of Charlotte, Vermont is chosen.

1970   President Nixon signs Fort Lawton bill into law.

Native-American group storms Fort and claims ownership.

Seattle School District seeks Fort Lawton buildings for educational uses, but is denied.

King County claims reversionary rights to 151 acres of Fort Lawton, but claim is denied.

Opposition causes Navy to withdraw request for 110 acres of Fort Lawton.

Under pressure US Coast Guard withdraws request for 44 acres of Fort Lawton.

Army Reserve moves training from Harbor Island to renovated Fort Lawton buildings.

Mayor Wes Uhlman appoints Citizen's Advisory Committee for Fort Lawton Park.

1971   General Services Administration (GSA) declares 425.75 acres of Fort Lawton as surplus.

Mayor Uhlman tells GSA the City is determined Fort will become a park. He says the City rebuffed Audubon Society's request for 200-acres and to others including skeet shooters, equestrians, golfers, and soccer players.

Bureau of Indian Affairs (BIA) seek 30 acres of Fort property for United Indians of All Tribes Federation (UIATF) Indian Cultural Center (ICC) but later withdraws request asking that an ICC area be included in the Park plans.

City applies for Fort Lawton for park and recreation uses.

President Nixon announces 426 acres of Fort Lawton available for park uses.

Army builds 3,800-foot chain link fence to enclose remaining Fort property. Sen. Jackson intercedes and it is removed.

UIATF artist, Lawney Reyes, sketches plans for ICC. Plan later expands in size and impacts.

Under pressure the US Prisons Bureau withdraws request for Fort Lawton property.

Seattle architect Jack Morse calls for a boulevard entrance to Fort Lawton Park.

American Kiteflyer's Association wants Park area reserved for kite flying, but is denied.

Army Corps of Engineers lists West Point for yacht moorage. Moorage is located elsewhere.

Metro forms liaison committee with Park advocates to make sewage plans compatible with the Park.

Seattle allows Metro permit to build a sludge-dewatering basin at West Point beach. It is later removed and the beach is restored.

1972   Kiley Master Plan for Fort Lawton (Discovery) Park is submitted to the City.

City agrees to lease 19 acres for the ICC.

Newly-named Discovery Park opens to the public.

Metro receives ownership of 40 acres at West Point from Army and a 100-year lease from State Department of Natural Resources for 40 tideland acres.

President Nixon's daughter, Tricia Nixon Cox, presents deed for 391 acres of Fort to City.

The Seattle Rhododendron Society asks for 20 acres of Fort Lawton for a "Rhododendron Forest." It was later built elsewhere.

The Magnolia Action Planning Committee asks University of Washington landscape architecture class to study a boulevard entrance to Discovery Park.

Fort Lawton Won't Get Missiles; Two Kitsap County Sites Chosen

December 18, 1968.
The Seattle Times.

FORT LAWTON
PARK APPROACH

introduction

MAP   statement

February 14, 1973
Magnolia News *insert.*

1973 Burlington-Northern Railroad and the MCC celebrate the 100th Anniversary of Arbor Day by planting 180 incense cedars to beautify Discovery Park approaches.

MCC sponsors Seattle Beautiful Operation Triangle at 21st Avenue West and West Emerson Place to beautify approach to Discovery Park.

Senator Jackson dedicates Discovery Park calling it a "People's Park."

MCC challenges Metro's Auburn interceptor project. It would bring added Renton Plant sludge for discharging off West Point. (State later stops this practice.)

Chapel in the Pines is released to Park, adding an area of 2.5 acres.

1974 Kiley's 1974 Revised Master Plan updates 1972 plan.

Friends of Discovery Park (Friends) organize to oppose an initiative for a golf course on the south bluff area of Fort Lawton.

1975 Army announces a 151 upland acres of Fort Lawton is surplus to federal needs.

Seattle Park Board opposes golf course initiative. Later the voters defeat it.

City and UIATF sign lease for a 19-acre ICC.

MCC sponsors Seattle Beautiful Triangle Park at 32nd Avenue West and West Government Way to beautify Discovery Park approaches.

Discovery Park Loop Trail is designated National Urban Recreational Trail.

1976 Landmark's Board-Park Board committee meets to decide dispute over Park Historic District. They review 25 buildings containing more floor space than Seattle's city hall.

UIATF propose a People's Lodge for the first time, but is denied.

1977 UIATF's Daybreak Star Center opens.

Environmental groups led by Thomas O. Wimmer ask Metro to remove the West Point plant if secondary treatment is required and build a plant elsewhere.

GSA releases additional 127 acres of Fort Lawton to the City, bringing Park to 535 acres.

1978 City Council votes to preserve only two Fort Lawton historic buildings.

Taproot Theater Company asks for the Fort Lawton Chapel on the Hill, but request is denied.

Army Chief of Chaplain's recommends Fort Lawton Chapel be released to the Park.

1979 Seattle-King County Health Department director warns of pollution on West Point beach.

Marine Animal Resource Center seeks property at West Point for a seal rescue center after being refused property in the Park, but is denied.

1980 UIATF seeks the Coast Guard antenna site. Under terms of lease agreement they are not to ask for property outside the ICC boundaries. Request is denied.

1981 A cougar loose in Discovery Park closes Park. He is captured and returned to the Cascades.

1982 Proposal for reuse of Park's "historic buildings" meets opposition. It brings traffic into the Park's interior and allows commercial rentals.

Park Superintendent Walter Hundley calls for arbitration of UIATF lease violations.

Park Department plans West Central Maintenance Center at Discovery Park, but facility is later placed outside the Park.

1983 Washington State Department of Ecology (DOE) grants Metro a waiver from secondary treatment.

City Council considers a "sale and lease back plan" for the Discovery Park historic buildings as a tax credit plan, but opposition defeats it.

1984 Washington Environmental Council, Legal Advocates of Washington, and Friends join Puget Sound Water Quality Defense Fund (PSWQDF) in lawsuit against Metro expansion.

The State DOE requires Metro to go to secondary treatment.

The Jackson Memorial Viewpoint is dedicated in Discovery Park.

1986 To date hundreds of cities have received park property from the "Fort Lawton Bill."

A Washington Trust for Historic Preservation suit stops historic building demolition.

Mayor Charles Royer calls for a new secondary treatment plant outside the Park to preserve the natural beauty of West Point and its value to future generations.

Donald S. Voorhees criticizes proposed Discovery Park Development Plan.

UIATF People's Lodge proposal includes Olympic-sized swimming pool, a 5000-seat arena, and 8 acres of Park for 250 more parking spaces, but is denied.

1977 Series.
Argus Magazine.

1987 Thomas Wimmer, leader of the PSWQDF, dies at age 77.

1988 City Council approves plan level permit for Metro expansion at West Point.

PSWQDF, LAW, "Friends," and WEC appeal permit to the Washington State Shoreline Board.

The Park Department establishes the Discovery Park Memorial Fund.

U.S. District Judge John Coughenour rules the City must review Historic Building decision.

Park planner Dan Kiley takes City to task saying, "…the city emasculated my Master Plan without giving me a chance to review it…Because of all this I do not consider this my Master Plan anymore, and therefore, do not have a loyalty to it."

City Council votes to save the facades of several historic buildings, but with no uses inside.

1989 Judge Voorhees dies July 7.

Discovery Park Memorial Fund raises $34,800 in donations. Money is added to the Park's visitor center funds.

1990 Park staff memo calls UIATF application to the Federal Administration for Native Americans for funds to plan the People's Lodge "explosive." This proposal surfaced by chance in 1993.

National Oceanographic and Atmospheric Administration says studies find Metro and Seattle guilty of Puget Sound pollution. They find diseased fish off West Point.

Mountain bikers ask to use all Park trails but are kept only on paved trails.

Hang gliders ask for a special area on south bluffs, but are denied.

Northwest Golf Magazine tries again for a golf course in south meadow area but fails.

Citizens challenge City Light's proposal to build a vault in the Kiwanis Ravine and bring power lines through. This begins a successful effort to protect a Great Blue Heron nesting and wildlife habitat in the ravine and to preserve a wildlife corridor to the Park.

1991   Settlement agreement signed by environmental and civic groups with Metro and the City.

Paul Frandsen, Discovery Park manager, leaves the Park for new park position in California.

Advanced Wastewater Treatment Citizens Advisory Committee organized to meet Settlement Agreement goals to remove digesters, reduce plant size and open beaches for public use.

Park Department locates West Central Maintenance facility off-site ending plan to place it in Discovery Park.

1992   City Light moves proposed vault from the Kiwanis Ravine to a site near Commodore Park. A street-end park was built over it.

1993   The Environmental Education Association of Washington names Discovery Park as having the "outstanding community based environmental education program" in the state.

Metro allots $30 million for the Shoreline and Park Improvement Fund.

Discovery of a Native American midden (refuse heap) slows secondary construction.

Magnolia News

Council OKs West Point expansion

Opponents vow to continue fight

By Alan Gallick

March 2, 1988
Magnolia News.

UIATF plans a 148,000-square foot People's Lodge in Discovery Park.

Senator Slade Gorton proposes building a 140,000-square foot joint Army-Navy Reserve Center at Fort Lawton. The plan meets opposition.

Friends of Seattle's Olmsted Parks seek SPIF funds for boulevard entrance to the Park.

UIATF asks for Sand Point Naval Station property being declared surplus.

Washington Wildlife and Recreation Program approves $351,000 to purchase Kiwanis Ravine property. Other funds bring total to $750,000.

1994   UIATF seeks space in Naval Readiness Center building on South Lake Union.

Citizens and Senator Gorton discuss problem of adding Navy reservists to Fort Lawton.

Citizens object to helicopters disturbing eagles and nesting Great Blue Herons.

Navy Captain D. H. Moses refuses to move Navy Mini-Mart from Park to Fort Lawton.

City Councilmember Jan Drago proposes three off-leash dog runs in Discovery Park but they are eliminated. Dogs on-leash are allowed in Discovery Park.

1995   Daybreak Star sewer line breaks. City Council says the lease requires the UIATF to repair it. The UIATF says, "The center leases the property from the city ($1 a year). It is the city's responsibility." Council appropriates funds but requires repayment which is never made.

Friends oppose use of Metro's sludge (bio-solids) on the Park's meadows and application is stopped.

1996   P-Patch members seek a park site for transfer of their Interbay program, but are denied.

The Navy Reserve Director says moving the Naval Reserve to Fort Lawton does not enhance the Reserve's mission capability and a location is found elsewhere.

Citizens unearth a 1993 UIATF request to the City to add 150-180 acres of Discovery Park to the ICC for a 21st Century Master Plan—A Native American "Commons." The plan includes social services and the 9.5 acre "500" military area expected to be surplus. (The federal deed does not allow social services in the Park. These needs were provided for elsewhere in the City.) In the same request the UIATF asked for City support to gain "charter status" for federal recognition.

Police horse patrol will move from Discovery Park and paddock area to be restored as habitat.

1997 Metro completes construction of secondary treatment plant.

1998 The Save Discovery Park Coalition fights size and impacts of UIATF proposed People's Lodge.

Citizens learn from BIA office in Portland that "charter status" means recognition of Indian tribes. A UIATF request for "charter status" had renewed fears of casino gambling.

1999 DCLU loses 1,000 citizen comments on the UIATF's People's Lodge proposal.

DCLU releases Draft Environmental Impact Statement on UIATF People's Lodge.

City hearing examiner overturns DCLU's decision ruling People's Lodge's use is as a museum.

UIATF appeal city hearing examiner's decision to King County Superior Court.

King County Council votes to build third treatment plant. West Point will not expand.

2000 UIATF leader Bernie Whitebear dies from colon cancer, July 16.

Army Reserve dedicates new reserve building now reduced in size and impacts.

UIATF People's Lodge appeal remains on hold.

July 13, 1998.
The Seattle Times.

Paul Bunyan's golf ball. This Cold War air defense radar now tracks routine aircraft traffic for the Federal Aviation Administration. Photo by Monica Wooton, 2000.

A Certain Clout: The Magnolia Community Club

By Monica Wooton

"In a city known for its strong neighborhoods, Magnolia and the Magnolia Community Club (MCC) stand out, and their success hasn't come by accident. The formula is simple . . . just enough people with talent and resources who have been willing to devote years to the MCC, giving it a clout that exceeds its sheer numbers."[1]

A quick look down the past presidents roster demonstrates why the MCC has always been strong: Lady Willie Forbus, John Mucklestone, Barbara McIntosh, Pat Cook, Joel Haggard, Ken Schubert, and Janet Anderson—all very busy and successful in their "real" lives of politics, law, accounting, and real estate. Yet, all have stepped up to serve as Club presidents to handle the issues of their neighborhood through the unusually active organization of the Magnolia Community Club.

Jan Kumasaka, a former City planner, said of the group in 1987: "They are a very interesting bunch of people. Very protective . . . They are affluent enough and educated enough to know what to do. They get their facts and they know the right buttons to push to get their way. They are a good role-model for other community groups."[2]

In 1959, in an open letter to Magnolia, Eyrle Day, MCC president at the time, wrote: "[The] Magnolia Community Club is not only the Voice of Magnolia, but it performs many functions that the individual citizen could not hope to do. It acts as the liaison between our community and the City proper—your problems have the strong backing of the Club and thereby carry added weight and exert maximum influence with City officials."[3]

The Magnolia Community Club can trace some origins to a club formed in 1921 as the Magnolia Bluff Improvement Club. Those Club minutes give an interesting view of the ongoing history. It started out with strict boundaries that ended up excluding its own vice president from being a member. An entry dated February 3, 1925, reads: "Any person residing in the Magnolia Bluff district, or owning property . . . in the described district shall be eligible for membership."[4] In 1939, the Club officially became the Magnolia Community Club and received its "Articles of Incorporation."[5] The books of official record are chock-full of business, with the occasional dance or annual picnic plans of years gone.

Opposite: Caroline Alabach, Magnolia Community Club Trustee, offers a welcoming smile, newsworthy literature, and Club memberships to Magnolia neighbors at the SummerFest 2000. Displays of MCC projects including: the expansion of the Library, work on the Magnolia Bridge for expanding traffic demands because of Immunex moving to the area, and Magnolia's new history book are showcased at the booth. Photo by Roy Scully, 2000.

The very first page of minutes reveals members of the community who came together to talk about establishing a school for the neighborhood children. The stories from then until now, include scribblings on the thin, aged pieces of notebook paper in handwritten ledgers and letters, mimeographed minutes, and computer-generated documents. All reveal the same message, this is a community that looks to preserve its perceived quality of life: demands for bus service, streets and sidewalks, sewer repairs, and the critical bridges. The MCC has evolved through the years addressing more complicated issues such as fighting Metro's secondary sewage treatment plant, struggling against mandatory school busing, and working to preserve park land such as Smith Cove Park.

For all of the complaining one sometimes hears about the MCC vocalizing complaints, it is a fact that Discovery Park, only three bridge entrances, the Locks, the Interbay trains, Piers 90/91, and the sliding slopes surrounding the neighborhood are real reasons for concern. For several years even air-noise has escalated to intolerance for some residents. This is a club surrounded with issues, metaphorically and quite literally. It works to demonstrate a sense of pride and duty, and to maintain the quality of Magnolia life and neighborhood safety and appeal for the long term.

Club membership did not grow dramatically in the late 1990s. With mothers working and families trying to keep up the pace of the double-income society and expensive taxes for their little piece of Magnolia, it has been harder to find the volunteers of old such as Heidi Carpine, Ed Mueller, Pat Cook, Howard Vierling and first club president Dr. H. T. Harvey. Meanwhile, working the hot issues is still in the hands of those with the burning desire to serve on the MCC Board. Past MCC president Scott Smith sums his MCC service up nicely: ". . . I felt I had an obligation . . . a lot of people have that attitude here. They are going to put down roots, and there's no better way to participate than to get involved in these kinds of issues."

The MCC 2000 Board of Trustees lives the break-neck speed lives we've all come to know in the early twenty-first century, yet they have made time to volunteer. Dedicated to what he considers almost a mission, Mike Rees has spent countless hours with airport officials. He has discussed the controversial issues of alternate cargo flight paths over Puget

The first page of minutes recorded by The Magnolia Bluff Improvement Club in 1921. Many history records are in the MCC History Committee Archive. Courtesy of Magnolia Community Club History Committee Archive.

Sound with the Federal Aviation Administration and Boeing Field representatives. Mike has volunteered in an effort to curtail escalating airplane noise over Magnolia Bluff. His statistics show a problem for Magnolia that has worsened, and he wanted to sleep nights without the noise of the 5 a.m. cargo runs that have awakened him and the thousand of residents who have signed his petitions. Lindsay Brown, a mom and lawyer, has volunteered as MCC Web site designer. She had long-term concerns that spurred her to join the Club, specifically schools and the disposition of the Briarcliff School property in her neighborhood. Since its closure in the 70s, it has attracted both graffiti and rats. Betty Ivie, MCC vice-president and businesswoman, has co-edited the MCC newsletter with her husband Bill for several years.[6] The Ivies have produced a professional club newsletter that reflects the serious and influential nature of the MCC's business, containing in-depth reports on Club issues and actions.

All of the Magnolia citizens who have participated in the MCC truly are the "Voices of Magnolia." So it is still as Eyrle Day said of participation in the Club more than 30 years ago.

The MCC has evolved into holding a general membership meeting every second Tuesday of the month to address issues important to Magnolia residents. In early 2000, one such issue was the planned traffic overpass to relieve traffic congestion at the bottom of the Magnolia Bridge anticipated with the construction of the new Immunex complex. (An additional one to two thousand cars were expected to clog Elliott Avenue and the Magnolia Bridge even with some kind of road improvement and rerouting.) The MCC has looked at the issue since the late 1990s. By mid-2000 it was still not satisfied that the City planners had a good grasp of Magnolia's traffic needs, such as retaining the freedom for residents to access the Magnolia Bridge without stops. The MCC has gone back to the City engineers many times to clarify information and City plans, and has invited them to at least three public meetings in order to educate Magnolia residents on the issue. The quick commute to and from downtown is one of the attractions of Magnolia residency.[7]

The first bank book of the Club and other artifacts document the Club's history and activities. They provide concrete evidence of the Club's existence and original minutes through 1972 provide interesting and accurate details of the past history of the MCC. Courtesy of Magnolia Community Club History Committee Archive.

This kind of tenacity and demand for municipal accountability has earned the MCC some unflattering names downtown, and some residents consider the Club to be overly zealous and unable to accept change. The MCC remains unfazed. It knows its job: to get to the bottom of whatever is proposed for this neighborhood, and approve the plan if it enhances the community or to work to change it so that it will.

In addition to the monthly general meeting, Board Members meet the third Tuesday of each month to present information, answer questions and receive

feedback on the various issues being worked. This is when motions are passed or defeated and the discussions are often lengthy and detailed in order to make the "right" choice on behalf of Magnolia residents.

From "Gray to Green" is one program which the MCC has been working. The overgrown weeds and crumbling asphalt that make up the playfield behind Magnolia School could be renovated into a park/playfield. While the MCC supported the effort in its initial phase, it has surveyed the surrounding neighbors about potential uses for the site and for potential impacts such as light spillage and parking. The neighbors have become very involved in the process, and the MCC wanted to be certain the residents are well served by the program before "Gray to Green" gets its full support.

The great spaces that the MCC has saved as park land also give a great feeling of ever-present nature to the neighborhood. Discovery Park's loop trail, the blue heron rookery at Kiwanis Park, Commodore Park at the Locks, the salty freshness of a walk at Smith Cove Park make it all a very special neighborhood—one the MCC feels is worth fighting for to maintain the quality of life that is Magnolia.

Through the years many personalities have contributed unique talents to the MCC. Take Les Cowan. He was Club President in 1975. He is a listener. A former US Air Force colonel, he has no problem making a hard decision, but one feels he really wants the information and personal opinions from others first. He would sit devotedly, eye-to-eye, spending the time to hear what a resident would have to say. In relating his experiences with the MCC, he takes a nonchalant attitude, saying that it was a "*looong*" time ago, and brings up an anecdote or two.

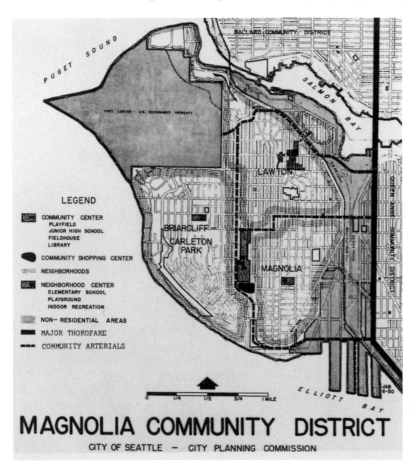

LEGEND

COMMUNITY CENTER
PLAYFIELD
JUNIOR HIGH SCHOOL
FIELDHOUSE
LIBRARY

COMMUNITY SHOPPING CENTER

NEIGHBORHOODS

NEIGHBORHOOD CENTER
ELEMENTARY SCHOOL
PLAYGROUND
INDOOR RECREATION

NON-RESIDENTIAL AREAS

MAJOR THOROFARE

COMMUNITY ARTERIALS

MAGNOLIA COMMUNITY DISTRICT

CITY OF SEATTLE — CITY PLANNING COMMISSION

Les loved Aleua Frare. "Just in her 70s, a little lady in tennis shoes who wanted to write the history of *MAGNOLIA Yesterday and Today*. And, she did it almost single handedly, tirelessly" he chuckled. Les hired Robert Slagle to illustrate the book. He also helped get the copyright, and was most proud of the fact that it was accepted as an official Bicentennial project and could proudly bear the logo of the American Bicentennial Celebration on the cover and title page. The MCC used the book as a premium give-away to all members who paid dues of $3. Many were sold, and eventually a second printing was made of the book and sold out.[8]

Les also dealt with one of the most far-reaching issues the MCC has ever had to deal with: the signing of the Treaty of Magnolia, an agreement of rights and responsibilities between the Port of Seattle and the Magnolia community in 1983. His calm, earnest manner fit such a large political task appropriately.[9]

Chet Sundt loved his year as president in 1962. He's a bubbly man, quick with a joke, and a lively speech pattern. He remembers as a beginning toastmaster he would start each and every meeting with a joke toastmaster style, and was proud to begin his meetings on that kind of note. That year the Club "had a kinda quiet" year. His wife Norma, who attended the meetings with him, agrees. They both found the experience very positive and full of memories of "good Magnolia people."[10] He and Norma were involved many years with club duties.

Chet's earlier years were filled with Magnolia history as he and his family resided in the brew master's house at 3219 22nd Avenue West in 1925, two blocks from Clauson Brewery, which ceased operation because of Prohibition. The brewery is where they got firewood, daring not to slip and fall between the rotten floor beams they teetered across while avoiding the big stagnant pools of water on the floor to get to the wooden wall boards.[11]

Chet attended and graduated from Interbay Grade School in 1931. In 1935, he was a Queen Anne graduate. He was a paperboy his entire childhood, starting with the oddly-colored green paper called the *Union Record*, the pink *Seattle Star*, and graduating to a *Seattle Times* route in his high school years. Every penny of the money went to the family kitty to provide for the basics. Chet remembers the trestle systems of Interbay, and walking like on a tightrope the north trunk sewer line, a pipe that carried sewage above ground. He recalls that fertilizer for the garden was obtained through Marymount Dairy.[12]

Chet's history on Magnolia has made him feel attached to the neighborhood. His MCC presidency was a labor of love, in his day there were no board meetings to deal with, just the general meeting for all Magnolia residents. That seems to fit Chet's people-loving style, because he liked the crowds to meet and greet. He was also instrumental in getting Dick Bringloe to do a rendering of the Village—past to present—that became a merchandising piece for Magnolia businesses to advertise their services and to give Magnolians a glimpse of the past. (This piece is updated for this book!) Chet is proud of it all, his Magnolia past and his past MCC presidency.

Ursula Judkins' favorite part of her years as MCC president in 1991 and 1992 was the signing of the Settlement Agreement on Secondary Treatment at West Point because of the clause stating that the

Les Cowan, President of the MCC in 1975. Courtesy of the Cowans.

Chet and Norma Sundt fondly recall the days of the Club. Chet was a long-time member, treasurer, and then '62-'63 president. Norma never missed a meeting. The archives are full of Chet's good deeds with the MCC. Photo by Monica Wooton, 2000.

Ursula Judkins is visiting the artist shop where the charming Discovery Park leaf patterned sidewalks were designed. She has been extremely active in the MCC and last year was the recipient of a special award for her outstanding service. Photo courtesy of Ursula Judkins.

plant would never be increased in size. It had been a long fight for the MCC and the words "preclude future expansion" made it worth it to her. To this day, she considers it a responsibility to insure those words are kept, constantly reminding residents and County representatives of their promise.[13]

She considers her tenure as MCC president to be an honor and a most positive two years, adding that she often felt she wasn't always up to the heavy responsibilities of the job. However, she always managed with extensive homework, constant meetings, friendships with those in powerful positions (who respected her), community members who mentored her, and a powerful ball-point pen. She credits another Past President, Scott Smith, as really making a difference in her realizing her own abilities as a MCC president.

Ursula is quick to smile then slip into a furrowed brow of thought. The issues she speaks of are serious to her, her representation of Magnolia a big job on her mind. And she's hooked. She has been a trustee nearly every year since her presidency, giving invaluable background information to newcomers and continuing to serve on MCC committees. Ursula is an avid letter writer and organized keeper of records. She can put her hands on the information she needs to explain an issue, and doesn't stop until all possibilities for solutions have been exhausted. She is a bit stubborn, and this has paid off in her work for the MCC. She was pleased to see the 28th Avenue West reservoir get a lid and have West Manor Park built over it. She goes there for exercise and to relax, and feels that it is a great use of creative space for nature. Ursula was named citizen of the day in 1999 by Seattle Mayor Paul Schell for her volunteer efforts on behalf of the Magnolia community.

The fourth annual tree planting of the MCC, under the direction of Steve Erickson. The event is a great success every April. It is a day of joyful camaraderie and beautification of our neighborhood. Photo by Heidi Carpine, 2000.

As written in *The Seattle Times/Seattle Post-Intelligencer* in 1987, "Magnolia seems very close to the small town that many residents envision themselves living in. Perhaps that's what makes Magnolia so special. In the midst of a big city, Magnolia still feels intimate— its Community Club still manageable."[14]

Today, bags of scattered mini-Mars bars are on the president's table for sharing, the monthly donated thermos of coffee from a Magnolia small business stands by, members with blue ball-point pens and binder paper are following the meeting and taking notes. They will go home, get to their computers eventually, and make recommendations regarding the Chamber's new clean-up project, the moratorium on floatplane permits on Elliott Bay or the MCC's position on cellular antennas in residential areas. "Manageable" or not, the Magnolia Community Club volunteers do what they have always done: protect Magnolia and its residents.

Monica Wooton served on the Magnolia Community Club as a member of the Board of Trustees for 18 months during 1997-1999. She served as the Chair of the History Committee. Along with Mimi Sheridan, Historian, Jose Montaño, President, and Susan Stern, Vice-President, she agreed to update the written Magnolia history. Monica has served as project manager for Magnolia: Memories & Milestones, *developing its format and writing team. With more than 20 volunteers, aged 26 to 90, working on the project with dedication and delight, she believes strongly the work is a real tribute to volunteerism and dedication on the part of Magnolia residents. She feels very fortunate to have had this rare opportunity and is thankful to all who have worked to make the project such a special experience and keepsake for Magnolians— a perfect MCC project!*

PAST PRESIDENTS

1924-26	Dr. H. T. Harvey	1963-64	Wm. T. Moore
1926-28	Samuel H. Furber	1964-65	Wm. Armstrong
1928-29	E. W. Wood	1965-66	John Mucklestone
1929-30	A. S. Knight	1966-67	Howard Vierling
1930-32	F. W. Carlson	1967-68	Pat Cook
1932-33	Burt Owen	1968-69	Ed Currier
1933-34	V. L. Sylliassen	1969-70	Eyrle Day
1934-35	Iner C. Nelson	1971	Bob Kildall
1935-36	H. C. Roberts	1972	Ed Mueller
1936-37	Chester W. Hills	1973	John Sears
1937-38	George Mathieu	1974	Barbara McIntosh
1938-39	Hugh Bell	1975	Leslie Cowan
1939-40	Linus Pearson	1976	Granville Gillett
1940-41	Earl A Phillips	1977	Robert Hall
1941-42	Fred I Rowe	1978	Scott L Smith
1942-43	A. C. Jephcott	1979	Joel Haggard
1943-44	S. N. Greenleaf	1980	Lee Bass
1944-45	Guv P. Locker	1981	Janet Anderson
1945-46	Vernon G. Latimore	1982	Bobbie King
1946-47	Michael K. Copass	1983	Veda Jellen
1947-48	Wm. T. Beeks	1984	Ken Schubert
	Paul D. Mackie	1985	John Mahlum
1948-49	R. Steve Sasnett	1986	Mike McGavick
1949-50	Lady Willie Forbus	1987	Heidi Carpine
1950-52	Howard Kroehl	1988	Rich Patton
1952-53	John James	1989	John Rasmussen
1953-54	A. E. Stephan		Nancy Kroening
1954-55	Norman Allen	1990	Nancy Debaste
1955-56	C. G. Flannigan	1991-92	Ursula Judkins
1956-57	Fred Hullen	1993	Tim Washburn
1957-58	Fred Hoover	1994	Allan Potter
1958-59	Murray Furguson	1995	Tammy Zinsmeister
1959-60	Wolcott Denison	1996	Don Erickson
1960-61	J. E. Mathiasen	1997	David Doherty
1961-62	Jack Rooney	1998-99	Jose Montano
1962-63	C. A. Sundt	2000	Susan Stern

1990 Census Data For Magnolia (Zip 98199)

POPULATION

Total	18,262
Male	48%
Female	52%

AGE DISTRIBUTION

0-4	5-9	10-14	15-19	20-24	25-34	35-44	45-54	55-64	65-74	75-84	85 plus	18 plus
6%	4%	4%	3%	5%	19%	20%	11%	9%	11%	7%	2%	84%

Median age 39.4 years

1999 MAGNOLIA POPULATION AND HOUSEHOLD (ESTIMATES)

Current Tract	Housing Units	Occupied Housing Units	Vacancy Rate %	Household Population	Household Size	Total Population
56.00	2736	2671	2.38	6190	2.317	6190
57.00	2683	2593	3.35	5491	2.118	5539
58.01	2545	2426	4.68	4250	1.752	4250
58.02	2542	2387	6.10	4267	1.788	4272
Totals	10,056	10,077	4.13	20,198	1.993	20,251

Source: Puget Sound Regional Council

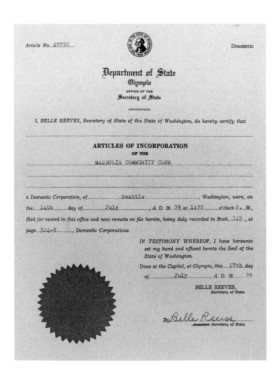

Official document of incorporation of the MCC-1939. MCC Historical Committee Archive.

HOUSEHOLDS

Number of households	8,753
Average household size	2.08
# of non-family households	3,946

FAMILY INCOME

Less than $15,000	8%
$15,000 to $24,999	10%
$25,000 to $34,999	14%
$35,000 to $49,999	17%
$50,000 to $74,999	27%
$75,000 and over	25%
Median family income	$51,236
Per capita Income	$22,265

FAMILY HOUSEHOLDS

Number of families	4,807
Average family size	2.7
Married couples	85%
Male householder	4%
Female householder	11%
Households with children	35%

Selected Highlights of Magnolia Community Club Activities 1921-2000

1921: Named Magnolia Bluff Improvement Club. Passed a motion to get a new bathhouse at Magnolia Beach and bus service. Demanded a schoolhouse.

1922: Dues sixty cents per quarter with a 10-cent refund if meeting attended with membership ticket. Voted a free load of wood for the church.

1924: The Carleton Park Improvement Club was formed at a meeting at Arthur Phinney's real estate office. Dr. H.T. Harvey was elected as the first president. Magnolia had about 4,000 residents.

1932: The Carleton Park Improvement Club was renamed the Magnolia Community Club and the area covered was expanded to include the Bluff. The MCC had 160 members.

1933: The MCC was responsible for the cessation of logging in Magnolia.

1939: The MCC is formally incorporated on July 17, and the first set of bylaws adopted.

1940: Zoning along the Ship Canal all the way to Shilshole Bay was made industrial. The MCC and Lawton Wood Neighborhood Council induced the City to change the zoning west of Fishermen's Pier to multi-family, which was later changed to residential.

1943: The first Library comes to Magnolia.

1946: In the days before environmental awareness, the City agreed to pour oil on the ground near the end of the Number 24 bus route to reduce dust.

1952: The MCC became the first tenant in the Magnolia Community Center and held the first meeting there. The MCC had been instrumental in the development of the Center.

1954: The MCC successfully obtained a post office for the Village.

1956: Dumping in Kiwanas Ravine, north of Government Way, was successfully stopped.

1959: The City agreed to rename the Garfield Bridge to the Magnolia Bridge.

1964: A newly-designed Library located at 34th Avenue West replaces the original Library in the Village.

1967: The City agreed to reroute a sewer line that dumped straight into Elliott Bay by Wolfe Creek to the Interbay pumping station. The MCC sponsored the 50th Anniversary Celebration of the Locks, and it started a fund to acquire the land for Commodore Park, on the south side of the Locks, to prevent apartments from being built and views destoyed.

1969: The Community Planning Survey resulted in the Magnolia Action Planning Committee, to prevent incompatible development.

1969-1973: Another skirmish in the battle for a Magnolia swimming pool, which began in 1921. This time, Queen Anne got the nod.

1973: The MCC chooses the name for Discovery Park after championing the park since 1924.

1974: The Port of Seattle makes a formal proposal to develop Pier 90/91. The MCC files suit against the Port - eventual settlement results in the Treaty of Magnolia.

1977: First Metro Environmental Impact Statement (EIS) on the Regional Water Quality Plan starts the Battle for West Point.

Betty and Bill Ivie editors, MCC Newsletter.

Magnolia Community Club

NEWSLETTER
JANUARY 2000

PMB #136 • 3213 WEST WHEELER • SEATTLE, WASHINGTON 98199 •(206) 283-1188

OFFICERS

President
Susan Stern

1st Vice President
Betty Ivie

2nd Vice President
Ursula Judkins

Treasurer/
Membership
Rob Wilson

Recording Officer
Open

Past President
Jose Montaño

TRUSTEES
Caroline Alabach
Mark Bloome
Alan McLean
Mike Rees
Michael Allen
Lindsey Brown
Don Erickson
Bill Ivie
Michael Letourneau
Eileen Ridgway

Newsletter
Bill Ivie
Betty Ivie

PRESIDENT'S MESSAGE

Happy New Year to you and with it, the birth of a New Century. The Magnolia Community Club has been around for the major portion of the 1900's. We have accomplished many incredible deeds.

In the year 2000 there will be much to do. The Historical Committee will be publishing the second book (the first was written in 1975) about Magnolia. The discussion about disposition of the Briarcliff Elementary School building and property continues with the Seattle Public School District. The UIATF People's Lodge in Discovery Park, to be or not to be, that is the question. The Seattle Parks and Recreation Department is planning a "Gray to Green" project at Magnolia Elementary (African American Academy), which could mean more open space and play fields. Will the Magnolia Library get its share of library funds, and how will those funds be used at our library? Aviation noise and the battle with King County International Airport to quiet the noise over our heads continues as the prosperous Puget Sound area attracts more commercial and freight flights. Tree planting will occur in the Spring and ongoing care of the Madrones and vegetation on Magnolia Boulevard remains.

Building the West Galer Street flyover to move car and truck traffic in and out of the new Immunex complex in addition to Magnolia traffic will result in some traffic disruptions. West Point Sewage Treatment Plant appears safe from expansion, but it took many hours of hard work by the MCC to help make this a reality. Will there be antennas on the Dravus Street Water Tower, on homes, on public/business buildings affecting our views, health and property values?

In addition to the controversial issues, I hope we can have a lot of fun along the way. The revitalization of the Village by the Magnolia Chamber is coming along nicely (notice the MCC bench in front of the Post Office?). The monthly MCC General Meetings social time has been a great success. With your help we would like to add a "Children's Social Area" staffed by teenagers to watch the younger ones so the parents can attend a General Meeting.

I know you are enjoying the Newsletter (thank you, Betty and Bill Ivie and all contributing reporters!). We have many great projects to be done by the Greatest Seattle Neighborhood – Magnolia! I hope to see you at our monthly General Meetings and wish you and your family a joyful New Year.

Susan Stern, President

-1-

MAGNOLIA
Yesterday and Today

by
Aleua L. Frare

Illustrations by
Robert L. Slagle

Commemorating the
50th Anniversary
of the
Magnolia Community Club

Author: Aleua Frare, 1975.

MCC Historical
Committee Archive.

MCC Historical
Committee Archive.

1978: Neighbors on 36th Avenue West, between West Emerson Street and Government Way West, petition for street closure to through traffic, citing danger to children and inadequacy of road to handle arterial traffic. A spot rezone attempt at the old grocery story on 28th Avenue West, across from the reservoir, is thwarted. Senator Henry Jackson is honored by the MCC at the Commodore Park dedication.

1980: West Point Sludge Lagoon removed after proving a failure, MCC had fought for removal. Discussion of Terminal 91 alternative issues proposed, and Pier 91 uses discussed again. Ship Canal award to MCC for Fish Ladder in conjunction with Locks remodel, Commodore Park and MCC participation.

1981: Discussion of the possibility of alternative uses of Blaine Junior High, if surplused and closed as a Middle School. Magnolia Elementary Schools: Lawton, Briarcliff and Magnolia combined with redistricting, boundaries now running east/west instead of north/ south for enrollment. US Post office relocated. Pea Patches at Interbay, for Magnolia and Interbay residents begins. Golf Course at Interbay is also approved by MCC. Pier 90/91 proposal as container port is not supported by MCC. Instead, the MCC favors placement of Navy Fleet and NOAA there. Part of Discovery Park becomes a Historic District.

1982: MCC studies Draft Environmental Impact Statement (DEIS) for proposed Terminal 90/91 uses as it moves forward. Discovery Park Master Plan studied and policy developed to stop hang gliding off the Dunes or anywhere else in the Park. Liquor guidelines reviewed and firmly established regarding the Park, as well. Chempro tanks at the piers emmited odors that affects Magnolia residents, MCC investigates. MCC opposes "add a rental" to single-family housing. Blaine is closed as middle school.

1983: MCC by-laws researched and amended. Two low-income housing buildings on Magnolia are approved. MCC moves to neither support nor fight Marina development. School busing and pairing with south-end schools started: Briarcliff paired with Hawthorne; Lawton with Dearborn Park. Large Metro Transit questionnaire is begun citywide, MCC participates. An agreement is reached on short fill at Terminal 91 during litigation between Port and MCC. Neighborhood Advisory Council (NAC) formed—Magnolia, Queen Anne and the Port in regular oversight meetings, one result of that agreement and neighbors disfavored reactions of the grainery project done on the waterfront by the Port.

1984: Golf Course development begins at Interbay. Four Mile Rock, off Perkins Lane, is discovered as an illegal dumping ground for toxic wastes. MCC works against this. Burlington Northern Railroad becomes a source of noise pollution again and with aircraft over-flights, MCC begins battle to stop noise pollution in Magnolia. Proposed alternate route to Elliott Bay Marina, at 32nd West access by Marina opposed as unacceptable to neighborhood traffic patterns. Marina questionnaire is released to Magnolia residents to get a feel for sentiment and scope of acceptance of proposal.

1985: Amendments are made to previous agreement on short fill at piers. MCC does not get involved in Bus Tunnel debate. Four Mile Rock waste dumping is proposed as a possible litigation case. Shoreline Master Plan presented, MCC reviews parts relevant to Magnolia. Bus shelter added to Magnolia Bridge entrance for resident use. MCC does not oppose the marina construction.

1986: Pier 90/91 container issue revisited. Magnolia Bridge under goes major needed repairs. Study of Fishermen's Wharf/Terminal redevelopment plans issued. Metro Sewage Plant at Interbay as an option to Metro proposal's for West Point, not supported by MCC (in a joint agreement with Queen Anne.) Marina (EIS) is ruled insufficient, and they make new proposal to move project 280 feet east.

1987: Four Mile Rock is closed to dumping. Metro Sewage secondary treatment public hearing, MCC participates and opposes this for West Point. Historic building determination at Discovery Park process begins. Horse patrol is proposed to be move out of the park. MCC opposes this. Issues of the year: recycling plans for City, pier as container ports again, water quality issues, septic tanks on Magnolia. MCC opposes Bed and Breakfast proposal for neighborhoods.

1988: Thorndyke Avenue median beautification matching funds project begins. Litigation over secondary treatment at Metro is begun by MCC. More development of full-service golf course at Interbay proposed. Four Mile Rock is cleaned up as part of mitigation of toxic waste problem. Eagle's nest is discovered in Discovery Park. MCC opposes Bed and Breakfasts in single family homes again.

1989: Container port discussions continue with Port and Club. Seaplane noise added to noise pollution issue. Thorndyke beautification continues. Signs posted on Magnolia beaches warning that eating shellfish from Magnolia shores is dangerous, due to pollution. MCC donates own money for obtaining matching funds for grants to write and see Magnolia receive for projects. Lawton School rebuilding begins. West Point Metro issues continue.

1991: MCC President Ursula Judkins signs the Settlement Agreement, on February 19, officially ending the Club's 14-year conflict with Metro on secondary sewage. Construction at West Point begins. MCC brings long list of alleged Metro permit violations to the attention of the City Council in the fall.

1993: The proposal for a People's Lodge at Discovery Park raises concern.

1994: MCC participates in promotion and distribution of a poster relating to neighborhood diversity. The Club studies and reports its position on a City zoning change for smaller housing units and mother-in-law apartments.

1995: Discussions of the Immunex Project begin in earnest. The neighorhood district council is re-organized. The Esplanade development proposal is submitted and the building permit is eventually denied. Burke Gilman trail alterations occur.

1996: The Immunex Project readies to move next to Magnolia. The Magnolia Bridge overpass is proposed. The City proposes a Comprehensive Plan. The Magnolia Neighborhood Plan Survey is carried out. The West Point secondary sewage treatment plant is dedicated. The street tree-planting project starts for the first year. The Club publicly comments on the Seattle Commons Park Proposal. The Seattle Pacific University soccer stadium is discussed and street improvements to Dravus Street are accomplished. Discussion of a third runway at "Sea-Tac" begins by the Port of Seattle; the MCC provides preliminary response. King County Airport (Boeing Field) is expanded. The Magnolia Bridge gets some seismic refitting.

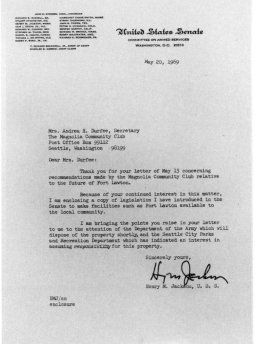

MCC Historical
Committee Archive.

1997: A serious slide on the west side of the Magnolia Bridge causes bridge closure. Airplane noise issues are formalized for discussion; the Roundtable, with affected communities and King County Airport participate. Briarcliff School property is first talked about being sold to private interests. An overpass is proposed for Immunex employee traffic over Magnolia Bridge. The Port of Seattle repairs Pier 91. The Ballard Interbay North Manufacturing and Industrial Center plan is reviewed. A specific maintenance plan for landscaping on the Boulevard is developed.

1998: Airplane noise over Magnolia becomes a formal issue. Roundtable discussions continue. The second tree planting takes place. The Dravus Bridge retrofitting causes traffic problems; the MCC talks to the City. The idea of a comprehensive neighborhood plan is proposed and a survey is done, including future ideas for Briarcliff property uses. The Magnolia Library and MCC discuss expansion of the facility. Commercial cellular radio antennas in areas zoned residential are questioned. King County Council starts discussions on expanding the West Point Sewer Treatment Plant again putting in jeopardy the "no expansion" agreement. Review of the Ballard Interbay North Manufacturing and Industrial Center continues.

1999: The airplane noise issue escalates. The King County International Airport Master Plan is released. *Magnolia: Milestones & Memories* is initiated by the MCC. A flyover on the Magnolia Bridge is proposed to facilitate traffic to the Immunex complex. Expansion at West Point will not occur; a new plant will be built in the North End. The United Indians of All Tribes Foundation (UIATF) ask for more property than the Discovery Park Master Plan allows. Tree planting is completed. A serious slide at the bottom of the Magnolia Bridge causes bridge closure again, extensive repairs and costs, traffic re-routed.

2000: The Club works on the library expansion, design and funding. The "Gray to Green" proposal to transform old properties into playfields is studied. Elliott Avenue West traffic impacts are studied due to considerable construction. Discussions continue with the school district on the fate of the Briarcliff School property. *Magnolia: Milestones & Memories* is published.

Submitted by MCC for publication.

MCC Historical
Committee Archive.

A Malsed Magnolia Millennium Moment

By Rick Malsed

This article appeared in the Magnolia News *December 29, 1999.*

As my stroll down the reflective road of the closing century begins, a Magnolia lifetime provides many special moments. Please recognize that these memories don't actually start at the beginning of the passing millennium, but rather my first Magnolia encounter of the century was coming home from Virginia Mason Hospital in May 1944.

The first Bluff encounter I can remember is standing in our front yard at 30th Avenue West and Grover Street during the '49 earthquake—obviously an event shared around town and therefore not an exclusive Magnolia event, it nevertheless still qualifies as No. 10 on my list of Top 10 Magnolia Millennium Moments.

Before continuing, maybe you'd like to compile your own list of memories and impressions from the almost-past century of Magnolia life. If so, try thinking about life here in four categories: "Millennium Moments," your overall best memories from the Bluff, "Most Missed from Magnolia," the no-longer-present aspects of life here that you most miss as we enter the 2000s, "Glad They're Gone," the changes in Magnolia you most appreciate and "Century-End Best of Magnolia," your favorite Magnolia features that have survived the past century (or part thereof).

Let's start with celebrating what's not here for Y2K New Year's Eve.

Top 10 Glad They're Gone from Magnolia

10. Noon Wednesday air raid siren test (the Cold War's over?).

9. The Post Office at 15th and Garfield (behind the billboard)—the present crew of guy and gal eaglets just seem to fit so perfectly being here in the Village rather than down on 15th!

8. The Interbay open-burning garbage dump.

7. Jane Fonda and her fellow protesters camped at 36th and Government Way when the Army surplused Fort Lawton.

6. Above-ground power and phone lines on some of the Bluff (just wish their visual pollution was absent from all of Magnolia).

"Century-End Best of Magnolia – The People."
Malsed
Photo by Monica Wooton, 2000.

5. Standing water on the Magnolia Playfield.

4. Village merchant security man "Fred the door shaker"—he'd pass through the Village carefully checking each merchant's door to assure they were locked, then place a little folded piece of white paper in the door crack - its absence later would indicate if someone entered the business between Fred's inspections. Trouble was, some kids would follow him and remove the little papers so that by now he'd certainly be totally beside himself and it's much kinder that technology has now filled the crack.

3. Unchecked raw sewage piped into Puget Sound around the Bluff.

2. Red fire alarm call boxes on the telephone poles at every corner—I wanted one so badly that if they hadn't disappeared on their own, there's a good chance that the Devil might have made me try to requisition one and that by now I'd be the guest inmate columnist for the *Magnolia News*.

1. And, number one glad it's gone from Magnolia: The stop-and-go intersections (before the overpass and underpass) on 15th at Garfield, Dravus and Emerson, which adequately handled the '40s and early '50s traffic but would fail today's two-plus car family test to and from the Bluff.

Bonus Wish It Was Gone: Port of Seattle Grain Elevators from Magnolia
(and Queen Anne) views.

Top 10 Most Missed from Magnolia

10. Fort Lawton and the cannon fired at 5 p.m. daily.

9. Johnny's Pasture.

8. The No. 19 Carleton Park bus.

7. Passion Pit without any street lights.

6. Phone numbers that start with "ATwater."

5. The door between the Medical-Dental Building and the men's suit department in Frederick and Nelson (Mom and Dad met while working at F&N, and without them I'd have no Magnolia memories, so this qualifies on my Magnolia list).

4. The Goat's Trail and the homes lost to the slides at Perkins Lane's south end.

3. Street lights made with a regular light bulb hanging from the center of a round, wavy tin hat (I've heard, but can't personally confirm, that this design made it exceptionally easy to break the bulbs with the toss of a rock or dirt bomb—by even the poorest of aims).

2. The Village bowling alley and lunch counter. First, in grade school days every Saturday afternoon, then on Friday nights during the three years at Blaine Junior High School, followed by high school dates, and then young marrieds' nights out without the kids.

Number One Most Missed from Magnolia: the Magnolia Theater.
When recently asked by his-publisherness, Dillon, to recall some of the movies seen at the art deco, flower-covered picture palace, I realized it wasn't the enchanting, never-ending serial superheroes, nor the double features with cartoons and newsreel, nor the first-run releases that makes the Magnolia Theater the most missed. It's most missed because of all that it meant as a life-long social cornerstone for us and our community.

Although some time about 1976, the curtain came down for the last time, the ageless socializing that took place in the presence of its charming silver screen flickers, wide aisles, special priced lounge seats, real butter popcorn, and extra second-floor lobby and crying room is top of my warm keepsake memories of Magnolia's now-missing bests!

So here we are, ready to look at Malsed's Magnolia Millennium Moments, at least for this century.

TOP 10 ALL TIME MALSED'S MAGNOLIA MILLENNIUM MOMENTS

10. 1949 Earthquake.

9. Ballard Shake Mill fire viewed from the Navy-housing complex east of 28th.

8. Yo-yo contests at J&J Pharmacy.

7. Columbus Day Storm and the day after walk through all the downed trees and limbs.

6. Two-week summer Canadian cruise on Magnolia's Explorer Scout troop's 65-foot *S.E.S. Propeller*, with Skipper Barney Bruce.

5. First kiss—Penny Packard in the hall closet during a Briarcliff friend's party the folks let me host.

4. KUAY closing—never another Grizzly football, basketball or baseball score reported on the 11 o'clock news.

3. A lifetime around the Bluff—30th & Grover, 3200 block of 43rd, Magnolia Boulevard & Dravus, 45th West, 31st West duplex (my first property), Lawton Way, Cottage Lynn (next door to my folks first house here—unknown when I purchased it), Magnolia Way, 28th near my "Mag Pres" baptism site, Perkins Lane & Raye St, and post Y2K— who knows?

2. Michael Morris Malsed and Michelle Marion Malsed, born in the '60s to parents living on West Lawton Way.

1. And number one Malsed's Magnolia Millennium Moment—My May Day Magnolia garden wedding to Christine Drake ('99).

So now let's close the century-ending year with our best:

CENTURY-END BEST OF MAGNOLIA

The people of Magnolia.

The homes and yards of Magnolia.

The merchants of Magnolia.

Our charming blend of life together here on our Magnolia island.

Happy New Millennium (or part thereof) on Magnolia!

"Our charming blend of life here on our Magnolia Island." Photo by Monica Wooton, 2000.

Courtesy Rick Malsed and Queen Anne/Magnolia News, *Mike Dillon publisher.*
Freelance writer Rick Malsed has lived on Magnolia since 1944, and is a monthly columnist for the Magnolia News.

Magnolia Village
and how it grew

BY
DICK
BRINGLOE

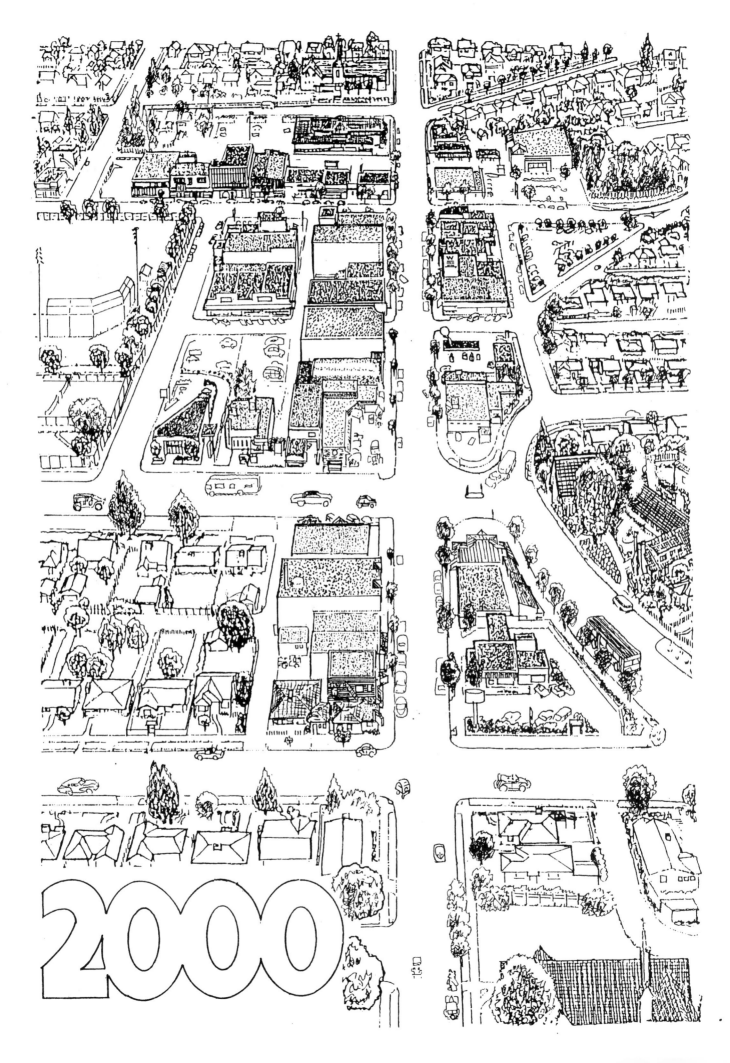

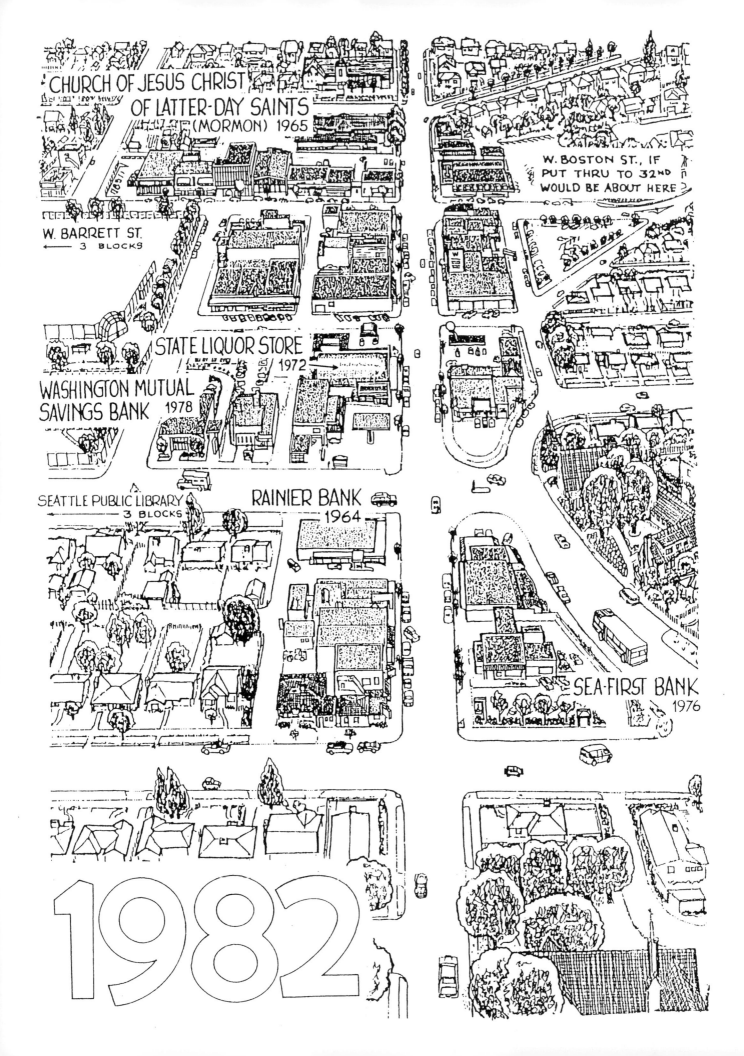

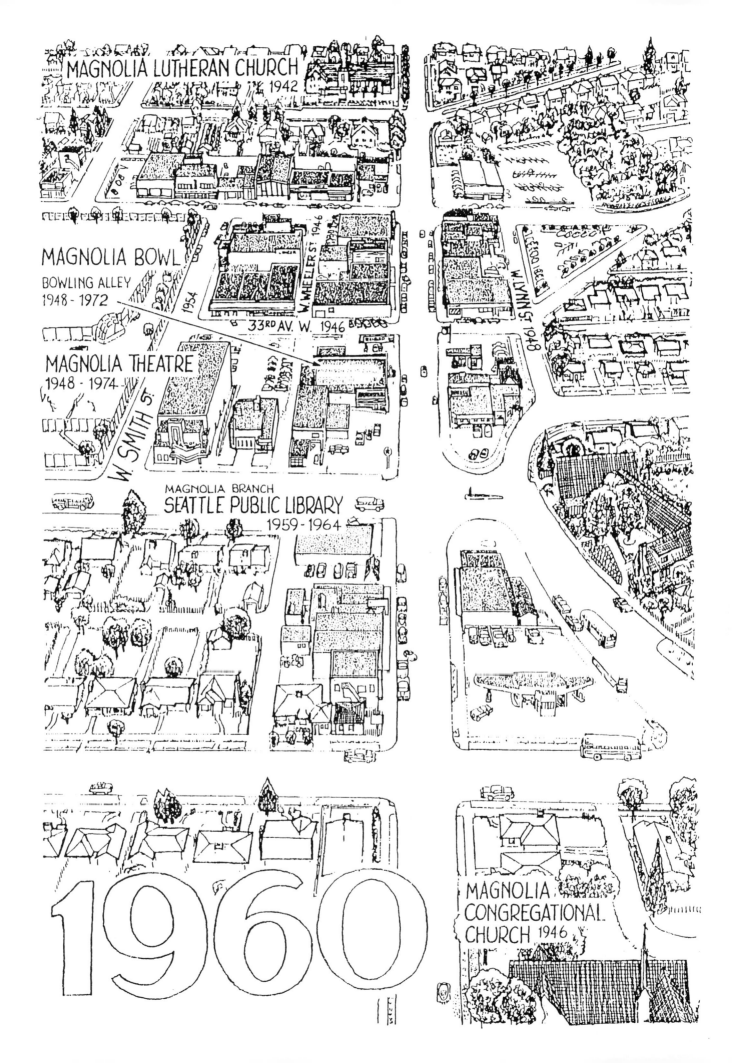

MAGNOLIA LUTHERAN CHURCH 1942

MAGNOLIA BOWL

BOWLING ALLEY 1948 - 1972

1954

33RD AV. W. 1946

W. WHEELER ST. 1946

W. DOSBON ST.

W. LYNN ST. 1948

MAGNOLIA THEATRE 1948 - 1974

W. SMITH ST.

MAGNOLIA BRANCH
SEATTLE PUBLIC LIBRARY 1959 - 1964

1960

MAGNOLIA CONGREGATIONAL CHURCH 1946

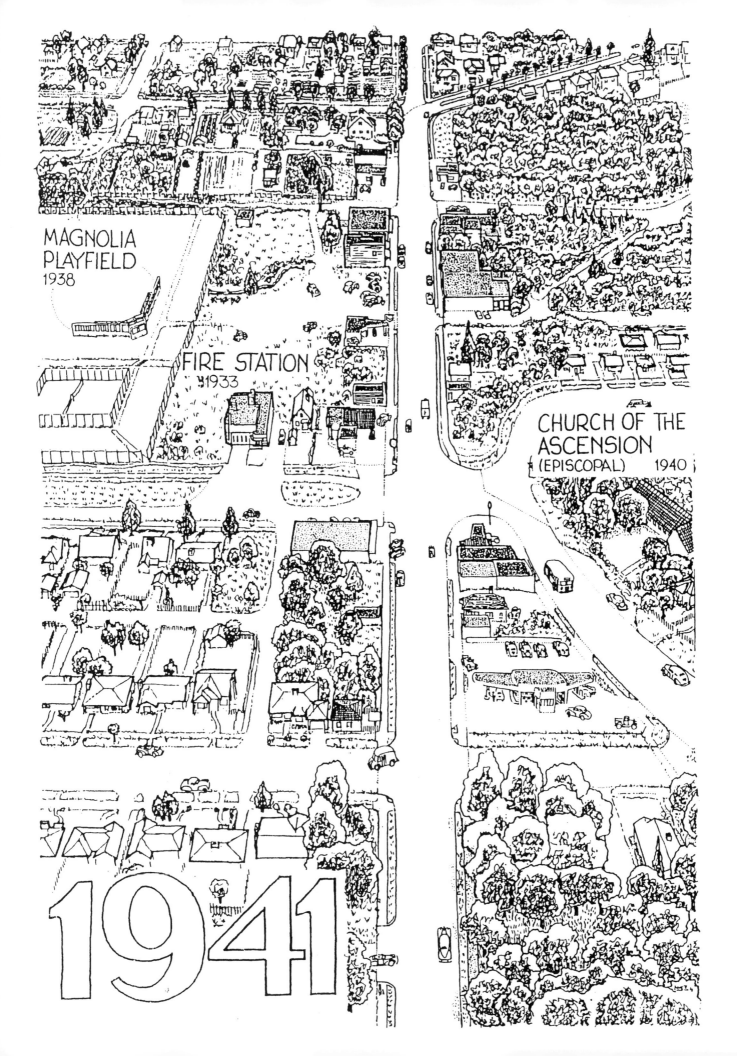

MAGNOLIA
PLAYFIELD
1938

FIRE STATION
1933

CHURCH OF THE
ASCENSION
(EPISCOPAL) 1940

1941

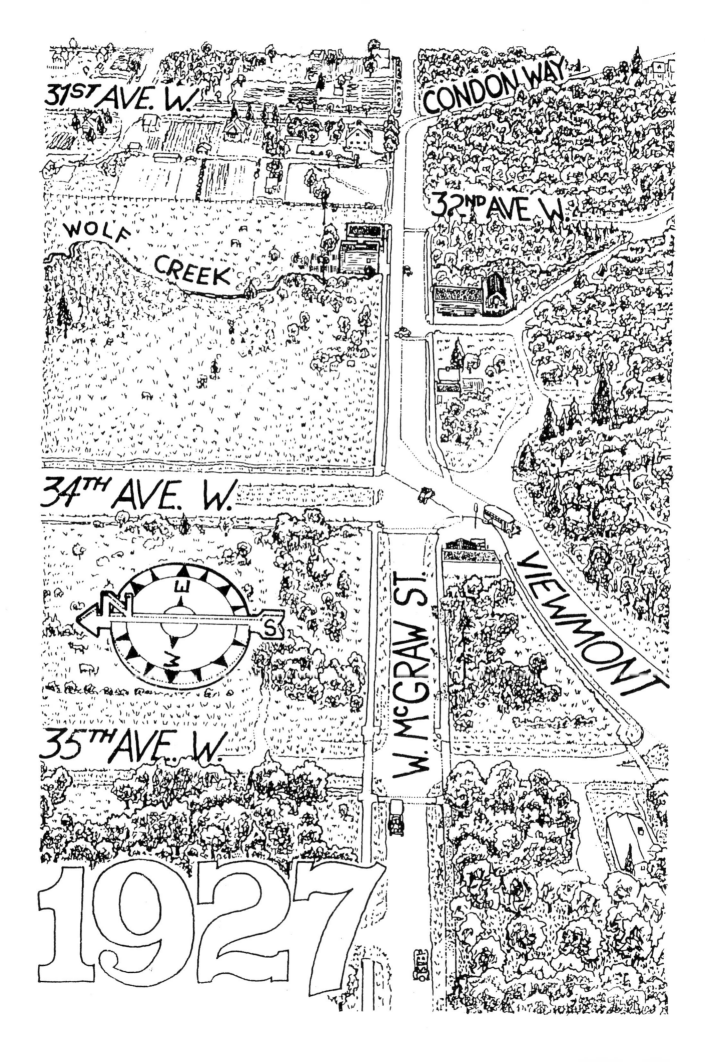

Since 1948

Le Roux

MAGNOLIA VILLAGE

Fine Apparel for Men & Women

MICHAEL SMITH
ALEXANDRA SMITH

3220 W. McGraw St. · **283-0377** · Seattle, WA 98199

Since 1993

CATERING & TAKE-OUT
CELEBRATIONS TO GO

2434 32nd Avenue West Seattle Washington 98199 Tel: 206.286.8755

MADISON DRAPERY

MC

CARNOLIA CLEANERS

SINCE 1938

Richard Turner

3412 West McGraw   (206) 284-2855
Seattle, WA 98199   Fax (206) 284-0616

SZMANIA'S

Pronounced "Smahn-ya's"

R E S T A U R A N T

Since 1990

3321 W. McGraw   Ludger & Julie Szmania
Seattle WA 98199   Chef/Owners
206.284.7305   www.szmanias.com
Fax 206.283.7303   E-mail: ludger@szmanias.com

MAGNOLIA INSURANCE AGENCY INC.

Est. 1954

GEORGE M. ANDERSON, JR.

TEL: (206) 284-4886
FAX: (206) 281-8688
RES: (206) 283-7486

3424 WEST McGRAW STREET · P.O. BOX 99085 · SEATTLE, WASHINGTON 98199

NIKOS GYROS

SINCE 1996

Nikos Gyros
2231 32nd West
Seattle, WA 98199
(206) 285-4778

COLDWELL BANKER

BAIN ASSOCIATES

Carol Batchelder
Associate Broker

Paula Ross   Linda Keylon
Realtor   Realtor

2560 32nd Ave. West
(206)283-3604
Serving Magnolia since 1963!

Since 1989

Janet Haberbush
Managing Broker

Business 206-284-8989 ext. 600
Fax 206-284-2184
E-mail jhab@windermere.com

Windermere

Magnolia | Windermere Real Estate/Wall Street, Inc.
3214 West McGraw St., Suite 102
Seattle, Washington 98199

Magnolia Chamber of Commerce

Since 1949

Working for the Community

(206) 284-5836

3213 WEST WHEELER, NO. 518 · SEATTLE, WASHINGTON 98199

Ric's Automotive & Texaco Inc.
3317 West Government Way
Seattle, Wa 98199 • 285-1761
Fax No 285-0246

Since 1958

RIC KASTNER
Owner

TEXACO

Since 1979   ORDER TO TAKE OUT

AUTHENTIC CHINESE CUISINE

GIM WAH

RESTAURANT & LOUNGE

3418 WEST McGRAW
(Magnolia District)
Seattle, Washington 98199

284-7000

Since 1949

Magnolia T.V., Inc.

3800 - 34TH AVE. WEST
SEATTLE, WA 98199
(206) 282-2712
(206) 284-5696 FAX

Porcelain Gallery

SINCE 1973

2426 32nd Avenue West
Seattle, WA 98199
Phone: 206/284-5893
Fax: 206/284-5260
www.porcelaingalleryinc.com

Edward**Jones**®

Caroline Alabach
Investment Representative

3205 West McGraw Street
Seattle, WA 98199
206-282-3426
www.edwardjones.com

Serving Individual Investors Since 1871

In Magnolia since 1988

Magnolia Garden Center

SINCE 1950

3213 West Smith Street
Seattle, Washington 98199
telephone 206·284·1161
fax 206·284·0081
maggarcen@aol.com

LPL

FINANCIAL SERVICES

Marc S. Scharr
Investment Advisor Representative

3202 W. Lynn St.
Seattle, WA 98199
Office: (206) 283-7198
Fax: (206) 283-7238

Since 1994

Linsco/Private Ledger   Member NASD/SIPC

**Founded
in Magnolia
in 1990**

206.281.8040
4001 21st Ave. W.
3217 W. McGraw St.

Roasters of Award-Winning Coffee
Available in the Finest Establishments

Magnolia Ace Hardware
2420 32nd Avenue West
Seattle, WA 98199
Phone: (206) 282-1916

Carolyn L. Conn
Manager

Tim Clark
Assistant Manager

Kregg Wilson
Assistant Manager

ACE

Since 1927

Magnolia Glass, Inc.

We Specialize in Vinyl Windows and Installation

*Insulated Glass * Mirrors * Shower Doors * Table Tops
Storm Windows * Screens * We fix broken windows*

3139 Government Way
Seattle WA 98199

206 283-3239 Phone
206 281-8440 Fax

*Here to serve you: * Earl Balder * Don Evans * Earl Odion
Ted Kovacevic * Doug Perdang * Amanda Turner/Office Mgr.*

Since 1973

MAGNOLIA'S BOOKSTORE

Since 1991

3206 W. McGraw
Seattle, WA 98199

(206) 283-1062

SINCE 1977

QUALITY
AND
REASONABLE

FREE
ESTIMATES

HOLMSTROM'S FAMILY PAINTING

INTERIOR & EXTERIOR

LICENSED - BONDED - INSURED

BOB HOLMSTROM
#HOLMSFP012P7

(206) 284-1376

PENHOLLOW MARKETS

In Magnolia Since 1960

3830 34th Ave West • Seattle, WA 98199
(206) 283-2710 - FAX (206) 283-0248

(W) **Washington Mutual**

Hank Erkenbeck
Assistant Vice President
Manager

Since 1977

2424 34th Avenue W   phone   206.461.3075
Seattle, WA 98199   fax   206.554.2709

34th Street Garage
Quality Work at Reasonable Cost

Gene Mayer, Owner

2410 - 34th Avenue West
Seattle • Washington • 98199
(206) **283-3448** phone
facsimilie   (206)   284-6880

Since
1991

SINCE 1955
3221 WEST MCGRAW
MAGNOLIA VILLAGE
SEATTLE, WASHINGTON 98199
PHONE 206-285-9756
FAX 206-352-3212
E-MAIL: blackthornepub@aol.com

BLACKTHORNE
Village Pub

CHRIS KOLSCEY   NEIL REEDER
DANTE PONCE   WALLY ROBINSON

SECRETARIAL ASSISTANTS
since 1973
Scanning ♦ Transcription ♦ Desktop Publishing
Photocopies ... Fax ... Email ... Reports
Resumes ... Brochures ...Newsletters ... Proposals
Manuals ...Flyers ... Spreadsheets ... Databases

3214 West McGraw Suite 103
Seattle Washington 98199
Tel 206/282-0158 ♦ Fax 206/282-9544
email sa@mcgoldrick.com

Village PLUMBING
282-4303

repair & remodeling specialists
family plumbers since 1890

**The above Magnolia businesses
generously supported the publication
of this book. Thank you.**

Donations To Book Project
as of October 28, 2000

$10-$49 Friends

Lynne Bivona and Jim B. Murray

Lindsay Brown and David Zapolsky

Heidi A. Carpine

Jill A. and Kevin G. Connell

Nadine K. Hale

Leslie A. Hargus

Susan Corcoran and Jonathan A. Hay

The Jepson Family

Granny Gillette

Bonnie Jepson

Cristy and W. C. Robert Lancaster

Leona M. and James A. LePenske, Jr.

John and Liv Mahlum

Louise and Richard Major

Fred and Mia Mann

Faye B. and Robert A. Matter

Eleanjor and Walter J. Minor

Belle and Carl B. Molander

Diane G. and Daniel Oneal

Queen Anne/Magnolia News

Robert L. Sharp

J. William Keithan, Jr.

Dan Kerlee

Ruth M. and Robert E. Kildall

Russ and Marion Langstaff

Delbert W. Loder

Marco J. Magnano, Jr.

The past Magnolia Historical Society

Mrs. and Dr. William L. Malcomson

Virginia M. Mason

Barbara and Jose Montano

Lynne R. and James D. Penhollow

Prolab (In Kind)

Rainbow of Magnolia Landscaping Inc.

Jean D. Rassbach

Bett Samuelsen

Ron and Joan Santucci

Mimi Sheridan

Teresa B. and Vincent H. Stecker

Mary S. and Dean D. Thornton

70th US Army Reserve (In Kind)

Jerome E. Vetosh

Joan B. and Robert K. Wilson

$50-$249 Donor

Phyllis M. and George M. Anderson

Magnolia Branch of Bank of America

Sharon and Mark Bloome

Seanna M. Browder and Paul A. Marti

Vada May and Jack R. Corkery

Doris M. and Col. Leslie W. Cowan

Lorene E. Currier

Discovery Park (In Kind)

Mary Kay and Joel E. Haggard

Rob Hitchings

Shirlee J. and L. Monty Holmes, Sr.

Toni and Robert Hutchinson

Louis Isquith, DDS

Ursula Judkins

$500 or More Patrons

Virginia Baxter

Exchange Facilitator Corporation

The Helmick Family

For Dottie, who would have loved this project and would have been knee-deep in the work and support of it!

Magnolia Ace Hardware Co.

(In Memory of Dottie Helmick)

Magnolia Community Club

Alyson McGregor

Rosealma and Cdr. Scott L. Smith

Susan Stern

Hal and Shirley Will

Jon and Monica Wooton

If your name has been inadvertently left out please contact the Magnolia Community Club, with your receipts of donated items and value. We will issue an in-kind receipt for tax purposes to you. We are sincerely sorry for any omission.

The main perpetrators.

Front to back, left to right. 1st row: Joy Carpine (and Petey), Hal Will, John Hendron. 2nd row: Scott Smith, Monica Wooton, Patty Small, Roy Scully. 3rd row: Jonathan Wooton, Joan Santucci, Rob Hitchings, Shirley Will, Betty Ivie. 4th row: Gail Perterson-Martini,

Cindy Howell, Rob Wilson. Back row: Steve Erickson, Nancy Worssam, Dan Kerlee. Invisible: Claudia Callan, Bob Kildall, Rick Mulsed, Sisi Sedgewick, Mimi Sheridan, Sam Sutherland.

Works Cited Bibliography

INDIANS ON MAGNOLIA BEFORE 1915 (No numbered endnotes for this piece.)

Ballard News Tribune. "Passport to Ballard The Centennial Story."

Buerge, David M. *Seattle in the 1880s.* Historic Society of Seattle & Kings County 1986.

---, "Seattle 3000 B.C. – 1851 A.D." *The Weekly.* 17 Dec. 1980: 16-25.

---, "From Whulj to Chu'ba a Guide to Tracing the Tracks of the First Seattlelites." *The Weekly.*
20 May 1981: Section 2, 1-5.

---, "The Lost Tribes of Lake Washington Reconstructing the Prehistory of the Lake People." *The Weekly.* 1-7 Aug. 1984: 29-33.

---, "Lost Seattle: Our Shameful Neglect of a Rich Archeological Past." *The Weekly.* 6-13 Mar. 1985: 32-35.

---, "The Eastside's Indian War: Who Would Control Puget Sound? . . . " *Eastsideweek.* 12 July 1985: 12-17.

---, "Seattle's Delta Country." *Seattle Weekly.* 15 July 1992: 23-28.

---, "Any there there?" *Seattle Weekly.* 18 June 1997: 25-29.

Dorpat, Paul. *Seattle, Now and Then.* 2nd ed. Seattle: Tartu Publications, 1984.

Eckrom, J.A. *Remembered Drums A History of the Puget Sound Indian Wars.* Walla Walla: Pioneer Press Books, 1989.

Harmon, Alexandra. *Indians in the Making Ethnic Relations and Indian Identities Around Puget Sound.* Berkeley: U. of California Press, 1998.

Holm, Bill. *The Box of Daylight Northwest Coast Indian Art.* Seattle & London: University of Washington Press, 1983.

Larson, Lynn L., and Dennis E. Lewarch, eds. *The Archeology of West Point Seattle, Washington, 4,000 Years of Hunter-Fisher-Gatherer Land Use in Southern Puget Sound Vol. 1, Part 1.*

Newell, Gordon, and Don Sherwood. Totem Tales of Old Seattle. Seattle: Superior Publishing Company, 1956.

Spencer, Robert, and Jesse D. Jennings, et al. *The Native Americans.* New York: Harper & Row Publishers, 1965.

Stewart, Edgar I. *Washington Northwest Frontier, Vol. II.* New York: Lewes Historical Publishing Co., 1957.

Thompson, Nile. "Salmon Bay Charlie, Last Headman of the Lake People." *Columbia.* Summer 1991: 34-37.

Tollefson, Kenneth D. "Reflections on Traditional Indian Subsistence Living." *Columbia.* Fall 1993: 13-17.

Vouri, Mike. "Raiders from the North." *Columbia.* Fall 1997.

Wilke, Steve, Principal Investigator, Karen James, Project Ethnohistorian. "An Archeological Evaluation of the Fort Lawton Historic District, Seattle." Report of the City of Seattle Department of Parks and Recreation, July 1984.

MAKING HISTORY? MAGNOLIA'S FIRST PIONEER

1 Graff, Ione Smith. Manuscript CUA-UW N PAM1124. March 1958. 1.

2 ---. Manuscript. 2.

3 ---. Manuscript. 2.

4 Bagley, Clarence. *History of Seattle From the Earliest Settlement to Present Time. Vol. 2.* Chicago: S.J. Clarke Publisher. 1916. 847.

5 Graff, Ione Smith. Manuscript. 1.

6 ---. Manuscript. 2.

7 Bagley, Clarence. *History of Seattle From the Earliest Settlement to Present Time. Vol. 2.* 846.

8 Graff, Ione Smith. Manuscript. 3.

9 Wade, Tom. *Magnolia News.* 3 Mar. 1981. 8.

10 Graff, Ione Smith. Manuscript. 3.

11 Jensen, Eva. *Transition from School to Community.* Self-published.

12 Wade, Tom. *Magnolia News.*

13 Graff, Ione Smith. Manuscript. 3.

14 ---. Manuscript. 4.

15 ---. Manuscript. 5.

16 ---. Manuscript. 4.

17 Bagley, Clarence. *History of King County, Washington. Vol. I.* S.J. Clarke Publisher. 1929. 41.

18 Wade, Tom. *Magnolia News.*

19 ---. *Magnolia News.*

20 Graff, Ione Smith. Manuscript. 3.

21 Wade, Tom. *Magnolia News.*

22 Sucher, David. *Puget Sound Access.* 1973. 6.

23 Dorpat, Paul. "Smith: The Cove and the Man." *Now and Then.* 1984. Essay No. 48.

24 Wade, Tom. *Magnolia News.* 8.

25 ---. *Magnolia News.* 8.

26 Bagley, Clarence. *History of Seattle From the Earliest Settlement to Present Time.* Vol. 2. 849.

27 Graff, Ione Smith. Manuscript. 5.

28 "Maritime Week Observers pay tribute to Henry Smith." *The Seattle Times.* 20 May 1978.

29 Graff, Ione Smith. Manuscript. 6.

30 ---. Manuscript. 7.

31 ---. Manuscript. 9.

32 ---. Manuscript. 9.

33 ---. Manuscript. 8.

34 ---. Manuscript. 8.

35 ---. Manuscript. 10.

36 ---. Manuscript. 11.

37 ---. Manuscript. 9.

38 ---. Manuscript. 10.

39 ---. Manuscript. 11.

40 ---. Manuscript. 11.

Rural Magnolia: A Pastoral Time

1 Deeds Map of City of Seattle. Circa 1880s.

2 Reinhartz, Kaye. *Queen Anne community on the hill.* Seattle: Queen Anne Historical Society, 1993.

3 ---.

4 ---.

5 Frare, Aleua L. *MAGNOLIA Yesterday and Today.* Magnolia Community Club, 1976. 9.

6 ---.

7 Reinartz, Kaye. *Queen Anne Community on the Hill.*

8 Sucher, David (as told by Henry Smith). "From the Earliest: Land Use . . ." The Asahel Curtis Sampler. Photographs of Puget Sound Past. 1973. 6.

9 Plat Maps, Pleasant Valley Neighborhood. City of Seattle. City Assessor's Office, 1888.

10 Dweyer, Joe. *Atlas of Washington Agriculture.* Washington State Department of Agriculture, 1963. 3.

11 ---. *Atlas of Washington Agriculture.* 8.

12 ---. *Atlas of Washington Agriculture.* 3.

13 Wade, Tom. "The forgotten doctor-and his Smith Cove legacy." *Queen Anne/Magnolia News.* 18 March 1981. 8.

14 Denny, Arthur. *Pioneer Days on Puget Sound.* Fairfield WA: Ye Galleon Press, 1965. 49.

15 Deeds Map of City of Seattle. Circa 1880s.

16 Pixel, Rebecca. "Farming in Magnolia." E-mail to Monica Wooton, 27 Oct. 1999.

17 Frare, Aleua L. *MAGNOLIA Yesterday and Today.* Magnolia Community Club, 1976.

18 Young, Shirley Allen. Personal interview. 25 April 2000.

19 Wyse, Cy. Personal interview. 30 Aug. 1999.

20 Gustufson, Emery. *Queen Anne News.* "The Passing Scene." 2 July 19.

21 ---. Personal interview. 23 May 1999.

22 ---.

23 ---.

24 Peterson, Ray. "Farm Days of Mine." E-mail to Monica Wooton, 15 April 1999.

25 Evans, Elizabeth. "Knut's Dairy is Still Going Strong." *The Seattle Times.* 18 April 1965. 5.

26 ---.

27 ---.

28 Will, Hal. *I'member.* Self-published. Limited Edition. June 1994. 14.

29 Elder, Phyllis. Telephone interview. November 1999.

30 ---.

31 ---.

32 ---.

33 Holmes, Monty. Personal interview. 15 Sept. 1999.

34 ---.

35 ---.

36 ---.

37 ---.

38 ---.

39 ---.

40 ---.

41 ---.

42 Photo of Shillstead Home and Property Description. Photographer unknown. Discovery Park Archive.

43 Holmes, Monty. Personal interview. 15 Sept. 1999.

44 Montano, Barbara. Personal interview. 15 Sept. 1999.

45 ---.

46 Samuelson, Bett. Personal interview. 11 April 1999.

47 ---. *Family History*. Self Published. 1980-1990

48 ---.

GATEWAY TO WAR, GUARDIAN FOR PEACE: FORT LAWTON

1 NARA Pacific Alaska Region. "Re: request for info from record group (338) Ft. Lawton 1942-." E-mail to Robert Hitchings. 12 Feb. 2000.

2 NARA College Park, Md. "Re: request for info from record group (338) Ft. Lawton 1942-." E-mail. 22 Feb. 2000.

3 Epley, William W. *America's First Cold War Army*. Institute of Land Warfare (NSA). August 1999.

4 Personal interviews with USA veterans. 1959-1960.

5 Epley, William W. *America's First Cold War Army*.

6 ---. *America's First Cold War Army*.

7 *The Seattle Times*. "War Causes Big Rise in Port Volume." 13 Aug. 1950. A-6.

8 ---. 13 Aug. 1950.

9 ---. 13 Aug. 1950.

10 Penman, Keith. Specialist First Class, USA (Ret.). "Re: The role that Fort Lawton played during the Korean War." E-mail to Robert Hitchings. 16 Feb. 2000.

11 Epley, William W. *America's First Cold War Army*.

12 Penman, Keith. E-mail to Robert Hitchings.

13 Hitchings, A.C., major USA (Ret.). Personal interview. 2 April 2000.

14 Strauss, Joseph, captain USAF (Ret.). Personal interview. 7 April 2000.

15 Rabe, Robert, major USA (Ret.). Personal interview. 29 April 2

FISHERMEN'S TERMINAL: MILLION-DOLLAR INDUSTRY

1 "Passport to Ballard, The Centennial Story." *Ballard News-Tribune*. 1988.

2 City of Seattle Report. An Archeological Evaluation of the Fort Lawton Historic District, Seattle. July 1984.

3 ---.

4 Passport to Ballard.

5 Tucker, F.C. Seattle Public Library Map. 1884.

6 Ballard News-Tribune. July 26, 1902.

7 Passport to Ballard.

8 Minutes of the regular meeting of Port Commission. 13 Dec. 1911.

9 Minutes of Special Meeting of Port Commission. 26 Jan. 1912.

10 Port of Seattle Commission Records.

11 First Annual Report of the Port Commission. 31 Dec. 1912.

12 Port of Seattle data. Undated.

13 Port of Seattle data. Undated.

14 Port of Seattle Commission data.

15 Seattle Post-Intelligencer. 11 Jan. 1914.

16 Ballard News-Tribune. 27 Sept. 1932.

17 Port of Seattle records. Undated.

18 Museum of History and Industry. Seattle.

19 Port of Seattle document. Undated.

20 Port of Seattle data. Undated.

21 Regal, Charles. *Seattle Post-Intelligencer.* 9 Sept. 1949.

22 Port of Seattle report. Undated.

23 Dwyer, James D. Fishermen's Terminal Redevelopment. 20 May 1986.

24 Port of Seattle data. Undated.

25 The Seattle Fishermen's Memorial Committee. Seattle.

26 Anschuetz, William. Personal interview. Spring 2000.

27 Osborn, Jeff. Personal interviews. 2000.

28 Fishermen's News. Vol. 55 No. 8 and 9. August and Sept. 1999.

29 2000 Business Plan Summary. Port of Seattle.

30 Our Living Oceans. U.S. Department of Commerce. June 1999.

31 ---. U.S. Department of Commerce.

32 ---. U.S. Department of Commerce.

33 NOAA Technical Memorandum NMFS-F/SPO-41. U.S. Department of Commerce. 1999.

34 Hare, Steven. Phone interview. 23 Feb. 2000.

35 Washington Department of Fish and Wildlife annual reports. 1984, 1985,1986,1995,1997, 2000.

36 ---. Annual reports.

37 ---. Annual reports.

38 ---. Annual reports.

39 Commercial Salmon License Buy-Back Program. Washington Department of Fish and Wildlife. April 1999.

40 1999 Commercial Salmon License Buyback Survey. Washington State Department of Fish and Wildlife. 5 June 2000.

41 ---. Washington State Department of Fish and Wildlife.

42 Endangered Species. National Council for Science and the Environment Publication I810009. December 1999.

43 Gudette, Karen. "State timber board adopts new regulations." *Seattle Post-Intelligencer.* 21 Jan. 2000.

44 "Feds declare disaster for ground fish." Seattle Post-Intelligencer. Staff report. 20 Jan. 2000.

45 Technical Report No. 40, The Pacific Halibut: Biology, Fishery and Management. International Pacific Halibut Commission. 1998.

46 Trumble, Robert J. Personal interviews. 1999.

47 ---. Personal interviews.

48 Our Living Oceans.

49 Osborn, Jeff. Personal interviews. 1999.

BEACHES, BERRIES AND BASEBALL

1 Bishop, Mary Sutlovich. Personal interview. 23 March 2000.

2 Deal, Alvara Forbus. Personal interview. 27 March 2000.

3 Gilkerson, Connie Collins. Telephone interview. 3 April 2000.

4 Wicklund, Helen Horn. Personal interviews. 20 March 2000.

5 Allen, Shirley Young. Personal interview. 25 April 2000.

6 Axley, Mary Pat Woolfolk. Personal interview. 23 March 2000.

7 Cannon, Geraldine Heiser. Personal interview. 21 March 2000.

8 Denney, Mary McGovern. Personal interview. 20 March 2000.

9 Mary McGovern Denney interview.

10 Carlson, Audrey Clark. Personal interview. 22March 2000.

11 Deal, Alvara Forbus. Personal interview. 27 March 2000.

12 Carlson, Audrey Clark. *A Century of Transition in School and Community*. Seattle:
   Seattle Public Schools, 1987.

13 Alvara Forbus Deal interview.

14 Geraldine Heiser Cannon interview.

15 Shirley Young Allen interview.

16 Mary McGovern Denney interview.

17 Brown, Vernice Monsey. Personal interview. 20 March 2000.

18 Alvara Forbus Deal interview.

19 Shirley Young Allen interview.

20 Mary Sutlovich Bishop interview.

21 Geraldine Heiser Cannon interview.

22 Wicklund, Helen Horn. Personal Interview. 20 March 2000.

23 Mary Sutlovich Bishop interview.

24 Audrey Clark Carlson interview.

25 Axley, Mary Pat Woolfolk. Personal interview. 23 March 2000.

26 Alvara Forbus Deal interview.

27 Mary McGovern Denney interview.

28 Mary Sutlovich Bishop interview.

29 Pennington, Mary Louise Mitchell. Personal interview. 21 March 2000.

30 Mary Louise Mitchell Pennington interview.

31 Geraldine Heiser Cannon interview.

32 Geraldine Heiser Cannon interview.

33 Mary Sutlovich Bishop interview.

Brand New Feminism: Forbus Family

1 Ellington, Anne. "PROFILE: Lady Willie Forbus." *The Bar Review*. September 1985. 5.

2 Hogle, Dale Forbus-Shoemaker. Personal interview. 16 June 2000.

3 Ellington, Anne. "PROFILE: Lady Willie Forbus." *The Bar Review*.

4 Hogle, Dale Forbus-Shoemaker. Personal interview.

5 ---. Telephone interview. 3 July 2000.

6 ---. Personal interview. 16 June 2000.

7 ---.

8 ---.

9 ---. Telephone interview. 3 July 2000.

10 ---. Personal interview. 16 June 2000.

11 ---.

Dumb Stunts and Grade-School Memories

1 Hansen, Robert. Personal interview. 3 Sept. 1999.

2 Jones, Albert. Personal interview. 15 Sept. 1999.

3 Sloan, Sherman, Jr. Personal interviews. 8 Sept. 1999 and 15 Sept. 1999.

4 Clark, Robert. Phone interview. 16 Sept. 1999.

5 Shrewsbury, Robert. Personal interview. 22 Sept. 1999.

6 Will, Edward. Phone interview. 16 Sept. 1999.

7 Holcomb, Alice Whalley. Personal interview. 17 Oct. 1999.

8 Fraser, Tom. Personal interview. 7 Sept. 1999.

9 Minard, Laury. Personal interview. 15 Oct. 1999.

10 Minard, Nancy Norton. Personal interview. 15 Oct. 1999.

11 Thomas, Jean Allyn. E-mail to Hal Will. 30/31 Oct. 1999.

12 Langstaff, Russ. Personal interview. 20 Sept. 1999.

13 Elder, Phyllis Paul and Elder, Robert. Phone interview. 25 Sept. 1999.

14 Morgan, Allen. Phone interview. May 2000.

15 Andrew, Geri Marty. Phone interview. 15 Oct. 1999.

16 Bell, Jean Martin. E-mail to Hal Will. 15 Oct. 1999.

17 Timberlake, Patricia Jephcott. Phone interview. 17 Sept. 1999.

18 Jeffery, Robert. E-mail to Hal Will. 20/21 Sept. 1999, 9 Dec. 1999.

The Village

1 Watchie, Jeanne. "Early platting of Magnolia – part of a colorful area." *Magnolia News*. 7 Oct. 1970.

2 Chambers, Jack and Ralph. Personal interview. 25 Aug. 1999.

3 Dillon, Matt. "Denton and Delorez Rossell are Magnolia originals." *Magnolia News*. 31 May 2000.

4 Watchie, Jeanne. "Magnolia early days." *Magnolia News*. 16 Sept. 1970.

5 "History Notes." *Magnolia News*. 16 Mar. 1969.

6 Magnolia Library Highlights. Magnolia Library flyer. Oct. 1991.

7 American Library Association News. 17 Apr. 1966.

8 Brindle, Pinky Kearney. Personal interview. 20 Apr. 2000.

9 LaRussa, Gloria. Personal interview. 8 June 2000.

10 Malsed, Rick. "It takes a Village." *Queen Anne and Magnolia Almanac.* 1999.

11 Smith, Bob. Personal interview. 2 Apr. 2000.

12 Frare, Aleua L. *Magnolia Yesterday and Today.* Magnolia Community Club History Project. Sept. 1975.

13 Taft, Patricia. Personal interview. 3 Mar. 2000.

14 Rusch, Hedy. Personal interview. 12 Apr. 2000.

15 Strachem, Margaret. "Magnolia Builds for the Future." *The Seattle Times.* 7 Apr. 1946.

16 Bomerngen, Jan. Personal interview. 15 Feb. 2000.

17 "Liquor store being protested." *Magnolia News.* 22 Oct. 1959.

18 Coughlin, Dan. "Magnolia proudly fights urban invasion." *Seattle Post-Intelligencer.* 6 Nov. 1978.

MAGNOLIA'S WOODEN TRESTLES

1 *Baist's 1908 Seattle Real Estate Atlas*

2 Don Sherwood Parks History Collection. Pos. 2696-20. Item 29330. Photographer: Olmsted Associates, Inc. May 1903.

3 James Patrick Lee. Photo #771, 8 May 1912.

4 Seattle Engineering Department. Negatives 2296, 2299 and 2300.

5 "SEATTLE BRIDGES BURN, Replacements Will Cost City $250,000." *The Seattle Times.* 1 July 1924.

6 "WORK TO BEGIN ON VIADUCT." *Seattle Post-Intelligencer.* 12 June 1928.

7 Seattle Engineering Department. Negatives 7218, 7219 and 7223.

8 Don Sherwood Parks History Collection. Negative 7506.

9 Seattle Engineering Department. Negative 2430. 17 July 1914. Negative 2780. 5 March 1915. W&S Negative 20639. 16 November 1911.

CRITICAL CONNECTION: BRIDGE TO THE BLUFF

1 Frare, Aleua. *Magnolia Yesterday and Today.* Seattle: Magnolia Community Club, 1975.

2 Stimmel Hill, Mary Ann. Telephone interview. 30 Sept. 1999.

3 "Survey of Interbay Dump Settlement." Advisory Committee on Social Security to Board of County Commissioners King County Washington. August 1937.

4 Carleton Park Improvement Club minutes. 11 Oct. 1932. 165.

5 Nagley, C.N. "To Mr. J.D. Blackwell, City Engineer." 2 July 1924.

6 Carleton Park Improvement Club minutes. 13 May 1926. 20.

7 Magnolia Bluff Seeks Permanent Bridge Over Cove." *The Seattle Times.* 27 Sept. 1925.

8 "Magnolia Bluff Dwellers Demand Permanent Span." *The Seattle Times.* 4 Oct. 1925.

9 ---. *The Seattle Times.* 4 Oct. 1925.

10 "Magnolia Bluff Residents Fight For New Bridge." *The Seattle Times.* 14 Oct. 1925.

11 ---. *The Seattle Times.* 14 Oct. 1925.

12 "Magnolia Bridge Petition Presented City Council." *The Seattle Times.* 26 Oct. 1925.

13 "Magnolia Bluff People Protest Bridge Estimate." *The Seattle Times.* 20 Nov. 1925.

14 ---. *The Seattle Times.* 20 Nov. 1925.

15 "Magnolia Bridge Project Before Council Monday." *The Seattle Times.* 3 Dec. 1926.

16 ---. *The Seattle Times.* 3 Dec. 1926

17 "Council Approves Permanent West Garfield Bridge." *The Seattle Times.* 7 Dec. 1926.

18 "Garfield Bridge Plans Approved by Council Body." *The Seattle Times.* 15 April 1927.

19 ---. *The Seattle Times.* 15 April 1927.

20 Carleton Park Improvement Club minutes. 13 Sept. 1927. 53.

21 Judkins, Ursula. Personal interview. 15 July 2000.

22 ---. Personal interview. 15 July 2000.

23 Carleton Park Improvement Club minutes. 11 Nov. 1930. 116.

24 City of Seattle, Office of City Engineer invoice. 1 Oct. 1930.

25 Phelps, Myra L. *Public Works in Seattle: A Narrative History of the Engineering Department 1875 – 1975.* Seattle: Kingport Press, 1978.

26 Will, Hal. Telephone interview. 9 Dec. 1999.

27 Hartman, W. A. "To Mr. J. W. A. Bollong, c/o Street Department." 26 April 1934.

28 Magnolia Community Club Resolution. 12 June 1934.

29 "Traffic Signal to Replace Sign." *The Seattle Times.* 19 Nov. 1940.

30 Plan Number 782-94, Seattle Transportation Archives.

31 Arnold, Cecil C. Report CF 237586, Box 34 of City Clerk Reports and Studies, series 1802-D9. 23 June 1959.

32 Plan Number 782-100, Seattle Transportation Archives.

33 Denison, Walcott. "To Mr. Roy W. Morse, Chief Engineer." 12 Dec. 1959.

34 Henry, E.G. "To Honorable City Council." 27 Jan. 1960.

35 City Ordinance #89307

36 Magnolia Community Club minutes. 6 Sept. 1960.

37 Plan Number 782-131, Seattle Transportation Archives.

38 Yanagimachi, Frank. Personal interview. 8 Dec. 1999.

39 Williams, Marla. "Magnolia Bridge reopens today, weeks early." *The Seattle Times.* 8 May 1997.

40 Yanagimachi, Frank. Personal interview. 8 Dec. 1999.

41 Williams, Marla. "Magnolia Bridge reopens today, weeks early." *The Seattle Times.* 8 May 1997.

42 Yanagimachi, Frank. Personal interview. 8 Dec. 1999.

43 Beers, Carole. "Bridge closure snarls up Magnolia Neighborhood." *The Seattle Times.* 10 Feb. 1997.

44 O'Denius, Nancy. Telephone interview. 5 Dec. 1999.

45 Schubert, Ruth and Ho, Vanessa. "Mountain of 'pudding' smashes into bridge." *Seattle Post-Intelligencer.* 3 Jan. 1997.

46 Williams, Marla. "Magnolia Bridge reopens today, weeks early."

47 Yanagimachi, Frank. Personal interview. 8 Dec. 1999.

48 ---. Personal interview. 8 Dec. 1999.

49 ---. Personal interview. 8 Dec. 1999.

50 ---. Personal interview. 8 Dec. 1999.

51 Anderson, William and Allwine, Herb. Personal interview. 7 April 2000.

52 Shannon & Wilson. *Geotechnical Report, Garfield Street Landslide.* June 1999. 1.

53 Anderson, William and Allwine, Herb. Personal interview. 7 April 2000.

54 Anderson, William. Phone interview. 26 April 2000.

55 ---. Phone interview. 26 April 2000.

56 Anderson, William and Allwine, Herb. Personal interview. 7 April 2000.

57 Anderson, William. Phone interview. 26 April 2000.

58 ---. Phone interview. 26 April 2000.

59 Anderson, William and Allwine, Herb. Personal interview. 7 April 2000.

60 Anderson, William. "Re: Magnolia Bridge East Slide." E-mail to Joy Carpine.
   26 April 2000.

61 Anderson, William and Allwine, Herb. Personal interview. 7 April 2000.

62 Anderson, William. Phone interview. 6 July 2000.

63 ---. Phone interview. 6 July 2000.

64 Rees, Ted. Telephone interview. 26 Sept. 2000.

65 Anderson, William and Allwine, Herb. Personal Interview. 7 April 2000.

The Twenty-Year Battle for West Point

1 Morgan, Brandt. *Enjoying Seattle's Parks.* Seattle Washington: Greenwood Publications,
   1979.

Pioneer Family Who Helped Build Magnolia

1 Miner, Eleanor and Walter. Personal interview. 3 Dec. 1999.

2 Warren, James and William McCoy. *Highlights of Seattle History.* Historical Society of
   Seattle and King County. Seattle: 1982.

3 Meiner's Homestead Booklet 100th Anniversay of the Darrington Homested.
   Self-published. 1999.

4 World Book Encyclopedia Vol. 8 H. Field Enterprise Corporation. Chicago, 1961.

5 Meiner's Homestead Booklet 100th Anniversay of the Darrington Homested.
   Self-published. 1999.

6 Miner, Eleanor and Walter. Personal interview. 28 Oct. 1999.

7 Miner, Eleanor and Walter. Personal interview. 19 Aug. 1999.

8 Jenson, Eva. *Transition School to Community.* Self-published. 1987.

9 Meiner's Homestead Booklet 100th Anniversay of the Darrington Homested.
   Self-published. 1999.

10 Miner, Eleanor and Walter. Personal interview. 28 Oct. 1999.

11 Miner, Eleanor and Walter. Personal interview. 19 Aug. 1999.

12 Frare, Aleua L. *Magnolia Yesterday and Today.* Magnolia Community Club Publication.
   Sept. 1974.

13 Miner, Eleanor and Walter. Personal interview. 19 Aug. 1999.

14 Miner, Eleanor and Walter. Personal interview. 28 Oct. 1999.

15 Miner, Eleanor and Walter. Personal interview. 19 Aug. 1999.

16 Gillman, Tami. Personal interview. Summer 1999.

17 Miner, Eleanor and Walter. Personal interview. 19 Aug. 1999.

18 Meiner's Homestead Booklet 100th Anniversary of The Darrington Homestead.
   Self-published. 1999.

19 ---.

HISTORY OF DISCOVERY PARK

1 Kiley, Dan. *Fort Lawton Park Plan*. Seattle Park Department. 1972. 13.

2 ---. Fort Lawton Park Plan. Appendix A.

3 ---. Fort Lawton Park Plan. 14.

4 Federal Lands for Parks and Recreation Act of 1970.

5 Fort Lawton, Discovery Park. Seattle Department of Parks and Recreation. Undated.

6 Preamble to the 1974 Lease Agreement between the United Indians of All Tribes
   Foundation and the City of Seattle.

7 Kiley, Dan. Fort Lawton Park Plan. 1.

8 Morgan, Brandt. *Enjoying Seattle's Parks*. Seattle: Greenwood Publications. 1979. 109-111.

9 "If and When . . . Natural park at Ft. Lawton?" *Magnolia News*. 20 Mar. 1969. 1.

10 Gilje, Svein. "Fort Lawton Won't Get Missiles; Two Kitsap County Sites Chosen." *The
   Seattle Times*. 18 Dec. 1968. 1.

11 Sawyer, Richard. "Ft. Lawton tightens laws." *Magnolia Journal*. 8 Oct. 1969.

12 "Ft. Lawton Still Open, Despite Bus-Shelter Shift." *The Seattle Times*. 10 Oct. 1969. 3.

13 Gilje, Svein. "Fort Lawton-Area Residents Cite Harassment by M.P.s." *The Seattle Times*.
   23 Oct. 1969. A-1.

14 Whitney, Stephan R. *Nature Walks in & around Seattle*. Seattle: The Mountaineers,
   1987. 69.

15 Magnolia Community Club documentation. 29 Apr. 1969.

16 Tawresey, Virgina Bishop. *J.G.Cougar's Great Adventure*. Seattle: Storytellers Inc., 1993.
   11.

17 Brown, Charles E. "West Point Lighthouse Marks 100th Shining Year." *The Seattle Times*.
   17 Nov. 1981. B2.

18 ---. "West Point Lighthouse Marks 100th Shining Year."

19 "Lighthouse Reaches 100th year." *Magnolia News*. November 1981.

20 Bagley, Clarence B. *The History of Seattle. Vol. 1*. Chicago: The S.J. Clarke Publishing
   Company, 1916. 12-13.

21 Olmsted, John. 1910 sketch of Fort Lawton.

22 Philips, Myra L. *Public Works in Seattle, A Narrative History. The Engineering Department
   1875-1975*. Kingport Press: 1978.

23 Stewards of the Waters: A retrospective on wastewater treatment at Seattle's West Point.
   King County Department of Metropolitan Services. 1998. 6.

24 ---. "Stewards of the Waters . . . " 37-38.

25 Leccese, Michael. "A Point Well Taken." *Landscape Architecture Magazine*. June 1999.

26 Murray, John S. "Publisher's Corner." *Queen Anne News*. 20 Mar. 1968. 2.

27 Woodward, Walt. "Aquarium, Ft. Lawton Park, Marine Parkway Go Together." *The
   Seattle Times*. March 1968.

28 ---. "Aquarium, Ft. Lawton Park, Marine Parkway Go Together."

29 ---.

30 Braman, James. "To Alfred Petty." 2 Mar. 1972.

31 *Argus Magazine*. 17 Nov. 1980.

32 Manning, Harvey. *Footsore 1. Walks and Hikes Around Puget Sound*. Seattle: The
   Mountaineers.

33 Articles of Incorporation of the Friends of Discovery Park. Article II. December 1974.

A Certain Clout: The Magnolia Community Club

1 Nelson, Robert. "A Lesson in Protectionism." *Seattle Times/Seattle Post-Intelligencer*. Pacific
   Magazine. 27 Dec. 1987: 5,6,9,14,18.

2 ---, "A Lesson in Protectionism." *Seattle Times/Seattle Post-Intelligencer*. Pacific Magazine.
   27 Dec. 1987: 5,6,9,14,18.

3 Eyrle, Dan. "An Open Letter to Magnolia Residents." *Magnolia News*. 9 Sept. 1970: 28.

4 ---, "An Open Letter to Magnolia Residents."

5 Official Magnolia Community Club Minutes 1939 - 1945. 17 July 1939: 11.

6 MCC Officer and Trustee Roster. 1999.

7 Ivie, Betty and Bill. Magnolia Community Club newsletters. May 2000/Oct. 1999.

8 Cowan, Les. Personal interview. 30 Sept. 1999.

9 Magnolia Community Club. Select Highlights of Activities 1924 – 2000.

10 Sundt, Chet and Norma. Personal interview. 4 Dec. 1999.

11 Chet and Norma Sundt interview.

12 Chet and Norma Sundt interview.

13 Judkins, Ursula. Personal interview. 11 May 2000.

14 Nelson, Robert. "A Lesson in Protectionism." *Seattle Times/Seattle Post-Intelligencer*, Pacific
   Magazine. 27 Dec. 1987.

Index